WHEN WE SPEAK
OF FREEDOM

RADICAL LIBERALISM

IN AN AGE OF CRISIS

The Joseph Rowntree Reform Trust has supported this work in recognition of the importance of the issue. The facts presented and views expressed in this report are, however, those of the authors and not necessarily those of the Trust. www.jrrt.org.uk

WHEN WE SPEAK
OF FREEDOM

RADICAL LIBERALISM
IN AN AGE OF CRISIS

Edited by
Paul Hindley & Benjamin Wood

Beecroft Publications
Leeds

When We Speak of Freedom:
Radical Liberalism in an Age of Crisis

Published in 2025 by
Beecroft Publications
72 Waterloo Lane
Bramley, Leeds LS13 2JF
www.beecroftpublications.co.uk

on behalf of
The John Stuart Mill Institute
Reg. charity: 1010395

Funded by the Joseph Rowntree Reform Trust

A CIP catalogue record for this book is available from the
British Library

ISBN 978-0-9930909-9-8

Production editor, design and typography: Elizabeth Bee

Contents

Foreword

This book is the product of almost two years work by supporters of the John Stuart Mill Institute (JSMI). Founded in 1992 the Institute seeks to stimulate debate on issues of public concern. Inspired by the liberal philosopher John Stuart Mill (1806-1873), the Institute prizes freedom of the individual, supports responsible democratic participation and continues to develop a coherent tradition of thought on political, economic and social issues in the 21st century.

The JSMI has charitable status and is independent of any political party. It seeks to apply the values of liberty and participation to present day problems and to educate those who are interested in public policy. The Institute asserts the importance of applying a principled approach to contemporary issues, both nationally and internationally. The Institute also values the principle of individual and collective liberty, and societies which support flourishing individuals and thriving communities.

This volume covers a wide variety of subjects. Some of these subjects may strike the reader as unusual, or even out of place, but liberalism infuses our lives in all its dimensions including religion, the arts and architecture, and culture as well as economics and politics. We cannot however embrace all possible issues in a book of 20 essays, but the volume attempts to offer a rich overview of perspectives.

Liberalism comes in many colours – from Hayek to Hobhouse, from Mill to Grimond, from Locke to Beveridge. Liberal values have constant relevance and application but can, at times, be in conflict one with another. This requires liberals and liberalisms of all complexions not to be dogmatic but to conduct their political discourse in a spirit of reasonableness and tolerance of other viewpoints.

Grand ideologies may come and go – often the creatures and victims of fashion – but liberalism endures.

In an age in which liberal democracies are being shaken by populism, unreason, conspiracy theories and fake news, this collection of essays is intended to make the case for a deep revitalisation of liberal politics. The general message of the collection is clear. It is incumbent on all liberals to address contemporary political issues, short and long term, with a principled approach reinterpreting liberal values with courage and ambition in the face of adversity and widespread cynicism.

Liberals would also do well to remember the remark attributed to one of the 20th century's greatest Liberals, John Maynard Keynes, who is credited with saying 'When the facts change, I change my mind – what do you do?' Thus liberals need constantly to rethink their views, both now and in the future. The liberalism of these pages is not defensive, but positive, constructive and challenging.

As always liberals remain committed to the rule of law and to due democratic and judicial process – not that these are exempt from the need for enormous improvement, as many of the contributors demonstrate. Similarly, we are unrepentant internationalists and supporters of global political and economic institutions however imperfect.

There are some themes which stand out in the book. One is about the redistribution of power from the centre, and from oligarchs and oligopolies down to real communities and to individuals. There is the repeated insistence that the distribution of power must be comprehensive, encompassing political, economic, social and cultural spheres. Another theme concerns the need to rebuild trust in politics by developing more mechanisms to enlist citizen participation. This will doubtless demand much more honesty from politicians about the policy choices available to governments at all levels.

Alongside this, there is an implicit demand in the book which concerns our conduct as individual citizens. We have to learn, as individuals and societies, to live in a manner which is environmentally sustainable, if human life on this planet is to remain remotely tolerable. This will require leadership, imagination and trustworthiness. Confronted with ecological breakdown, we cannot look to our political masters alone. A better way of life must be worked out together, sustained from the grassroots.

The Institute is hugely indebted to the two joint editors of this book, Paul Hindley and Ben Wood, who have worked long and hard to make this collection ready for publication. We hope that you will find these essays stimulating and that, having read the contents, you will agree that not only is liberalism is very much alive and well, but that the contributions you will find here are worthy of liberalism's distinguished ancestors.

Dr Alan Butt Philip
Convenor, John Stuart Mill Institute trustees

If you would like to support the work of the John Stuart Mill Institute or seek further information about it, please visit the Institute's website at www. jsmi.org.uk or write to the John Stuart Mill Institute, 1 Whitehall Place, London SW1A 2HE.

Acknowledgements

This project formally began in October 2023 over wine and sandwiches at the home of Elizabeth Bee and Michael Meadowcroft. A small group of us talked contemporary politics, memories of liberal triumphs past, and our hopes for the future. This book is suffused with the warmth, intellectual curiosity, and hospitality of that first meeting.

All the authors give their personal views, which are not necessarily those of the editors, the John Stuart Mill Institute or of the organisations to which they belong.

We thank the authors who volunteered their time, passion and expertise to this vital enterprise. In this time of cynicism and exhaustion, you have summoned hope, vision, and humanity.

Editorship is not an isolated affair but draws upon wide webs of sympathy and support. Firstly, our upmost thanks must go to the John Stuart Mill Institute and its trustees for putting their faith in us. We hope the present volume has repaid that trust handsomely. We would like to particularly thank Liz Bee for the immense amount of work that she has undertaken to bring this book to light. Our task would have been impossible without her keen eye and critical input.

Special thanks are reserved for Alan Butt Philip, Michael Meadowcroft and Ian MacFadyen for their tireless support, advice and encouragement. Gratitude goes to the Joseph Rowntree Reform Trust for generously supporting the production and distribution of this book. We hope it accords closely with the Trust's tradition of radical conscience, political reform and democratic participation. Last, but certainly not least, we would like to thank our families and loved ones for supporting us through this process, especially Ann Hindley, Richard Hindley and Stephen Wood for their love, support and patience.

Paul Hindley and Benjamin Wood

1

Introduction:
The Crisis of Democracy

Michael Meadowcroft

A century ago, at the general election of 1924, Britain transitioned from being a two-party Conservative/Liberal country to being a two-party Conservative/Labour country. In this electoral shift something of immense value found itself eclipsed. Monuments of its achievements were scattered all over early 20th century Britain. Old-age pensions, experiments in public works, and progressive taxation on land and capital, were fragments of a much larger political creed, which placed its hopes in the flourishing of individuals in communities organised at a human scale. As the *Liberal Yellow Book* of 1928 summarised this ethic:

> The measures we advocate in all these things spring from one clear purpose. We believe with a passionate faith that the end of all political economic action is not the perfecting of this or that piece of mechanism or organisation, but that individual men and women may have life and that they have it more abundantly.[1]

Such a generous politics, in its attentiveness to the preciousness of the individual, was habitually averse to the reduction of democracy into static blocks of occupation, caste or class. Against the distortions of sectional interests, many liberals sought to appeal to the decency, the intelligence and conscience of each citizen on the basis of a shared human interest. In adopting this attitude, liberals attempted to model their highest goods; those of participation, diversity, and dialogue. This draws us to an important point about the character and techniques of liberalism. However important coherent policies are, for liberals the end does not justify the

---

1   From *Britain's Industrial Future* (1928) quoted in *Political Parties and the Party System in Britain: A Symposium*, ed. Sydney Dawson Bailey (Hansard Society, 1952:1979), p. 89.

means. Enforcing change with insensitivity or caprice, often undermines the value of the change itself. Important alterations require the citizen's consent, particularly when they are necessary but unpopular. A liberalism inattentive to the needs and wishes of persons is no liberalism at all. This attitude was vividly expressed by Friedrich Schiller in his response to the excesses of the French Revolution:

> When the artist lays hands upon the formless mass in order to shape it to his ends, he has no scruple in doing it violence. The natural material he is working merits no respect for itself, his concern is not with the whole for the sake of the parts but with the parts for the sake of the whole. The political or educational artist, however, must learn to approach his medium with genuine respect for its individuality and potential for dignity and beware of damaging its natural variety.[2]

Liberalism's reflexive distrust of uniformity and zeal may be appealing, but does the present epoch have any use for tender political artists? Certainly, there have been from time to time in Britain flurries of electoral life from a Liberal or Liberal Democrat Party (not least at the 2024 general election), but these moments of renewed activity have never threatened the dominance of a left-right duopoly, into which the electoral realities from 1924 onwards skilfully guided political debates henceforth. What then is the character of these two political poles? Since 1924, UK electors have been presented with a straightforward contest between the organising power of the state or the innovative capacity of the market. Complex matters of policy have been shrunk into a two-sided conversation regarding the relative merits of collectivism or laissez-faire. The existence of a distinctive third political force that embraced a view of society that did not fit at any point of the left-right spectrum was ignored with much implicit or innocent connivance of liberals themselves, not least because they felt it made them relevant and, to be fair, the debate, at least superficially, had its virtues.

Whilst continued economic growth seemed inexorable in Western economies, it was possible to 'buy off' public discontent through higher levels of material wellbeing. In the broad confines of Britain's Conservative and Labour parties, it was possible to pursue a compromise between left and

---

2   Friedrich Schiller, *Essays*, ed. Daniel O. Dahlstrom and Walter Hinderer (Bloomsbury Academic, 1993), p. 94.

right in a moderate version of social democracy, christened 'Butskellism'[3] by *The Economist*. Underpinning this convergence of principles was the work of two visionary liberals, John Maynard Keynes and William Beveridge.[4] Their influence gave the unfortunate impression however that liberalism had become the common property of all democratic parties. Whatever great service liberalism had performed in forming and sustaining open societies, as an independent political party, it was commonly regarded as an electorally spent force. However, as the East Asian economies flourished, undercutting the West in many areas of manufacturing, both parties increasingly floundered. At times, the duopoly was moved effortlessly towards extremes, rooted in the perverse belief that the problem in Britain was a lack of ideological purity rather than changing social and material conditions. But in their purist extremes these parties revealed who and what they had become. Instead of representing a broad base of moral, geographical, aesthetic and community opinion, they were mere ciphers for economic doctrines. As the liberal Roger Fulford observed in 1959: 'Life bounded by purely economic limits is in fact the negation of Liberalism. Yet the conservatives and socialists contrive to give the impression that economic policy – if not the sole object of their existence – is the most sensitive point in their lives.'[5] In an era of rapid environmental degradation, this point is worth revisiting. Many of life's key problems cannot be reduced to economic values like profit and loss.

Political philosophies that live by economic success die from its lack. The public has become used to each generation having a higher standard of living than its predecessor. Consequently, we have become habituated to think of our present cohort of politicians as failures on the basis that they cannot increase all fortunes simultaneously. They continue to promise bounty and it refuses to appear. But is this really what is sought? Society's emphasis on financial advancement as a key indicator of success (and the increasing difficulty in achieving it) is leading to widespread dissatisfaction and social unrest, fed by the apparently ever-increasing gap between the highest and

---

3   See Peter Kerr, *Postwar British Politics: From Conflict to Consensus* (Routledge, 2001), p. 46.
4   See William Beveridge, *Social Insurance and Allied Services* (The Beveridge Report), CMD 6404, 1942: https://www.nationalarchives.gov.uk/education/resources/attlees-britain/beveridge-report/ [Accessed 15/6/2024]. William Beveridge was Liberal MP for Berwick-upon-Tweed, 1944-45.
5   Roger Fulford, *The Liberal Case* (Penguin Books, 1959), p. 97.

lowest paid. Vivid evidence of the malign influence of economism was seen starkly at the recent general election. The Conservative government continually produced figures showing the vast sums it had spent on public services. But when voters looked around them they saw sewage in rivers, potholes in streets, delays in health treatment and a proliferation of foodbanks. There is undoubtedly an economic context to this social decay, but its roots run much deeper. It is all a question of what we love and cherish as a society. If there is no acceptance of the inherent value of police, teachers and public servants, the shared realm of politics is likely to deteriorate. Only a society that values individual men and women for what they are rather than what they might acquire can reverse the decline in community life.

Alongside the economisation of society, the last fifty years has seen the accelerating bureaucratisation of society throughout the Western world. Whether administered by politicians of the state or the market, the attempt to prop up the right/left duopoly has produced a wilderness of strictures and guidelines, to the neglect of local communities. The socialist and conservative views of society are locked into rules and regulations which are handy for bureaucrats but are unrelenting for individuals. When Margaret Thatcher came into office in 1979, she abolished the use of discretion when considering Supplementary Benefit claims from poor and needy individuals. Until then, when Armley constituents came to me for help in appealing against a refusal to help with particular needs, such as shoes for children, fares to go to hospital or to visit a sick relative, I would argue it was a case in which the official should have discretion.[6] In just about every case the (then) DHSS would give in before the hearing. Then, as if overnight, the avenue of discretion was removed. For liberals, eliminating local remedies is not merely inefficient and cruel, but a diminution of community. If we run down the capacities of local government, for short-term gains, we are merely storing up deep social problems in the long run. During the 1981 urban riots in Brixton (and a number of other cities), an article in *The Economist* offered a highly liberal analysis premised upon the need for a vibrant local democracy. As the article remarked:

---

6   Poverty does not conform to exact bureaucratic levels and liberals therefore prefer David Donnison's definition: 'Poverty is the inability to live with dignity in one's own community.'

One common aspect of the riot areas is that all have suffered for decades because politicians and their planning advisers have removed from them their natural community leaders. Local councils have used central funds to buy up, often compulsorily, anyone with a financial stake in the community – homeowners, shopkeepers, landlords, small businesses – to add their property to the council's land bank pending comprehensive redevelopment. Such individuals are the first to be offered the money and favourable housing nominations to move out of the area, if only because they are the most independent and mobile citizens. The effect has been to break the economic and social ties which bind the community together, ties which also help to police it.[7]

It is neither hasty nor fanciful to suggest the presence of similar dynamics at work in the London riots of 2011. Behind these eruptions is a vital political truth: there is more to public life than individual wealth. There is collective wealth, crystalised in local institutions and services. Essential to the health of democracy is thriving municipal government. Together with civil society and its plethora of voluntary bodies, local government is the guarantee of pluralism, participation and of a healthy democracy. It has, alas, been killed off almost imperceptibly over the past 75 years by its powers being taken away one by one. Only when one looks back is the real situation apparent. In 1948 many large cities, controlled gas, electricity, water, a hospital, some social security, police, fire service, ambulance, schools, further education, some higher education, local transport and even airports – all of which have now been centralised or privatised. What is more, local government cannot even today spend almost all of the money it raises locally without the permission of central government. The nonsense of such abuse of power is seen when the central government sets up a potholes fund! It is all part of the desire from both left and right to control more and more of the individual citizen's life and to inhibit innovation and diversity. Despite fine words before last July's election, one of the first actions of the new Labour government has been to force local authorities to build the houses the government dictates for their areas, when all that they need is the resources. Liberalism sees devolution of power and the encouragement of local initiative as a benefit and as a bulwark against the abuse of power. Repairing local democracy requires the

7   Nick Harmon, *The Economist*, 18 July 1981 vol. 280, part 1 (digitised 14 October 2008), p. 28.

jettisoning of the rule of ultra vires, under which a local council has to find explicit legal authority for what it intends to introduce, and the embrace of intra vires, whereby a council can do anything not formally prohibited by law. In the raising of local finance it should be up to a council to determine what it believes it can persuade its electors to support. The Localism Act 2011 included this provision in principle, but it has been little used.

Renewing politics

There is evidence that the tide of economism and bureaucracy is beginning to turn. The long crisis of social democracy in post-industrial economies presents liberalism with a unique opportunity to place its radical vision before an exhausted public. As the British sociologist and philosopher, Ralf Dahrendorf[8] observed, somewhat prophetically, in the late 1970s:

> The issue today is not how to be social democratic… [The] issue is what comes after social democracy. If this is not to be a Blue, Red or Green aberration, it will have to be an imaginative, unorthodox and distinctive liberalism, which combines the common ground of social-democratic achievements with the new horizons of the future of liberty.[9]

In this account, we must acknowledge the innovations of social democracy in its day, following the radical policies of the Asquith/Lloyd George reforms of the 1906 government (National Insurance-based universal public healthcare, workplace protections, and state investment in welfare and education), but entrench these advances along liberal lines. Yet, the question remains; are we prepared for this new stage of political life? Should there be any pessimism as to the electorate's inherent liberalism; one need only consider the public response to the Covid pandemic. Four essentially liberal attitudes came to the fore. First, the sympathy and interaction shown by and between individuals; second, the sense of community generated

---

8   Ralf Dahrendorf, 1929-2009; Director, London School of Economics 1974-84; Liberal (FDP) Baden-Württemberg (Länder) and Bonn (Federal) parliaments; Minister of State in the Foreign Office in Bonn; EEC Commissioner for External Relations and Foreign Trade, and, later, for Science and Education between 1970 and 1974; Warden, St Antony's College, Oxford, 1987-97; created Liberal Democrat Life Peer, 1993.

9   Ralf Dahrendorf, *After Social Democracy* (The Liberal Publication Department, 1980), p. 20.

by shared need; third, a renewed awareness of the importance of public services in containing the social emergency; and fourth, the pressing reality of internationalism, through the acknowledgement that borders were irrelevant to the virus. The crisis regenerated certain political values which a few years before seemed moribund, including a renewal of interest in reversing the disasters of Brexit in a new liberal internationalism. This subtle realignment has not been without electoral consequences. With the lack of a powerful alternative, the blinkered left/right view of politics finally ran out of road at the 2024 UK general election when the polls showed that public trust in politicians had reached an all-time low. It is no coincidence that the long electoral decline of liberalism has coincided with a crisis of economic legitimacy and deepening political disengagement. The present two-party domination may not have produced our current crisis of political meaning, but it has certainly deepened it. As Emmy van Durzen argues vividly in this volume, the solutions to our multiple crises are not to be found in crass materialism, but in a revitalisation of human values like community, care and friendship. In different degrees each of us is a mixture of selfishness and altruism. Other political philosophies require dedication to one or the other. But only liberalism recognises the moral ambivalence in each of us. Two devils wrestle in the human heart. Within a society based on human values one pressing task of the politician is to enhance altruism and diminish selfishness. The temptation of egotism can be valued for its gifts of initiative and self-drive, but its manifest excesses must be tempered by the better angels of mutuality and social conscience.

But the roadblocks to such a rich social and political recovery are profound. The first obstacle concerns the problem of liberal self-understanding. Such is the ingrained ubiquity of a left/right spectrum that liberals have all too often compromised with this political shorthand, treating left/right as synonymous with progressive versus reactionary. But this is a mistake, one which readily traps liberalism inside the same barren fiscal debates as traps social democrats and conservatives. Liberal politics has to take note of economics (not least because all the services crucial to society depend on significant sums of money), but liberals do not define success or failure purely in terms of economic output. More vital for liberalism is the quality of human relationships, and the ability of politics to accommodate intelligently our joys, hopes, and affections by taming and channelling power. For too long liberals instead of rejecting it, have accepted the left/right line as if it were immutable, and this is the key point. If one is seeking a 'short-hand' placement for political liberalism, it sits towards the southern end of a vertical line, stretching from vast concentrations of power at the northern end to a creative diffusion of power at the other end. As the British Liberal Party constitution of 1936 expressed it: 'The Liberal Party exists to build a Liberal Commonwealth, in which none shall be enslaved by poverty, ignorance or unemployment. Its chief care is for the rights and opportunities of the individual, and in all spheres it sets freedom first.'[10]

However, as this volume proves, there are risks in endeavouring to sum up liberal ideology in a series of vague slogans. As Helena Rosenblatt and Helen McCabe both illustrate in their chapters, any description of liberalism needs to transcend elementary binaries like individuals and communities, altruism and initiative, and embrace complexity. This invites us into an important practical and philosophical task. To begin to reverse the dire lack of public trust in politics will require liberals to enter into discussion with the public on a more intellectually rigorous basis than the current sloganising and short-termism offered by day-to-day politics. In particular, liberals need to engage citizens on the basis of their vision of a better society; one informed by liberality, solidarity, initiative and creativity. These values need to underpin all policy. To shift from the embedded focus on hollow economic values to an awareness of rich human values will inevitably take time – and considerable explanation and persuasion. My 25 years of working with new and emerging democracies across the world vividly underlined my awareness that unless a country's political parties are based on some semblance of philosophy its democracy is not sustainable for any length of time. Certainly we know that 'liberation' movements, such as the Scottish National Party, or parties based on a single divisive issue, such as in Northern Ireland, are precarious in the long term. We need to ensure that our actions are sustained by deep roots.

But if ideological incoherence is a considerable hindrance to the flourishing of liberal politics, so too is a public weariness with the many half-baked positions which have been christened 'liberal' by both supporters and detractors alike. One response from a significant section of the public, weary of the failure of liberals to emphasise human values, has been to blame external causes – foreigners, immigrants, shirkers – and turn to parties

---

10 Liberal Party, *The Constitution of the Liberal Party* (Liberal Publication Department, 1936), p. 3.

that feed on populist and nationalistic sentiment. Such parties promise undeliverable solutions, but they do speak to a profound despair. It is all redolent of Weimar Germany. Out of the ruins of a dysfunctional democracy sprang the Nazi party. At the 1924 election the Nazi party polled just 2% of the vote but by 1933 it was in office; polling 43%.[11] Today's millennial generation is the first whose families have no inherited consciousness of the Nazi atrocities and is less alarmed by parties that promote sub-Nazi views. Faced with such political threats, only a society based on liberal values can combat growing prejudice and narrow nationalism. This liberal alternative is not just a variant of existing parties on the left/right spectrum but a distinct philosophy in its own right, with a political radical ethos and practice which long predates the rise of the British Labour Party at the beginning of the 20th century. Of what did this tradition consist? Painting this background in vivid colours, Eugenio Biagini has recalled:

> In 1883, the radical journalist W.E. Adams described community self-government and community representation 'as the essence of all political liberalism that is worthy of the name'... In contrast with the old Thatcherite or 'Newt Gingrichite' stereotypical image of 'Victorian values' – meaning individualism, self-help and *laissez-faire* – and the endorsement of similar myths by some socialist historians... politics in the nineteenth century 'was not primarily about individual rights, but the representation of his community'.[12]

One logical outgrowth of this attitude, particularly in working-class areas, was a progressive emphasis on syndicalism. The political logic was plain. If citizens were ever to rise above the threat of demagogues, lords, and tyrants, they needed greater control over their economic life. For at least a century, British liberals have insisted that employees in larger companies should become active partners and, particularly, shareholders and have the ability to appoint the directors. The object of these measures was not merely to tame capital, but to socialise it in the true sense of the world. As *The Yellow Book* expressed it:

11   See Larry Eugene Jones, *Hitler versus Hindenburg: The 1932 Presidential Elections and the End of the Weimar Republic* (Cambridge University Press, 2016).
12   Eugenio Biagini, 'Citizenship, liberty and community,' in *Citizenship and Community: Liberals, Radicals and Collective Identities in the British Isles*, ed. Eugenio Biagini (Cambridge University Press, 1996), p. 1.

> [The] remedy to [contemporary conditions] in our view is not con-
> centration in the hands of the State but the diffusion of ownership
> throughout the community. We stand not for public ownership but for
> popular ownership. The aim must be not to destroy the owner-class,
> but to enlarge it.[13]

The record where co-ownership has grown organically from innovation and from developments within a company is excellent. The psychological impact of a setting in which employees have a direct interest in the actual processes and performance of their workplace is often transformational. Replacing the adversarial roles of owners/management and unions by co-operation and mutualism permits the humanisation of work and the taming of unaccountable bureaucracy. As ever, scale is a significant factor in the success or failure of these enterprises. It should be readily acknowledged that co-ownership becomes more difficult and complex as a company becomes larger than is feasibly comprehended by those involved. Larger companies inevitably require more formal structures and good union practice, including works councils as intermediaries. It is my contention that greater workplace participation is equally as important as local government as a means of strengthening democratic processes.

Nevertheless, it should be admitted that there are structural barriers in the British case, which makes such a rich democratic politics difficult to build. The first-past-the-post electoral system entrenches the current major parties and embeds the constricting left/right axis. Under current conditions voters who dissent from the political binary are left with an unpalatable choice between negative and tactical voting. The decreasing turnout at all elections suggests that the electorate has an increasing sense of disillusion with the effectiveness of the democratic system to be responsive to their views.

The superficial tendency to see change only as 'proportional rep-resentation' with an acceptance of one system or another of party lists needs to be rejected as giving even more powers to party hierarchies rather than to voters. A change to the Single Transferable Vote (STV) is needed, under which the voter expresses his or her preferences, in party terms or on other grounds, in a multi-member constituency. Not only does STV greatly

---

13 Liberal Industrial Inquiry, *Britain's Industrial Future: Being the Report of the Liberal Industrial Inquiry of 1928* (Ernest Benn Limited, 1928), p. 243.

improve proportionality and accountability, but it also obviates the need for tactical voting and disincentivises purely negative voting. For liberals, electoral reform is a necessary first step in imagining a politics beyond the poles of market and state.

The world we wish to build

In *The Environment: A Liberal Party Report* (1972) it was observed that: 'Once the basic needs of food and shelter are met, man's greatest satisfactions are to be found in love, trust and friendship, in beauty, art and music and in learning, none of which are served by the mythology of growth for its own sake.'[14] But turning this insight into a practical reality will be no easy task. It requires nothing less than reconfiguring the aspirations and objects of a whole mode of governmental and commercial civilization. Long ago, J.S. Mill observed the link between economic organisation and social values. Reflecting on the possibility of a world beyond the scramble for indiscriminate production, Mill observed:

> It is scarcely necessary to remark that a stationary condition of capital and population implies no stationary state of human improvement. There would be as much scope as ever for all kinds of mental culture, and moral and social progress, as much room for improving the art of living, and much more likelihood of it being improved, when minds ceased to be engrossed by the art of getting on.[15]

Here Mill introduces us to a subversive thought. For too long we have assumed that getting on means more output, higher productivity and the accrual of vaster concentrations of material wealth. However, that assumes that the only kind of worthwhile expansion for human beings concerns the satisfaction of ever more complex material wants. Mill begs to differ. A society, which no longer prioritises generalised and indiscriminate growth, need not be a community of cultural or spiritual stagnation. We certainly want, Mill thinks, the kinds of 'getting on' which means children are fed

---

14 The Liberal Party, *The Environment: A Liberal Party Report* (Liberal Publication Department, 1972), p. 3.
15 John Stuart Mill, 'Of the Stationary State,' from *Principles of Political Economy*, Book IV, Chapter VI, https://www.panarchy.org/mill/stationary.1848.html [Accessed 15/6/2024].

and the elderly cared for but that is not accomplished merely by 'more'. Resources must be organised, not merely thoughtlessly piled up. The most crucial area that requires such intellectual rigour is the urgent need to reverse the effects of climate change. This cannot be effected without constraints on the economic development of each of us, but the consequences of not acting will be disastrous, even more so for poorer, low-lying countries such as Bangladesh and many Pacific islands. The required 'green imperative' is a response to the environmental analysis and must underpin every policy and every action.

This urgent task confronts us with a basic problem of moral priorities which cannot be circumvented through technology. Where does true security and prosperity lie? For liberals the answer cannot be greater acquisition. Often our material outputs feel as vain as Egyptian mausoleums. Aimless expansion may appeal to plutocrats and warmongers, but it should have little appeal to those committed to liberty. Freedom is more than material growth, keeping up with the Joneses, or grasping at technological power. The present Labour government's near-obsession with general and unfocused growth suggests not merely faulty policy, but a void of philosophical reflection. It appears that the Labour Party finds it nearly impossible to speak of principles which are non-material and non-instrumental. Like the Conservatives, they are caught in a soulless scramble for resources, the purpose of which they do not define. They are attempting to run a machine for its own sake, and not for any higher purpose.

This lack of moral reflection speaks to a deep hollowness at the heart of our politics. Some years ago, the economist Fritz Schumacher put the matter starkly. He suggested that we cannot ground social peace on the dream of universal prosperity, since such a condition would only be attainable 'by cultivating such drives of human nature as greed and envy, which destroy intelligence, happiness, serenity, and thereby the peacefulness of man.'[16] Limitlessness is not heroic; it is suicidal and self-defeating. Far more courageous is learning to live within recognisable ecological and material bounds. This means in part, learning to take delight in what we already possess, and what we are able to preserve. We must also acquire the wisdom to reorientate our lives away from the validations of wealth and instead seek opportunities for self-development. For liberals, such a way of life, one

---

16 F.E Schumacher, *Small is Beautiful: A Study of Economics as If People Mattered* (Vintage Books, 1993).

concerned with the enrichment of personality, is far superior to any nebulous goal of unbounded wealth. To ween ourselves off this destructive myth we must return to the old virtues of generosity, moderation, self-mastery, and friendship. These qualities are worth defending. Liberals have no desire to be ruled by power seekers or those obsessed with wealth.

In pursuing a vigorous and coherent environmental policy, we must avoid shallow sectarianism. It diminishes the impact of the green imperative to claim to be the preserve of a single political party. It must be a shared effort, which brings together all the parties alongside civil society. Certainly, many of the policy changes needed today to produce a sustainable and convivial society will not be immediately popular. That is not to say that the electorate would therefore vote against their promotion. Particularly with better citizenship education and more intellectual rigour from political leaders there is a great deal of evidence that voters will support 'right thinking' proposals, even if they are intrinsically sceptical about them. Patrick Devlin, from his extensive experience as a judge, made the comparison between juries and the electorate. He pointed out in his 1965 book,[17] that because juries have to act collectively, have the case being tried set out carefully to them and have their final decision put into effect, they vote for a 'right' decision and not for prejudices. He argues that if the politicians treated the electorate in the same way, in effect as a giant jury, they could expect a similar considered response. Citizen's assemblies go some way towards this, as used in the Republic of Ireland.

Perhaps the most difficult change for liberals to accomplish concerns our society's deep attachment to the rat race and the alluring promises held out by 'meritocracy'. The term was invented by the sociologist Michael Young in his book *The Rise of the Meritocracy* (1958). Originally written for the Fabian Society, the book was largely rejected by the Fabian left because of the way it gave this positive sounding term such a negative gloss. The radicalism at the heart of Young's book lay in his willingness to question dominant ideas of social satisfaction and advancement. In the increasingly technocratic world of the 1950s, progress came to mean the advancement of a highly educated workforce, trained and selected through the rigour of formal qualifications, fenced in by all-important examinations. In this account, drastic economic inequality was permissible if, and only if, people's

---

17   See Patrick Devlin, *The Enforcement of Morals* (Oxford University Press, 1967).

place in the social strata reflected an individual's intelligence combined with effort. But Young could not reconcile himself to such a narrow conception of value. The new professionalised education system certainly made the selection of specialists more efficient in some respects, but by necessity, such a social production line manifestly disadvantaged those who could not be neatly fitted into the bounds of a technical or specialist role. However, more crucially, by pressing human beings into academic bands and professional divisions, Young suggested that his contemporaries had devalued much of what makes life worthwhile. As Young expressed the matter: 'Were we to evaluate people, not only according to their intelligence and their education, their occupation, and their power, but according to their kindliness and their courage, their imagination and sensitivity, their sympathy and generosity, there could be no classes.'[18]

The lesson for contemporary liberals is a stirring one. We will never have an open and classless society, unless or until, we have left behind the desire to excel based on brute comparison. The object of any just community, as Young himself conceded, must be 'the tolerant society, in which individual differences are actively encouraged as well as passively tolerated, in which full meaning was at last given to the dignity of man.'[19] Instead of rising up or falling down a professional or income-based hierarchy, '[every] human being would…have equal opportunity…to develop his own special capacities for leading a rich life.'[20] We desperately need a society capable of recognising that fact. In our education system and in our common life together, we need a larger and wider conception of social value. As John Ruskin would remind us:

> There is no wealth but life. Life, including all its powers of love, of joy, and of admiration. That country is the richest which nourishes the greatest numbers of noble and happy human beings; that man is richest, who, having perfected the functions of his own life to the utmost, has also the widest helpful influence, both personal, and by means of his possessions, over the lives of others.[21]

18 Michael Young, *The Rise of the Meritocracy* (Transaction Publishing, 1958:1994), p. 156.
19 Young, *The Rise of the Meritocracy*, p. 159.
20 Young, *The Rise of the Meritocracy*, p. 159.
21 John Ruskin, 'Unto The Last,' in *The Genius of John Ruskin: Selections from His Writings,* ed. John D. Rosenberg (University of Virginia Press, 1997), p. 270.

What might it mean to take this intuition seriously? Principally we are summoned to foster a society in which beauty and community are just as politically pressing as health or education. The modern world should never have separated wellbeing and aesthetics, much less wrenched economy from notions of the social good. In renewing our politics, technique is not enough. We need the breathing space to ask ourselves why we strive, and crucially, what we strive for. For liberals, there is no greater intellectual mission. Freedom cannot thrive in a community obsessed only with 'means'. We need grand ends and compelling principles to make a better life and make a better politics.

Bibliography

Bailey, Sidney Dawson, ed. *Political Parties and the Party System in Britain, A Symposium*. Hansard Society, 1952:1979.

Bee, Elizabeth, Kamran Hussain, Ian MacFadyen, and Michael Meadowcroft, eds. *The Yorkshire Yellow Book 2019: Essays on a Liberal future for Yorkshire and the Humber*. Beecroft Publications, 2019.

Beveridge, William. *Social Insurance and Allied Services* (The Beveridge Report). CMD 6404, 1942. https://www.nationalarchives.gov.uk/education/resources/attlees-britain/beveridge-report/ [Accessed 15/6/2024].

Biagini, Eugenio, 'Citizenship, liberty and community.' In *Citizenship and Community: Liberals, Radicals and Collective Identities in the British Isles*. Edited by Eugenio Biagini. Cambridge University Press, 1996.

Dahrendorf, Ralf. *After Social Democracy*. The Liberal Publication Department, 1980.

Devlin, Patrick. *The Enforcement of Morals*. Oxford University Press, 1967.

Fulford, Roger. *The Liberal Case*. Penguin Books, 1959.

Harmon, Nick. *The Economist*, 18 July 1981 vol. 280, part 1, digitised, 14 October 2008.

Jones, Larry Eugene. *Hitler versus Hindenburg: The 1932 Presidential Elections and the End of the Weimar Republic*. Cambridge University Press, 2016.

Kerr, Peter. *Postwar British Politics: From Conflict to Consensus*. Routledge, 2001.

Liberal Industrial Inquiry. *Britain's Industrial Future: Being the Report of the Liberal Industrial Inquiry*. Ernest Benn, 1928.

Liberal Party. *The Constitution of the Liberal Party*. Liberal Publication Department, 1936.

— *The Environment: A Liberal Party Report*. Liberal Publication Department, 1972.

Mill, John Stuart. 'Of the Stationary State.' From *Principles of Political Economy*, Book IV, Chapter VI. https://www.panarchy.org/mill/stationary.1848.html [Accessed 15/6/2024].

Ruskin, John. 'Unto The Last.' In *The Genius of John Ruskin: Selections from His Writings*. Edited by John D. Rosenberg. University of Virginia Press, 1997.

Schiller, Frederich. *Essays*. Edited by Daniel O. Dahlstrom and Walter Hinderer. Bloomsbury Academic, 1993.

Schumacher, F.E. *Small is Beautiful: A Study of Economics as If People Mattered*. Vintage Books, 1993.

Young, Michael. *The Rise of the Meritocracy*. Transaction Publishing, 1958:1994.

2

Imagining a Liberal Future

Benjamin Wood

A map of the world that does not include Utopia is not worth even glancing at, for it leaves out the one country at which Humanity is always landing. And when Humanity lands there, it looks out, and, seeing a better country, sets sail. Progress is the realisation of Utopias.[1]

In an era of acute economic, environmental and political crisis, what should liberal politics aim for? The question is not arcane, nor rarified, but increasingly pressing. In its orbit are carried perennial matters of urgency, including the meaning of freedom, the role of government, alongside the character and purpose of economics. If liberals are to play any decisive role in shaping these terrains of human endeavour, they must know where they seek to go, and what they value most in both life and politics. They must have not merely policies, but an answer to the opening query, 'what is it that you hope for?' They must cultivate the capacity to imagine a liberal future, a far shore which orders their principles, renews their energy, and sustains their ideals. To resolve this existential problem of ultimate aims, we should in the first instance turn our minds to the recent past. One of the treasures of political autobiography are the memoirs of Jo Grimond (1913-1994), leader of Britain's Liberal Party, from 1956 to 1967 (and again briefly in 1976). While Grimond never achieved high office, he was a keen intellectual, with a hinterland spanning art, literature and history. Unlike his contemporaries Harold Wilson and Edward Heath, he was not by temperament a political fixer or party-manager. He was rather a deep thinker, who possessed an uncanny capacity to look beyond immediate political crises, and ask deep questions about the structure, direction, and goals of contemporary politics.

1   Oscar Wilde, 'The Soul of Man Under Socialism,' in *The Complete Works of Oscar Wilde Volume IV: Criticism: Historical Criticism, Intentions, The Soul of Man*, ed. Bobby Fong, Joseph Bristow and Ian Small (Oxford University Press, 2000), p. 247.

In an age when public questions had become colonised by a breed of bland Keynesian technocrats, he thought of politics in unfashionably grand terms. He was not afraid to talk about the ideals of civilisation, the threats of barbarism, or the horrors of crass materialism. Grimond found in the ideals of the ancient Greeks (if not always in their practice) a compelling fable which allowed him to diagnose many contemporary ailments. At its best, he thought the Athenian conception of the polis (rooted in shared citizenship, participation, and responsibility) provided a dynamic model for contemporary liberal democratic politics. In the alluring light of ancient democracy, Grimond turned to the politics of the 20th century and found them wanting. In the final chapter of his memoir, he strikes a startlingly pessimistic note:

> We have succumbed to the worship of the great idol of 'more'. Technical and economic determinism, blind to human values, now decides where we must go. Science and machinery, we are told, under the bureaucracies will conjure up more and more of everything. Our role is to sit up and beg, being content with whatever [is] thrown us. The Christian and Greek teachings which although seldom followed point towards the right way, are now derided. The Greeks taught the delight of self-expression, play, creation, art. They treated human communities as heirs of past triumphs and guardians of the future. They and their Christian successors hoped that we might by adding to its heritage leave the world a better place.[2]

Against this august Greek-Christian sensibility, Grimond detected a rising coarsening of Western societies, driven by an instrumental attitude to people and nature. In a world where the bottom-line was all, industrialists, technicians and managers found ever more ingenious mechanisms for piling up riches, but paid little attention to the quality of politics, the state of our friendships, or the vibrancy of our public ideals. As Grimond lamented: 'We see now a cult of barbarism, with airlines ticketed out with the most expensive planes available, in the burning up of energy, in the scramble for new gadgets, and the trampling down of non-conformity. Human beings are discounted.'[3] There is something in this litany of pessimism which recalls the past destruction of civilisations. In the age of Pericles, Athens

2   Jo Grimond, *Memoirs* (Heiman, 1979), pp. 294-5.
3   Grimond, *Memoirs*, p. 295.

felt itself to be the centre of the world. Its art, riches, and culture spoke of an untouchable greatness. Yet, as Thucydides chronicles in his *History of the Peloponnesian War*, there was a cankerous worm at the heart of the Athenian polis. Sumptuousness bred arrogance, security bred recklessness, learning bred foolishness. In this spirit of Thucydidean pity Grimond tells his readers living in a latter-day Athens:

> Looking around London it is uglier, dirtier, more expensively and more incompetently run than it was ten years ago. Many of the people in the Underground railway look like refugees from a prison camp. The standard of life may statistically be rising but it is difficult to discern greater well-being in either the homes or faces of most people. A certain mulish worry seems a prevalent expression. Yet their avowed inability, in spite of the vast armoury of tools now at their disposal, to conduct affairs economically or competently does not prevent our governors from essaying constant interference in our lives when it suits them.[4]

What shall we make of such a dire portrait? Almost immediately after writing, Grimond's mournful assessment took on a peculiar strangeness, pushing against a dominant story of progress and prosperity. After 1989, Western politicians heaved a collective sigh of relief. The Soviet Union had disintegrated, Germany had been reunified, and the Western economies were beginning to recover from the cycles of stops and shocks which had characterised their sluggish performance since the mid-1970s. Britain, after the painful dysfunctions of Thatcherism, was beginning to settle into something like an ideological consensus. John Major, the moderate Tory, was the perfect representative of a country grown weary of ideological crusades and hard economic medicine. Yet, Grimond sensed, against the shallow instincts of many political commentators, that underneath this new shiny consumer society were deep and unaddressed contradictions. In the midst of Britain's deep post-Brexit malaise. it might be time to admit that the doom-saying of Grimond possesses some profound truths. On paper we are one of the richest countries on earth, surrounded daily with technological marvels, but the country feels anxious, shabby, spent of purpose, and sick with both insecurity and the shallow prosperity of the few. But herein lies the key point. The formation of Brexit Britain was

4   Grimond, *Memoirs*, p. 293.

never just a technical question of being part of a political and trading bloc. It always was an existential question about political meaning. What are our lives together for? Where are we going? How do we navigate a world where most of us feel practically helpless to effect change? Can the country be better than this? This is precisely why the cynical Brexiteer cry of 'take back control' spoke to many. In our rapidly changing world an increasing number of people feel scared, anchorless, without a sense of home, and with little sense of a future. What tools should we use to understand the state of decay we appear to be in? How do we translate Grimond's talk of Greek ideals into a diagnosis for our own times? What needs fixing so we avoid something akin to a Thucydidean collapse? To address these quandaries, I propose to read Grimond's sorrowful petition of decay through the work of Hannah Arendt (1906–1975). Like Grimond, Arendt was a student of the Greeks. Confronted with the alienation and technological horrors of the 20th century, Arendt sought a rebirth of old ideals. She desired the best of the old Greek city, purged of its slavery and thirst for domination. At a time when our island feels like its inexorably sinking into a sea of sorrow and memory, Arendt throws us something of a lifeline, just as Grimond spells out the character of the storm. In clasping hold of this raft, we can discover not only remedies for our immediate troubles, but a means of re-energising half-forgotten liberal ideals of participation, self-creation, and civic dignity. These values, among others, have the capacity to anchor us in ways that consumerism, and fantasies of endless prosperity simply cannot.

Hannah Arendt in hollow streets

Perhaps the best place to begin is to consider what Grimond calls 'the idol of "more"'. By excavating the roots of modern consumerism, we might discover much of what is driving our increasingly fraught and fraying politics, not only in Britain, but in the post-industrial West more generally. How is it, that many contemporary British people are surrounded by relative safety and convenience and yet feel hateful, afraid, and disconnected from one another? Today, Arendt is known primarily as the great theorist of totalitarianism, but this ignores her other substantial contributions to political thought. Of particular concern in Arendt's work is the way in which liberal-democratic ideals of participation and citizenship, have given way to an apolitical purchaser society of toil and consumption. As Arendt observes in *The Human Condition* (1958): 'The modern age has carried with it a theoretical glorification of labour and has resulted in a factual transformation of the whole of society into a labouring society.'[5] In this valorisation of labour what does Arendt think has been lost? In her view, capitalist worker-states have lost the capacity to think beyond the narrow confines of economic necessity, towards 'the "beautiful," that is, with things neither necessary nor merely useful…the life devoted to the matters of the *polis*, in which excellence produces beautiful deeds.'[6] Frenzied activities of production and consumption increasingly replace the seeking after virtuous modes of life, and the perfection of the political community. And while equality is proclaimed as the primary ideal in such a society, worker-equalitarianism is merely an expression of the conformist levelling required by the logic of mass-production and mass-distribution. Our sameness is increasingly a result, not of a sense of togetherness as citizens, but the outcome of economic standardisation. We walk down the same bleak streets, with the same clone shops, in increasingly identical homes. A longing for the betterment of the community, has been largely replaced by the acquisition of things.

Nonetheless, as widespread poor mental health testifies, this work-society is not meeting deep human needs. What are these needs? They are illustrated in two probing questions, 'Does my life matter?' 'Am I making a difference to anything?' Judging by the rise of what the anthropologist David Graeber has called 'bullshit jobs', a growing number of people say 'no' to both vital questions. In this pervasive state of anomie what is left to hold onto? Responses to such meaning-deprivation are various, but one reaction in particular preoccupied Arendt, namely the racial ideology of the Far Right. In the absence of strong local and civic identities, Arendt believed that people sought to inherit their way into belonging and mattering through an appeal to ethnic myths. This desire becomes violent and totalitarian when people are willing to escape meaninglessness at any price. The seedbed of such a politics is, according to Arendt, a condition of widespread loneliness. As Arendt notes in *The Origins of Totalitarianism*:

> What makes loneliness so unbearable is the loss of one's own self which can be realized in solitude but confirmed in its identity only by the trusting and trustworthy company of my equals. In this situation, man loses trust

---

5   Hannah Arendt, *The Human Condition* (University of Chicago Press, 1958: 1998), pp. 4-5.
6   Arendt, *The Human Condition*, p. 13.

in himself as the partner of his thoughts and that elementary confidence in the world which is necessary to make experiences at all. Self and world, capacity for thought and experience are lost at the same time... What prepares men for totalitarian domination in the non-totalitarian world is the fact that loneliness, once a borderline experience usually suffered in certain marginal conditions like old age, has become an everyday experience of the ever-growing masses of our century. The merciless process into which totalitarianism drives and organizes the masses looks like a suicidal escape from this reality.[7]

Politics without polis

How does this speak to our own context? In the wasteland of austerity, a housing-shortage, stuttering pay, and insecure jobs, one can see Britain plummeting into rootlessness. While we have not yet sunk into totalitarian conditions, it may be justly asked whether we have any adequate defences against such forces when and if they arrive. Bluntly, we no longer have the institutions to root us, and in the ruins, hatred and suspicion continues to grow. In the heated, sometimes poisonous debates concerning immigration, we are offered a glimpse of a possible future, one in which an atomised community of strangers turns on the helpless outsider to relieve its own loneliness. How did we get here? Fintan O'Toole, in his book *Heroic Failure: Brexit and the Politics of Pain*, chronicles how the welfare state of 1945 gave the weary people who had lost an empire a noble and ennobling vision of caring for the sick, protecting the old, and educating the young. The mixed economy held the promise of a mighty compromise between capital and labour, state-socialism, and market discipline.[8] Yet, as post-war optimism mutated into economic pessimism in the late 1970s and early 1980s, people felt increasingly cheated by this grand vision. As Grimond reflected on its shortfalls in 1978: 'What is true is that collectivism has been the dominant strain in British (and indeed in Western) thinking for the last forty years or so. This has affected social services, as it has all sides of politics. State or bureaucratic socialism has won the day over varieties of Christian or democratic socialism such as syndicalism. Control of officials on behalf of the public has been largely accepted.'[9] Far from improving the public welfare, Grimond contended that

---

7   Hannah Arendt, *The Origins of Totalitarianism* (Penguin, 1951:2017), pp. 626-7.
8   Fintan O'Toole, *Heroic Failure: Brexit and the Politics of Pain* (Apollo, 2018), p. 19.
9   Jo Grimond, *The Common Welfare* (Maurice Temple Smith, 1978), p. 70.

the extension of officialdom had increased patronage, corruption, and the dependence of civil society and the private sector on state-handouts.

Thatcherism, in its valorisation of Victorian values, attempted to correct this situation by insisting on self-reliance and civic responsibility. Yet in an era of mass-advertising, and the credit card, these ideals soon degenerated into crass consumerism, and the glorification of selfishness. As Margaret Thatcher later confided to her friend, the Labour MP Frank Field, she expected her party's slashing of tax rates to herald a new age of civic engagement and philanthropy – when (in high Tory fashion) the rich would once again take care of the poor. The fact that this promised land of civic responsibility did not emerge bewildered her.[10]

The rapid deindustrialisation of Britain in the 1980s did not herald a new Victorian age. The rich of the Home Counties prospered, while the rest of the country creaked and withered. Thatcher's miscalculation was to make a significant contribution towards our present malaise. In the world after Thatcherism and New Labour, it is not entirely clear what holds this island together. In a country where shopping seems more central than citizenship, people can feel themselves to be profoundly alone, displacing their disconnection with an ever more bewildering profusion of consumer goods. For Arendt, such a state of affairs is always unsatisfactory, because it degrades the dignity of the individual person. It reduces the rights-bearing citizen to a passive creature of consumption, incapable of virtue, creativity, or purpose. We could be so much more, but the apolitical domain of the shop window invites us to divert our energies from the city to ourselves, from collective, to private concerns. As Arendt notes disdainfully: 'In Greece…it was the ever-frustrated ambition of all tyrants to discourage the citizens from worrying about public affairs, from idling their time away in unproductive *ago-reuein* and *politeuesthai*, and to transform the *agora* into an assemblage of shops like the bazaars of oriental despotism.'[11]

Here we observe the deep material roots of our powerlessness. In advanced post-industrial societies, most of us are not the fulfiller of our own needs. We wait to be satisfied by corporations and government agencies. We do not feel any ownership over the world about us. We do not believe we have

---

10   Frank Field, 'What would Thatcher do today about . . . the rich,' *The Times*, 18 April 2013, https://www.thetimes.com/article/582a8b7e-ca6b-4905-935c-449859462239 [Accessed 12/12/2024].

11   Arendt, *The Human Condition*, p. 160.

the capacity to perform any deeds that will endure or produce any beauty that will last. The impersonality of modern organisation renders us a passive cog in wheels we can neither control, nor comprehend. In such conditions of isolation, the banner of Brexit and the heroic nationalist myth becomes irresistible. In a polis that has become empty of politics, the flag becomes a talisman against the sense that we belong nowhere. But, in the end, this talisman, this flag, presents an 'imaginary community'. It is a pleasant piece of poetry, a myth which is increasingly refuted by experience. It does not really meet people's sense of meaninglessness; it only masks it. How does Arendt think we can escape from the existential senselessness of the work society? Looking back to ancient Athens, Arendt argues that the only cure is a society in which civil participation is felt to be the preserve of all citizens, not just elected officials or selected technocrats. This is the cure, she argues, not merely to public meaninglessness, but an answer to those demagogues who would take advantage of our fear and loneliness for their own political ends. Since the very early days of her philosophical career, contemporaries found Arendt hard to characterise. Sometimes she sounded like a conservative. She relished in the aristocratic ideals of Athenian society and longed for some version of their return. Yet, she often sounded like a socialist, railing against the alienations and indignities of a mechanised de-humanised society. At other times, Arendt sounded like an inveterate anarchist. In the human life stripped of dignity by crowds, mobs, and bureaucracies, she discerned the source of the many horrors of the 20th century. In truth, it seems Arendt thought all these streams were fruitful avenues through which to repair politics. What held these tendencies together was her contention that there was no long-term future for the consumer worker-state, whether Capitalist or Soviet. Politics must be rethought if modern human beings were to avoid futility and despair. As she wrote at the beginning *of The Human Condition*:

> Closer at hand and perhaps equally decisive is another no less threatening event. This is the advent of automation, which in a few decades probably will empty the factories and liberate mankind from its oldest and most natural burden, the burden of labouring and the bondage to necessity. Here, too, a fundamental aspect of the human condition is at stake, but the rebellion against it, the wish to be liberated from labour's 'toil and trouble', is not modern but as old as recorded history. Freedom from labour itself is not new; it once belonged among the most firmly established privileges

of the few. In this instance, it seems as though scientific progress and technical developments had been only taken advantage of to achieve something about which all former ages dreamed but which none had been able to realize.[12]

The labouring society and its discontents

Underlying Arendt's remarks is the important classical distinction between 'work' and 'labour'. For the philosophers (most prominently Aristotle) work is what we build a meaningful life around. Work refers to those acts which connect the present with the future, foster beauty and meaning for ourselves and others. Labour by contrast involves those needful activities that are required to keep one alive. They are not sources of meaning, but blunt expressions of biological need. It was Aristotle's contention that the life of necessity was always lower in the scale of human goods to the life of work because the latter allowed the individual freedom to care about his city and the people in it. A life of drudgery dedicated to the production of goods was for Aristotle incompatible with the political and outward-facing life of the citizen. The activity of the workman was the domain of the apolitical slave. As Aristotle expressed this idea in *Politics*: 'any task, craft, or branch of learning should be considered vulgar if it renders the body or mind of free people useless for the practices and activities of virtue. That is why the crafts that put the body in worse condition and work done for wages are called vulgar; for they debase the mind and deprive it of leisure'.[13] Despite the welcome elimination of mass-slavery in modern cultures, Arendt believed that latter-day technological societies are nonetheless surprisingly grim because they have largely departed from the Greek separation between labour and work. Instead of giving human beings the opportunity to perfect themselves through politics, the pressures of contemporary money-making reduce the horizons of many people to a narrow range of concerns. Instead of seeking out a good life, modern people are so bombarded with prices, goods, and expenditures that these commercial matters begin to absorb all their attention. Their minds become so fixated on the acquisition of material things that they cease to look for moral, aesthetic, or intellectual satisfactions. As a consequence, the deep joys of human experience (friendship, connection,

12 Arendt, *The Human Condition*, p. 4.
13 Aristotle, *Politics*, 1337 a10–11, trans. C.D.C. Reeve (Hackett Publishing, 1998), p. 228.

creativity, learning) are constantly being crowded out. As the cultural critic Walter Benjamin once summarised this predicament:

> The freedom of conversation is being lost. If, earlier, it was a matter of course in conversation to take interest in one's interlocutor, now this is replaced by an inquiry into the cost of his shoes or of his umbrella. Irresistibly intruding on any convivial exchange is the theme of the conditions of life, of money. What this theme involves is not so much the concerns and sorrows of individuals, in which they may be able to help one another, as the overall picture. It is as if one were trapped in a theatre and had to follow the events on the stage, whether one wanted to or not—had to make them again and again, willing, or unwilling, the subject of one's thought and speech.[14]

Here we are introduced to a peculiarly modern form of impoverishment. The office worker may inhabit clean and well-regulated surroundings, but her daily activities consist in a series of meaningless tasks that trap her life in the drudgery of labour.[15] She is a colleague and co-worker, but she does no useful work (in the Aristotelian sense). The demands of the workplace (e-mails, reports, and meetings) leave her without the time or energy to consider the community she is part of. Her job, its daily commute and inflexible routines actively isolates her from a sense of the 'public'. The same well-organised deprivation is equally discernible in the case of the night-time shop-worker, the delivery driver, or the personal care assistant. Labour absorbs not merely time, but life-energy, not simply attention, but possibility. And as Arendt's remarks signpost, automation holds out the distinct possibility of the restoration of meaningful work. Instead of giving our lives over to the rat-race of career-orientated consumption, we can again start thinking of society and politics as terrains for purpose, care, and connection. In a world where the factory (and office) is increasingly empty, politics can become something we do as leisure, not in-between work. In this renewed vision of the polis, we can care about our common choices, not as an anxious after-thought, but as a daily reality. In such a post-acquisition society, a thousand forms of social life could be given the space to flourish.

---

14 Walter Benjamin, *One-Way Street*, trans. Peter Demetz (Harvard University Press, 2016), p. 37.

15 Arendt, *The Human Condition*, p. 151.

In past centuries the majority laboured so the few could pursue their life-projects. Artists, priests, legislators and philosophers worked for lasting glory, while the majority toiled in hateful servitude. Now we are on the cusp of a world without paralysing need and senseless slog.

Of course, the municipal socialist and collectivist anarchist would be at home in such a future. Insofar as the money-society cloaks hopelessness and violence of all kinds, the end of worthless labour represents the deepest hopes of many a leftist utopia. Yet, we should not underestimate the extent to which such a vision responds to the deepest needs of the patriotic conservative. It was the philosopher Michael Oakeshott who argued that conservatism always prefers 'the familiar to the unknown, to prefer the tried to the untried, fact to mystery, the actual to the possible, the limited to the unbounded, the near to the distant, the sufficient to the superabundant, the convenient to the perfect, present laughter to utopian bliss.'[16] Yet, there is nothing more utopian, nothing more obsessed with the unbounded and the distant, than our consumer-society. In its constant fixation on future satisfaction, it depreciates the present, the actual and the concrete. How can any true love of country be born when our lives are marred by insecurity, anxiety, and greed? How can the cult of 'more' even come close to the love of place? Arendt's return to old political ideals, offers a route of escape. In a society where labour is no longer the defining activity of life, the patriot may rediscover the love of locality as an actual feeling, not a mere notion preserved in a flag. The bombastic neo-liberalism of the 1980s and 1990s has obscured this vision from us. For too long, ideologues and commentators have defined freedom in terms both egoistic and materialistic. We have forgotten an older idealistic conception of liberty, one that includes the virtues of love, care, and fellowship. As the radical liberal philosopher T.H. Green argued in his *Prolegomena to Ethics* (1890):

> Now the self of which a man thus forecasts the fulfilment, is not an abstract or empty self. It is a self already affected in the most primitive forms of human life by manifold interests, among which are interests in other persons. These are not merely interests dependent on other persons for the means to their gratification, but interests in the good of those other persons, interests which cannot be satisfied without the consciousness that

16 Michael Oakeshott, 'On Being Conservative', in *Rationalism in Politics and Other Essays* (Liberty Fund, 1991), pp. 408-9.

those other persons are satisfied. The man cannot contemplate himself as in a better state, or on the way to the best, without contemplating others, not merely as a means to that better state, but as sharing it with him.[17]

In this account of the political life, we begin, not with the abstractions of economics, private ego, or sprawling nations, but first and foremost, with the transformative power of human relationships. It is for Green, only by loving what is concrete, human, and interdependent, that we can discover the meaning of what the liberal theorists have called 'self-realisation'. No tools, objects or structures can serve as a surrogate for genuine sociality. Even 'freedom' cannot serve its purpose (that of expanding personal possibilities) if it is cut off from the lives and needs of others. The one who seeks genuine liberty, says Green, is she who knows that the lives of others are necessarily included in any quest for a higher, better self. All increases in the spheres of thought and action always depend upon deep social roots. Here notions of reciprocity and obligation are more than merely burdens or constraints on an otherwise boundless individual. They are a means of enlarging, crystalising, and perfecting the self that heeds them. In webs of sympathy we become more ourselves and not less. We move from symbols, generalities, and gestures to the marrow of politics; persons in repeated encounter, loving, speaking, loathing, contending, but never walking away from the repeated demand to live together.

Glancing a further horizon

The one small garden of a free gardener was all his need and due, not a garden swollen to a realm: his own hands to use, not the hands of others to command.[18]

The vision of society sketched above is undoubtedly liberal in its most compelling sense. It assumes not merely liberty as an end in itself, but cherishes a civic liberality, a generosity of spirit which seeks its full actualisation in and through the lives of others. By cherishing transformative leisure, locality, and the hunger for meaning, such a politics would provide the most benign climate imaginable for liberal ideals to flourish. But unlike

17   Thomas Hill Green, *Prolegomena to Ethics* (Clarendon Press, 1890), §199, p. 210.
18   J.R.R. Tolkien, *The Lord of the Rings* (HarperCollins, 2005), p. 901.

its consumerist counterpart which terminates in the acquisition of 'things', this hoped-for liberal citizen is defined by her sociability, her capacity to give and create, not merely consume, and amass. In his more optimistic moments, Grimond saw a new world emerging from the husk of the old. At its centre was the image of a vibrant and self-conscious citizenry, animated by altruism, personal affection, and a deep reverence for self-government. Looking back over the previous half-century of hierarchical state-control and corporate power, Grimond observed how poverty and rootlessness had not been overcome, but in some areas had substantially deepened. Higher growth rates and greater consumer variety had not generated the peace and unmatched security foreseen by its architects. The true answer to these deep woes lay, thought Grimond, in a wholesale renewal of local life. As he noted in 1983: 'If the opportunities of the poor are to be enhanced by more resources, we must build up from local communities. The sphere of local government must be more carefully defined, but each community should be encouraged to develop the way of life best suited to it within that sphere.'[19] This meant, said Grimond, 'decentralisation of decision-making, of government, of industry, of the social services, of education.'[20] Rejected were industrial monoliths and soulless office blocs.

Enthusiastically embraced was 'the active participation of individuals'[21] who intended to craft institutions that suited their specific needs. In Grimond's utopia, life was to be organised on a comprehensible human scale, a world hospitable to street-level management, networked groups, and bottom-up initiatives. Thus, Liberal politics, in Grimond's idiosyncratic model, involved the giving over of social and economic space to those instincts of sympathy, solidarity and initiative for which state-bureaucracies and corporate management find little immediate use.

For his part, Grimond believed that the bare bones for such a decentralised culture were already a reality in the late 1980s. Arendt's world of empty factories was swiftly coming to pass. Traditional heavy industry was dying, while at the same time a new class of professional workers began to emerge. Extractive industries were increasingly capital intensive but employed fewer and fewer full-time workers. Harold Wilson's 'white-hot heat of technology' was, as prophesied, felling all before it. Reflecting on

19 Jo Grimond, *A Personal Manifesto* (Martin Robinson, 1983), p. 161.
20 Grimond, *A Personal Manifesto*, p.160.
21 Grimond, *A Personal Manifesto*, p.160.

Britain's economic position in 1978, Grimond noted: '[At] the time of writing we are bedevilled by what is optimistically considered a temporary lack of work, we may have to resign ourselves to a higher level of unemployment than was once thought necessary.'[22]

Not all was doom and gloom, however. In the ashes of the workers-state Grimond believed that something like 'socialism without a state' might yet spring up to replace it. Echoing the politics of Robert Owen, Grimond argued for a pluralist political settlement capable of replacing the gigantic forces of centralising government and corporate enterprise. People would find renewed purpose, not through the agitation of their desires, but through the possibility of involvement in the life of the community. Through a network of local institutions, co-operatives and unions, Grimond saw a way to break with the crass materialism and political apathy of the modern world. Yet, as Grimond was at pains to point out, his liberal syndicalism was not the workers-state of conspicuous consumption reborn. Any effort expended in the new state of plenty should not be an end in itself, but as a means to 'play, self-expression, dancing, enjoyment, and tolerance.'[23] Underpinning Grimond's post-labour society was the right of every citizen to be paid a minimum income.[24]

Such a scheme would not only protect people against poverty[25] but expand the range of voluntary activity. Not only would such citizens have a greater opportunity to care for the needy but would be freer to devote themselves to activities that would enrich community life, including art and the maintenance of local amenities like libraries, theatres, and ad hoc forms of community education. Noting the modern rise in self-employment, Grimond speculated optimistically: 'Self-employment must include, indeed largely consist of, work for the community.'[26] Cities, once designed for the requirements of industrial workers and office-bound bureaucrats, could finally be refashioned to accommodate a greater range of pastimes and pleasurable pursuits.[27]

---

22 Jo Grimond, *The Common Welfare* (Maurice Temple Smith, 1978), pp. 49-9.
23 Grimond, *The Common Welfare*, p. 139.
24 Grimond, *The Common Welfare*, p. 42.
25 An excellent summary of Jo Grimond's Basic Income Scheme can be found in The Parliamentary Debates (Hansard), House of Lords official report, volume 465, pp. 290-291.
26 Grimond, *The Common Welfare*, p. 147.
27 Grimond, *The Common Welfare*, p. 147.

After centuries of indignity, Grimond believed that the West could again find its centre of gravity in the agora, and its promise of a life of beauty and significance. In the possibility of vacant offices and museum factories, Grimond discerned the contours of a richer life within our grasp. What have such grand plans got to do with our present social and political malaise? I contend that we cannot understand the pathologies of ultra-populism, nativism, and rising authoritarianism unless we address deep human needs – the need to belong, to create, to mould, to matter.

People are angry because they feel homeless, bereft of significance, and without anchor in a rapidly changing world. Unless we rise to the challenge of our present conditions, the multiplying contradictions of our age will swallow us whole. Such an undertaking appears politically urgent in Britain as our system of government stutters and strains under the weight of structural inertia. Yet, such a project is needed in all the post-industrial economies. The factories continue to empty, the amount of necessary labour keeps shrinking, and yet, we continue to sustain the worker-state, dimly aware of the misery we are in. There must be a better world than this. Both Grimond and Arendt articulate a resolute refusal to be diverted from the possibility of a larger, fuller life. No facsimile of politics should ever be accepted for the real thing. Either the polis is based on participation or there is no polis. Either we find ways of enhancing beauty and meaning, or we will sink into greed, violence, and loneliness. Citizenship must mean more than a flag and a passport but personify an invitation into a shared project of civic betterment. This then is the generous ideal towards which liberals should move. We must harness our wealth and technology to the cause of community and leisure, individuality, and fellowship. This is our task; this is our challenge.

Bibliography

Arendt, Hannah. *The Human Condition.* University of Chicago Press, 1958: 1998.
— *The Origins of Totalitarianism.* Penguin, 1951:2017.
Aristotle. *Politics.* Translated by C.D.C. Reeve. Hackett Publishing, 1998.
Benjamin, Walter. *One-Way Street.* Translated by Peter Demetz. Harvard University Press, 2016.
Field, Frank. 'What would Thatcher do today about… the rich.' *The Times,* 18 April 2013. https://www.thetimes.com/article/582a8b7e-ca6b-4905-

935c-449859462239 [Accessed 12/12/2024].

Green, Thomas Hill. *Prolegomena to Ethics*. Clarendon Press, 1890.

Grimond, Jo. *The Common Welfare*. Maurice Temple Smith, 1978.

— *Memoirs*. Heiman, 1979.

— *A Personal Manifesto*. Martin Robinson, 1983.

O'Toole, Fintan. *Heroic Failure: Brexit and the Politics of Pain*. Apollo, 2018.

Oakeshott, Michael. *Rationalism in Politics and Other Essays*. Liberty Fund, 1991.

Tolkien, J.R.R. *The Lord of the Rings*. HarperCollins, 2005.

Wilde, Oscar. *The Complete Works of Oscar Wilde Volume IV: Criticism: Historical Criticism, Intentions, The Soul of Man*. Edited by Bobby Fong, Joseph Bristow and Ian Small. Oxford University Press, 2000.

3

Individuality and the Common Good

Helena Rosenblatt

John Stuart Mill is best known today for his passionate advocacy of individual liberty. His essay, *On Liberty* (1859), is celebrated as one of the most powerful defences of individual freedom ever written and is what has earned him a hallowed place in the liberal canon. Neither the state nor society, Mill declared, should be permitted to impose its values on individuals: 'The only freedom which deserves the name is that of pursuing our own good in our own way.'[1] If one sentence encapsulates Mill's thought, this is it.

However, Mill's thoughts on freedom are more complex and nuanced than this sentence suggests, because he did not advocate freedom just for freedom's sake. He had a moral goal in mind. Mill was not only a famous philosopher, political economist, and politician, but also, and like many 19th century liberals, a social critic and moralist. He intended the freedom he advocated to foster a morally progressive citizenry, one that strove to contribute to the public good. It was for this reason that he championed 'individuality' (a word he repeated 17 times in *On Liberty*) and never 'individualism'. It behoves us to understand why this distinction matters. The distinction is particularly important today, as we grapple to understand what freedom means in our modern society at the level of the individual, the economy and society in general.

Today, 'individualism' evokes many positive values, such as self-reliance and independence. In the realm of politics, it evokes a belief in the sanctity of individual rights. In this, individualism can be regarded as the opposite of collectivism. In Mill's day, however, the word carried mostly negative connotations. It connoted license and selfishness, and the disregard for the norms and traditions that made society possible and held it together. Liberals

---

1   John Stuart Mill, 'On Liberty,' in *'On Liberty' and Other Writings*, ed. Stefan Collini (Cambridge University Press, 2012), p. 16.

before Mill, such as Benjamin Constant (1767-1830) and Madame de Staël (1766-1817), avoided the word completely. Constant endorsed 'individuality' instead. In his masterpiece, *Democracy in America*,[2] Alexis de Tocqueville (1805-1859) called individualism a modern form of selfishness and warned his readers that democracy would only make it grow. Mill, who reviewed both volumes of Tocqueville's book favourably, agreed. Mill rejected both self-interestedness and individualism, which he likened to the rampant competition that exists in a dog-eat-dog world. Individualism meant:

> …each one for himself and against all the rest. It is grounded on opposition of interests, not harmony of interests, and under it every one is required to find his place by a struggle, by pushing others…[3]

Individuality, however, meant something altogether different. In his introduction to the Cambridge University Press edition of Mill's *On Liberty*, Stefan Collini tells us that Mill's essay should be seen as 'the single most eloquent, most significant and most influential statement of the irreducible value of human individuality'.[4] But what did Mill actually mean by individuality? He never proffered an exact definition, perhaps because he expected his 19th century readers to understand what he meant. Today, we can surmise his meaning from the rest of his essay. A human being is 'progressive', he writes, and, as such, is meant to 'grow and develop' intellectually and morally.[5] Individuality is the result of this growth. It is closely related to 'character';[6] and together they foster a flourishing life and happiness.

Mill meant something special by happiness. Although a utilitarian and a follower of Jeremy Bentham (1748-1832), he did not share Bentham's views on happiness and was not a hedonist in the normal sense of the word. Like Bentham, Mill did not build his defence of the individual on the foundation

---

2   Alexis De Tocqueville, *Democracy in America, II:I*, trans. Henry Reeve, Project Gutenberg: https://shorturl.at/eDSwe [Accessed 4/12/2024].

3   John Stuart Mill, 'The Claims of Labour,' in *The Collected Works of John Stuart Mill*, vol. 4, ed. John M. Robson (University of Toronto Press, 1963-91), p. 379, as quoted in C. Heydt, 'The Ethics of Character: John Stuart Mill on Aesthetic Education,' PhD dissertation (Boston University, 1994), p. 184.

4   Stefan Collini, 'Introduction,' *On Liberty and Other Writings*, p. vii.

5   Mill, *On Liberty*, pp. 14, 60.

6   'Character' is a word used at least 40 times in *On Liberty* alone.

of natural rights but believed instead that any rights had to be underwritten by the happiness they brought about to both the individual and society. Where Mill disagreed with Bentham was in his belief that there were higher (intellectual and emotional) and lower (physical and material) pleasures. It was the pursuit of the former that fostered individuality and led to personal fulfilment. Mill also differed from Bentham when it came to moral duty and virtue. Unlike Bentham, who did not regard disinterestedness as a necessary good or goal, Mill argued that a person who lacked virtue would be unable to contribute constructively towards the general good of society. Virtue was both a 'good in itself' and 'conducive to the general happiness'.[7] There was an important condition, however, and it was that virtue should always be freely chosen, never coerced. Choosing virtue voluntarily resulted in a higher form of personal happiness. This reminds us that the goal of Mill's individual liberty was not just to improve individuals, but society as a whole. The cultivation of individuality and the promotion of the public good were inextricably connected.

This does not mean that Mill trusted the public to make decisions for the individual, however. Many today assume that *On Liberty* is primarily about the need to limit government intrusion into the lives of individuals, but this is a simplification and mischaracterisation of the essay's intended message. Mill rebelled against '*social* tyranny'[8] as much, or even more, than '*political* despotism'.[9] '[T]he yoke of opinion' he wrote, 'could often be heavier than the law'.[10] Indeed, it was 'more formidable than many kinds of political oppression'.[11]

Growing up in a Victorian society, Mill had experienced firsthand not just the restrictive force of its laws, but also its conventions. As a youth, he was arrested for distributing information about birth control. As an adult, he was ostracised for his relationship with Harriet Taylor. Throughout his life, he felt obliged to remain silent about his unorthodox religious beliefs. Society's straightjacket was even worse than the state because it was so hard

---

7   Quoted in Julia Driver, 'The History of Utilitarianism,' in *The Stanford Encyclopedia of Philosophy*, ed. Edward N. Zalta and Uri Nodelman (Winter 2022 edition), https://plato.stanford.edu/archives/win2022/entries/utilitarianism-history/ [Accessed 1/11/2024].
8   Mill, *On Liberty*, p. 8, emphasis added.
9   Mill, *On Liberty*, p. 9, emphasis added.
10   Mill, *On Liberty*, p. 12.
11   Mill, *On Liberty*, p. 8.

to escape. It penetrated into one's life, 'enslaving the soul itself.'[12] Public opinion was self-righteous and intolerant. Oppressive conventions turned human beings into 'sheep' or 'ape-like' imitators.[13] State and society worked together to 'prevent the formation of any individuality.'[14] All of this was preventing social progress.

For individuals to develop and improve themselves and their society, the shackles on their minds had to be removed and diversity, even eccentricity, positively encouraged. Individuals should be free to express their ideas and pursue their own 'paths.'[15] They should be permitted to make their own choices, engage in 'experiments in living'[16] and learn from these.

> He who does anything because it is the custom, makes no choice. He gains
> no practice either in discerning or in desiring what is best. The mental
> and moral, like the muscular powers, are improved only by being used.[17]

Freedom of expression was particularly important because it led to a diversity of opinion, which Mill thought was essential for the discovery of 'truth'.[18] The 'collision of opinions'[19] led to the improvement of both individuals and society. Even 'eccentricity' was good, while conformity presented a 'hindrance to human advancement.'[20] The desire to improve society permeates all of Mill's major work. A major problem was selfishness:

> One of the commonest types of character among us is that of a man
> all whose ambition is self-regarding: who has no higher purpose in life
> than to enrich or raise in the world himself and his family; who never
> dreams of making the good of his fellow-creatures or of his country an
> habitual object…[21]

---

12   Mill, *On Liberty*, p. 11.
13   Mill, *On Liberty*, pp. 67, 59.
14   Mill, *On Liberty*, p. 8.
15   Mill, *On Liberty*, pp. 59, 72, 89.
16   Mill, *On Liberty*, p. 81. 'Experiments' on pp. 57, 64, 81, 106, 110.
17   Mill, *On Liberty*, p. 59.
18   Mill, *On Liberty*, p. 20.
19   Mill, *On Liberty*, p. 53.
20   Mill, *On Liberty*, pp. 67, 49.
21   John Stuart Mill, *Inaugural address, delivered to the University of St. Andrews*, (Longmans, 1867), p. 90.

It was imperative to cultivate 'the feelings and capacities which have the good of others for their object'.[22] He sought ways to encourage 'the more unselfish public spirit and calmer and broader views of duty'.[23] However, Mill was certain that allowing individuals more liberty would be a step in the right direction because 'when each person becomes more valuable to himself, he is capable of being more valuable to others'.[24] Reducing selfishness and improving society was not an easy task. Individuality was a difficult thing for any individual to achieve. It required the courage to be different, the willingness to make choices, and to accept responsibility for their consequences. It meant thinking for oneself, which most human beings find painful. Mill devoted a considerable amount of thought to finding solutions to this problem. He enlisted the help of women and religion.

The role of women

Mill's feminist views are well-known and appreciated. Drawing on many years of collaboration with his intellectual partner, and eventual wife, Harriet Taylor, he argued for the full equality of women, including the right to vote. In *On Liberty*, Mill calls 'the almost despotic power of husbands over wives' an 'evil' that must be abolished.[25] In 1867 he made a speech in the House of Commons advocating 'The Admission of Women to the electoral franchise' and two years later he published the now famous *The Subjection of Women*. In it, he likened marriage to a form of 'slavery' and declared that there should be 'perfect equality' between men and women.[26]

Mill's progressive stance on the issue, so rare in its time, had much to do with his desire to foster individuality and the advancement of society. Women's legal subordination was 'wrong in itself' but also because it was 'one of the chief hindrances to human improvement'.[27] He rejected the idea that women's natures predisposed them to only domestic roles. '[W]hat is now called the nature of women is an eminently artificial thing – the result of forced repression in some directions, unnatural stimulation in others.'[28]

---

22 Mill, *On Liberty*, p. 63.
23 John Stuart Mill, 'The Subjection of Women,' in *'On Liberty' and Other Writings*, ed. Stefan Collini (Cambridge University Press, 2012), p. 213.
24 Mill, *On Liberty*, p. 63.
25 Mill, *On Liberty*, p. 104.
26 He refers to women's 'slavery' 13 times.
27 Mill, *The Subjection of Women*, p. 119.
28 Mill, *The Subjection of Women*, p. 138.

Denying women a free choice as to how to lead their lives and confining them to the management of the household stunted their moral and intellectual capacities. The men responsible for this did so out of base motives and any happiness that resulted were of the lower kind. Granting equality to women would allow them to develop themselves and acquire character too. Moreover, as in the case for men, it would be a gain for society as a whole. As equal partners, they would help in the 'moral regeneration of mankind'.[29] Mill did not deny women's primary role in the family, an institution that he believed had a 'direct influence on human happiness'.[30] However, the only way a family could be the 'school of moral cultivation' is if it became a 'society between equals'.[31] Only a family 'justly constituted'[32] could teach the necessary virtues.

A new religion

Along with women's rights, Mill believed that a reformed religion would be necessary to regenerate society. In *The Utility of Religion*, published posthumously in 1874, he restated his belief that the moral advancement of humanity required reducing selfish impulses. However, by focusing men's thoughts on the afterlife, Christianity only made them more selfish and disconnected from a sense of duty to their fellow men. Like all 'old religions', Christianity degraded man's intellect and character. What was needed, was a 'Religion of Humanity' that would cultivate in individuals 'a deep feeling for the general good'.[33] This would be a secular creed focused on fostering a 'high tone of mind'[34] and a sense of duty towards the welfare of all humanity.

The economy

Regenerating mankind meant adopting a moral attitude to the economy. Mill was not a consistent or staunch advocate of laissez-faire. He had a far more complex position on the economic role of the state than is often recognised and recommended considerably more state 'interference' than is commonly acknowledged. In *On Liberty*, he distinguished between two kinds of actions: self-regarding and other-regarding ones. The first kind affected only the agent,

29 Mill, *The Subjection of Women*, p. 211.
30 Mill, *On Liberty*, p. 108.
31 Mill, *The Subjection of Women*, p. 159.
32 Mill, *The Subjection of Women*, p. 16.
33 John Stuart Mill, 'Utility of Religion,' in *The Collected Works of John Stuart Mill*, vol. 10, ed. J.M. Robson (Routledge and Kegan Paul, 1985), p. 241.
34 Heydt, 'The Ethics of Character.'

while the latter affected other people as well. When it came to self-regarding actions, Mill argued that 'there should be perfect freedom' from coercion.[35] When it came to other-regarding actions, however, he thought that some laws and regulations would likely be necessary. For example, the state might legitimately regulate the sale of alcohol to ensure against fraud. But the state should not be permitted to prohibit its consumption.

Over time, Mill's belief in laissez-faire declined further. His later writings even suggest a sympathy for socialism, or at least for some form of mixed economy. He was sympathetic to the goal of reducing economic inequality and improving the welfare of the working class. In his *Principles of Political Economy*, he supported progressive taxation and the redistribution of wealth. He also favoured workplace regulations and limits to workers' hours. Mill's attraction to aspects of socialism only grew over time, as can be seen in the changes he made to the second and third editions of his *Principles of Political Economy*. He became ever more sensitive to social problems that were caused by a 'grand failure of the existing arrangement of society'.[36] What was ultimately needed, Mill came to believe, was social transformation. In 1866, he entered parliament as a Liberal and fought hard against any policies based on the principles of laissez faire.

For social transformation to occur, however, Mill thought that people's mindsets first had to be changed. Ever the moralist, he believed people needed to stop being selfish. One of the lessons of the 1848 revolutions in Europe, which he observed closely, was that people's minds had to be prepared if socialist ideas were to have a chance of succeeding. A 'real amelioration in the intellectual and moral state'[37] of mankind was necessary. This was once again why individual freedom was so very necessary. Only freedom could bring about moral reform.

Colonialism

Georgios Varouxakis rightly calls Mill 'the most open-minded, the most cosmopolitan and the least parochial of mid-Victorian political thinkers'.[38]

---

35 Mill, *On Liberty*, p. 74.

36 John Stuart Mill, preface to the third edition of *Principles of Political Economy*, in *The Collected Works of John Stuart Mill*, vol. 2, ed. John M. Robson (University of Toronto Press, 1965), p. 102.

37 John Stuart Mill, 'Autogiography', in *The Collected Works of John Stuart Mill*, vol. 1, ed. John M. Robson (University of Toronto Press, 1984), p. 244.

38 Georgios Varouxakis, 'Empire, Race, Euro-Centrism: John Stuart Mill and

For this, Mill should be celebrated. On the other hand, he supported British rule in India, which many today see as a glaring contradiction. After all, in *On Liberty*, he emphatically stated that: 'Each is the proper guardian of his own health, whether bodily, or mental or spiritual.'[39] 'Each' apparently did not apply to Indians. Mill himself did not find his support for British imperialism contradictory. He justified British rule on the grounds that Indians were, in his mind, incapable of benefiting from the liberty he espoused for English men and women. But he was not a racist. The incapacity of Indians to govern themselves was due not to any inborn deficiency in their intellectual or moral faculties but simply a product of historical circumstances. India was one of many 'backward states' that existed at a lower level of development than Europeans. Like children, they were immature and therefore needed both protection and education.

> Those who are still in a state to require being taken care of by others, must be protected against their own actions as well as against external injury…A ruler full of the spirit of improvement is warranted in the use of any expedients that will attain an end, perhaps otherwise unattainable.[40]

Mill's support for the minimal interference of governments in the lives of individuals thus did not apply to Indians. Civilised and civilising despots were necessary to rule and educate them before they could govern themselves. Hence, Mill's now infamous statement that:

> [d]espotism is a legitimate mode of government in dealing with barbarians, provided the end be their improvement, and the means justified by actually effecting that end. Liberty, as a principle, has no application to any state of things anterior to the time when mankind have become capable of being improved by free and equal discussion.[41]

These words are especially disappointing considering that Mill knew, or should have known, India well. At the age of 17 he became an employee of

---

his Critics,' *Utilitarianism and Empire*, ed. Bart Schultz and Georgios Varouxakis (Lexington Books, 2005), p. 149.
39 Mill, *On Liberty*, p. 16.
40 Mill, *On Liberty*, p. 13.
41 Mill, *On Liberty*, p. 13.

the East India Company and remained one for roughly half his life. But it was also in that capacity, and precisely because of his knowledge of India, that he appreciated the role the company could play in improving India's infrastructure, health care system and educational institutions.[42] It is also to be recalled that while he thought that Indians needed to be civilised and improved, he thought his own compatriots needed to be as well.

Conclusion

Liberalism is often described as an ideology overly focused on the rights of the individual at the expense of the community. Liberals are accused of promoting a selfish and atomising belief-system that dissolves the bonds of family and community. As I have shown elsewhere, this is a gross mischaracterisation of liberal thought.[43] In Mill's thinking, liberty is necessary for the moral growth of the individual, which should bring forth more enlightened citizens who are capable of seeing the intersection of individual and societal growth. In this essay, I have tried to show that, like many other 19th century liberals, John Stuart Mill was invested in promoting 'individuality' rather than 'individualism'. He, too, lamented the selfishness he saw all around him and tried to find ways to understand and combat it. He believed that enhancing individual liberty was a way to create morally responsible human beings able and willing to improve both themselves and their societies. His was a liberalism that was socially aware and committed to the public good. It has much to inspire us today.

Bibliography

Driver, Julia. 'The History of Utilitarianism.' In *The Stanford Encyclopedia of Philosophy* (Winter 2022 edition). Edited by Edward N. Zalta and Uri Nodelman. https://plato.stanford.edu/archives/win2022/entries/utilitarianism-history [Accessed 1/11/2024].

Gibbins, John. 'J.S. Mill, Liberalism and Progress.' In *Victorian Liberalism: Nineteenth Century Political Thought and Practice*. Edited by Richard Bellamy. Routledge, 1990.

42 Mark Tunick offers a compelling interpretation of Mill's views on imperialism and how they accord with the rest of his thought in 'Tolerant Imperialism: John Stuart Mill's Defense of British Rule in India,' *The Review of Politics* vol. 68, issue 4 (2006): pp. 1-26.

43 Helena Rosenblatt, *The Lost History of Liberalism from Ancient Rome to the Twenty-First Century* (Princeton University Press, 2018).

Heydt, C.M. 'The Ethics of Character: John Stuart Mill on Aesthetic Education.' PhD dissertation. Boston University, 1994.

Kahan, Alan. *Aristocratic Liberalism: The Social and Political Thought of Jacob Burckhardt, John Stuart Mill and Alexis de Tocqueville.* Transaction, 2001.

Kurer, Oskar. *John Stuart Mill: The Politics of Progress.* Garland, 1991.

Mehta, Uday S. *Liberalism and Empire: A Study in Nineteenth-Century British Liberal Thought.* University of Chicago Press, 1999.

Mill, John Stuart. 'Autobiography.' In *The Collected Works of John Stuart Mill,* vol. 1. Edited by John M. Robson. University of Toronto Press, 1984.

— 'The Claims of Labour.' In *The Collected Works of John Stuart Mill,* vol. 4. Edited by John M. Robson. University of Toronto Press, 1963-91.

— *Inaugural address delivered to the University of St. Andrews.* Longmans, 1867.

— *'On Liberty' and Other Writings.* Edited by Stefan Collini. Cambridge University Press, 2012.

— 'Principles of Political Economy.' In *The Collected Works of John Stuart Mill,* vol. 2. Edited by John M. Robson, University of Toronto Press, 1965.

— 'The Subjection of Women.' In *'On Liberty' and Other Writings.* Edited by Stefan Collini. Cambridge University Press, 2012.

— 'The Utility of Religion,' In *The Collected Works of John Stuart Mill,* vol. 10. Edited by John M. Robson. Routledge and Kegan Paul, 1985.

Robson, John. *The Improvement of Mankind: The Social and Political Thought of John Stuart Mill.* University of Toronto Press, 1968.

Rosenblatt, Helena. *The Lost History of Liberalism from Ancient Rome to the Twenty-First Century.* Princeton University Press, 2018.

Skorupski, John, ed. *Cambridge Companion to Mill.* Cambridge University Press, 1998.

Tocqueville, Alexis de. *Democracy in America, II:1.* Translated by Henry Reeve. Project Gutenberg: https://www.marxists.org/reference/archive/de-tocqueville/democracy-america/ch27.htm#p2 [Accessed 4/12/2024].

Tunick, Mark. 'Tolerant Imperialism: John Stuart Mill's Defense of British Rule in India.' *The Review of Politics* vol. 68, issue 4 (2006): pp. 1-26.

Varouxakis, Georgios. 'Empire, Race, Euro-Centrism: John Stuart Mill and his Critics. In *Utilitarianism and Empire.* Edited by Bart Schultz and Georgios Varouxakis. Lexington Books, 2005.

4

Liberalism, Land and Democracy

Christopher England and Andrew Phemister

It was the summer of 1886 when *The Times* reported with alacrity: 'There is war in Tiree.'[1] This dramatic statement could well have been considered journalistic hyperbole, were if not for the fact that a detachment of 125 Royal Marines had been dispatched to the small Hebridean island. The marines sailed from Plymouth aboard the troopship *HMS Assistance* to support the delivery of eviction notices, following a failed attempt days earlier when the Duke of Argyll's agents, accompanied by 20 policemen, had been driven back by 300 crofters armed with sticks and stones. Nor was it the first time in recent years that the Scottish Isles had witnessed British military force applied in defence of landlords' rent rolls. On Skye just a few years earlier, the enclosure of common grazing land at Glendale on the north of the island and subsequent complaints of trespass had eventually spiralled, prompting the arrival of the gunboat *HMS Jackal*, followed by the arrest and trial of the supposed ringleaders.

On Skye, as on Tiree, threats of eviction and arrest were met with a collective determination to protect access to the land. In what became known as 'The Battle of the Braes', crofters burned summonses and defied attempts to arrest leaders of the local Highland Land League. Marching the eight miles south from the town of Portree, the 50 Glaswegian police officers, who had been seconded for the unenviable task of arresting the summons incendiaries, were perturbed by the eerie silence on their way to the Braes district of Skye. It was a silence suddenly broken by a crowd of women 'with infuriated looks', who began 'shouting at the pitch of their voices, uttering the most fearful imprecations, hurling forth the most terrible vows of vengeance against the enemy'.[2] On their call, stones began to rain down on

---

1 'The Crofters in Tiree,' *The Times*, 24 July 1886.
2 Alexander Mackenzie, *The Isle of Skye in 1882-1883; Illustrated by a Full Report of the Trials of the Braes and Glendale Crofters at Inverness and Edinburgh*

the lowland constabulary, followed by direct attacks with 'sticks and flails'. Here, as elsewhere in Scotland and in Ireland where the conflict over the right to land had come to a head in the 1880s, women played a prominent role in the protests and were often 'the most troublesome assailants'.[3]

The violence meted out on Skye and Tiree toward landlord authority and its agents from the state, dramatic though it was, represented only a minor skirmish in a wider global conflict over land. Not confined to Britain and Ireland, the long land war encompassed peasant uprisings in Spain and Italy; it involved French farmers and American labourers, revolutions in Mexico and Bolivia; and it was central to questions of colonial power and self-determination across the Global South. Increasing trade connections, combined with a rapidly expanding but volatile American economy, prompted an agricultural depression in the 1870s that brought the land question to the fore in the subsequent decade. Yet it was in no way a novel problem. At its root, matters of political sovereignty had always been material. An issue of access to resources, ultimately shaped, in the final analysis, by the question of who owned the land. The 'land question', as it was commonly termed in the 19th century, has been the foundational question in the history of political thought, and one with profound implications for liberalism.

The Duke of Argyll, who owned the whole island of Tiree, had been engaged in a conscious effort to extirpate crofter smallholdings there since the 1840s. His plan for improvement, as he saw it, was also one of expulsion and removal from the land. As with many other liberal-minded 'improving' landlords, the duke's replacement of people with sheep eradicated communities in the name of economic growth and a utilitarian conception of land that rejected its social character. A leading Liberal statesman, Argyll's position as one of Britain's largest landowners placed him at the forefront of the defence of private property in land at what seemed like a particularly precarious moment for it.[4] In 1877, four years before he resigned from Gladstone's cabinet in protest at the Irish Land Act, a signal political moment that heralded the beginning of the social liberal state, Argyll penned a critique laying out his concerns about the slew of 'elaborate investigations into the history of land tenures'

(A & W Mackenzie, 1883), p. 29.
3   Mackenzie, *The Isle of Skye*, p. 3.
4   John W. Mason, 'The Duke of Argyll and the Land Question in Late Nineteenth Century Britain,' *Victorian Studies* vol. 21, no. 2 (1978): pp. 149-170.

that questioned the very nature of property in land.[5] Written for that bastion of free trade liberalism, the Cobden Club, Argyll explained that land was like any other form of property. Not only should land be freely bought, sold and rented like any other property, but its private ownership by individuals was the very cornerstone of liberalism and progress. Popular alienation from the land was simply a natural condition of material development.

The internal battle for land

That same year a very different character was putting pen to paper. An autodidact who had worked as a mechanic and a sailor before turning his hand to journalism, and whom the Duke would dismissively deride as the Prophet of San Francisco, was developing a book that would set out a very different liberal position on land. Henry George's *Progress and Poverty* would be published in late 1879, and had a transformative, global impact. The roll of influential fin de siècle revolutionary leaders who turned to George for assistance defining their vision of a decolonised world – including Sun Yat-sen, José Marti, José Batlle y Ordóñez – suggests that, until the Russian Revolution, it was George's land reform, rather than Marx's communism, that was destined to shape the Global South. George articulated, and attempted to resolve, the critical paradox at the heart of the relationship between liberalism and the land: that private ownership of this finite and foundational resource actually undermined both the field of individual freedom and activity, as well as the right to property itself. All the supposed virtues of the 19th century liberal individual: moral character, political independence, financial probity, and hard work were undermined by private monopolisation of the land. His work rejected the idea of property in land on 'the very principle of the right to property'.[6] It was, in George's telling, the landlords themselves who violated property rights.

No other issue so clearly and consistently marked the boundaries of the radical liberal tradition as the question of property in land. As the land conflict exploded in the 1880s, it exposed this perennial tension – inescapable for a political ideology which prioritised self-possession and personal freedom – over how access to the earth should be organised. As Locke had

---

5   George Campbell, *Essay on the Commercial Principles applicable to Contracts for the Hire of Land* (Cassell, Petter & Galpin, 1877), p. 1.
6   Eugenio Biagini, *Liberty, Retrenchment and Reform: Popular Liberalism in the Age of Gladstone, 1860-1880* (Cambridge University Press, 1992), p. 10.

pointed out, locating a right of ownership in human creations set the land apart as distinct. The problem of how to accommodate this distinctiveness would have far-reaching implications for conceptions of justice, rights, and freedom. During the 1880s George and Argyll would publicly debate private property in land, their disagreements coming to represent definitive statements of wildly divergent approaches to political freedom. Their discussions represented two contrasting visions of liberal politics which the land question, over and above almost any other political issue, had laid bare.

Ever torn between the twin poles of freedom and equality, liberal politics, in both its classical and social variants, had an ambivalent relationship to participatory democracy, which was by necessity circumscribed either by capital or the state.[7] For both of these liberal traditions the distinctiveness of land was rejected, and it was to be either commercialised or managed like any other form of property. Yet for the radical liberal tradition access to land was a right that was both inherent to an individual, and universal to all. It saw that only by ensuring this access could popular democracy be protected from both the unceasing acquisition of personal wealth and the authority of the state. For radical liberals, land was the key to aligning individual freedom with collective egalitarianism, and the heartbeat of a morally coherent political economy.

This was also a popular demand, rooted as much, if not more so, in the practices of access and collective custom than in any theories of ownership or arguments about rights. Among the most striking features of the radical liberal approach to land as a unique, communal resource was how closely it seemed to align with popular conceptions of economic justice – an observation made as frequently by vociferous critics as by sympathetic supporters. As E.P. Thompson observed, from at least the mid-17th century through to the 1880s, 'working-class Radicalism remained transfixed' by the question of land.[8] From the Diggers to the Chartists, the land was a site where both political and economic freedom could be realised. While agrarian visions of decentralised democracy (that tied personal independence

---

7   Inevitably this is a rough typology. Classical liberals tended to focus on the sanctity of individual contracts as the cornerstone of freedom, while social liberals viewed state and society as a complex integrated organism (a common metaphor) that needed carefully management to facilitate individual development.

8   E.P. Thompson, *The Making of the English Working Class* [1963] (Penguin, 1981), p. 105.

and economic self-sufficiency to a levelling egalitarianism) had been the cornerstone of radical thought, it was the forms of peasant protest, as on Skye and Tiree, but just as evident in Galway, Salerno or Andalucía, that made this evident in practice. Mass trespass, fence breaking, ploughing and sowing enclosed land were common means of asserting collective claims on land. As one of the crofters asserted after his arrest on Skye:

> If I was going to jail for a sheep or for a lamb, you might be very sorry. But, as it is, you ought to be very glad. For we go to uphold a good cause; we go to defend the widow and the fatherless, and the comfort and needs of our hearths and homes.[9]

Land, democracy and soul

Despite the most fevered claims of the conservative press, this kind of agrarian agitation was not particularly socialistic, but rather directed toward securing collective sufficiency, survival, and freedom. Indeed, for many conservative thinkers, among the most concerning facets of the agrarian radicals' analysis of land ownership was its widespread resonance; its striking correspondence with popular conceptions of justice and fairness. The problem was, one commentator remarked, that many people 'who are by no means Socialists, appear to entertain some vague suspicion that it may be true'.[10] The roots of this popular resonance lie, at least in part, in the close connection between agrarian radicalism and Christianity. Not only was there a shared corpus of Christian discourse, but there was also a theological core to the argument for common ownership of the land, too. George's work, which was 'so percolated with religious phraseology and so profusely adorned with Scriptural quotations', was able to connect far and wide through this shared religious language, accessible to Catholic and Protestant alike.[11] Not only had the land been made by God, but it had been created with a purpose – human sustenance and survival. Marketising and commodifying land was consequently a rejection of this purpose, 'not only an injustice and a wrong', as the Irish Bishop Thomas Nulty of Meath put

9   John Macpherson, quoted by the *Inverness Courier*, and cited in Mackenzie, *The Isle of Skye*, p. 124.
10   William Hurrell Mallock, *Property and Progress, Or a Brief Enquiry into Contemporary Social Agitation in England* (G.P. Putnam's Sons, 1884), p. 126.
11   William Edward Hartpole Lecky, *Democracy and Liberty* vol. II [1896] (Longmans, Green, and Co., 1903), p. 357.

it, but 'an impious resistance to the benevolent intentions of the Creator'.[12] Back on Skye, Reverend Donald MacCallum, a committed Land Leaguer known as the Prophet of Waternish explained the issue in identical terms to his own parishioners:

> The land is our birth-right, even as the air, the light of the sun, and water belong to us as our birth-right. Man cannot live without a part of the land. We cannot go up with the birds and take up our abode beyond the clouds. We cannot go down to the bottom of the sea and live with the whales. And even could we, the lairds would claim us as their property, as they claim the birds and the fishes. They are the lords of sky, earth and sea… If the law can keep us from any part of the land, it can keep us from the whole. If the law that can do that is right, then God created us in vain with bodies that cannot live without a part of the earth. Do you know why there are no sun-light leaguers? It is because the sun cannot be bought and sold.[13]

This connection, the purposeful relationship between human bodies and the land, went quite far back. It was Aquinas who had set out that the natural world had been divinely bestowed to all humans in common. The connection between the land and the right to life had also always been a political one. This was not just a question of property or economic equality, but also a matter of justifying authority: if property in land was a common inheritance, the state's power over it was pre-emptively restrained. In this way, universal and natural rights to land were deeply threatening not only to private property, but to political absolutism, as thinkers such as Hobbes and Machiavelli had recognised. It was in the 17th century that radical rights theorists began to develop these premises of self-preservation into proto-democratic arguments.[14] Was the allocation of natural resources simply a matter of political stability? Or did humans have pre-existing claims to land that were rooted in the fact of their human existence and divine right to life? In these early-modern arguments, we can see how the issue

12   Thomas Nulty, *The Land Question: Letter of the Most Rev. Dr. Nulty, to the Clergy and Laity of the Diocese of Meath* (Joseph Dollard, 1881), p. 14.

13   Donald MacCallum, Speech at Fairy Bridge, Skye, 13 May 1884, in *Addresses by the Rev. Donald MacCallum* (Duncan Cameron, 1884), pp. 4-5.

14   Richard Tuck, *Natural Rights Theories: Their Origin and Development* (Cambridge University Press, 1979).

of land tended to drive individualist propositions into deeply radical and even communitarian conclusions that were hostile to the idea of absolute ownership. This ambiguity with regard to property in land was sufficiently discomfiting that it prompted the English jurist William Blackstone to note, in the mid-18th century, that 'we seem afraid to look back to the means by which [landed property] was acquired' because 'accurately and strictly speaking, there is no foundation in nature or natural law, why a set of words upon parchment should convey the dominion of land'.[15] Blackstone, whose *Commentaries on the Laws of England* defined English Common Law for both British and American statesmen, could find no solid ground to rest his belief in landed property, an uncertainty that only fuelled utilitarian solutions that rejected any unique quality to property in land.

While Blackstone may have cautioned against what he saw as pointless and potentially dangerous philosophical speculation about land, the relationship between property ownership and political freedom, long contested, became a more pressing and concrete concern in the wake of American independence. The new republic itself became a site of possibility because the question of land ownership appeared to be less constrained than in Europe, where regardless of any conjecture on the origins of property, nearly all land was laden with centuries of written title and the weight of thick vellum deeds. The former colonists set about debating the foundations for an ideal republic and drawing deeply on the republican suspicion of inequality in political life, Thomas Jefferson emerged as the patron saint of US agrarianism. For Jefferson, widespread ownership of farms preserved the economic independence and civic virtue necessary for self-governance:

> Corruption of morals in the mass of cultivators is a phenomenon of which no age nor nation has furnished an example. It is the mark set on those, who, not looking up to heaven, to their own soil and industry, as does the husbandman, for the subsistence, depend for it on the casualties and caprice of customers. Dependence begets subservience and venality, suffocates the germ of virtue, and prepares fit tools for the designs of ambition.[16]

---

15 William Blackstone, in *The Commentaries on the Laws of England*, vol. II, *Of the Rights of Things* [1765], ed. Robert Malcolm Kerr (John Murray, 1876), pp. 1-2.
16 Thomas Jefferson, 'Notes on the State of Virginia,' in *The Complete Jefferson*, ed. S.K. Padover (Duell, Sloan and Pearch, 1943), p. 678.

After the election of 1800, Jefferson's Democratic-Republican Party eclipsed the Federalist Party because of support from the swelling population of the Trans-Appalachian West. Even when the federal government resorted to burning down squatters' homes, the ardour of settlers did not cool; George Washington opined that nothing would stop them 'short of a Chinese wall or a line of troops'.[17] In contrast to federalists, who often tried to cobble together large estates out of public lands to model themselves disinterested aristocrats, Jefferson designed the Northwest Ordinance to cleanly divide the Great Lakes region into small plots accessible to yeoman farmers.

Land and the politics of the future

The radicalism of the American Revolution had been predicated on a refusal of the dead hand of past generations. Established, monarchical, absolutist systems of power were swept away so that rational man could make the laws anew. For Jefferson, this temporal priority applied to the land, which was, as he famously wrote to James Madison in 1789, possessed only momentarily and provisionally on the basis of human need rather than in perpetuity by ancient deed. His model of a diffuse property-owning agricultural republic was not the only interpretation that could be drawn from these premises, however, and several writers went further. Spurred by the American Revolution, radicals in Britain also began to articulate a more explicit critique of land ownership. Some of these critiques were academic and others polemical, and they emerged from a range of different class and socio-economic backgrounds. William Ogilvie, a Professor of Humanity at King's College, Aberdeen, published his *Essay on the Right of Property in Land* in 1781. Anticipating the familiar rhetorical angle adopted by Donald MacCallum on Skye a century later, Ogilvie pointed out that land was a common inheritance in which all were due an equal share 'little different from that which he has to the free use of the open air and running water'.[18] While Ogilvie's anonymous contribution was theoretical and abstract, and of no political danger despite its wide circulation in learned circles, others were less guarded. Thomas Spence, a Newcastle schoolteacher who delineated a utopian vision of decentralised parish communes through

---

17　Gordon Wood, *Empire of Liberty: A History of the Early Republic, 1789-1815* (Oxford University Press, 2009), p. 121.
18　William Ogilvie, 'Essay on the Right of Property in Land,' repr. in *The Pioneers of Land Reform: Thomas Spence, William Ogilvie, Thomas Paine*, ed. Max Beer (G. Bell and Sons, 1920), p. 35.

which the possession of land would be democratically regulated, would have a longer trajectory of influence on early 19th century British radicals. It is no surprise to find in his arguments, however, the same critiques of the corrupting influence of commerce common to republican radicals. At the same time, his claims were again founded on the familiar basis of the necessity of land to human life. 'There is no living but on land', Spence explained, so that 'what we cannot live without we have the same property in as our lives'.[19] Furthermore, Spence's argument that working people had been cut off from the 'Rights of Nature', extended beyond matters of mere survival. Sustenance itself was insufficient recompense for the loss of these rights, which also represented a claim to participate democratically in the wider community. In one political tract, Spence narrated a conversation with a forester who had stopped him gathering nuts in a wood. Accused of trespass and theft in the Duke of Portland's woods, Spence replies to the forester: 'these nuts are the spontaneous gifts of Nature ordained alike for the sustenance of Man and Beast.' Since 'nature knows no more of him than of me [...] the Duke of Portland must look sharp if he wants any nuts'. Yet this exclusion had a political bearing too, as Spence continued:

> What must I say to the French, if they come? If they jeeringly ask me what I am fighting for? Must I tell them for my country? For my dear Country in which I dare not pluck a Nut? Would not they laugh at me? Yes. And do you think I would bear it? No: Certainly I would not. I would throw down my Musket saying let such as the Duke of Portland, who claim the Country, fight for it, for I am but a Stranger and Sojourner, and have neither part nor lot amongst them. This reasoning had such an effect on the Forrester that he told me to gather as many nuts as I pleased.[20]

Fewer figures embody the transatlantic nature of this agrarian radicalism, and its intertwined political and economic dimensions, as clearly as Thomas Paine, whose life and career stretched across both continents. Paine, appointed by the fledgling US confederation to negotiate with the Iroquois during the revolution, observed that American Indians lived

---

19 Thomas Spence, repr. In Henry Hyndman, ed., *The Nationalization of the Land in 1775 and 1882* (E.W. Allen, 1882), p. 10.
20 Thomas Spence, *The Restorer of Society to its Natural State; In a Series of Letters to a Fellow Citizen* (Thomas Spence, 1801), p. 19.

better than the European poor, concluded that this was because they held land to be the 'COMMON PROPERTY OF THE HUMAN RACE', and argued that the landowners who had monopolised the fruits of development owed the community a ground-rent.[21] Paine's proposals for recompensing non-property owners for both their lost natural inheritance in the land, and the socially created value of private property, aimed to be less disruptive and more conducive to commerce and industry. They would prefigure, in many respects, the theory put forward a century later by Henry George. Paine's ideas, developed in his 1797 pamphlet *Agrarian Justice*, made clear just how central equality of property had to be in a functioning democracy – more than this, however, his claims for the materially disenfranchised to have a share in 'natural' property were rooted in the theft of their original entitlement. This was not a humanitarian or welfare argument, or one based on social expediency, but about reclaiming an inheritance. While this was common to most agrarian claims, it also clashed awkwardly with a burgeoning liberal utilitarianism and Paine, like Spence, was soon marginalised.

The marginalisation of these arguments for common rights led land reform down a path consistent with the Duke of Argyll's pro-proprietarian logic, so that the freedom of land for some could often mean unfreedom for others. Jefferson embodied this contradiction. While Jefferson often romanticised indigenous culture, he took for granted that white settlement in the Louisiana territory would displace native peoples. Jefferson successfully pushed for the abolition of the transatlantic slave trade, but accepted slavery in the Louisiana territory, laying the groundwork for a deadly domestic slave trade that drove the profitability of slavery in the mid-Atlantic, where it had been in decline. The racial and gendered boundaries of citizenship became more pronounced with time, until Jacksonian populism in the 1820s rested claims for the equality of white men on their presumed superiority to others. In 1821, New York dropped property qualifications to vote for white men, only to raise them for black men.[22]

21 Thomas Paine, *Agrarian Justice* (Booksellers of London and Westminster, 1797), p. 7.
22 Robert Kennedy, *Mr. Jefferson's Lost Cause Land, Farmers, Slavery, and the Louisiana Purchase* (Oxford University Press, 2003); Edward Baptist, *The Half Has Never Been Told: Slavery and the Making of American Capitalism* (Basic Books, 2014); Wood, *Empire of Liberty*, pp. 394-399; Van Gosse, *The First Reconstruction: Black Politics in America From the Revolution to the Civil War,* (University of North Carolina Press, 2021), p. 376.

Yet, when the Argentine education reformer Domingo Sarmiento toured the United States in the 1840s, he observed that its egalitarian distribution of land had crafted a nation in which 'you will have to hide your sceptres, crowns, and golden trinkets to present yourself before the Republic'.[23] During the colonial era, American society was riven by quasi-feudal class divisions usually predicated on inherited status; court proceedings were bogged down with extended wrangling over whether a plaintiff merited the title of 'gentleman'. The scarcity of land meant that in some New English towns at least one third of married couples remained in the households of their parents, with the continuous threat of disinheritance enshrining patriarchal authority as the reigning social paradigm. To seek employment outside of this household meant submitting to laws that framed servants as, in many respects, the property of their employer, legally subject to violent correction and barred by law from leaving their employer, marrying, or acquiring property. Even free people were generally clients of landed elites who, in return for leasing land or patronising a business, expected their dependants to elect them to office. Political office was thus tied to the financial ability of propertied elites to mobilise clients. Elections became pro forma ratifications of families that monopolised the same public offices over generations. Land created the possibility of economic, social, and political independence, and as citizens of the newly formed nation moved West and easily met property qualifications for voting, a more democratic culture formed.[24] While large speculators cobbled together vast estates in the West, these did not convey political power amid an electorate of small, independent farmers who occasionally used heavy taxes to punish idle ownership of land. As a sign of a new balance of power emerging in the young republic, Ohio's first congressman, elected in 1803, owned just 385 acres, which he worked himself.[25]

By the 1830s, US land reformers began to assemble cross-class support for the expansion of democratic rights. Urban workers, supporting the National Reform Association (NRA), advocated that land in the public domain be

---

23 Domingo F. Sarmiento, *Sarmiento's Travels in the U.S. in 1847*, trans. Michael Aaron Rockland (Princeton University Press, 1970), pp. 164-5, 179-180.
24 Gordon Wood, *The Radicalism of the American Revolution* (A.A. Knopf, 1992), pp. 21, 25, 53, 55-92; Karen Orren, *Belated Feudalism: Labor, the Law, and Liberal Development in the United States* (Cambridge University Press), 1991.
25 Wood, *Empire of Liberty*, pp. 116-121, 364; Paul Gates, *The Jeffersonian Dream: Studies in the History of American Land Policy and Development*, ed. Paul Gates and Allan G. Bouge (University of New Mexico Press, 1996), pp. 84-88.

given freely to farmers who promised to use it. Most land reformers intended to continue their careers as urban artisans but speculated that opening a Western safety valve would reduce the numbers of, and increase the wages of, urban workers.[26] Working-class land reformers often differed with middle-class abolitionists over whether releasing enslaved persons into an economy governed by land monopoly would constitute substantive progress, but they generally supported the abolition of slavery. George Henry Evans, who organised the NRA, inspired the wealthy abolitionist Gerrit Smith to donate 200,000 acres to black farmers in upstate New York.[27] After the Mexican-American War, southern aspirations to spread slavery into newly acquired territory further united land reformers, who feared that wealthy planters would monopolise the land, with critics of slavery. Together, these two groups formed the foundation for anti-slavery politics, in first the Free-Soil Party, and then later, the Republican Party.[28]

The National Reform Association's utopian scheme for the resettlement of urban workers on the land, where restrictions on landholding would stabilise model participatory democracies of independent farmers and artisans, was not uniquely American. In its wide support base, from labourers and farmers to artisans and professionals, the NRA were, according to one observer, 'neither more nor less than English Chartists transported to this country'.[29] This was not a surprising claim given the centrality of the land issue to British radicals in the 1840s, and even less so given that a co-founder of the NRA had been the Irish Chartist Thomas Ainge Devyr. Devyr, a curmudgeonly and acerbic character, thought that a popular democratic-republican government could only be constructed on 'the beneficent designs of God and Nature'; that is, by accepting that 'the land was indisputably given to supply the natural wants of man' and could not be possessed beyond this.[30] While the Chartist Land Plan had been

26 Jamie Bronstein, *Land Reform and Working-Class Experience in Britian and the United States, 1800-1862* (Stanford University Press, 1999), p. 61.
27 Bronstein, *Land Reform and Working-Class*, pp. 93-96.
28 Eric Foner, *Free Soil, Free Labor, Free Men: The Ideology of the Republican Party Before the Civil War* (Oxford University Press, 1995); Adam Tuchinsky, *Horace Greeley's New-York Tribune: Civil War-Era Socialism and the Crisis of Free Labor* (Cornell University Press, 2009).
29 Sidney Pollard, 'Nineteenth-Century Corporations: Community Building to Shopkeeping,' in *Essays in Labour History*, ed. Asa Briggs and John Saville (Palgrave Macmillan, 1967), p. 74.
30 Thomas Ainge Devyr, *Our Natural Rights: A Pamphlet for the People* [1835] (Devyr, 1842), p. 3.

much less ambitious and successful than its American equivalent, it was the cornerstone of the movement.[31] Political rights were downstream from the economic exploitation that flowed from the unequal distribution of land. As the Chartist newspaper *The Poor Man's Guardian* explained: 'We consider that the monopoly of land is the source of every social and political evil.'[32]

Slavery, freedom and land

In the US, the emancipation of enslaved persons after the Civil War reinforced the connection between land ownership and freedom. When President Andrew Johnson returned land to confederates, the freed people who were expelled from farms leased to them by the federal government on Edisto Island petitioned for homesteads, by highlighting the dire consequences of being propertyless in the land of their former enslavers: 'we are at the mercy of those who combined to prevent us from getting land… We can only do one of three things Step into the public road or the sea or remain on them working as In former time and subject to their will as then.'[33] Some freed people escaped sharecropping and found a measure of freedom in the West. In Oklahoma, persons formerly enslaved by the Cherokee acquired tribal land that served as the foundation for the vibrant Greenwood District, often referred to as 'black wall street'. When the community was burned down in a race riot in 1921, black ownership of the land allowed it to survive despite intense pressure from local elites to expel its residents and establish Tulsa as a homogenously white city. In his autobiography, Nat Love chronicled his experience working alongside white cowboys as they fattened cattle on the open range and herded them to railheads. The unfenced plains offered black cowboys like Love an unusual level of equality during a time when workplace segregation barred people of colour from many opportunities. When the introduction of barbed wire made it possible for the wealthy to divide these vast commons into large ranches, Love was pushed into work as a Pullman Porter, a job for which only black men were hired, and above which no black man working on the railroads could rise. The closing of the open range forced Love into a segregated workforce under the purview

31 Malcolm Chase, "'Wholesome Object Lessons": The Chartist Land Plan in Retrospect,' *The English Historical Review* vol. 118, no. 475 (2003): pp. 59-85.

32 *Poor Man's Guardian*, p. 148, 4 April 1834, quoted in Malcolm Chase, *The People's Farm: English Radical Agrarianism, 1775-1840* (Oxford University Press, 1988), p. 8.

33 Jonathan Levy, *Freaks of Fortune* (Harvard University Press, 2012), p. 124.

of monopoly capitalism, mirroring the way in which the privatisation of federally confiscated land in the South had delivered freed people back into the subjugation of the planter class.[34]

Due to absent southern representation in Congress, land reformers secured victory during the Civil War with the Homestead Act of 1862, which allowed citizens to claim 160 acres of public domain for a small filing fee if they stayed on the land for five years (three, if they were veterans). The Homestead Act, however, failed to limit speculative usages of land; the federal government simultaneously distributed 125 million acres of land to corporations girding the nation with rail. The Timber Culture Act, which granted land to owners who planted trees in the inhospitable plains, secured millions of acres for speculators who failed to deliver the forest growth, and instead sold land to developers. Approximately six out of ten homesteaders did not remain on their property for the five years required by the law to claim it. Some packed up and moved on, others purchased the land in advance, and many others, acting as speculators, sold their claim as development sparked demand. Nevertheless, nearly a million and a half homesteaders claimed land under the law. The world's largest democracy was carved into perfect squares that reflected neither natural geography nor the market, but rather the bureaucratic logic of government surveyors animated by a philosophy of equal rights to land.[35]

Property relations and democratic action

In 1851, the minor Scottish aristocrat Sir George Makgill, otherwise known as the 9th Baronet of Kemback and Fingask, sat down at his desk in a fashionable town house on Claremont Crescent in Edinburgh's wealthy New Town to write a small pamphlet about the land question. Unnerved by recent events across Europe (the revolutions of 1848 and the public interest there

---

34 Anthony Wood, *Black Montana, Settler Colonialism, and the Erosion of the Racial Frontier* (University of Nebraska Press, 2021), pp. 69-72, 169-198; Douglas Flamming, *African Americans in the West* (Bloomsbury Publishing, 2009), pp. 57-90; Victor Luckerson, *Built From the Fire: The Epic Story of Tulsa's Greenwood District, America's Black Walls Street* (Random House, 2023).

35 Richard White, *The Republic for Which It Stands: The United States during Reconstruction and the Gilded Age, 1865-1896* (Oxford University Press, 2017), pp. 120, 141-2; Fred A. Shannon, 'The Homestead Act and the Labor Surplus', *The American Historical Review* vol. 41, no. 4 (1936): pp. 637–651; Gates, *The Jeffersonian Dream:*, pp. 40-52; Andro Linklater, *How an Untamed Wilderness Shaped the United States and Fulfilled the Promise of Democracy* (Penguin, 2003).

in communist ideas) he was nevertheless reassured that in Britain, 'no one of note among us has attempted to raise doubts on fundamental questions, or to challenge the principles on which our law of property is based'. There was one exception, however, to this general observation, and that was when it came to land. So, while 'the notion of property in general, and as applied to moveables, is perhaps as strict, and as firmly footed [...] as in any other civilised nation; but a vague opinion seems to prevail that property in land stands upon a wholly different footing'. Not only this, but all classes of people, including the commercial and manufacturing sections of society, he worried, seemed to possess 'an undefined but pretty general notion that the right of a landowner is something of a much more questionable kind than that to any other kind of property'. Even many landowners, he explained, seemed a little unsure of themselves, and betrayed an uncertainty as whether holding land as private property was truly justified, 'as if the defenders were not altogether sure of the soundness of their position, and shrunk from provoking too close a scrutiny'.[36]

But it was not just events in Europe that had unsettled Makgill and provoked his small tract. It was another event in 1848, the publication of John Stuart Mill's *Principles of Political Economy*, that Makgill blamed for the confusions over land ownership. 'The confusion of ideas that prevails regarding land-property' was due to the doctrine of rent, the idea that income from land was not due to either labour or abstinence; not to the making of things nor to the lending to others the things you had made. This was the basis of Mill's argument, that the land, by which he meant all the raw natural materials of the earth, were not made by humans, and did not themselves increase by human labour. Land was to be owned in common precisely because it was not one of those things that should be absolutely owned by individuals because they made them. It was precisely because people had a right to their own lives and the things they had made, that Mill argued: 'when the sacredness of property is talked of, it should always be remembered that this sacredness does not apply in the same degree to landed property. No man made the land'.[37] Land was an elemental necessity

---

36 George Makgill, *Rent No Robbery: An Examination of Some Erroneous Doctrines Regarding Property in Land* (William Blackwood, 1851).

37   John Stuart Mill to C. E. Norton, 24 September 1868, in *The Letters of John Stuart Mill*, ed. Hugh S. R. Elliot, vol. II (Longmans, Green, and Co., 1919), p. 123; John Stuart Mill, 'Advice to Land Reformers,' *The Examiner*, 4 January 1873.

to all humans, and its purpose was to provide for human life. Therefore, as Mill explained, this point should set the boundaries of its possession. 'Now, when we know the reason of a thing, we know what ought to be its limits,' he explained. 'The limits of the reason ought to be the limits of the thing. The thing itself should stop where the reason stops.'[38] It was this argument, put forward effectively and prominently by Mill, that would essentially form the basis of most subsequent liberal arguments for land reform.

During the 1880s Henry George appropriated Mill's land tax for an urban environment, modernising land reform to reflect the inequality spurred by private ownership of city lots. As a newspaper editor in San Francisco, George had seen inequality grow amid the ample resources of the West. Dividing land equally into 160 acre lots hardly promised substantive equality in a community where 'there are lots that will sell for more than would suffice to pave them with gold coins.'[39] By taxing the full rental value of this land, the government would encourage speculators to sell, making it easier to take, but harder to hold, land. The full rental value of land would be socialised to support the development of public infrastructure, education, and welfare.

George built a movement that, until it lost influence in the 1920s, served as a motor for democratisation and liberalisation. At the time, Gilded Age inequality inspired a progressive backlash against rights rhetoric and an embrace of technocratic expertise that sometimes veered toward scepticism about democracy. H.L. Mencken once joked of Theodore Roosevelt that: 'He didn't believe in democracy; he believed simply in government.' According to Mencken, Roosevelt 'was for a paternalism of the true Bismarckian pattern… His instincts were always those of the property-owning Tory, not those of the romantic Liberal.'[40] In contrast to Roosevelt, who had taken part in efforts to limit the voting rights in New York City, George, who edged out the future president to secure second place in the New York mayoral race of 1886, fought to establish a secret ballot, and his followers were at the forefront of movements to introduce direct legislation. After George's death his lieutenant, Louis Post, assumed control of the movement's leading publication and promoted an expansive vision of equal rights, joining the

---

38   John Stuart Mill, 'Tract on the Right of Property in Land, Land Tenure Reform Association' [1873], in Elliot, The Letters of John Stuart Mill, p. 388.

39   Henry George, Progress and Poverty (National Single Tax League, 1879), p. 239.

40   H.L. Mencken, 'Roosevelt: An Autopsy,' in Prejudices: Second Series (Jonathan Cape, 1921), pp. 123-4.

National Association for the Advancement of Colored People and, during his stint as Assistant Secretary of Labor, leading efforts against racial discrimination in First World War industries. The principle that land was not an entitlement that should be monopolised forever, but a collective good that owners should be incentivised to dispense with, mirrored a vision of citizenship that was similarly open and hostile to inherited privilege.[41]

The egalitarian character of Georgism grew in a cross-class coalition of supporters whose commitment to equal access to land reflected a wider belief in equal opportunity. The movement built on a constituency that the historian Robert D. Johnston called the radical middle class, upwardly mobile urban artisans and professionals concerned about high rent, but also with strong support among working class constituents who needed the services that land value taxation could fund.[42] George identified as a working man but drew the category broadly to include all those – manual labourers and professionals – who lived by labour rather than monopolising rent. In Australia, Georgists were prone to transgress the social boundaries of class by wearing eccentric clothing or alternating between bourgeois and working-class styles of dress.[43] In the United States, the Colored Farmers Alliance, concerned about sharecropping, was the first major organisation to endorse George's single tax, and many middle-class former abolitionists, such as William Lloyd Garrison II, joined George believing that land monopoly had prevented freed people from securing the equality that emancipation promised.

Populist democracy comes of age

As George captured international attention, the alternative tradition of a wide land ownership spurred agrarian revolt that would undermine an American party system representing the interests of industrial elites. From 1870 to 1880, grain exports grew from $68 million to $226 million, dwarfing manufacturing exports, and all but ending the famines that had periodically ravaged Europe. But the result of this agricultural boom was that within a four-year period domestic wheat prices fell by half, a crisis exacerbated by the hard money policies of the Republican Party. In 1892, the People's Party (or Populist

41 Christopher England, *Land and Liberty: Henry George and the Crafting of Modern Liberalism* (Johns Hopkins University Press, 2023).
42 Robert Johnston, *The Radical Middle Class: Populist Democracy and the Question of Capitalism in Progressive Era Portland* (Princeton University Press, 2006).
43 Melissa Bellanta, 'Transcending Class? Australia's Single Taxers in the Early 1890s,' *Labour History* no. 92 (2007): pp. 17-30.

Party) was formed to demand a more favourable deal for agriculture and to support farmers joining agricultural marketing cooperatives to establish economies of scale. Populists spoke in romantic terms about democracy and the danger that the concentration of wealth posed to it. Populism brought economic debates back into a political discourse that had been dominated by identarian disputes over ethnicity, religion, and region – often mediated by the festering animosities of the Civil War. By adopting populist politics, William Jennings Bryan captured the Democratic Party and transformed it into a substantial alternative to the big business platform of the Republican Party. In this way, peasant proprietorship could be said to have reinvigorated democratic discourse in the United States.[44]

Populist democracy though, with its social basis in small proprietorship, would often be circumscribed by the exclusive class boundaries of ownership, ultimately devolving into a parochial interest group. While populism united small and large farmers, it failed to incorporate tenants, reinforcing overlapping boundaries of race. The Farmers' Alliances opposed the strikes of black cotton workers. On the local level, alliances lobbied against funding black schools, fought for laws that would punish 'unfaithful' black tenants, and colluded against leasing land to black farmers so they could be coerced into work for wages. Although the Populist Party platform offered rhetorical support to the labour movement, the Farmers Alliance eventually eliminated dual membership with the Knights of Labor to ensure that black farm labourers were not inadvertently incorporated into their movement through an alliance with labour unions. In 1920, Charles Macune, who had organised the Farmers' Alliance movement, accounted for is decline: 'its very success from a business point of view obviated the necessity of its existence.'[45] Despite occasional efforts to build broad, democratic coalitions and the infusion of some radical intellectuals, populism was principally driven by the narrow business interests of farmers. It evaporated when they had solidified their position as a powerful special interest lobby.

A similar story unfolded on the other side of the Atlantic. The 1892 Small Holdings Act was introduced by Lord Salisbury's Conservative

44 White, *The Republic for Which It Stands*, pp. 219-220; John D. Hicks, *The Populist Revolt: A History of the Farmers Alliance and the People's Party* (University of Minnesota Press, 1931); Michael Kazin, *A Godly Hero: The Life of William Jennings Bryan* (Knopf, 2006).
45 Charles Postel, *The Populist Vision* (Oxford University Press, 2007), pp. 40-41, 75, 180, 275, 284.

administration in an attempt to buttress and expand a rural propertied class resistant to further change. In Ireland, where conflict over the land had been a semi-permanent feature of national life, the heightened upheavals of the Land War from 1879 started a legislative process of state-assisted purchase for tenant farmers that was inaugurated by William Gladstone's 1881 Irish Land Act. Though often driven by radical rhetoric about popular access to the land (the Irish Land League's Michael Davitt was in close accord with Henry George's analysis of the situation), the ultimate result of the liberal intervention was to consolidate land and political power in a rural nationalist middle-class.

The radicals' hopes for a universalised and egalitarian settlement to the land question were also foreclosed in Britain. Energised by the formidable land wars in Ireland and the Scottish Highlands, liberal politicians of all stripes took an increasing interest in the land, but tended to view it in terms of welfare, municipal reform, or further government oversight, rather than as a fundamental issue of natural justice or political power. Access to land was framed as a palliative solution for physical and mental health, as in the Commons Preservation Movement, or as a problem of economic nationalism: appeals were made to the 'patriotic resonance' of the English countryside and its role in preserving 'racial' health rather than any egalitarian universalism.[46] Alleviating poverty through minimum agricultural wages, improved rural housing, increased land taxation, greater use of uncultivated land, or smallholder allotments involved a recognition of serious problems, but even the most dramatic of proposals tended to consign the land question to what Arnold Toynbee categorised as 'problems of administration'.[47] For Jesse Collings, whose plan in the liberal 'Radical Programme' of state assisted peasant smallholdings went further than most, the simplest solution was to 'confer upon the State larger powers in these

---

46   Paul Readman, *Land and Nation in England: Patriotism, National Identity, and the Politics of Land, 1880-1914* (The Boydell Press, 2008), pp. 206-7; Jan Marsh, *Back to the Land: The Pastoral Impulse in Victorian England from 1880-1914* (Quarter Books, 1982), pp. 39-45.

47   Arnold Toynbee, *'Progress and Poverty', A Criticism of Mr. Henry George, Being Two Lectures Delivered in St. Andrew's Hall, Newman Street, London* (Kegan Paul, Trench and Co., 1883), p. 24; See also: Thomas Hill Green, *Liberal Legislation and Freedom of Contract* (Slatter and Rose, 1881); Charles Bradlaugh, *Compulsory Cultivation of Land: What it means, and why it ought to be enforced* (Freethought Publishing, 1887).

matters than she now possesses'.[48] Indeed, as Liberal MP Richard Haldane explained in the Commons, many schemes of liberal reform were intended to head off the threat posed by those who wished to nationalise the land.[49]

The New Deal and after

During the 20th century, US land reform, as George had imagined, shifted focus to metropolitan housing, but only reinforced small proprietorship. By 1920, more than half of Americans lived in urban areas. Franklin D. Roosevelt, who looked to Jefferson as his lodestar, declared amid the unrest of the Great Depression that: 'A nation of homeowners, of people who won a real share in their own land, is unconquerable.'[50] In 1933, F.D.R. signed legislation granting the Home Owners Loan Corporation the power to refinance the mortgages of families at risk of default, engineering a model for federal intervention in housing that became permanent with the establishment of the Federal Housing Administration (FHA) in 1934. These federal programmes not only spread access to homeownership but also ensured that homeownership entailed some sort of merger of town and country – appraisers regularly warned against offering loans in neighbourhoods where 'lots are small' or there was 'an appearance of congestion'.[51] The FHA systematically discriminated against prospective buyers in minority neighbourhoods, reinforcing strict residential segregation and racial wealth disparities. But sponsorship of suburban homeownership was a popular policy that, in crossing class boundaries, solidified support for Roosevelt's 'Herrenvolk social democracy'[52] when much of the world was gravitating toward authoritarian nationalism. The historian Kenneth Jackson observed that:

---

48 Jesse Collings, 'The Radical Programme', *Fortnightly Review* vol. 34, no. 201 (1883): p. 445.

49 Richard Haldane, HC Deb, 4 May 1892, vol. 4, col. 78. See also Ian Packer, *Lloyd George, Liberalism and the Land: The Land Issue and Patry Politics in England, 1906-1914* (Boydell and Brewer, 2001), p. 30.

50 Kenneth Jackson, *Crabgrass Frontier: The Suburbanization of the United States* (Oxford University Press, 1985), p. 190.

51 Jackson, *Crabgrass Frontier*, p. 201.

52 Sometimes called master-caste democracy, it refers to a system of government where political institutions and processes are dominated by a single ethnic group. The flipside of such a system is the active disenfranchisement of other ethnic groups. Examples include 19th century America and Apartheid South Africa. For a useful discussion of the concept see Ronald Weitzer's *Transforming Settler States Communal Conflict and Internal Security in Northern Ireland and Zimbabwe* (University of California Press, 2023), pp. 32-34.

'suburbanisation was an ideal government policy because it met the needs of both citizens and business interests and it earned the politicians' votes.'[53] In 1959, when the US highlighted its culture at the American National Exhibit in Moscow, Richard Nixon used a model suburban home at the exhibit to present Russian premier Nikita Khrushchev with the case for superiority of the US system. By the Cold War, even Republicans had adopted state sponsored small proprietorship as the epitome of democratic culture.

Suburbanisation provided a stable basis of support for liberal democracy, that was, like populism, structured around the exclusive parameters of ownership. Amid the racial tensions of the emerging civil rights movement, suburban communities proved largely inhospitable to far right, fascist organisations. When President Richard Nixon appealed bluntly to racism with his southern strategy, southern suburbs instead elected moderate Democrats who embraced integration. Yet, southerners responded to integration by withdrawing in droves from public institutions – pools, parks, transit, and even schools. Claiming freedom of association, whites embraced more private lifestyles rooted in suburban families. Patterns of residential segregation enforced by federal policy were normalised as natural achievements in the marketplace. Moral panics around drug use created a suburban legal regime focused on rehabilitation that contrasted starkly with an urban regime of persistent harassment and incarceration – a segregated legal system structured around the disparate geographies of homeownership and tenancy. Propertied suburbanites had little sympathy for authoritarian responses to civil rights that would have undermined the liberal world order in which they had obtained comfortable stability. But the exclusive character of landownership drew social boundaries that justified restrictions on equal citizenship, as it had done, to varying degrees, since the founding of the republic.[54]

Proprietarian land reform reached the pinnacle of its global influence during the Cold War but faltered due to an overreliance on top-down bureaucratic management. In the post Second World War world the United

---

53 Jackson, *Crabgrass Frontier*, p. 216.
54 Kevin Kruse, *White Flight: Atlanta and the Making of Modern Conservatism* (Princeton University Press, 2007); Lisa McGirr, *Suburban Warriors: The Origins of the New American Right* (Princeton University Press, 2001); Matthew Lassiter, *The Silent Majority: Suburban Politics in the Sunbelt South* (Princeton University Press, 2006); Matthew Lassiter, *The Suburban Crisis: White America and the War on Drugs* (Princeton University Press, 2023).

Nation's Food and Agriculture Organization (FAO) served as a clearing house for expertise on land reform, promoting broadcast ownership as a democratic third way between communism and inegalitarian markets. For the English and American social scientists who staffed the FAO, land reform had proven itself the path toward economic autonomy and democracy. It also had enormous popularity in the decolonising Global South, where even Marxism, a theory predicated on the inevitable hegemony of the industrial working class, morphed into a form of agrarianism under the tutelage of Mao Zedong.

The FAO provided technical assistance to the Global South in mapping land for redistribution, advising farmers in best practices, and disseminating the research of agrarian thinkers, like India's Samar Ranjan Sen. However, hopes for land reform faded by the end of the 1960s; even with technical assistance from the United Nations the state capacity to map land for equitable redistribution was lacking. India, one of the best prospects for land reform, instead saw the owners of great estates circumvent land limitation laws by hiding their property in the hands of distant relatives.[55] A notable success story was Taiwan's 1953 land-to-the-tiller programme. Though the programme was intended to shore up rural support for the Kuomintang party's authoritarian government,[56] it nevertheless facilitated democratisation. Government purchase and redistribution of large estates undermined the power of land owning elites and created a new class of small owners who became more engaged in grassroots politics.[57] In Latin America, where the legacies of Spanish colonialism ensured that two-thirds of farmland was owned by a mere one percent of the population, the handful of states that established some land reforms – Uruguay, Argentina, and Chile – developed better standards of living and more stable political systems.[58]

---

55 Jo Guldi, *The Long Land War: The Global Struggle for Occupancy* Rights (Yale University Press, 2021), p. 314; Julia Lovell, *Maoism: A Global History* (Bodley Head, 2019).

56 The Kuomintang (KMT) is a Chinese political party that ruled mainland China from 1927 to 1949 prior to its relocation to Taiwan as a result of the Chinese Civil War.

57 Kevin Wei Luo, 'Redistributing Power: Land Reform, Rural Cooptation, and Grassroots Regime Institutions in Authoritarian Taiwan,' *Comparative Political Studies* vol 58, issue 2 (2024): pp. 1-34.

58 Andro Linklater, *Owning the Earth: The Transformative History of Land Ownership* (Bloomsbery, 2013), pp. 324, 326.

While land reform has assembled cross-class support for democratic institutions, simple ownership has also broadened support for systems that continue to exclude more marginalised groups. This result was foreseen by the British Chartist George Julian Harney, a supporter of Spence's plan for communal ownership, who noted in 1850 that breaking up landed estates would only mean that 'those who had money to buy land would become landlords, and every such landlord, whether lord of fifty or fifty thousand acres, would become a conservative – the sworn enemy to further changes.'[59] One leading model for democratisation posited by Daron Acemoglu and James Robinson hypothesises that societies dominated by rent-seeking elites favour conservative, autocratic government to protect their privileges, whereas societies in which all people have the capacity to reap the fruits of their labour, embrace openness and dynamism.[60]

Shortly before his death in 1865, indeed on the occasion of his last public speech, the great free trade advocate and leader of the Anti-Corn Law League, Richard Cobden told an audience that 'a League for Free Trade in Land, just as we had a League for Free Trade in Corn', was now an economic and social necessity.[61] In defiance of Harney's prescient observation, or perhaps in accord with it, many liberal approaches to the land question from the mid-19th century onward embraced a free trade solution that, by integrating it more fully into the market, furthered its commodification, and therefore the division between those with access and those without. The radical liberal vision of land, so ably articulated by Mill and George, was also plundered from the opposite direction, becoming subsumed within a centralised, utilitarian politics of social welfare that largely excised its participatory and democratic implications. Historically speaking, the relationship between liberal politics and the land question has been one of paradox and contradiction. Thomas Jefferson rejected the absolute ownership of land, arguing that 'the earth belongs in usufruct to the living'. During his time as an ambassador in Paris, he witnessed the poor begging for sustenance outside of the large, unused estates of aristocrats and called for governments to 'tax the higher portions of property in geometrical

59 Bronstein, *Land Reform and Working-Class Experience*, p. 36.
60 Daron Acemoglu and James Robinson, 'Rents and Economic Development: The Perspective of Why Nations Fail', *Public Choice* vol. 181, no. 1/2 (2019): pp. 13–28.
61 Speech at Rochdale, 23 November 1864, quoted in *Richard Cobden and the Land Tax* (English League for the Taxation of Land Values, n.d.), p. 1.

progression as they rise'. 'Legislators', he observed, 'can't invent too many devices for subdividing property.'[62] Yet, in practice, Jefferson inspired proprietarian land reforms that underwrote new boundaries of exclusion. In 2023, when homeowners formed Montanans Against Densification to block the construction of apartments, they called for barring renters from their communities by evoking an ideal of single-family housing that had been sponsored by federal home loan programs on land gifted by the federal government. A widened land ownership had, perhaps, facilitated the rise of liberal democracies' more tepid iterations, but had fallen short of the equality that radical liberals aspired to.

Land. ecology and a right to life

Access to land and the earth's natural resources may always have been fraught, but climate catastrophe and ecological collapse promises to make it the most grave and urgent question of all. Even though billionaires might choose to build bunkers in New Zealand, individual ownership of the land offers no protection for humanity in the face of the global conflict, instability and deprivation that may face us. The scale and complexity of the problem can seem to be irreconcilable with liberal commitments to individual rights and ponderous democratic deliberation. How is it possible to preserve participatory democracy when not only the existence of a stable political order, but indeed survival of the natural world itself, appears to require setting aside such messy and dangerous freedoms, and the challenge of achieving democratic consensus, for the greater good? Yet some answers present themselves from the radical agrarian tradition. This politics, which focused on the right to life and framed its arguments around the demand for self-preservation and the needs of the human body and mind, required access to land and to political collaboration. It was a collective expression of individual rights that could never lose sight of the limitations imposed by humans' environment, whether natural or social. Expanding this idea to encompass our future as well as our present, this powerful demand for self-preservation might help us think about what we need, as human animals, to sustain a habitat that will promote our own flourishing and fulfilment.

---

62 Linklater, *Owning the Earth*, pp. 208-209.

Bibliography

Acemoglu, Daron, and James A. Robinson. 'Rents and Economic Development: The Perspective of Why Nations Fail.' *Public Choice* vol. 181, no. 1/2 (2019): pp. 13-28.

Baptist, Edward. *The Half Has Never Been Told: Slavery and the Making of American Capitalism*. Basic Books, 2014.

Bellanta, Melissa. 'Transcending Class? Australia's Single Taxers in the Early 1890s.' *Labour History* no. 92 (2007): pp. 17-30.

Biagini, Eugenio. *Liberty, Retrenchment and Reform: Popular Liberalism in the Age of Gladstone, 1860-1880*. Cambridge University Press, 1992.

Bradlaugh, Charles. *Compulsory Cultivation of Land: What it means, and why it ought to be enforced*. Freethought Publishing, 1887.

Bronstein, Jamie L. *Land Reform and Working-Class Experience in Britian and the United States, 1800-1862*. Stanford University Press, 1999.

Campbell, George. *Essay on the Commercial Principles applicable to Contracts for the Hire of Land*. Cassell, Petter & Galpin, 1877.

Chase, Malcolm. *The People's Farm: English Radical Agrarianism, 1775-1840*. Oxford University Press, 1988.

— '"Wholesome Object Lessons": The Chartist Land Plan in Retrospect.' *English Historical Review* vol. 118, no. 475 (2003): pp. 59-85.

Cobden, Richard. *Richard Cobden and the Land Tax*. English League for the Taxation of Land Values, n.d.

Collings, Jesse. 'The Radical Programme.' *Fortnightly Review* vol. 34, no. 201 (1883): p. 445.

Devyr, Thomas Ainge. *Our Natural Rights: A Pamphlet for the People* [1835]. T.A. Devyr, 1842.

England, Christopher. *Land and Liberty: Henry George and the Crafting of Modern Liberalism*. Johns Hopkins University Press, 2023.

Flamming, Douglas. *African Americans in the West*. Bloomsbury Publishing, 2009.

Foner, Eric. *Free Soil, Free Labor, Free Men: The Ideology of the Republican Party Before the Civil War*. Oxford University Press, 1995.

Gates, Paul W. *The Jeffersonian Dream: Studies in the History of American Land Policy and Development*. University of New Mexico, 1996.

George, Henry. *Progress and Poverty*. National Single Tax League, 1879.

Gosse, Van. *The First Reconstruction: Black Politics in America From the Revolution to the Civil War*. University of North Carolina Press, 2021.

Green, Thomas Hill. *Liberal Legislation and Freedom of Contract.* Slatter and Rose, 1881.

Guldi, Jo. *The Long Land War: The Global Struggle for Occupancy Rights.* Yale University Press, 2021.

Haldane, Richard. HC Deb, 4 May 1892, vol. 4, col. 78.

Hicks, John Donald. *The Populist Revolt: A History of the Farmers Alliance and the People's Party.* University of Minnesota Press, 1931.

Hyndman, Henry, ed. *The Nationalization of the Land in 1775 and 1882.* E. W. Allen, 1882.

Jackson, Kenneth T. *Crabgrass Frontier: The Suburbanization of the United States.* Oxford University Press, 1985.

Jefferson Thomas. 'Notes on the State of Virginia.' In *The Complete Jefferson.* Edited by S. K. Padover. Duell, Sloan and Pearch, Inc., 1943.

Johnston, Robert. *The Radical Middle Class: Populist Democracy and the Question of Capitalism in Progressive Era Portland.* Princeton University Press, 2006.

Kazin, Michael. *A Godly Hero: The Life of William Jennings Bryan.* Knopf, 2006.

Kennedy, Robert. *Mr. Jefferson's Lost Cause Land, Farmers, Slavery, and the Louisiana Purchase.* Oxford University Press, 2003.

Kerr, Robert Malcolm, ed. *The Commentaries on the Laws of England,* vol. II, *Of the Rights of Things* [1765]. John Murray, 1876.

Kruse, Kevin. *White Flight: Atlanta and the Making of Modern Conservatism.* Princeton University Press, 2007.

Lassiter, Matthew. *The Silent Majority: Suburban Politics in the Sunbelt South.* Princeton University Press, 2006.

— *The Suburban Crisis: White America and the War on Drugs.* Princeton University Press, 2023.

Lecky, William Edward Hartpole. *Democracy and Liberty,* vol. II *[1896].* Longmans, Green and Co., 1903.

Levy, Jonathan. *Freaks of Fortune.* Harvard University Press, 2012.

Linklater, Andro. *Measuring America: How an Untamed Wilderness Shaped the United States and Fulfilled the Promise of Democracy.* Penguin 2003.

— *Owning the Earth: The Transformative History of Land Ownership.* Bloombery, 2013.

Lovell, Julia. *Maoism: A Global History.* Bodley Head, 2019.

Luckerson, Victor. *Built From the Fire: The Epic Story of Tulsa's Greenwood*

District, America's Black Walls Street. Random House, 2023.

Luo, Kevin Wei. 'Redistributing Power: Land Reform, Rural Cooptation, and Grassroots Regime Institutions in Authoritarian Taiwan.' *Comparative Political Studies* vol 58, issue 2 (2024): pp. 1-34.

MacCallum, Donald. *Addresses by the Rev. Donald MacCallum.* Duncan Cameron, 1884.

Mackenzie, Alexander. *The Isle of Skye in 1882-1883; Illustrated by a full report of the trials of the Braes and Glendale Crofters at Inverness and Edinburgh.* A & W Mackenzie, 1883.

Makgill, George. *Rent No Robbery: An Examination of Some Erroneous Doctrines Regarding Property in Land.* William Blackwood, 1851.

Mallock, William Hurrell. *Property and Progress, Or a Brief Enquiry into Contemporary Social Agitation in England.* John Murray, 1884.

Marsh, Jan. *Back to the Land: The Pastoral Impulse in Victorian England from 1880-1914.* Quarter Books, 1982.

Mason, John W. 'The Duke of Argyll and the Land Question in Late Nineteenth Century Britain.' *Victorian Studies* vol. 21, no. 2 (1978): pp. 149-170.

McGirr, Lisa. *Suburban Warriors: the Origins of the New American Right.* Princeton University Press, 2001.

Mencken, H.L. 'Roosevelt: An Autopsy.' In *Prejudices: Second Series.* Jonathan Cape, 1921.

Mill, J.S. 'Advice to Land Reformers.' *The Examiner,* 4 January 1873.

— *The Letters of John Stuart Mill,* vol. II. Edited by Hugh S.R. Elliott. Longmans, Green, and Co. 1919.

— 'Tract on the Right of Property in Land.' In *The Letters of John Stuart Mill,* vol. II. Edited by Hugh S.R. Elliott. Longmans, Green, and Co. 1919.

Nulty, Thomas. *The Land Question: Letter of the Most Rev. Dr. Nulty, to the Clergy and Laity of the Diocese of Meath.* Joseph Dollard, 1881.

Ogilvie William. 'Essay on the Right of Property in Land.' Reprinted in *The Pioneers of Land Reform: Thomas Spence, William Ogilvie, Thomas Paine.* Edited by Max Beer. G. Bell and Sons, 1920.

Orren, Karen. *Belated Feudalism: Labor, the Law, and Liberal Development in the United States.* Cambridge University Press, 1991.

Packer, Ian. *Lloyd George, Liberalism and the Land: The Land Issue and Patry Politics in England, 1906-1914.* Boydell and Brewer, 2001.

Paine, Thomas. *Agrarian Justice*. Booksellers of London and Westminster, 1797.

Pollard, Sidney. 'Nineteenth-Century Corporations: Community Building to Shopkeeping.' In *Essays in Labour History*. Edited by Asa Briggs and John Saville. Palgrave Macmillan, 1967.

Postel, Charles. *The Populist Vision*. Oxford University Press, 2007.

Readman, Paul. *Nation in England: Patriotism, National Identity, and the Politics of Land, 1880-1914*. The Boydell Press, 2008.

Sarmiento, Domingo Faustino, *Sarmiento's Travels in the U.S. in 1847*. Translated by Michael Aaron Rockland. Princeton University Press, 1970.

Spence, Thomas. *The Restorer of Society to its Natural State; In a Series of Letters to a Fellow Citizen*. Thomas Spence, 1801.

Shannon, Fred. A. 'The Homestead Act and the Labor Surplus.' *The American Historical Review* vol. 41, no. 4 (1936): pp. 637-651.

Thompson, E.P. *The Making of the English Working Class* [1963]. Penguin, 1981.

Times, The. 'The Crofters in Tiree.' 24 July 1886.

Toynbee, Arnold. *'Progress and Poverty', A Criticism of Mr. Henry George, Being Two Lectures Delivered in St. Andrew's Hall, Newman Street, London*. Kegan Paul, Trench and Co., 1883.

Tuchinsky, Adam. *Horace Greeley's New-York Tribune: Civil War-Era Socialism and the Crisis of Free Labor*. Cornell University Press, 2009.

Tuck, Richard. *Natural Rights Theories: Their Origin and Development*. Cambridge University Press, 1979.

Weitzer, Ronald. *Transforming Settler States Communal Conflict and Internal Security in Northern Ireland and Zimbabwe*. University of California Press, 2023.

White, Richard. *The Republic for Which It Stands: The United States during Reconstruction and the Gilded Age, 1865-1896*. Oxford University Press, 2017.

Wood, Anthony. *Black Montana, Settler Colonialism, and the Erosion of the Racial Frontier*. University of Nebraska Press, 2021.

Wood, Gordon. *Empire of Liberty: A History of the Early Republic, 1789-1815*. Oxford University Press, 2009.

— *The Radicalism of the American Revolution*. A.A. Knopf, 1992.

5

Loneliness, Trust and Freedom

Emmy van Deurzen

One of the great 21st century challenges is to manage the tension between freedom and individualism on the one hand and the needs of the community and society on the other hand. This is not something we are currently handling very well in our global village, perhaps because the liberal values needed to address this tension are not currently clearly in view. Liberal ideas have become suspect to many, in an age where neo-liberalism has made political freedom look like a dangerous excuse for the unimpeded tyranny of the economically privileged elite, whilst personal freedom has become equated with rampant consumerism. This has led to a crisis of confidence in both individualism and politics. If we are to address this problem, we need to start by redefining freedom and its role in human existence, in a way that makes sense to our contemporaries. To do so we have to look at freedom and its corollaries of loneliness, isolation, choice and responsibility in the round, considering their many complex implications. Freedom without its counterpart of responsibility and without awareness of the human need for safety in a supportive community is an empty concept. In a society that tends to polarise opinion, rational debate has failed to address this need for a balanced, considered and realistic approach. When people are confronted with a society that appears unwilling to address the intricate and paradoxical nature of human existence, they are tempted to give up, because they know in their bones that those who are in power are not speaking about the things that truly matter.

Mental health impact

The mental health crisis we are witnessing around the world is a good indicator of this malaise. It does not mean that the world population is mentally ill. It means that there is a generalised sense of discomfort and hopelessness about the situation human beings find themselves in. Many people are now inclined to withdraw from a socio-political world in which they do not think they can play any part and where they deeply mistrust those in power. As they withdraw into isolation, contenting themselves with superficial consolations and reducing their social world to the inevitable virtual connections, the meaning of life narrows. Suicide rates, anxiety and depression, which are at an all-time high (even beyond 1941 levels) are a witness to this state of affairs. The number of antidepressants prescribed per year has more than tripled over the past two decades, from 18.4 million in 1998 to 70.9 million in 2018 in the UK alone, as can be seen from the longitudinal study on the trends and variations in antidepressant prescribing in English primary care.[1] There are over 47,000 deaths by suicide in the EU alone[2] and it is estimated that 40 million Americans are affected by anxiety each year.[3] The World Health Organization's (WHO) statistics are startling, with approximately 280 million people in the world suffering from depression.[4] WHO also reports that 1 in 8 people around the world is afflicted with a mental health disorder.[5] This means that 970 million people are struggling with anxiety and or depression at any one time.[6]

The solution does not just lie in better mental health care. It has to come from cultural and societal changes. Yet, the public's faith in bringing about positive change through politics is at an all-time low. People are cynical about philosophical liberalism because they perceive it as a despotic choice and connect it in their minds with the abuse of power that is so rife, rather than with their personal rights as was the case in John Stuart Mill's time. When

1.   Paul Bogowicz, Helen J Curtis, Alex J Walker et al., 'Trends and variation in antidepressant prescribing in English primary care: a retrospective longitudinal study,' *BJGP Open* vol. 5, no. 4 (August 2021), https://bjgpopen.org/content/5/4/BJGPO.2021.0020 [Accessed 16/7/2024].

2   Eurostat, 'Deaths by suicide in the EU down by 13% in a decade,' https://ec.europa.eu/eurostat/web/products-eurostat-news/w/edn-20240909-1 [Accessed 7/1/25].

3   NAMI, 'Anxiety Disorders,' https://www.nami.org/about-mental-illness/mental-health-conditions/anxiety-disorders/ [Accessed 7/1/25].

4.   World Health Organization, *Depressive Disorder Fact Sheet*, 31 March 2023, https://www.who.int/news-room/fact-sheets/detail/depression [Accessed 16/7/2024].

5.   World Health Organization, *Mental Disorders: Key Facts*, 8 June 2022, https://tinyurl.com/2f2n4sbb [Accessed 16/7/2024].

6.   World Health Organization, *Mental Health Gap Action Programme guideline for mental, neurological and substance use disorders*, 3rd ed., November 2023, https://www.who.int/publications/i/item/9789240084278 [Accessed 16/7/2024].

the crowd has drowned out a person's voice, she is more likely to choose to stay mute and keep her head down than to engage in political debate or to clamour for greater freedom or the right to be heard. Addressing the mental health crisis is not just about finding remedies. It is about addressing the root cause of this lack of emotional stability and contentment in the world. It is important to understand why so many people give up. This is centrally relevant to politics.

Lack of trust

In a culture where might is right and everything is measured and calculated, politicians have learnt to think in terms of quantitative statistics, facts and figures, rather than in terms of quality of life and personal concerns. They often forget that they are addressing individuals, rather than groups and they tend towards groupthink, aiming to appeal to the widest possible audience. Populism now rules politics and makes it much harder for politicians to think clearly about the values and realities that people are dealing with. They forget about the people whose daily lives are lived in the margin of politics and who are sceptical of the words they hear. They address the imaginary individual that has been construed and described to them by their advisers. In the day-to-day world of ordinary people, political discourse often seems irrelevant and insincere. Politics is a show, a competition and a shouting match and does not reach through to the individual person's true concerns. An unbridgeable divide is created between the people and the politicians. Politicians are tempted to lie or exaggerate when confronted with this abyss, promising the earth and delivering very little. This erodes public respect ever further and many now experience the ruling classes as untrustworthy, self-promoting and out of touch with their reality.

Politicians forget that the people who withhold their vote are not just negligent, ignorant, or lazy. They are voting with their feet against a system in which they feel that the dice are loaded. Not participating in democracy has become a way to affirm displeasure in politics. Democracy is perceived as a sham rather than as a highly desirable value. When people feel they have more to lose than to gain from exercising their democratic rights, they will naturally prefer not to engage at all, not even by raising their voice in protest. Many do not bother, because they do not believe they can make a difference, and they do not believe that their opinion matters. This does not mean that the silent majority is content with its lot; it simply means that many have given up on the political process. They observe what happens and they feel justified in switching off from it. It is now possible for individuals to feel isolated from the world, condemned to obscurity and loneliness, whilst at the same time watching those who make the decisions on their screens, despairing about the world. What these people feel is not the impotency they may have felt in John Stuart Mill's day, it is rather a disdain for the political process, which they consider not to be relevant to them. People have learnt to interpret life as a game and the political game is not seen as a realistic pathway towards freedom or improvement.

Polarisation

In this climate of self-isolation and cynicism, worldviews become increasingly polarised.[7] There is little subtlety in the opinions that are projected into the world by the media. There is less refined debate than ever before. Pundits tend to posture. We see fewer dialogues between experts and more enflamed debates between celebrities. The emphasis is on what is eye catching or likely to produce a sound bite. Political figures turn themselves into caricatures or amplify the impact of the measures they propose. Social media have given people access to the means of engaging in political battles in emotive ways. Reflective thought is often further reduced in this way and arguments are displaced by opinionated assertions. The more people lose touch with their self-worth and the less they feel heard, the more likely they are to hold their opinions with thoughtless obstinacy. Exchanges turn into fights, rather than into opportunities for nuanced and fair dialogue. It is the loss of that disciplined thinking about the issues that increasingly puts people off political engagement. They prefer to live in their own bubble, which seems sufficient to them, as long as they have the resources to pay the rent, mortgage, food and bills. Engaging in debate is too dangerous, if each side is allowed to misrepresent the situation and lies are often left unchallenged. The post-truth era that brought us Trump as president of the US and Brexit in the UK, eventually led to new wars and widespread social unrest in Europe and the Middle East. The polarisation that appears to dominate the world reverberates in people's private worlds, where they often experience

7.   See Kirk J. Schneider, *The Paradoxical Self: Toward an Understanding of Our Contradictory Nature* (Insight Books, 1999), alongside Schneider's subsequent studies: *The Polarized Mind: Why it's Killing Us and What We Can Do About it* (University Professors Press, 2020) and *Life-Enhancing Anxiety: Key to a Sane World* (University Professors Press, 2023).

themselves as being at the mercy of others who are not rational or willing to consider the issues in a balanced and fair-minded manner. This leads to a pop psychology of identity politics, character assassination and cancel culture. People now frequently give up on human relations all together, withdrawing into a hard shell. They have alternative worlds to live in, through the fantasy universes of gaming, of substance use, or of the entertainment of social media or Netflix binges. This tendency towards polarisation and psychological warfare against those who are perceived as enemies, is insinuating itself into politics too. People are losing the capacity to think in a more attentive and tolerant manner. Intolerance divides society and creates a fertile ground continually more populist and right-wing politics.

Totalitarianism

Such populism easily flows into totalitarianism. When people feel isolated and have the sense that they do not matter, they will uncritically follow leaders who promise the moon and sound as if they have their best interests at heart. As Arendt said in her book *The Origins of Totalitarianism*:

> What prepares men for totalitarian domination in the non-totalitarian world is the fact that loneliness, once a borderline experience usually suffered in certain marginal social conditions like old age, has become an everyday experience of the ever-growing masses of our century.[8]

This remark is more relevant today than it was in the fifties. Madeleine Albright[9] elaborated on this idea and showed how easy it is to tip a society into cruelty, when politicians divide people against each other and capitalise on their isolation and lack of understanding of the political process. In the UK, throughout the Brexit debates we saw how neatly people could be manipulated into voting against their own interests, simply by misinforming them and playing on their insecurities. By appealing to their natural fears of intruders and misrepresenting reality in significant ways, exaggerating dangers and failing to show realistic predictions of what can be expected; a crowd can be stampeded into obedience. Naomi Klein, in her book *The Shock Doctrine*, demonstrated how such methods can be cynically applied by

8.   Hannah Arendt, *The Origins of Totalitarianism* (Harvest Book, 1951:1966), p. 176.
9.   See Madeleine Albright, *Fascism: a Warning* (William Collins, 2019).

those who practice disaster capitalism, once they realise that people who feel insecure and who are faced with disasters will willingly accept dominance by authoritarian leaders.[10] I have illustrated how such experiences create ever further distance between human beings and how this emotional isolation leads to anxiety, depression and despair.[11]

Loneliness and isolation

To feel lonely is to be cut-off from others and to experience yourself as not belonging. Often this feeling can be generated by not being able to make yourself understood. Loneliness is one of the scourges of contemporary society and is at the root of many mental health problems. So many live in relative isolation within urban environments, where they are only connected via the internet and hardly even speak to their neighbours. Other people find society so consumerist, aggressive, loud, violent and embattled that they deliberately avoid it, though that disconnection leads to loneliness. When a mentality of dominance and competition is standard in our culture, it becomes a struggle to engage and find a place to fit into the world. This is particularly true for people who identify as belonging to a minority,[12] but there are many people who are born into relative ease, who nevertheless, end up perceiving the world as hostile and decide it is not worth the effort. They start mistrusting others and withdraw from the world. A longitudinal study, investigating adult development, has been carried out by psychologists at Harvard University since 1938.[13] This has followed several generations of two separate groups of people, sophomores (second years) at Harvard and boys from the poorest areas of Boston. Their health and mental health were studied continuously as they evolved through the decades, and some very interesting conclusions were drawn from all these data. There is overwhelming evidence that material possessions make little difference to people's lives in the long run, as long as you have your basic needs met. What matters more than anything is that your life feels meaningful. This will make all the difference as to whether a person feels life is fulfilling and

---

10. Naomi Klein, *The Shock Doctrine: The Rise of Disaster Capitalism* (Allen Lane, 2008).

11. Emmy van Deurzen, *Rising from Existential Crisis: Life Beyond Calamity* (PCCS Books, 2021).

12. See Dwight Turner, *The Psychology of Supremacy: Imperium* (Routledge, 2023).

13. Robert Waldinger and Marc Schulz, *The Good Life: Lessons from the World's Longest Scientific Study of Happiness* (Simon & Schuster, 2023).

worthwhile. Meaning is generated particularly through being in meaningful relationships. It is therefore all the more shocking that such a large percentage of people in contemporary society live in isolation. They do so largely because they do not trust other people anymore. The conclusion drawn by the researchers is that loneliness kills and that good lives are created and sustained by positive relationships and safe pleasant places to live. This is very much in line with the work of positive psychologists.[14]

It is isolation and lack of mutuality that creates most of the problems in the world. We are not talking about solitude, which is an entirely different matter. Solitude is the capacity to be sufficient in yourself and able to enjoy being on your own at times. Solitude is much improved by a capacity for contemplation and deep reflection. Solitude is necessary if you want to settle into a peaceful place in yourself.[15] Moreover, this in turn is necessary if you are going to be able to build good and trusting relationships based on mutuality and collaboration. Mill argued that solitude was essential to creating the imperfect democracy he believed in, and he was right about this.[16] He had less to contribute on loneliness as he lived in an era where people could cure their loneliness mostly by the way in which society was organised in smaller units. In the 21st century, loneliness has taken residence in people's hearts and minds and is no longer about physical distance. It has become an inner and relational form of alienation and isolation. This is a serious problem that we need to contend with if we are going to get people interested in democracy and engagement with politics. It is even more important if we are serious about creating a happier nation.

Liberalism

Mill understood that democracy is dependent on an increasing number of people being able and willing to reflect not only on their own life, but also on the life of the community. He might therefore have been baffled by political debates on social media. Today, more people than ever can, in principle, participate in shaping public opinion, but many feel cowed by the noise of social media, where the influencers and opinion shapers dominate the debate.

14. See Ed Diener and Eunkook M. Suh, eds., *Culture and Subjective Well-Being* (MIT Press, 2003).

15. Emmy van Deurzen, *Paradox and Passion in Psychotherapy*, 2nd ed. (Wiley, 1998:2015).

16. John Stuart Mill, *On Liberty, Utilitarianism and other Essays*, ed. Mark Philip (Oxford World's Classics, 2015).

There is a lack of disciplined structure, and we have not rebuilt our political system to evolve alongside this new global connectivity. We are, in principle, in a position to decentralise power and introduce online citizens assemblies as a means to involve people from all walks of life and backgrounds in democratic reflection and even in the political decision-making process, but we have done very little to make this happen. Instead, people are being ruled by algorithms, mathematical processes that decide how far their voices will reach, and what will come up on their timelines. There is a lack of dialogue about the fundamental values that are needed to create a functional global society in which freedom and responsibility are two sides of the same coin. When is the last time you saw a proper philosophical debate on television? Intellectual ideas are not explored carefully and responsibly in the media, but rather exploited cynically, for profit. As Mill and many others have long argued, the way to create a free society is by educating people. Giving people access to clear and critical thinking is increasingly seen as risky. Yet, there can be no freedom without understanding and without awareness of consequences, implications and responsibilities.

John Gray summarised the ideas of liberal thought very poignantly as being composed of four elements: individualism, egalitarianism, meliorism and universalism.[17] Mill was speaking up for those who were oppressed, including workers and women. He championed the cause of equality and human rights and showed the importance of human freedom and individuality at a time when such things were groundbreaking and much needed. But times have changed and from the second half of the 20th century onwards, individualism, egalitarianism, meliorism and universalism have become part of the daily diet of citizens who live with relative security and who watch the world's ups and downs from the protective bubble of their screens. Much of the cultural discourse, in movies and novels and games, portrays the personal struggle of an individual who is fighting against a group of individuals, a system or a society that is oppressing them. The implied objective is often that of achieving fairness, equality or improvement in a person's situation. This is too often achieved through violence, by wars, revolutions, or on a smaller scale, through crime. It is hardly surprising that there is an increasing problem of violence in a world where the political process is perceived as distorted, elitist and

---

17. See John Gray, *The New Leviathans: Thoughts After Liberalism* (Allen Lane, 2023).

oppressive. Consequently, conflict is becoming understood as an essential expression of personal power. Instead of seeing politics as a way to build a better world, people are more inclined to conclude that popular protest, strikes and obstructive actions are the most direct and ethical path towards having minority views heard.

Crisis of confidence

The Climate Crisis protests are a good example of this. They demonstrate that young people have lost trust in the way the world is being managed and organised.[18] They despair of their future and seek safe havens in which to hide away. They often perceive their elders, as having failed at protecting the environment and the planet. As Greta Thunberg says on the cover of her book: 'everything needs to change. And it has to start today.'[19] This is a sentiment echoed by many of the younger generation. An interesting study about the worldviews of young people, in twelve countries, showed that young people are often confused and hesitant about which worldview to adopt and that there is no current dominant worldview they champion, though they feel that things are very wrong. There is clearly a moral vacuum. We need a new moral vision, capable of harmonising the challenges and aspirations of young people. However, as Peter Nynäs et al. have observed, this is no easy task:

> The recent developments of societal polarisation, climate change, pandemics and warzones in Europe call for developing moral purposes and values in higher education students. Higher education students are not a homogeneous group – the divisions of worldviews and values of young people along an axis of universalism and self-direction versus tradition and conformity also apply to them.[20]

Young people largely no longer have the framework of religions to guide them and there is a huge need for a new secular moral framework that

18. Greta Thunberg, *No One is Too Small to Make a Difference* (Penguin Books, 2019).
19. Thunberg, *No One is Too Small.*
20. Peter Nynäs, Ariela Keysar, Martin Lagerström et al., *The Diversity Of Worldviews Among Young Adults: Contemporary (Non)Religiosity And Spirituality Through The Lens Of An International Mixed Method Study* (Springer, 2022), pp. 47-71, https://doi.org/10.1007/978-3-030-94691-3_3 [Accessed 7/9/2024].

can be applicable worldwide, one that can guide and inspire, without imposing rigidity. Pluralism and tolerance of other views is going to be an important part of the foundation of such a framework. This framework will need to address the challenges of liberalism in a way that is cogent, direct and relevant to young people, those who do not want to be subjected to the very same ideas that have blighted the world with industrialism and commercialism. Many will doubtless revolt against such ideas, feeling that these are erroneous, misconceived and dishonest, as they have obviously not worked out in practice and have not brought them any happiness or hope for a future. Freedom is no longer a driving value for people like this. They have become complacent in taking their many basic freedoms for granted and are far more sensitive to the dangers that surround them than to the options available to tackle them. The scientific faith in determinism that has underpinned society for the past centuries cannot easily be supplanted by older ideas of liberty and individuality. Young people have a strong sense of entitlement about their rights, but very little understanding of how such rights were acquired, or how they might be maintained and improved on.

The challenges of the future are great, and we can only face them if we understand that freedom is not a panacea. People frequently think of freedom in the negative: they believe that freedom is about liberating themselves from something. To free yourself from a yoke is a highly motivating purpose, but once you have achieved that freedom, it can be much harder to know what to do with it.[21] Engagement and commitment are an important counterweight to freedom in this respect and it is by making connections and commitments that we create a framework of meaning.[22] Mill argued that the only valid reason for interfering with a person's freedom should be to protect them from harm, but this no longer feels right. When people are alienated from their own awareness of freedom, it may be necessary to educate and protect them more from emotional, psychological or existential distress and confusion than from physical harm. To do so we have to talk about freedom and the realities that it brings with it. Freedom and community always go together. When they do not, there is a problem. Freedom and responsibility are two twins that are inseparable. One without the other cannot survive.

---

21 See Erich Fromm, *Fear of Freedom* (Routledge, 2001).

22 See Emmy van Durzen, *Psychotherapy and the Quest for Happiness* (Sage, 2009) and Roy Baumeister, *Meanings of Life* (Guildford Press, 1991).

Solidarity

When we live in little cells of self-sufficiency and we are inclined to be suspicious of others, criticising them profusely from the safety of our homes, it becomes much harder to have a sweeping sense of solidarity with those who are deprived of such privileges. During the pandemic, there was a brief flourishing of such solidarity, after it became clear to people that their lives might be at risk. However, this solidarity was more with the essential workers who kept life going and especially with the medical, nursing and caring professionals who were perceived as battling bravely to keep us all safe. This solidarity was also surprisingly short lived when it came to paying salary increases to these same essential workers. There were neighbourhood support schemes for the elderly or those who were shielding, but this diminished rapidly as vaccinations were rolled out. Similarly, there was an initial wave of solidarity when Ukraine was invaded by Russia and people suddenly felt scared at the thought of what Ukrainians were made to endure. We identified and opened our borders and offered hospitality to thousands of Ukrainians, but began to grow weary of this charity very rapidly when it was obvious that there might not be a quick end to the war and that Ukrainian citizens did not like being treated as refugees. There was deeply felt solidarity with the Israelis when they were cruelly attacked by Hamas in October 2023 and our hearts went out to those who had been taken hostage, or whose family members had been killed or taken hostage, but this sentiment was quickly changed into solidarity with the Palestinians who were under siege and who were being attacked in ways that were obviously excessive and extremely violent. It is not easy for people to be purposeful in their sense of solidarity, as their emotions are constantly being inflamed and agitated by what is portrayed in the media.

Nobody is thinking through the issues carefully. The discourse is largely reactive, and solidarity is triggered in the same way as we become empathetic of heroes in movies: only to become enamoured of another hero the next day. The kind of committed and enduring solidarity that wins political arguments as we saw in Poland in the eighties is less likely to happen now.

Community and democracy

You cannot build a credible democratic society, unless people are actively engaged with each other in deciding their own future. Democracy has become impotent in many Western societies. People are not clear anymore about what their role in their community is, and how or whether they could influence what happens locally, nationally and internationally. They are paralysed by the complexity of life and often not sure whether they are willing or able to contribute something of their own to their community, because they are not sure what they would gain from this in the end. People will contribute to a local foodbank or a project for someone who has been dealt a hard blow of fate, but they tire of such efforts and in the end, they feel compassion fatigue and they fear that they have been virtue signalling rather than having any kind of real connection or impact. As Joss Sheldon has playfully argued in a little book called *Democracy*, we have lost track of what true democracy looks like.[23] Crucially, we are out of touch with the sort of direct effect we might be able to have on how we are governed. Mostly people follow their leaders blindly and do not feel they can be the masters of their own destiny. When eleven female writers took on the topic of democracy,[24] they spoke about demagoguery, disappointment, and the need to start listening to nature and to each other and ourselves before we can reform democracy. In this book, Elif Shafak astutely describes democracy as a delicate eco-system of checks and balances, rights and needs, power and accountability. However, individuals have lost track of their contribution to that eco-system, for voting alone does not make you feel empowered. It is not just the natural world that needs protecting; it is the socio-political world too. Human beings more than ever seek to live a worthwhile life as a free individual, but to be held safe in a meaningful and peaceful community at the same time. Observing how easily such a tender equation is destroyed by war or other catastrophes makes people despair, because they do not know how to rebuild their communities in a worthwhile way.

Personhood, autonomy and freedom

Engaging with your society and community effectively is only possible if you have learnt to become a well-functioning unit of your own in a smaller group, usually in a family. Learning to observe your inner thoughts, feelings, sensations and intuitions is an important condition of the capacity to communicate about the things that actually matter to you. People will censor themselves as long as they believe that what they

---

23. Joss Sheldon, *Democracy: A User's Guide* (Rebel Books, 2020).
24. Margaret Atwood, Mary Beard, Erica Benner et al., *Democracy: Eleven writers and leader on what it is – and why it matters* (Profile Books, 2004).

experience is not important, or when they fear they will be ridiculed when they speak from the heart. This means that we have to educate people to think, read, dialogue and argue about the things that are important to them and connect this up to what is important to the wider world. We have to show children from very early on, how their contribution matters and how their particular strengths and talents can be put to good use in the group as well as appreciated. They also have to experience the satisfaction in taking responsibility for themselves and the common good. However, in the dynamic of many families and many schools what we observe is not learning for cooperation but for competition. Especially in their teens, throughout secondary education children are taught to observe each other critically and apprehensively, and they learn that their performance will be measured against that of others and that only the best will succeed. This not only inspires suspicion and aggression towards a world that will test you instead of showing you how to put your ability to good use, but it also trains people to be cynical about communal activity. We cannot all win, and many learn to give up.

We speak of the many freedoms people enjoy in contemporary society, but we forget to look at the many constraints they feel under. The importance of learning to recognise the whole spectrum of human existence, in all its paradoxical reality is something that we can learn from the discipline of existential therapy, which has evolved a pragmatic philosophy to live by.[25] The younger generation appreciates such clarity greatly and it would be hugely beneficial to make such ideas common currency, starting with simple and clear philosophical ideas about what it means to live well.[26] It would enhance young people's capacity to take a carefully responsible stance in the world and relate to themselves and each other with much greater understanding. The question people often find hard to address is not what they want to be free from, but what it is they want to be free for.[27] Many people are drawn

---

25. See Hannah Arendt, *The Human Condition*, 2nd ed. (University of Chicago Press, 1958:2018). Also, refer to Victor E. Frankl, *The Doctor and the Soul: From Psychotherapy to Logotherapy*, 3rd ed., trans. R. Winston & C. Winston (Vintage Books, 1986); and Irvin D. Yalom, *Existential Psychotherapy* (Basic Books, 1980).
26. For such philosophical insights, see Simon Blackburn, *Being Good, a short introduction to ethics* (Oxford University Press, 2003); and Julian Baggini and Peter S. Fosl, *The Ethics Toolkit: A Compendium of Ethical Concepts and Methods* (Wiley Blackwell, 2007).
27. Emmy van Durzen, *The Art of Existential Freedom: Guide to a Wiser Life* (Penguin, 2025—in press).

into unrealistic desires, pursuing a hedonistic or achievement focused lifestyle. Some feel the pain of inner confusion and find it hard to make sense of the contradictions and suffering they observe in the world. These are things we can remedy.

Choice and responsibility

As we have argued above, if human beings are going to seek to live better lives, they will have to start by revisiting the basic question of what it means to be a person, an individual and a member of a democratic society. What can we do with our lives? What can we achieve for ourselves and what can we hope to contribute to our culture and the world of the future? Is freedom the starting point, or the objective, or is freedom perhaps an emerging property and side effect of living in the right way? How many people have any idea about what it means to live a good and meaningful life? Our existential philosophies have been largely replaced by the urgency of the search for happiness or success, which is continually promoted by the zeitgeist.[28] It takes a lot of learning to understand the situations we find ourselves in and to reflect on how we would like to use our lifetime, not just for our own enjoyment, but for the purpose of creating a better world. If you don't know what is possible, you cannot exercise your human rights, or your freedom. If you have not learnt to question what is right and wrong or to think about what makes for a good human existence, you are unlikely to be able to use your freedom to make the best choices. We often have politics without philosophy these days, and in the same way we have lives without thoughtfulness. People are good at manipulating technology, but much less good at knowing themselves, understanding each other or making life choices in a knowledgeable and responsible way.

Into the future

If we want to extricate ourselves from the current mental health crisis as well as build a better and more balanced world for the future, we are going to have to address these existential issues. This is undoubtedly something that takes us back to the ideals of liberalism, for it is about re-establishing the balance between the individual and society, freedom and responsibility, solitude and solidarity. In a world where the global village needs to find a more equitable and pleasant way for people to co-exist and thrive into the

28. Emmy Van Durzen, *Psychotherapy and the Quest for Happines*.

long distant future, a new form of liberalism is an indispensable necessity, not a luxury.

We know much more about human beings than Mill did in the 19th century, and we can adjust our scope and manner of approaching the issues. As French poet Paul Valéry once put it, it is the task of the mind to produce the future.[29] The mind takes in sensory information and emotional responses and takes its time to ponder how best to respond. It thinks slowly about the world when it is at its best and it thinks fast in a crisis.[30] As Daniel Dennett said, a mind is fundamentally an anticipator, an expectation-generator.[31] Human beings will always be better at sensing the future that suits them best. AI can provide the facts and can generate a range of possibilities in a much faster manner, but the slow and mature thinking of a free mind is inimitable. This is what people know, deep in their hearts and they will always wish for a future in which they can continue to exercise that freedom of thought, feeling and choice. Politicians may be able to frighten people into believing that they will be at the mercy of forces beyond them, but people will always know that they are part of an ordered universe. Each of us is a thinking animal and an element of nature. We are capable of deciding about our own fate, taking into account the whole situation and its conflicting forces. Politicians who can engage people with the kind of hope for the future, that involves human beings in making more of their capacity for deliberation and freedom, by a joint commitment, will fare well. Those who will use scare tactics may temporarily gain ascendency but in the end, truth and liberty will tell.

Conclusions

What do you want to be free for? Are we willing to consider how to create a better human civilisation by facing up to our contradictions, our conflicts and our crises? Alternatively, are we just seeking to rearrange deckchairs while the ship is sinking? If we have the courage to come to an existential worldview that can rise above opposing ideologies and provide people with a robust framework from which to craft meaningful lives, interrogating

---

29. *Paul Valéry: An Anthology*, ed. James R. Lawler, trans. David Paul (Princeton University Press, 1977).
30. Daniel Kahneman, *Thinking, Fast and Slow* (Penguin Books, 2012).
31. Daniel Dennett, *Kinds of Minds: Towards an Understanding of Consciousness* (Basic Books, 1996:2013).

reality and truth and owning up to their responsibility, the sky is the limit. However, this will require much determination to think things through instead of going down well-trodden paths, trying to make the future fit into a repetition of an ever more cramped past. It will require bringing more philosophy and psychology into politics.

Bibliography

Albright, Madeleine. *Fascism: A Warning*. William Collins, 2019.

Atwood, Margaret, Mary Beard, Erica Benner, et al. *Democracy: Eleven writers and leaders on what it is – and why it matters*. Profile Books, 2004.

Arendt, Hannah. *The Human Condition*, 2nd ed. University of Chicago Press, 1958:2018.

— *The Origins of Totalitarianism*. Harvest Book, 1951:1966.

Baggini, Julian, and Peter S. Fosl. *The Ethics Toolkit: A Compendium of Ethical Concepts and Methods*. Wiley Blackwell, 2007.

Baumeister, Roy. *Meanings of Life*. Guildford Press, 1991.

Bogowicz, Paul, Helen J. Curtis, Alex J. Walker, et al. 'Trends and variation in antidepressant prescribing in English primary care: a retrospective longitudinal study'. *BJGP Open* vol. 5, no. 4 (August 2021).

Blackburn, Simon. *Being Good, a short introduction to ethics*. Oxford University Press, 2003.

Dennett, Daniel. *Kinds of Minds: Towards an Understanding of Consciousness*. Basic Books, 1996:2013.

Deurzen, Emmy van. *The Art of Existential Freedom: Guide to a Wiser Life*. Penguin, 2025—in press.

— *Paradox and Passion in Psychotherapy*, 2nd ed. Wiley, 1998:2015.

— *Psychotherapy and the Quest for Happiness*. Sage, 2009.

— *Rising from Existential Crisis: Life Beyond Calamity*. PCCS Books, 2021.

Diener, Edward, and Eunkook M. Suh eds. *Culture and Subjective Well-Being*. MIT Press, 2003.

Eurostat. 'Deaths by suicide in the EU down by 13% in a decade'. https://ec.europa.eu/eurostat/web/products-eurostat-news/w/edn-20240909-1 [Accessed 7/1/25].

Frankl, Victor E. *The Doctor and the Soul: From Psychotherapy to Logotherapy*, 3rd ed. Translated by Richard Winston and Clara Winston. Vintage Books, 1986.

Fromm, Erich. *Fear of Freedom*. Routledge, 2001.

Gray, John. The New Leviathans: Thoughts After Liberalism. Allen Lane, 2023.

Kahneman, Daniel. *Thinking, Fast and Slow*. Penguin Books, 2012.

Klein, Naomi. *The Shock Doctrine: The Rise of Disaster Capitalism*. Allen Lane, 2008.

Mill, John Stuart. *On Liberty, Utilitarianism and other Essays*. Edited by Mark Philip. Oxford World's Classics, 2015.

NAMI, National Alliance on Mental Illness. 'Anxiety Disorders.' https://www.nami.org/about-mental-illness/mental-health-conditions/anxiety-disorders/ [Accessed 7/1/25].

Nynäs, Peter, Ariela Keysar, Martin Lagerström, et al. *The Diversity Of Worldviews Among Young Adults: Contemporary (Non)Religiosity And Spirituality Through The Lens Of An International Mixed Method Study*. Springer, 2022. https://doi.org/10.1007/978-3-030-94691-3_3 [Accessed 7/9/2024].

Schneider, Kirk J. *Life-Enhancing Anxiety: Key to a Sane World*. University Professors Press, 2023.

— *The Paradoxical Self: Toward an Understanding of Our Contradictory Nature*. Insight Books, 1999.

— *The Polarized Mind: Why it's Killing Us and What We Can Do About it*. University Professors Press, 2020.

Sheldon, Joss. *Democracy: A User's Guide*. Rebel Books, 2020.

Thunberg, Greta. *No One is Too Small to Make a Difference*. Penguin Books, 2019.

Turner, Dwight. T*he Psychology of Supremacy: Imperium*. Routledge, 2023.

Valéry, Paul. *Paul Valery: An Anthology*. Edited by James R. Lawler. Translated by David Paul. Princeton University Press, 1977.

Waldinger, Robert, and Marc Schulz. *The Good Life: Lessons from the World's Longest Scientific Study of Happiness*. Simon & Schuster, 2023.

World Health Organization. *Depressive Disorder Fact Sheet*, 31 March 2023. https://www.who.int/news-room/fact-sheets/detail/depression [Accessed 16/7/2024].

— *Mental Disorders: Key Facts*, 8 June 2022. https://www.who.int/news-room/fact-sheets/detail/mental-disorders [Accessed 16/7/2024].

— *Mental Health Gap Action Programme guideline for mental, neurological and substance use disorders,* 3rd ed., November 2023. https://www.who.int/publications/i/item/9789240084278 [Accessed 16/7/2024].

Yalom, Irvin D. *Existential Psychotherapy*. Basic Books, 1980.

6

The Radical Politics of
John Stuart Mill

Helen McCabe

John Stuart Mill believed 'the social problem of the future' was 'how to unite the greatest individual liberty of action, with a common ownership in the raw material of the globe, and an equal participation of all in the benefits of combined labour'.[1] This is a problem we have not yet solved. Attempts at common ownership (e.g. in Soviet-style communism) are associated with significant restrictions on individual liberty of action; but neoliberal experiments in 'the greatest liberty of action' for owners of capital have not led to equal participation of all in the benefits of combined labour (with a global unemployment rate of 4.9% in 2024[2]), and the benefits to those who *are* working being very unevenly shared, especially from a global perspective, with 719 million people living in extreme poverty by the end of 2020.[3] The greatest freedom for some has led to massive inequalities in wealth for all, with a tiny fraction of the world's population owning 'the raw material of the globe', and global capital. Moreover, Mill's criticisms of 19th century capitalism on the grounds of how unfree it made workers still, in many cases, stand,[4] notwithstanding great strides in the political freedoms of workers and women, 'the greatest liberty of action' is not enjoyed by all.

Mill identified this problem in the 1840s, and we might think that it reflects an old-fashioned attitude and the preoccupations of mid-19th century political economy. But in more modern terms, he means that the

---

1   John Stuart Mill, *Autobiography*, *Collected Works of John Stuart Mill* I (University of Toronto Press, 1983), p. 239.
2   'Indicators and data tools', International Labour Organization, https://ilostat.ilo.org/data/ [Accessed 18/11/2024].
3   'Global Progress in Reducing Extreme Poverty Grinds to a Halt', World Bank, https://www.worldbank.org/en/news/press-release/2022/10/05/global-progress-in-reducing-extreme-poverty-grinds-to-a-halt [Accessed 18/11/2024].
4   John Stuart Mill, *Principles of Political Economy*, *Collected Works of John Stuart Mill* II and III (University of Toronto Press, 1963), pp. 208-9.

great challenge society faces is how to combine maximal individual freedom with social and economic equality. I open with this because modern radical liberals do need to engage with this social problem, and find solutions to it. Mill was right that this *is* a problem – perhaps even *the* problem – and both history and our contemporary world clearly show that partial answers (liberty without equality, or vice versa) cause suffering, disillusionment, unrest, and desperation. This is even more the case when we also consider environmental concerns: production and social organisation as we currently know them, and have known them since Mill's own day, are creating a world in which the 'benefits' of combined labour increasingly cannot be participated in at all in some areas of the world, and 'the raw material of the globe' is spoiled, rendered uninhabitable, and destroyed.[5] This has significant implications for freedom, as well for justice and equality (and, potentially, the whole basis and feasibility of democratic political order).

Mill is probably most famous for his contributions to liberal theory around 'the greatest individual liberty of action' in his celebrated work *On Liberty*. In this piece he (and his wife, with whom he co-authored the essay[6]) argue that the only justification for restricting individual freedom of action must be 'self-protection' – that is, because the action would cause harm to others.[7] Paternalist reasons (i.e. a person's own – perceived or real – good) cannot be used to justify the use of power against an adult's will (if they are in the full possession of their faculties – i.e. not drunk, or so ill they don't know what they are doing). The scope of people's actions in what Mill calls 'a sphere… in which society… has, if any, only an indirect interest' which 'comprehend[s]… all that portion of a person's life and conduct which affects only himself, or if it affects others, only with their free, voluntary, and undeceived consent and participation' must be kept inviolate and not interfered with. Actions which stray outside that sphere should also be left unimpeded *except* where those actions cause harm to others.[8] This is the negative side of Mill's view of liberty: people must be left alone by the state, by public opinion, even by their friends, family and neighbours *unless* they

5   Mill was aware of some of these environmental issues as well, with sections on *Principles* recognised as raising (proto-)environmentalist concerns – see *Principles*, p. 756.
6   Mill, *Autobiography*, pp. 257-9.
7   John Stuart Mill, *On Liberty, Collected Works of John Stuart Mill* XVIII (University of Toronto Press, 1977), p. 223.
8   Mill, *On Liberty*, p. 225.

are causing harm to others. But there is also a positive side, the normative reason *why* this freedom is so important. Mill does not ground his theory in an abstract right to liberty: instead, he makes the case that there are significant social and individual benefits to freedom, and to being able to develop our individuality in whatever way we see best fit.[9] There has been a long-standing debate in liberalism about negative and positive freedom, but in Mill these are two sides of the same coin: the *value* of being free from constraint (be that legal, moral or social), and thus the reason that we should be so free, is that we are thereby able to develop our individuality unfettered.[10]

Most modern liberal societies are not as anti-paternalist as Mill's principle would suggest they ought to be. (For instance, most people think it is permissible for the state to enforce wearing seatbelts or cycle helmets solely on the grounds of the wearers' own good, though whether reasonable justifications could be given for this which would not *also* permit more paternalist laws than most people with agree with is a more vexed question!) But in the main, the very idea that there are areas of life (individual and collective) in which what we do ought not to be regulated by the state, or subject to coercion by public opinion, is less politically shocking (though, at heart, no less radical) in our own day than it was in Mill's. A clear example is in same-sex relationships, which (between men at least) were illegal in Mill's day, whereas now (in the UK, at least) same-sex marriage is legal and one's sexuality is a protected characteristic in law. Of course, this does not mean there is no homophobia, and that people do not still experience pressure, coercion and even violence from family and the wider public to 'change' or hide their sexuality (as recent debates about the need to ban so-called conversion therapy have shown). What is different is that such coercive, homophobic behaviour is now either illegal or (generally) seen as socially impermissible, and it is largely recognised that people's sex lives (so long as sex is consensual, voluntary and freely entered into by adults) are their own business, and not something which should be regulated by the state.

The sphere Mill delineates is still politically disputed in some cases, however. For instance, in the politically salient – one might even say toxic – case of access to abortion, some of the intractability of the dispute comes down to whether that act is one in which society legitimately could claim

---

9   Mill, *On Liberty*, pp. 224, 260-275.
10   There are also social benefits to allowing individual freedom, relating to progress and knowledge, on Mill's account.

to be acting in self-preservation on behalf of an unborn foetus, or whether it is a question solely of what Mill calls the 'sovereign[ty]' of a pregnant individual over 'their own body and mind'.[11] Though Mill was writing in the mid-19th century, the modern feminist slogan 'my body, my choice' reflects and reveals the contemporary salience of his views (and that they are radical, even today). Of course, as noted, his view could be invoked by both sides, showing that in some cases the 'sphere' he wanted to protect might be hard to define. Modern radical liberal politics needs to determine an answer to this question, and/or come down determinedly on one side or the other in terms of the interpretation of the liberty principle in this debate. (Or recognise that this principle alone is not sufficient, and marshal other radical liberal arguments for one side or the other.)

One thing it is important to note, though, is that the personal sphere that Mill identified over which society has no legitimate power (apart from to prevent harm) is not the same as the public/private distinction much (and rightly) criticised by feminist theorists. Mill is emphatically not saying that whatever happens at home or in the domestic sphere is none of society's (or any other individual's) business. Although Mill and other 19th century or first-wave feminists have been criticised for thinking only formal, legal reform was needed to ensure women's equality, Mill was aware of, as he puts it, 'the vast practical bearings of women's disabilities' and the 'mode in which the consequences of the inferior position of women intertwine themselves with all the evils of existing society and with all the difficulties of human improvement'.[12]

Here, Mill adopts what we would now call a social model of disability: it is nothing innate in *women* which 'disables' them, but the construction of society which will not let them engage as full (and fully responsible) citizens, from limits on their educational and employment opportunities, to refusing them political rights, to social assumptions (often internalised by women) as to their place (i.e. a second place) in society.[13] (Here, he also identifies the patriarchy as the structure which 'disables' women, though he does not use that word.) The 'inferior position' of women was a moral wrong, even if it was also a social fact (at the time), and something Mill worked hard to

---

11   Mill, *On Liberty*, p. 224.
12   Mill, *Autobiography*, p. 253.
13   John Stuart Mill, *On Marriage* and *The Subjection of Women*, *Collected Works of John Stuart Mill* XXI (University of Toronto Press, 1984).

try to improve in his lifetime, including by proper recognition that it was not *only* women's political rights and public life which needed improving. Indeed, he and his wife were two of the first political philosophers to engage directly with the issue of domestic abuse. They wrote scathing attacks on biased law, judges and juries in domestic abuse cases (including cases of murder, and also domestic abuse perpetrated by women, particularly against children and domestic workers), and campaigned for meaningful change in the law.[14] They denied that women (and children) were men's property, to be treated as they wished (including inflicting violence on them with impunity), instead upholding women's and children's right to live free from physical, emotional, psychological and financial abuse in their own home, and to be safe to leave not just if they were in danger, but if they did not wish to be married any longer (and able to get a divorce). Ideally, they wanted to see 'perfect equality' between the sexes, and this included ensuring women had the means to be economically independent, and support their children if a marriage broke down.[15] Society, in their view, in the shape of police and the legal system (as well as friends, neighbours, and family) should step in to prevent harm in the home, and it was a significant injustice that neither the state, nor society more broadly, did so (or felt it ought to do so) at the time.

This is still an issue with political significance today. A recent report for police chiefs in the UK regarding domestic violence reported there were four million male offenders (with one in ten people in England and Wales being victims, and one in 15 being perpetrators), and the Commissioner of the Metropolitan Police said, 'the scale of this is way beyond policing and the justice system'.[16] The Office for National Statistics estimated that 2.1 million people aged over 16 in England and Wales experienced domestic abuse in 2023: this more recent report suggests this was a significant under-

---

14 John Stuart Mill and Harriet Taylor, *The Acquittal of Captain Johnstone (and other related works), Collected Works of John Stuart Mill* XXIV (University of Toronto Press, 1986), pp. 865-6. See also John Stuart Mill and Harriet Taylor, *Remarks on Mr Fitzroy's Bill for the More Effectual Prevention of Assaults on Women and Children, Collected Works of John Stuart Mill* XXI (University of Toronto Press, Routledge and Kegan Paul, 1984), pp. 101-108.

15 Mill, *Subjection of Women, CW* XXI, p. 261.

16 Vikram Dodd, 'Met chief says millions of men are danger to women and girls in England and Wales,' *The Guardian*, 4 June 2024, https://tinyurl.com/mryr3smd [Accessed 18/11/2024].

estimation.[17] What is more, just as in Mill's own day, the attitudes of (some) police, judges, lawyers and jurors is shown in repeated reports to be as misogynist as they were in Mill and Taylor's own day, with rape myths and patriarchal attitudes perpetuated in, and by, courts and other mechanisms of state power on a regular basis.[18] The Independent Domestic Abuse Commissioner has called on all British political parties to take the issue seriously and deliver 'a bold vision,' pointing out that one in five voters will have faced domestic abuse, yet it hardly ever features in political discourse.[19] Domestic violence is a scourge that Mill and Taylor were well aware of, and one which truly radical liberalism would also tackle and forefront, given the detrimental impact such violence has on freedom for millions (as well as being a deep injustice in society). It is a central liberal tenet that the law ought to apply equally to all, and that everyone should have equal, and fair, access to it: Mill and Taylor were radical in revealing the extent to which this was not true for women, and sadly – and outrageously – it remains the case to this day.

It is also a central liberal tenet that people require basic security in order to enjoy liberty, and domestic violence undermines that security, depriving many of any opportunity to enjoy liberal rights or to freely develop their individuality. Mill and Taylor also pointed out wider political implications. If men think about their wives and children as property, which it seems they must in order to perpetrate such violence and enjoy exercising tyrannical power over them, then it excludes them from being good citizens in a democracy. Although Mill and Taylor supported the extension of the suffrage to all adult men and women, they were concerned about the possible outcomes of this happening, when so few people who would be granted political power were willing (or apparently capable) of exercising this power in an actually democratic (rather than tyrannical) way. Taylor pointed out that men who wanted the vote for other working men, but not for women, were radicals 'only because [they were]… not a lord', and

17 'Domestic abuse in England and Wales overview: November 2023,' Office for National Statistics, https://tinyurl.com/ycycyx8r [Accessed 18/11/2024].
18 See, for example, Crown Prosecution Service reports and advice on this issue: Crown Prosecution Service, https://tinyurl.com/ymnyxmdv [Accessed 18/11/2024] and also Crown Prosecution Service, https://tinyurl.com/y3tkjmrj [Accessed 18/11/2024].
19 Nicole Jacobs, *A Safer Future Without Domestic Abuse* (Domestic Abuse Commissioner for England and Wales, 2024).

just wanted power extending to them which was currently exercised *over* them – so they could misuse it in exactly the same way over people who would still be left powerless.[20] Again, this remains an issue for modern politics, and one where Mill and Taylor would both argue that people's private life *does* affect their fitness to exercise political power, from the vote itself to the highest political office. Aside from the specific question of how male politicians and voters view their wives or other dependants (and what this tells us about their likely actions in office), there is a wider question of the public perception of politicians as people only 'in' it for what they can get out of it. Modern liberal politics needs to engage positively with this issue, given the evident dangers of the public's loss of trust in *all* mainstream politicians.

One answer from Mill and Taylor about how to improve the outcomes of democracy is to give people more practice (as it were) in democracy. This is one reason that they were committed to the extension of democracy far beyond formal politics. In particular, they wanted to see its expansion into the workplace. As Bruce Baum has pointed out, this was an extension of their commitment to liberty from the political and social sphere into the economic.[21] 'The greatest individual liberty of action' included liberty in the workplace and in the hours spent at work.

Their anti-paternalism also applied to work as well: they were both vehemently opposed to popular theories (at the time) which argued that the poor (including the employed working classes) were rightfully dependent on their employers and landowners (their 'betters' in economic, social and political standing), and should remain so (which, in turn, put several duties of care on employers and landowners).[22] Mill and Taylor argued against the idea that a labouring and non-labouring 'class' was a fixed fact of economic (and political, and social) reality, saying:

---

20 Harriet Taylor, *Enfranchisement of Women*, *Collected Works of John Stuart Mill* XXI (University of Toronto Press, 1984), p. 397.

21 Bruce Baum, 'J.S. Mill and Liberal Socialism' in *J.S. Mill's Political Thought: A Bicentennial Reassessment*, ed. Nadia Urbinati and Alex Zakaras (Cambridge University Press, 2007), pp. 98-123; 'J.S. Mill on Freedom and Power,' *Polity* vol. 31, no. 2 (1998): pp. 187-216; 'J.S. Mill's Conception of Economic Freedom,' *History of Political Thought* vol. 20, no. 3 (1999): pp. 494-530.

22 Mill, *Principles*, pp. 758-62. It is these passages which Mill said were inspired by Taylor and, in the main, written in words 'taken from her lips'. (Mill, *Autobiography*, p. 255.)

I use those phrases in compliance with custom, and as descriptive of
an existing, but by no means a necessary or permanent, state of social
relations. I do not recognise as either just or salutary, a state of society in
which there is any 'class' which is not labouring; any human beings exempt
from bearing their share of the necessary labours of human life, except
those unable to labour, or who have fairly earned rest by previous toil.[23]

Mill and Taylor rip away the rose-tinted view spectacles of many proponents
of paternalism:

[N]o times can be pointed out in which the higher classes of this or
any other country performed a part even distantly resembling the one
assigned to them in this theory. It is an idealisation… All privileged and
powerful classes, as such, have used their power in the interest of their
own selfishness, and have indulged their self-importance in despising, and
not in lovingly caring for, those who were, in their estimation, degraded
by being under the necessity of working for their benefit.[24]

Moreover, they pointed out that 'working men' across Europe would simply
not put up with attempts at paternalism any longer: 'the working classes
have taken their own interests into their own hands' and tend to think
those interests are opposite to their employers'.[25] 'The poor have come out of
leading-strings, and cannot any longer be governed or treated like children.'[26]
On the one hand this meant that working people were demanding the vote
and other political rights. But it also meant that they were demanding
economic reorganisation, on the grounds not only of liberty but of equality
and justice. They saw their employers as unfairly taking the lion's share of
what the workers produced, and that, in general the 'produce of labour' was:

Apportioned almost in an inverse ration to the labour – the largest portion
to those who have never worked at all, the next largest to those whose
work is almost nominal, and so in a descending scale, the remuneration
dwindling as the work grows harder and more disagreeable, until the

23 Mill, *Principles*, p. 758.
24 Mill, *Principles*, p. 760.
25 Mill, *Principles*, p. 762.
26 Mill, *Principles*, p. 763.

most fatiguing and exhausting bodily labour cannot count with certainty on being able to earn even the necessaries of life.[27]

In the early 1840s Mill expressed a desire to see an end to antagonism and exploitation between workers and employers. He expressed a deep-seated hope for the 'raising of the labourer from the receiver of hire [i.e. a wage] – a mere bought instrument in the work of production, having no residuary interest in the work itself – to the position of being, in some sort, a partner in it'.[28]

Initially, this would be via profit-sharing arrangements, which Mill viewed as feasible and 'available as a present resource'[29] within current non-ideal circumstances. He wrote at length in *Principles of Political Economy* about examples of such schemes, and the benefits experienced by both workers and employers.[30] (A modern-day example on similar lines to some of those described by Mill would be *John Lewis* in the UK.) After the revolution in Paris in 1848, and the creation of the National Workshop scheme, along with a number of experiments not sponsored by the state, Mill became much more interested in the idea of producer cooperation, reading widely about these ideas in theory and practice, and writing about them at length in the next edition(s) of *Principles* (i.e. in 1849 and 1852).[31] He was also interested in experiments (mainly in England) in consumer cooperation (especially the success of the Rochdale Pioneers), but it was in producer cooperation that he (and Taylor) really saw scope for increasing the freedom of workers.

Workers' freedom was not simply a question of fewer regulations or rules in the workplace. In fact, Mill emphasised that many producer cooperatives had very strict rules for workers. What was important was that these rules were democratically determined, and self-imposed.[32] Instead of the unequal relationship of being a mere 'hire' or 'bought instrument'

27 Mill, *Principles*, p. 207.
28 John Stuart Mill, *Claims of Labour, Collected Works of John Stuart Mill* IV (University of Toronto Press, 1967), p. 382.
29 John Stuart Mill, *Chapters on Socialism, Collected Works of John Stuart Mill* V (University of Toronto Press, 1967). For more on this terminology, see Helen McCabe 'Navigating by the North Star: The Role of the 'Ideal' in John Stuart Mill's View of 'Utopian' Schemes and the Possibilities of Social Transformation', *Utilitas* vol. 31, no. 3 (2019): pp 291-309.
30 Mill, *Principles*, pp. 769-75.
31 Mill, *Principles*, pp. 775-94.
32 Mill, *Principles*, pp. 780-81.

obeying rules because they were enforced by employers over whom workers had no control and rarely any influence, workers in cooperatives were 'independent', mutually agreeing to work together. Work thereby exemplified the sovereignty and liberty that Mill and Taylor desired. In wage-labour (and, for that matter, salaried labour), power is enacted over workers arguably against their will, even where they have signed a contract, because they are in a very unequal position vis-à-vis the power of employers: whether to sign a contract may be a choice, but there is little room to negotiate the terms of it. (At the time, of course, there was little to no unemployment benefit, and also – in general – greater supply of labour than demand, especially in relatively low-skilled trades where workers were easily replaceable.) In producer cooperation, work becomes something which people engage in with the free, voluntary and undeceived consent of everyone else. Where rules of conduct are applied, then, they are freely and voluntarily consented to. Even where workers remain tied to one area, and one job, as under capitalistic wage-relations, they are freer if they are part of a cooperative. (Moreover Mill noted, in actual fact where rules are self-determined, they are often stricter than those employers can get away with imposing, and are adhered to more closely; 'and the voluntary obedience carries with it a sense of personal worth and dignity', unlike the outcome of obeying rules, generally because one has to, enforced by an employer, which can often be infantilising, and/or make people feel they are of little worth.[33])

Producer cooperatives also helped achieve two other of Mill's aims: they increased the number of people who exercised ownership of the raw materials of the globe (because capital, including land and raw materials, were held collectively by cooperatives, rather than by one or two rich capitalists and/or landowners); and they increased the number of participants in combined labour as well as – vitally – making the benefits of that labour more equally shared. Capitalists would no longer take the lion's share of the product of combined labour, but instead these would be shared among all cooperators. Mill defended capitalists' right to take this lion's share as a due return on their capital (which represented previous work and abstinence/self-discipline) under the rules of capitalism, but he equally ardently supported workers' rights to free themselves of paying this 'tribute' for the use of capital, and communally owning it themselves.[34] He was much less willing to respect

33 Mill, *Principles*, pp. 780-81.
34 Mill, *Principles*, p. 775.

the rights of landowners and those whose capital was owned merely by the lucky accident of their birth. He also accepted that all people were owed security as a basic principle of society, and so should be compensated for property if the state decided they should not own it anymore.[35]

The question of workers' freedom at work remains politically live. On the most extreme end, the United Nations' Sustainable Development Goals commit the global community to ending all contemporary forms of slavery,[36] but the International Labour Organization and Walk Free estimate that 49.6 million people were living in conditions of modern slavery on any given day in 2021 (an increase on 2017, in part due to the Covid-19 pandemic).[37] Similarly, 94 UN Member States appear not to have criminal legislation prohibiting slavery or the slave trade; 170 appear not to have criminalised the four institutions and practices similar to slavery banned in international treaties; 180 appear not to have enacted legislative provisions criminalising servitude; and 112 appear not to have put in place provisions for the punishment of forced labour.[38] Of course, these practices (and other forms of labour exploitation) also persist in places where they *are* illegal, but this lack of legal action shows the extent to which the issue has not even been tackled at a formal, state level. This should be an area of concern for all radical liberals, as should other policies which eradicate these practices.

At a less extreme end of the scale, there are on-going debates about precarity (e.g. 'zero-hours contracts'), working from home, and the extent to which workers can exercise autonomy in the workplace and are involved

---

35   It is for this reason that Mill supported paying compensation to people who had owned enslaved workers, after emancipation – a policy which has been much criticised in recent years. It is worth also noting, however, how much Mill felt was also owed to previously enslaved people, not least in order to ensure their on-going freedom in Southern States in America after the Civil War, where he foresaw a rapid re-exploitation of previously enslaved people unless they were granted not only political rights, but ownership of land and other key economic rights and benefits. Mill, *Principles*, p. 233.

36   United Nations, 'Sustainable Development Goals, Goal 8', https://sdgs.un.org/goals/goal8 [Accessed 18/11/2024]. Slavery and forced labour are covered in SDG 8.7.

37   'Global Estimates of Modern Slavery', Walk Free, https://www.walkfree.org/reports/global-estimates-of-modern-slavery-2022 [Accessed 18/11/2024].

38   Katarina Schwarz and Jean Allain, *Antislavery in Domestic Legislation* (University of Nottingham and Monash University, 2020).

in key decision-making processes. A key manifesto pledge for the Labour Party in 2024 is their so-called 'New Deal for Working People', with pledges to ban zero-hours contracts and fire and rehire practices.[39] This speaks to some of the same issues the concerned Mill and Taylor, recognising the importance of secure employment for freedom and flourishing, but even more radical plans could be developed by radical liberals for improving workers' freedom in the economic sphere.

To some extent, the line between worker and capitalist is more blurred than in Mill's day, with more workers owning stocks and shares (e.g. in savings, including their pensions) and their own homes (or, at least, having a mortgage on a home) than in the mid-19th century. However, most workers (especially across the globe) own little to no capital, just as in Mill's day. In 2022, Credit Suisse reported that the world's richest 1% of people owned 46% of the world's capital, while 52% of the world's population had less than $10,000 in personal wealth.[40]) Even if we look just at Britain, the Office for National Statistics estimated that in 2020, the richest 10% of households in Britain held 43% of all wealth, primarily in the form of private pensions and property.[41] However, the poorest 50% only held 9% of wealth, mainly in the form of physical items such as household possessions and vehicles.[42] Moreover, 'median net financial wealth in the group was zero, meaning that less than half of the poorest decile have financial assets such as savings and investments that outweigh their financial liabilities… Similarly, less than half of… this decile own property with positive equity or have any form of private pension'.[43] Women, people with disabilities, people identifying as bisexual, and people from most minoritised ethnicities were less likely to be wealthy than their white, male, heterosexual counterparts in the same region (and regions outside the South East were notably less wealthy than that area).[44] Many workers, even in modern Britain, are not owners of capital, and significant power imbalances exist between employers and those they

39 'Labour's Manifesto,' Labour Party, https://labour.org.uk/change/kickstart-economic-growth/#making-work-pay [Accessed 18/11/2024].
40 'Global Inequality,' Inequality.Org, https://inequality.org/facts/global-inequality/ [Accessed 18/11/2024].
41 'Distribution of individual total wealth by characteristic in Great Britain,' Office for National Statistics, https://tinyurl.com/zatjesk4 [Accessed 18/11/2024].
42 ONS, 'Distribution of individual wealth.'
43 ONS, 'Distribution of individual wealth.'
44 ONS, 'Distribution of individual wealth.'

employ (as well as other imbalances Mill and Taylor identified, such as
the problem of women's economic dependence on men). Arguably, the
same interpersonal problems that Mill identified also still exist between
employers and employees as well, with both sides looking to get as much
out of the other while giving as little as possible in return. This is also
something on which radical liberals should focus: liberalism may be
perceived as the ideology of capitalism, but a *radical* liberalism has to hold
out opportunities, hope, and solutions for those who do not own capital
as well as those who do.

Producer cooperation would not solve all these problems, but it would
radically change the economic landscape, and – over time – eradicate many
wealth inequalities. For one thing, it would change, and more equally share
the ownership of capital, decreasing inequalities caused by some people
owning capital and most people not owning it. For another, it would result
in higher wages for workers, at least some of which would be translated into
savings (including pensions). Mill also favoured restrictions on inheritance,[45]
but even without these, he saw cooperation eradicating inequalities related to
inherited wealth over time, especially as capitalists might feel they would get
a safer, and better, return on their capital through investing it in cooperatives
in return for an annuity (thus permanently transferring the capital to the
cooperative).[46] Producer cooperation therefore not only improved liberty,
but also ensured greater equality, as well as promoting more egalitarian and
democratic relations between people.[47]

Mill and Taylor were keen to emphasise that producer cooperation
would only achieve what they termed 'the nearest approach to social justice,
and the most beneficial ordering of industrial affairs for the universal good,
which it is possible at present to foresee' if 'both sexes participate equally
in the rights and in the government of the association'.[48] Although Mill has
been criticised for his apparently conservative views on married women
working, he was definitely committed to unmarried women's equal and
full involvement in the workplace, and in the management of industrial
concerns. Again, this echoes a contemporary problem, with the European

---

45   Mill, *Principles*, pp. 222-5.
46   Mill, *Principles*, pp. 793-4.
47   Helen McCabe, *John Stuart Mill, Socialist* (McGill-Queens University Press, 2022).
48   Mill, *Principles*, p. 794.

Commission estimating that only 67.6% of women were in employment in 2021,[49] and only 28% of people globally 'in the C-suite' being women in 2021.[50] In the UK, the female employment rate in 2023 was 72.1% compared to a male employment rate of 78.1%,[51] with 8% of women employed as managers, directors or senior officials, compared to 13% of men.[52] In the same year, the gender pay gap for all employees was 14.3% (based on hourly pay).[53]

Taylor pointed out the importance of women contributing to household income for their social standing (and safety in the home) as well as their independence, writing 'how infinitely preferable it is that part of the income [of a household] should be of the woman's earning, even if the aggregate sum were but little increased, rather than that she should be compelled to stand aside in order that men may be the sole earners, and the sole dispensers of what is earned', even if – overall – wages fall because of women's participation in the workforce (which increases the supply of labour).[54] This point is worth remembering by radical liberals who ought to continue to be exercised by the gender pay gap. Liberals should be encouraging women to enter the labour market, whilst also paying serious attention to the issue of the 'second shift', and the fact that women tend to do the vast majority of care and domestic work in the household, meaning they work longer hours (some paid, many unpaid) than men.[55] Affordable child-care, fair distribution of domestic work between genders, and recognition that domestic work *is* work are all feminist issues – but they are (or ought to be) radical liberal issues as well, if liberals really take freedom seriously.

This said, of course, both Taylor and Mill looked forward to a day when there would not be a 'market' for labour in the way they – and we – understand it, and where people would not be paid wages, but earn a share of the product of cooperative labour within a producer cooperative. They

---

49 'Women's situation in the labour market,' European Commission, https://tinyurl.com/4krr7tpv [Accessed 18/11/2024].

50 'Women in the Workplace 2024: The 10th-anniversary report,' McKinsey & Company, https://www.mckinsey.com/featured-insights/diversity-and-inclusion/women-in-the-workplace [Accessed 18/11/2024].

51 Brigid Francis-Devine and Georgina Hutton, *Women and the UK economy*, Research Briefing (House of Commons Library, 2024), https://researchbriefings.files.parliament.uk/documents/SN06838/SN06838.pdf [Accessed 18/11/2024].

52 Frances-Devine and Hutton, *Women and the UK economy*.

53 Frances-Devine and Hutton, *Women and the UK economy*.

54 Taylor, *Enfranchisement of Women*, CW XXI, p. 403.

55 Frances-Devine and Hutton, *Women and the UK economy*.

defended unequal divisions of that product on the grounds of recognised principles of justice (from giving more according to abilities to giving according to needs),[56] but strongly denied that sex (or gender) was a good ground for such inequality (or that, for instance, women would always 'need' less (or more) than men in return for their labour).

Mill likened the contemporary labour market to a race declared by a sadistic Roman emperor, in which 'those who came in hindmost should be put to death', noting that it would be no diminution of the evil of such a race that those who died were the slowest, weakest or oldest.[57] He defended competition between firms on the grounds of efficiency, entrepreneurship and equity for consumers, but did not see the same reasons as applying when it came to a market for labour.[58]

Producer cooperation is rarely mentioned as an alternative economic model in contemporary discourse, though of course there are some very successful (and relatively well-known) producer cooperatives in the world (for instance, MONDRAGON in the Basque region of Spain), and many people recognise issues in the contemporary economic system relating to the pursuit of profit and/or exploitation of workers. Despite the success of cooperation (particularly, but not solely, consumer cooperation) in the UK in the 19th century, its hey-day seems very much over, with cooperatives driven out of business by capitalist firms (and perhaps by a lack of investment or interest by workers themselves in this mode of working and organising production and consumption).

It may be that producer cooperation is not as feasible in our own day as it was in Mill's. Perhaps people are not so ready (or willing) to exit the capitalist economy via communal action (and self-discipline), perhaps the complexities of modern production mean it would be a great deal harder to do so than in Mill's day, where workers could save tiny amounts of capital and purchase, for instance, relatively simple tools. Individualism may be so hard-wired into our thinking that even though 5.51 million businesses in the UK (in 2023) were classified as small (i.e. had 0-49 employees) and a further 36,900 were classified as medium-sized (i.e. 50-249 employers), meaning

56 Mill, *Principles*, p. 203.
57 Mill, *Chapters on Socialism*, CW V, p. 713.
58 Joseph Persky has critically engaged with Mill's arguments, and the question of whether a labour market could really be eradicated under a sustainable system of producer cooperative socialism – 'Mill's Socialism Re-examined,' *Utilitas* vol. 32, no. 2 (2020): pp. 165-180.

that while over 99% of businesses[59] were of an ideal size for cooperation to be feasible, only 7,586 were actually co-operatives.[60]

In the UK 14 million people are members of a co-operative, but this is mainly consumer co-operatives, and/or mutual building societies.[61] The idea of producer cooperation, although not completely alien to UK workers, is still not familiar. There appear to be both economic and psychological barriers to entrepreneurial workers setting up co-operatives, even though research shows that co-operatives are more resilient, and more likely to last over five years, than privately-owned companies[62] (perhaps for reasons identified over 100 years ago by Mill, to do with worker 'buy-in', discipline, and dedication). In the current parliament, 43 MPs elected in 2024 are members of the Co-operative Party (which has been in an electoral pact with the Labour Party since 1927), making it the *de-facto* fourth largest party in parliament. Yet cooperative principles and modes of organising labour (as well as a more general cooperative outlook on how society ought to be organised, and to what end) seem to have little impact on the political agenda, not even of the Labour Party (though the 2024 manifesto does include an 'aim to double the size of the UK co-operative and mutuals sector, including in the energy sector'[63]).

This really is an area which radical liberals ought to be exploring and championing. Producer cooperation is a mode of realising freedom in the workplace, and democratic principles both within work and more widely in society, without – as Mill noted – needing much legislative action and certainly without doing violence to the existing system of property, law or finance. Commentators on the left may note that this is why it is doomed to fail, by not doing enough to destroy (or at least meaningfully change) the capitalist system. Conversely, Mill saw the very feasibility and 'availability' of producer cooperation as one of its inherent strengths – workers can do it *now*, and immediately improve (even transform) their position, opening up further possibilities of improvement and progress to come. If radical liberals are concerned about freedom, and *also* about core liberal values like

---

59 'Business population estimates for the UK and regions 2023: statistical release,' Department for Business & Trade, https://tinyurl.com/3pk38nvp [Accessed 18/11/2024].
60 Co-operatives UK, https://www.uk.coop/ [Accessed 18/11/2024].
61 Co-operatives UK.
62 Co-operatives UK.
63 Labour Party, *Change – Labour Party Manifesto 2024* (Labour Party, 2024).

security and due process, then they should be thinking more seriously about producer cooperation, and acting to see its extension to more workers, and workplaces – ensuring employers and capitalists 'play fair' and that workers have the necessary tools and education to make cooperation sustainable.

Producer cooperation is not the *only* means by which we might achieve the greatest liberty of action for all combined with communal ownership and equal participation in the benefits of combined labour, but it is a good start, along with proper recognition of feminist critiques of the public/private sphere, domestic violence, and women's employment (especially their unpaid employment as carers and domestic workers). Mill championed these issues in the mid-19th century: as we approach the middle of the 21st, it is time to revisit this element of his radical liberalism, not just in theory, but in practice.

Bibliography

Baum, Bruce. 'J.S. Mill and Liberal Socialism.' In *J.S. Mill's Political Thought: A Bicentennial Reassessment*. Edited by Nadia Urbinati and Alex Zakaras. Cambridge University Press, 2007.

— 'J.S. Mill on Freedom and Power.' *Polity* vol. 31, no. 2 (1998): pp. 187-21.

— 'J.S. Mill's Conception of Economic Freedom.' *History of Political Thought* vol. 20, no. 3 (1999): pp. 494-530.

Co-operatives UK. https://www.uk.coop/ [Accessed 18/11/2024].

Crown Prosecution Service. 'More to do to tackle rape misconceptions.' https://www.cps.gov.uk/cps/news/more-do-tackle-rape-misconceptions-and-lack-understanding-consent-cps-survey-finds [Accessed 18/11/2024].

— 'Rape and Sexual Offences.' https://www.cps.gov.uk/legal-guidance/rape-and-sexual-offences-annex-tackling-rape-myths-and-stereotypes [Accessed 18/11/2024].

Department for Business & Trade. 'Business population estimates for the UK and regions 2023.' https://www.gov.uk/government/statistics/business-population-estimates-2023/business-population-estimates-for-the-uk-and-regions-2023-statistical-release [Accessed 18/11/2024].

Dodd, Vikram. 'Met chief says millions of men are danger to women and girls in England and Wales.' *The Guardian,* 4 June 2024. https://www.theguardian.com/society/article/2024/jun/04/met-chief-says-millions-of-men-are-danger-to-women-and-girls-in-england-and-wales [Accessed 18/11/2024].

European Commission. 'Women's situation in the labour market.' https://commission.europa.eu/strategy-and-policy/policies/justice-and-fundamental-rights/gender-equality/women-labour-market-work-life-balance/womens-situation-labour-market_en [Accessed 18/11/2024].

Francis-Devine, Brigid, and Georgina Hutton. *Women and the UK economy*. Research Briefing. House of Commons Library, 2024. https://researchbriefings.files.parliament.uk/documents/SN06838/SN06838.pdf [Accessed 18/11/2024].

Inequality.Org. 'Global Inequality, https://inequality.org/facts/global-inequality/ [Accessed 18/11/2024].

International Labour Organization. 'Indicators and data tools.' https://ilostat.ilo.org/data/ [Accessed 18/11/2024].

Jacobs, Nicole. *A Safer Future Without Domestic Abuse*. Domestic Abuse Commissioner for England and Wales, 2024.

Labour Party. *Change – Labour Party Manifesto 2024*. Labour Party, 2024.

— 'Labour's Manifesto: Making work pay.' https://labour.org.uk/change/kickstart-economic-growth/#making-work-pay [Accessed 18/11/2024].

McCabe, Helen. *John Stuart Mill, Socialist*. McGill-Queens University Press, 2022.

— 'Navigating by the North Star: The Role of the 'Ideal' in John Stuart Mill's View of 'Utopian' Schemes and the Possibilities of Social Transformation.' *Utilitas* vol. 31, no. 3 (2019): pp. 291-309.

McKinsey & Company. 'Women in the Workplace 2024: The 10th-anniversary report.' https://www.mckinsey.com/featured-insights/diversity-and-inclusion/women-in-the-workplace [Accessed 18/11/2024].

Mill, John Stuart. *Autobiography*, Collected Works of John Stuart Mill I. University of Toronto Press, 1983.

— *Chapters on Socialism*, Collected Works of John Stuart Mill V. University of Toronto Press, 1967.

— *Claims of Labour*, Collected Works of John Stuart Mill IV. University of Toronto Press, 1967.

— *On Liberty*, Collected Works of John Stuart Mill XVIII. University of Toronto Press, 1977.

— *On Marriage* and *The Subjection of Women*, Collected Works of John Stuart Mill XXI. University of Toronto Press, 1984.

— *Principles of Political Economy*, Collected Works of John Stuart Mill II and III. University of Toronto Press, 1963.

Mill, John Stuart and Harriet Taylor. *The Acquittal of Captain Johnstone, Collected Works of John Stuart Mill* XXIV. University of Toronto Press, 1986.

— *Remarks on Mr Fitzroy's Bill for the More Effectual Prevention of Assaults on Women and Children, Collected Works of John Stuart Mill* XXI. University of Toronto Press, Routledge and Kegan Paul, 1984.

Office for National Statistics. 'Distribution of individual total wealth by characteristic in Great Britain.' https://www.ons.gov.uk/peoplepopulation andcommunity/personalandhouseholdfinances/incomeandwealth/ bulletins/distributionofindividualtotalwealthbycharacteristicingreat britain/april2018tomarch2020 [Accessed 18/11/2024].

— 'Domestic abuse in England and Wales overview: November 2023.' https://www.ons.gov.uk/peoplepopulationandcommunity/crime andjustice/bulletins/domesticabuseinenglandand walesoverview/ november2023 [Accessed 18/11/2024].

Persky, Joseph. 'Mill's Socialism Re-examined.' *Utilitas* vol. 32, no. 2 (2020): pp. 165-180.

Schwarz, Katarina, and Jean Allain. *Antislavery in Domestic Legislation.* University of Nottingham and Monash University, 2020.

Taylor, Harriet. *Enfranchisement of Women, Collected Works of John Stuart Mill* XXI. University of Toronto Press, 1984.

United Nations. 'Sustainable Development Goals, Goal 8.' https://sdgs. un.org/goals/goal8. [Accessed 18/11/2024].

Walk Free. 'Global Estimates of Modern Slavery.' https://www.walkfree. org/reports/global-estimates-of-modern-slavery-2022/ [Accessed 18/11/2024].

World Bank. 'Global Progress in Reducing Extreme Poverty Grinds to a Halt.' https://www.worldbank.org/en/news/press-release/2022/10/05/global- progress-in-reducing-extreme-poverty-grinds-to-a-halt [Accessed 18/11/2024].

7

Reviving the Spirit of Liberalism

Timothy Stacey

Whatever way you look at it, liberalism has taken a beating in recent years. Liberal values are openly opposed by authoritarians on the world stage. Within the liberal West, public discourse has radically polarised, and liberal parties are in decline. As the 20th century drew to a close, there was a widespread feeling that we were on a slow march to a progressive future. Today, nativism, racism and populism all seem entrenched. Regardless of people's ideological starting point, liberalism has become the political philosophy we love to hate. For conservatives, it's too woke. For traditionalists, it's spiritually vacuous. For communitarians, it's too rationalistic. For Marxists, it's capitalism by another name. Bombarded by this barrage of contradictory critiques, establishment politicians have tended to double-down and say that it is not liberalism but 'the deplorables'[1] who denounce it that need to be challenged. I take another tack.

My academic journey began in political theology. In the summer of 2011, I had just moved to London to pursue a PhD. From the confines of my north London apartment, I was trying to answer the question, 'How can we build solidarity in late liberal societies that are simultaneously Christian, secular, and religiously plural?' Then, on one sweltering summer evening, seemingly from nowhere for this out-of-touch daydreamer, news got around that there were riots happening. Most of the damage occurred in Tottenham, just a mile up the road. In the week that followed, an organisation called London Citizens sent community organisers to Tottenham High Street, to aid in the process of rebuilding the community. I had never in my life engaged in any form of grassroots action. But something called me to Tottenham that summer. It felt like a significant moment in time. Within weeks, I was feeling like quitting my PhD. 'Why study solidarity when I can do it?' I asked. But

---

1   A term used by Hilary Clinton in 2016 to describe Donald Trump supporters. See: 'Basket of deplorables,' https://en.wikipedia.org/wiki/Basket_of_deplorables.

my supervisor, Adam Dinham, urged me to stay. I didn't have to choose
between grassroots action and academia, he assured me. I could do both. My
actions could be my research. So began my journey into autoethnography. I
later consolidated my organising experience by spending time with Metro
Vancouver Alliance in Vancouver. I am now based at the Urban Futures
Studio, in Utrecht, the Netherlands, where I navigate between theory, policy,
and grassroots action, seeking to transform political processes by learning
from what ignites engagement at street level. This positioning has allowed
me to distinguish between liberal political ambitions and lived political
realities. With this perspective, I can accept that liberalism *as it is practiced
politically* is lacking in passion. But unlike its critics, I stress that this need
not be the case. Liberally oriented people are not heartless proceduralists.
They burn with an urge for justice. How to understand this disconnect?
Standing on the shoulders of grand theorists, I stress that liberalism splits
the public head and the private heart, making our politics and policymaking
emotionally illiterate, while allowing the confession of one's own truth to
take precedence over the need to compromise and build coalitions. But to
say that liberalism is wanting does not mean conceding that we must adopt
illiberal ideas, or even that we must, as some communitarians suggest,
recognise that civic spirit depends on the grassroots relationships fostered
by often illiberal communities, and thus that we must make exceptions for
them. Instead, our task is to reconcile head and heart without compromising
on liberal ideals: to bring a wave of passion back into the centres of liberal
politics and policy that is sufficient to extinguish the flames of division.
Enter the emotions, virtues, and spirit.

Understanding what is missing

Liberalism is a political philosophy with a thousand faces.[2] In North America
it is associated with the left. In the UK, it is more often associated with the
centrist Liberal Democrats. In Europe it invokes the neoliberalism that
began under Margaret Thatcher and continues to dog us today. Given this
complexity, some authors seek to clear the water by focusing on authors and
actors who self-identify as 'liberal'.[3] While illuminating, I find this approach

---

2   Jan Harald Alnes and Manuel Toscano, eds., *Varieties of Liberalism:
Contemporary Challenges* (Cambridge Scholars Publishing, 2014).
3   Helena Rosenblatt, *The Lost History of Liberalism: From Ancient Rome to the
Twenty-First Century* (Princeton University Press, 2020).

can inhibit us from critically reflecting on the underlying ideas giving shape to contemporary liberalism as it is practised.

Two roots are important. The first is the tradition of, in the name of peace and justice, expelling passions from public life. I call it the rational truth tradition. The second, intertwined with and enabled by the first, is that of cultivating one's own private truth. I call this the confessional truth tradition. We see early signs of the rational truth tradition in the later writing of Plato, where freedom and wisdom appear to be associated with the ability to transcend one's bodily passions and prejudices. It is those most capable of achieving such transcendence that are to rule. Almost two millennia later we see similar ideas being adopted, but for a very different reason. Amidst what came to be known as the European Wars of Religion, writers such as Grotius and Hobbes sought a purely rational basis for people to enter into a contract with the state. This writing becomes foundational to the Western model of secularism, the cornerstone of which is to develop policy at a principled distance from all religions. More than three centuries later, in the wake of the Second World War, this ideal is reinvigorated and expanded. Now, it is ideas of the good life that must be put to one side in the name of policies that are, at least in principle, agreeable to any rational person.

The problem with the rational truth tradition is twofold: first, it is lacking in that *je ne sais qoui* that makes us fall in love with political visions; second, it actually ends up fuelling exactly what it is designed to dispel: divisive public debate. In principle, the rational truth tradition is supposed to free up public space for a passionate, confessional truth. The confessional tradition emerged during the Reformation. In the works of Martin Luther, it is interior conviction by which one is justified, rather than obedience to church tradition or dogma. In the later writings of Rousseau, in the decades preceding the French Revolution, it is not merely the church but society as a whole that stifles people, by instilling in them a need for others' approval.[4] These developments are the forerunners of contemporary politics of confession, in which activists define their truth, marginalise those that refuse to sign up in full, and refuse to engage those with opposing views.

4   Francis Fukuyama, *Identity: The Demand for Dignity and the Politics of Resentment* (Farrar Straus & Giroux, 2018), chap. 3; Charles Taylor, *Sources of the Self: The Making of the Modern Identity* (Harvard University Press, 1992).

It is also here that liberalism seems so well-suited to capitalism: first, because access to private property allows one to opt out of oppressive communities. Second, because consumerism thrives on people's desire to perform their uniqueness.[5] Third, because compared with racism, homophobia, and totalitarianism, capitalism's threat to freedom is insidious. It does not overtly attack your right to be who you are – it just doesn't care if you have the land, resources or time to find out. This also speaks to why liberalism often seems ill-equipped to challenge capitalism: once capitalism has encouraged us to divide ourselves into distinctive subcultures, it can rule us with impunity. In the name of peace and justice, liberalism defines a space of political deliberation that is shorn of passion. But the result is that people lose interest in public identity and start to form ever-smaller elective communities without the strength collectively to stand up to the forces of oppression.

To reiterate, I am not suggesting that passion is absent from the history of liberal thought. It has been shown, for example, that Constant,[6] Mill[7] and Rawls[8] all emphasised the need to imbue the liberal project with passion. Even in the late 19th century, liberal politicians were already claiming that liberalism was in need of an emotional renaissance. But this stress on instilling passion *into* the liberal project, from the beginning, speaks to a tendency of liberalism in practice towards rationalist argumentation and passionless proceduralism. The world is awash with instances of politicians seeking to quash emotive political movements with rational argumentation – and losing. The anti-Brexit campaign stressed that Brits were 'better off in Europe'. The tone of such arguments was decidedly transactional and self-interested, lacking any shared appeal to a vision or a binding set of emotionally-charged public principles. I am not calling for liberal rationality or proceduralism

5   Luc Boltanski and Eve Chiapello, *The New Spirit of Capitalism*, trans. Gregory C Elliott (Verso, 2007).
6   Rosenblatt, *The Lost History of Liberalism*.
7   Michael Freeden, 'Liberal Passions: Reason and Emotion in Late- and Post-Victorian Liberal Thought', in *Politics and Culture in Victorian Britain: Essays in Memory of Colin Matthew*, ed. Peter Ghosh and Lawrence Goldman (Oxford University Press, 2006), p. 141, https://doi.org/10.1093/acp rof:oso/9780199253456.003.0009; Marlene Sokolon, 'Feelings in the Political Philosophy of J.S. Mill', in *Bringing the Passions Back In: The Emotions in Political Philosophy*, ed. Rebecca Kingston and Leonard Ferry (UBC Press, 2008).
8   Alexandre Lefebvre, *Liberalism as a Way of Life* (Princeton University Press, 2023).

to be abandoned. It is because of our passion for justice that we implement mechanisms that ensure a degree of fairness. Instead, I am suggesting that we must never lose sight of the passionate core driving our procedures, and the need to inspire passion in others.

Of course, this quick sweep of what is missing or obscured within the liberal tradition cannot be sufficient. That is an endless project to which many books, including my own, have been devoted.[9] But I hope I have provided enough of a diagnosis of liberalism's ills for readers to follow me on my mission: to resuscitate the spirit of political participation without compromising on liberal ideals. Surrounded by the forces of illiberalism both within and without, the task of this book, and of my contribution, is the reinvention and revival of the liberal project. Now is not the time to, as Yeats lamented, 'lack all conviction'. Now is not the time to deconstruct theoretically what liberalism is. Now is a time for reconstructing a vision of what liberalism might be; that is, to restore heart and soul to the centre of the liberal project. It is to this project that I now turn. To do so, I place grand theories of liberalism into dialogue with my own ethnographic experiences with policymakers and activists.

An emotional liberalism

Too often liberalism is framed as a soulless blueprint imposed on a passionate world. To counter this, I want to offer a new definition of liberalism that is emotively charged but still grounded in its political and intellectual history: liberalism is loving autonomy. By loving autonomy, I mean both the love of autonomy, and an autonomy whose characteristic feature is love. These are mutually reinforcing. Martha Nussbaum has stressed that 'all of the core emotions that sustain a decent society have their roots in, or are forms of, love.'[10] She explains that what she regards as the masculine, violent love of one's country must be balanced with a feminine, playful love. Playful love recognises that love for one's nation cannot survive without allowing for love of particular people and things. This is because it is through the love of

---

9   Timothy Stacey, *Myth and Solidarity in the Modern World: Beyond Religious and Political Division* (Routledge, 2018); Timothy Stacey, *Saving Liberalism From Itself: The Spirit of Political Participation* (Bristol University Press, 2022), https://bristoluniversitypressdigital.com/downloadpdf/display/book/9781529215502/9781529215502.pdf.

10 Martha C. Nussbaum, *Political Emotions: Why Love Matters for Justice* (The Belknap Press of Harvard University Press, 2015), p. 15.

my daughter, for example, that I acknowledge the vulnerability of younger women. I want to go a step further, however. For liberalism, it is largely *because* I have the freedom to spontaneously fall in love with whomever and whatever I desire that I am willing to die for my country or my cause. I can make love to whom I want, find meaning where I want, pursue what I want. And, in turn, that cause *is* the love of flourishing in its manifold forms. Liberal love is the rain that brings desert flowers into bloom. Offering unconditional grace, it waits to see, with delight, all the shapes and colours that arise. We fight, even die, for that rain. The liberal novelist E.M. Forster expressed this attitude in his essay *What I Believe:*

> …there lies at the back of every creed something terrible and hard for which the worshipper may one day be required to suffer, and there is even a terror and a hardness in this creed of personal relationships, urbane and mild though it sounds. Love and loyalty to an individual can run counter to the claims of the State. When they do—down with the State, say I, which means that the State would down me.[11]

Against abstract obligations, those of flags or national aggregates, liberals have repeatedly reaffirmed the primacy of the individual human being, in all its wonderful distinctness. But under liberalism, the love of particular people and things is intimately entwined with the abstract love of freedom. It is because I experience autonomous love that I love autonomy. And that love of autonomy is not only a selfish love of the principle that sets me free, but delight in the manifold forms of flourishing it enables. I die for my freedom, and I die for yours too. As the quote from Forster suggests, loving autonomy also has its shadow side: the hatred of oppression. Liberals experience rage when they feel that someone's autonomy is under threat. When a way of life appears to have been imposed from the outside, whether by an oppressive community or relation, or by economic circumstances, liberals go to war. In outline this implies, not merely that liberalism need not be straight-forwardly capitalistic, but further, that there are circumstances in which liberals must summon their most cherished values against extractive and abstract systems of accumulation. Of course, were loving autonomy merely about the cultivation of a burning, seemingly aimless desire, it would indeed

---

11   E.M. Forster, *What I Believe*, Hogarth Sixpenny Pamflets, No 1. (Hogarth Press, 1939), p. 8.

risk falling into the trap of individualism and fragmentation. This is why loving autonomy must be cultivated, as we shall now see.

A virtue-centred liberalism

A key critique of liberalism is that it is focused on procedure at the expense of virtue.[12] It is suggested, for example, that liberals are excessively focused on establishing just procedures, rather than on the kinds of qualities people should have. The consequences are twofold, first, we lose touch with what motivates people to do good. Second, because we can never anticipate the scenarios people will encounter, our rules will always fall short. Were this critique merely a matter of philosophical taste, it could be dismissed. But we frequently see dispassionate proceduralism emphasised in policy settings. As we have seen, the reasoning behind this comes from a good place: people are asked to park their subjective ideas about how a life ought to be lived in order collectively to find common goals that, at least in principle, are agreeable to everybody. Yet what I have found in my time working at street-level with people trying to build solidarity across ideological and class differences, is that the ability to compromise with different parties is not driven by reason. Instead, it is driven by love and strengthened by the practice of virtues. Let's name a few.

Faith. Liberals hold that achieving a degree of autonomy is possible, and that doing so makes one's life freer, richer, and more meaningful. Liberals accept that choice is limited by drives, genes, and socio-economic circumstances, but insist that it cannot be reduced to these.

Doubt. Liberals maintain that one's own truth is not, cannot be, *the* truth. If your truth were the truth, then you would merely be doing me the good grace of tolerating my differences and imperfections, as one does with the tempestuous toddler or trainee. But this wouldn't be loving autonomy. This would not be desert rain. It would be accepting autonomy. Liberals actively celebrate the notion that the divergent, queer, and marginalised may offer new insights into how life ought to be lived. Liberals are not relativists. They are open to the possibility that there may be just one good way of living, albeit with variations from time to time, place to place, and person to person. It is just that none of us has unique access to what that good way of living is. One way of understanding this is that the truth about

---

12   James Laidlaw, *The Subject of Virtue: An Anthropology of Ethics and Freedom* (Cambridge University Press, 2014).

the world recedes every time we seek to grasp it.[13] From things as big and abstract as democracy to things as seemingly tangible as trees. Humans are not passively receiving impressions but rather are always imperfectly constituting the world, first through the linguistic tools they receive, and then repeatedly through discussion and inward reflection.

Relationality. Liberals recognise that the freedoms they call for are relationally constituted or they are nothing. This is true at both fundamental and practical levels. Fundamentally, the right to self-expression is vacuous without the privilege of being listened to. Autosexuality aside, sexual freedom means very little if no one will have sex with you. And in practice, my freedom is dependent on the willingness of fellow citizens, politicians, lawyers, and judges recognising and fighting for it. But also at a practical level, my freedom depends on others' willingness to stand up for it. And so, my freedom demands that I must build strong bonds with those around me.

Compromise. Liberals recognise that sometimes they need to drop the attitude and embrace those they disagree with. Partly, this is because they know that they do not know the best way to live. But it is also because standing up to the forces of oppression means working with people whose beliefs and ways of life radically differ from our own.

Why do I name these characteristics virtues? Because like their ancient counterparts of moderation, charity or hope, they are habits of mind and body that unlock for us new terrains of human experience. Through them we can live radically enriched and enriching lives, which we couldn't live without them. And perhaps more starkly, and though as liberals we may not like to say so, we do judge people who lack in these virtues. Simply naming virtues, though, is not enough. Virtues cannot simply be argued for and wished into being. Instead, they are drawn from and kept alive in rich repertoires.

A spirited liberalism

As we have seen, many of those who identify as 'liberal' see it as antithetical to religion. They maintain that it is only by putting aside religion and ideology that we can embrace a politics in which all are welcome, regardless of background or belief. Yet just as I have stressed that liberalism is fuelled by emotions, and reinforced through the practice of virtues, these in turn are cultivated by what I call religious repertoires. I have elsewhere divided

---

13   Graham Harman, *Object–Oriented Ontology: A New Theory of Everything* (Pelican, 2018).

religious repertoires into magic, myths, rituals, and traditions. Here, for the sake of brevity, I focus on myths and rituals. By myths, I mean stories of great events and characters that shape one's understanding of how the world is, should, or could be. By rituals I mean routines and performances designed to bring one's character in line with how the world is, should, or could be.

The evocation of myths and rituals in a chapter about the deep structures of liberal politics is not as strange as it first seems. Liberalism's rationalist tradition itself is rooted in a myth: that of breaking free from the shackles of religion and ideology. Europe's so-called Wars of Religion[14] are a point of return for scholars. For pundits and politicians, the preferred points of reference are the Second World War and Holocaust, which are ritually recalled on an annual basis, the lives of the fallen commemorated in sacred spaces. Like Christ, they died for us. By chance, as I write, British prime minister, Rishi Sunak seems to have hammered the final nail into his own coffin by failing to attend the full D-day ceremony. Anti-Muslim hatred can be read in the reverse light. Women dressed in burqas become haunting symbols of a world we understand ourselves as having left behind. Religious repertoires underwrite our supposedly rational political lives. As soon as we recognise this, we can see the importance of identifying repertoires that might revive the liberal project. They are closer to home than we think. In a liberal society, repertoires must not be invented from above and imposed downwards. Any civil religion must be drawn from the diverse and autonomous lifeways it is intended to celebrate. For this reason, and to complement the work of theorists who offer creative suggestions from above,[15] my starting point has always been to attend to the repertoires that circulate among liberally-oriented people building solidarity across differences at street level: among community organisers in London and Vancouver.

Public Myths take on two forms: the first we might call 'god become human' myths. These are stories of charismatic leaders who, at great sacrifice and risk to themselves, further the cause of autonomy and justice. Figures such as Moses, Jesus, and Mohammed certainly come up when organisers engage with religious communities. But more live and exhilarating for

---

14 William T. Cavanaugh, "'A Twice-Told Tale": The Wars of Religion as Girardian Myth,' *Communio* vol. 45, no. 3–4 (2018); Barbara Diefendorf, 'Were the Wars of Religion about Religion?,' *Political Theology* vol. 15, no. 6 (1 November 2014): pp. 552–63, https://doi.org/10.1179/1462317X14Z.00000000099.
15 Martha C. Nussbaum, *Political Emotions*.

organisers themselves are the stories of Mahatma Gandhi, Nelson Mandela, Martin Luther King and Barack Obama. There is a profound wonder as to how these ordinary humans could achieve such extraordinary feats. These grand myths are supplemented by minor tales emphasising that ordinary is extraordinary enough: stories of regular people who in some way emulate these towering figures: a parent or friend, perhaps, who forewent fame or fortune to work in service of others. The second form that myths take is 'human becomes god': stories of downtrodden individuals who find their place in the world through the movement. An excellent but commodified example of such myths in popular culture is televised talent shows like *X-Factor* and *Pop Idol*. An ugly, overweight individual steps onto the stage, a living symbol of the forgotten and downtrodden. Miraculously, they turn out to have beautiful voices. Millions are drawn to tears. In UK politics, this narrative still has some traction in the form of the trade unionist-cum-politician.

I always find it amusing how more religious and spiritual interlocutors will scoff when I tell them that these stories can have the same function as do stories of Jesus. 'Such tales couldn't possibly rival *my* tradition' is the rebuttal, sometimes stated explicitly, sometimes implied. And yet, I hear the reverence in my friends' voices; I see the tears forming in their eyes, as they describe their heroes. What is more they are emulating their heroes, putting their bodies on the line. Their doubters are primarily armchair theologians. But more importantly still, what such critics are missing is the delight liberals take in the dignity and beauty of the ordinary person. Liberalism reminds us that alongside grand narratives, we are the beneficiaries of minor stories too – the smaller, often unrecorded tales, of ordinary kindness and ordinary courage, stories of intimate friendship, private laughter, domestic brokenness, and mundane reconciliation. These too mark and deepen a life. It was to these small stories of human communion and fellowship that Forster turned in his 1912 novel *Howards End*. This domestic drama about the history and inheritance of a single house was a story about the social condition of England, but more than that it was a story about what it meant to be a free and flourishing human being. As Forster expressed his holistic posture:

> …[Connect] the prose in us with the passion. Without it we are meaningless fragments, half monks, half beasts, unconnected arches that have never joined into a man. With it love is born, and alights on the highest curve, glowing against the grey, sober against the fire…

[Salvation]…was latent in his own soul, and in the soul of every man. Only connect! That was the whole of her sermon. Only connect the prose and the passion, and both will be exalted, and human love will be seen at its height. Live in fragments no longer. Only connect, and the beast and the monk, robbed of the isolation that is life to either, will die.[16]

What lessons do we find encased in this fusion of daily life and personal passion? Certainly, Forster teaches us that the ordinary is extraordinary enough. We need no grand dramas or transcendent causes to find something like nobility. Our ability to knit ourselves closely with others can enfold us in a better, grander way of living. But to structure these experiences, especially in ways that attend to others, we need rituals, points of symbolic anchor which can imbue our tenderness and attention with a stable context. The function of a good ritual is to allow somebody to shed aspects of their old self, to take on a new identity, and to perform that new identity in the world. This is crucial for movements because it allows individuals to be subsumed into and make sacrifices for the group. Love is transmuted from a rather feeble private sentiment into a dynamic cluster of public actions.

Some liberals, indebted to a lingering cultural Protestantism, have been suspicious of ceremonial activity, identifying ritual practice with automatic, irrational or slavish behaviour, easily contrastable with the rational and sober citizen of an ideal liberal state. But interestingly, we do not find this animosity in John Stuart Mill, one of the liberal tradition's pillars. Shaped by the sacred humanism of Auguste Comte, Mill became powerfully drawn to the notion of secular ceremonies that marked, memorialised and elevated human sympathy and solidarity. Here we see the most secular of Victorians rather incongruously investing his otherwise rational deliberative politics with a soul.[17] This latter notion of the sacralisation of the secular offers us an intriguing possibility in the present, namely the creation of new ritual forms which infuse liberal ideals with myth, meaning, and poetry. Liberal rituals must champion freedom, while revealing that freedom becomes most meaningful in community. Again, there is no point in being able to say what I want, unless someone is willing to listen. The substantial freedom that liberal rituals must convey is the freedom to be who you are *and still be held.*

---

16   E.M. Forster, *Howards End* (Blackwell, 1968), p. 18.
17   Alan P.F. Sell, *Mill on God: The Pervasiveness and Elusiveness of Mill's Religious Thought* (Wipf and Stock Publishers, 2012), p. 81.

Let me offer two vivid illustrations, one-to-ones and public dramas. Emerging in the American community organising tradition, one-to-ones were a pillar of Barack Obama's 2008 United States presidential campaign. Initially intended as a mode of recruitment, their power is derived from the fact they give each side the chance to tell their truth while the other listens intently. The best first step is to ask those present the simple question: what brought you here? They are then invited to find a partner to whom they can tell the story. Often, these encounters initiate 'man becomes god' stories. The participants sit across from one another and are asked to make eye contact. Sometimes instructions are given to listeners such as that only nonverbal utterances are allowed. In this intimate space, as each absorbs the other's emotions, something remarkable happens. For the speaker, sharing a deeply personal story, with the eyes of their interlocutor witnessing them, they experience a renewed self-worth: their story matters. For the listener, a deep feeling of empathy and connection is aroused. I like to see what happens in these encounters as the mutual discovery of what I call under-subjectivity. Liberal proceduralism tells us that to come to a consensus, we must rise above our own subjective experiences to find something objective. Conversely, by creating an intense experience of witnessing, one-to-ones invite participants beneath the story being told, towards the emotions being experienced. We are seeing their tears and their trembling hands, feeling their pain in our guts. We are no longer hearing a single person's story alone, but rather are feeling a human story: one of profound despair followed by newfound hope.

Public dramas on the other hand are designed to mimic and fuel the inherent spectacle of political life. They take myths and put them on the stage. Public dramas capable of galvanising the spirit of liberalism must draw on either 'god becomes human' or 'humans become god' myths. God becomes human dramas involve a charismatic leader holding court before an enormous audience, rallying them to the cause. Think, for example, of Martin Luther King's 'I have a dream speech' at the Lincoln Memorial, or Barack Obama's many campaign events in 2008. More complex are 'human becomes god' dramas. I witnessed many examples of these among community organisers in London and Vancouver. The event will normally begin with testimony: some particularly downtrodden citizens, the heroes, will take the stage to tell their story of hardship. The testifier starts off with a tremulous voice. But as the crowd wills them on, they audibly grow in confidence. They visibly find their voice in the community. And having imbued them with that power, the crowd too feels empowered. Next steps the potential villain onto the stage: the CEO of a business, or the politician, who has the power to alleviate the hero's suffering. If liberal politics and policy are once again to inspire widespread support, loving autonomy and the virtues through which it is sustained must be given space to thrive. Religious repertoires provide a tangible means of doing this. Politicians must identify, take ownership of, and circulate myths of great figures and ordinary people. Policymakers must adopt rituals into their practice, creatively encouraging sceptical members of the public to lose themselves in a collective process. Individuals must remember the art of receiving from the past and passing onto the future.

Conclusion

It is likely that the trajectories sketched will be open to a degree of mis-understanding, both from those willing to prosecute liberalism, and those seeking to defend it. So let me do my best to dispel any ambiguity. I am not arguing that we should understand liberalism in one way only, nor am I suggesting that all forms of procedural politics should be abandoned. Rather my posture is one of considered repair. If we are to retrieve what is best and most life-giving within liberal politics, while avoiding some of its pitfalls, we must draw into the orbit of our politics and practice those primordial terrains of connection and affection, ritual and roots that enable us to imagine and build community. This might be called a 'thick liberalism', a political account of freedom which refuses to render passion private. By necessity, such a posture should be counterpoised with 'thin liberalism', a position which tends towards procedural neutrality at the level of institutions and atomism at the level of society. Standing apart from such a threadbare conception of human life, stands a reinvigorated 'liberalism of somewhere'. In place of friendless universals and unmoored individualism, our discussion has touched on a much richer project, that of attaching principles of freedom and self-creation to particular persons and places. In such a politics we are invited to fall in love.

The invitation, for many, will be hard to accept of course, principally because of the proliferation of political rituals, which, over the course of the last century, have stood opposed to the formal institutionalism of liberal politics. In the mass rallies of Nazi Germany, the State Shinto of 1940s Japan, or the public cults of Maoist China, we see potent misuses of ritual. And yet, it is neither predetermined nor obvious that only totalitarian governments should benefit from appeals to the power of civil religion. In the liberal demonstrations too, there are a 'people', who must look beyond themselves if they are to know who or what they are. Only when we knit together the fragments of diverse human experience into wholes (without erasing the parts) can notions of freedom or democracy have any coherent meaning. Implied in such an emotive stance is a self-conscious strengthening of the emotions and virtues that give rise to liberal projects by identifying and reweaving alternative myths which model and embed examples of justice, care and friendship. In undertaking this task of imaginative bolstering, our cultural soils are rich: David's battles with Goliath, the ministry of Christ, the journey of Frodo and the struggles of Gandhi. In their sweep these stories offer us transformative archetypes and symbols upon which to hang larger lives of purpose, justice and compassion. By dwelling inside these magical moments, and the myths, rituals, and traditions that honour them, we can find the deep substance of political vocabulary and humanise otherwise abstract or impersonal institutions or structures. Moreover, we can discover models of virtue and self-giving which might otherwise be hard to find in our corporate and commercial imaginaries. In their moral power and relative rarity, we might discover fresh grounds for hope and courage.

Bibliography

Alnes, Jan Harald, and Manuel Toscano, eds. *Varieties of Liberalism: Contemporary Challenges.* Cambridge Scholars Publishing, 2014.

Boltanski, Luc, and Eve Chiapello. *The New Spirit of Capitalism.* Translated by Gregory C Elliott. Verso, 2007.

Cavanaugh, William T. '"A Twice-Told Tale": The Wars of Religion as Girardian Myth.' *Communio* vol. 45, no. 3–4 (2018).

Diefendorf, Barbara. 'Were the Wars of Religion about Religion?' *Political Theology* vol. 15, no. 6 (1 November 2014): pp. 552–63. https://doi.org/10.1179/1462317X14Z.00000000099.

Forster, E.M. *Howards End.* Blackwell, 1968.

— *What I Believe.* Hogarth Sixpenny Pamflets, No 1. Hogarth Press, 1939.

Freeden, Michael. 'Liberal Passions: Reason and Emotion in Late- and Post-Victorian Liberal Thought.' In *Politics and Culture in Victorian Britain: Essays in Memory of Colin Matthew.* Edited by Peter Ghosh

and Lawrence Goldman. Oxford University Press, 2006. https://doi.
org/10.1093/acprof:oso/9780199253456.003.0009.

Fukuyama, Francis. *Identity: The Demand for Dignity and the Politics of
Resentment*. Farrar, Straus & Giroux, 2018.

Harman, Graham. *Object-Oriented Ontology: A New Theory of Everything*.
Pelican, 2018.

Laidlaw, James. *The Subject of Virtue: An Anthropology of Ethics and Freedom*.
Cambridge University Press, 2014.

Lefebvre, Alexandre. *Liberalism as a Way of Life*. Princeton University Press,
2023.

Nussbaum, Martha C. *Political Emotions: Why Love Matters for Justice*. The
Belknap Press of Harvard University Press, 2015.

Rosenblatt, Helena. *The Lost History of Liberalism: From Ancient Rome to
the Twenty-First Century*. Princeton University Press, 2020.

Sell, Alan P.F. *Mill on God: The Pervasiveness and Elusiveness of Mill's Religious Thought*. Wipf and Stock Publishers, 2012.

Sokolon, Marlene. 'Feelings in the Political Philosophy of J.S. Mill.' In
Bringing the Passions Back In: The Emotions in Political Philosophy.
Edited by Rebecca Kingston and Leonard Ferry. UBC Press, 2008.

Stacey, Timothy. *Myth and Solidarity in the Modern World: Beyond Religious
and Political Division*. Routledge, 2018.

— *Saving Liberalism From Itself: The Spirit of Political Participation*.
Bristol University Press, 2022. https://bristoluniversitypressdigital.com/
downloadpdf/display/book/9781529215502/9781529215502.pdf.

Taylor, Charles. *Sources of the Self: The Making of the Modern Identity*.
Harvard University Press, 1992.

Wikipedia. 'Basket of deplorables.' https://en.wikipedia.org/wiki/Basket_
of_deplorables.

8

Beyond Neoliberalism

Matthew McManus

These evils then – great poverty, and that poverty very little connected with desert – are the first grand failure of the existing arrangements of society. The second is human misconduct; crime, vice, and folly, with all the sufferings which follow in their train. For, nearly all the forms of misconduct, whether committed towards ourselves or towards others, may be traced to one of three causes: poverty and its temptations in the many, idleness and disseverment in the few whose circumstances do not compel them to work; bad education, or want of education, in both. The first two must be allowed to be at least failures in the social arrangements, the last is now almost universally admitted to be the fault of those arrangements – it may almost be said to be a crime.[1]

Our tumultuous century has seen liberalism come under more pressure than it has in a long while. What makes this surprising is things weren't supposed to go this way. Taking a time machine back to 1989 you'd find authors writing glowingly or gloomily about the end of history and how liberal democracy had triumphed over all its geopolitical adversaries. This was also the moment of neoliberal ascendency domestically and internationally. A combination of unemployment and inflation, cresting conservatism, and a general sense that the socialist left was intellectually exhausted led Margaret Thatcher to declare there was no alternative but to upend the Keynesian welfare state. The promise, as Milton Friedman put it, was that by pursuing neoliberal freedom rather than equality we would get more of both. The decades since then have shown how readily this promise was broken, as soaring inequality has contributed to right populist and soft-authoritarian retrenchment. Right-populists like Trump and Liz Truss have

---

1   John Stuart Mill, *Principles of Political Economy with Chapters on Socialism,* ed. Jonathan Riley (Oxford University Press, 2008), p. 384.

doubled down on neoliberal economics à la gigantic tax cuts for the rich, debasing environmental regulations, and appointing anti-union officials wherever and whenever possible.[2] Such dire developments have led many of liberalisms enemies (and not a few of its friends) to ruminate out loud about whether political liberal projects have comprehensively failed.[3] The charges laid against liberalism seem severe, if contradictory: it is too libertine, not libertine enough, too fixated on identity politics, too universalistic to pay attention to identity, too egalitarian, nowhere near sufficiently egalitarian, too nihilistic, too moralistic, too democratic, and too separated from the masses. But at its heart I think the core problem is quite a bit simpler.

Liberalism, at least as it's been practised and perceived for the past four decades, has proven underwhelming. Many are no longer convinced of its promises, and those that are convinced tend to be liberalism's winners rather than its many losers.[4] The dirty secret liberals have to accept is that, to the extent liberalism is in a rut, it deserves it. Neoliberalism has proven as uninspiring as it was uninspired, a grab bag of all the worst features of the liberal tradition. But the failures of neoliberalism shouldn't entice us into imagining that liberalism as a whole has failed. What's required is for liberalism to once again inspire the sense of hope and optimism it was capable of at its birth; in a sense returning to what it once was and could be again.[5] This will mean recommitting to building societies that are genuinely defined by liberty, equality, and solidarity for all. In thinking through how to achieve this we can draw great insights from the quintessential liberal John Stuart Mill, particularly his liberal socialism. That Mill was a socialist has only recently become widely rediscovered.[6] Far from some idiosyncratic or contradictory dalliance, Mill saw a commitment to liberal socialism as harmonious-indeed completing the project of liberalism in the realm of

2   See Thomas Piketty, *Capital and Ideology*, trans. Arthur Goldhammer (The Belknap Press of Harvard University Press, 2020).

3   See Patrick Deneen, *Why Liberalism Failed* (Yale University Press, 2018) and Matthew McManus, *The Political Right and Equality: Turning Back the Tide of Egalitarian Modernity* (Routledge, 2023).

4   See Steven Pinker, *Enlightenment Now: The Case for Reason, Science, Humanism and Progress* (Penguin Books, 2018).

5   On this point see Samuel Moyn, *Liberalism Against Itself: Cold War Intellectuals and the Making of Our Times* (Yale University Press, 2023).

6   See Helen McCabe, *John Stuart Mill: Socialist* (Queens-McGill University Press, 2021), and my forthcoming book Matthew McManus, *The Political Theory of Liberal Socialism* (Routledge, 2025).

the economy. We have much to learn from Mill on these points, even if we shouldn't take his work uncritically. This chapter is divided into two core parts: the first will interrogate how liberalism became neoliberalism and in turn how neoliberalism led to systematic problems; the second part of the discussion will examine Mill's liberal socialism. I will conclude that Mill's pioneering liberal socialism is an ideal whose time has come and provides the right ideological framework to reject neoliberalism while pushing back against the wave of illiberal anti-egalitarianism.

What is liberalism?

Defining liberalism is a bit of a thankless task. For a political ideology which Alexandre Lefebvre rightly describes as akin to the water we swim in, there is a lot of ambiguity about its core principles, practices, and history.[7] (Very) right wing liberals like Ludwig von Mises seem eager to affirm the vulgar Marxist dismissal of liberalism as just an apologia for capitalism when they declare that the 'program of liberalism…if condensed into a single word, would have to read: *property,* that is, private ownership of the means of production…All the other demands of liberalism result from this fundamental demand.'[8] Edmund Fawcett is a bit more ecumenical when he describes liberalism as being committed to four key ideas. These are: an acknowledgement of social conflict, an inherent distrust of power, faith in human progress, and civic respect.[9] Back when he was a classical liberal, John Gray also defined the tradition through an appeal to four elements. Briefly, liberal politics was individualist, egalitarian, universalist and meliorist.[10]

Critics on left and right are of course considerably more venomous. Domenico Losurdo, pointing to a long history of liberal support for imperialism, slavery, colonialism and the Clintons, maintains we need to reject the common view of liberalism as being committed to liberty for all. Instead, Losurdo argues liberals distinguished between liberal subjects who deserve freedom, and the servile who either accepted or were fated

---

7   Alexandre Lefebvre, *Liberalism as a Way of Life* (Princeton University Press, 2024), p. 11.

8   Ludwig von Mises, *Liberalism* (Ludwig von Mises Institute, 2018), p. 19.

9   Edmund Fawcett, *Liberalism: The Life of An Idea,* 2nd ed. (Princeton University Press, 2018).

10   John Gray. *Liberalism,* 2nd ed. (University of Minnesota Press, 1995), p. xii.

for subordination.[11] Not to be outdone, Nietzsche developed an engaging iteration of the perversity thesis when he claimed 'liberal institutions immediately cease to be liberal as soon as they are attained' through their levelling egalitarianism. Liberalism is 'small, cowardly and smug' and in 'plain words' can be described as a 'reduction to the herd animal' and appropriate only for 'shopkeepers, Christians, cows, women, Englishmen and other democrats.'[12] An older John Gray echoes some of these objections from left and right in his rejection of hyperliberalism which is little more than a 'rationale for a failing variety of capitalism, and a vehicle through which surplus elites struggle to secure a position of power in society'.[13]

In the end I think it is better to follow Alan Ryan when he says that 'anyone trying to give a brief account of liberalism is immediately faced with an embarrassing question: are we dealing with liberalism or with liberalisms. It is easy to list famous liberals; it is harder to say what they have in common. John Locke, Adam Smith, Montesquieu, Thomas Jefferson, John Stuart Mill, Lord Acton, T.H. Green, John Dewey, and recent contemporaries such as Isaiah Berlin and John Rawls are certainly liberals – but they do not agree about the boundaries of toleration, the legitimacy of the welfare state, and the virtues of democracy, to take three rather central political issues.'[14] Consequently it is better to talk about liberalisms in the plural rather than liberalism.

Classical liberal, neoliberalism, and liberal socialism may all be described as part of the broader family of liberalisms which share a resemblance to one another, but like all families can differ from and even confront one another on many points. What unifying characteristics these different members of the liberal family have, I will not discuss here.[15] One reason for what Gray describes as liberalism's vast internal variety and complexity is that, rather like a family, it has a complicated history and has

11   Domenico Losurdo, *Liberalism: A Counter-History* (Verso Books, 2014), pp. 241-246.

12   Friedrich Nietzsche, *Twilight of the Idols and The Antichrist* (Penguin Books, 1990), pp. 103-104.

13   John Gray, *The New Leviathans: Thoughts After Liberalism* (Farar, Strauss and Giroux, 2023), p. 112.

14   Alan Ryan, *The Making of Modern Liberalism* (Princeton University Press, 2012), p. 21.

15   Curious readers can see my forthcoming book where I describe liberals as being committed to the shared principles of freedom and equality: McManus, *The Political Theory of Liberal Socialism*.

produced many offspring.[16] It's to this that I'll briefly turn before describing how we got to neoliberalism.

A brief history of liberalism's toos and fros

The term liberalism is widely seen as entering the political lexicon as late as the 19th century, so named after the Spanish liberales. But most people would date the development of core liberal ideas and practices back several centuries earlier. Marxists and socialists often paternity test proto-capitalist and bourgeois society in the 17th century as the mother of liberalism.[17] The conservative Max Weber and the socialist R.H. Tawney agree that the emergence of capitalism was important, but suggest that the spirit of Protestantism was crucial as well, perhaps even more so.[18] Truly ambitious political theorists like Nietzsche have dated liberal ideas about equality and liberty for all back to Christianity, with Nussbaum insisting even the Stoic tradition played an important role.[19]

Liberalism came into the world as a fighting ideology confronted by the entrenched power of the ancient regimes of Europe at their absolutist peak. One of the core arguments of early liberals was to insist on a certain degree of egalitarianism over and against the ontological social and political theories of their day. An emblematic example is Locke's famous dispute in the *First Treatise of Government* with Robert Filmer, author of *De Patriarcha*. Filmer insisted on the rights of hereditary monarchy on the basis of primogeniture: Adam was the first King granted authority by God, and the monarchs of Europe inherited their entitlement to rule from him. Against this, Locke followed Hobbes by insisting that, in a state of nature at the very least, all white men were in fact equal, including in their equal natural rights. These natural rights to life, liberty and property were sufficiently forceful and expansive that no one lost them, even when they transitioned to being citizens or subjects in civil society. In the event that a sovereign state interfered with them, individuals were entitled to rebel against it.[20]

---

16   Gray, *Liberalism*, p. xii.

17   See C.B. Macpherson, *The Political Theory of Possessive Individualism: Hobbes to Locke* (Oxford University Press, 1962).

18   R.H. Tawney, *Religion and the Rise of Capitalism: A Historical Study* (Angelico Press, 2021).

19   Martha Nussbaum, *The Cosmopolitan Tradition: A Noble But Flawed Ideal* (The Belknap Press of Harvard University Press, 2019).

20   For a discussion of the limitations of state power in Locke see *Two Treatise of Government* ed. Peter Laslett (Cambridge University Press, 1988), pp. 272-276.

This of course had revolutionary potential, and as Samuel Moyn reminds us, liberalism has a distinctly revolutionary history,[21] albeit one liberals often try to forget when arguing for the importance of law and order. The American, French, and Haitian revolutions were precursors to the Age of Revolution which would put absolutism on the ideological and geopolitical defensive – a shocking development which the political right has never forgotten.[22] Looking back at centuries of egalitarian ascendency and more or less consistent triumphs by liberals and later socialists, Russell Kirk in *The Conservative Mind* mused that conservatism had lost most of its major battles and been 'routed, but not conquered.'[23] But with success came the dilemmas of what to do with real power and influence. Alongside these 19th century political developments, changing economic conditions brought with them both opportunities and challenges. Many self-identified classical liberals look back on the 1800s as the idyllic period of the night watchman minimal state, which knew its place and facilitated freedom and market expansion.[24] They argue this was also a time period where the spread of liberalism across the globe, whether by imperialism or ascent, was a largely positive development which contributed magnificently to the spread of Enlightenment, markets and limited government.[25]

But this was also the period when socialism emerged as a new competitor for hearts and minds. Socialism was distinct from the reactionary ideologies liberals were very skilled at fighting by the 19th century. During this period the right often looked with a nostalgic register backwards and frequently lamented the spread of Enlightenment reason, denounced by Burke as an 'all-conquering empire of light and reason' which declared that a king was but a man.[26] By contrast socialism claimed to embody the mantle of progress and reason better than liberalism itself, and turned the claim of being reactionary and calcified back on bourgeois society. As Hobsbawm put it 'liberal ideology thus lost its original confident swoop – even the inevitability or desirability of progress began to be doubted by some liberals – a new

21 Moyn, *Liberalism Against Itself*.

22 See Eric Hobsbawm, *The Age of Revolution 1789-1848* (Vintage Books, 1996).

23 Russell Kirk, *The Conservative Mind: From Burke to Eliot* (Regnery Press, 2016), p. 257.

24 For an emblematic essay in this vein see Samuel Gregg. 'First Things and the Market Economy: A Reply to R.R. Reno,' *Public Discourse,* 20 September 2017.

25 See Pinker, *Enlightenment Now*.

26 Edmund Burke, *Reflections on the Revolution in France* (Oxford University Press, 2009), pp. 36-37.

ideology, socialism, reformulated the old eighteenth century verities. Reason, science, and progress were its firm foundation. What distinguished the socialists of our period from the champions of a perfect society of common ownership who periodically break into literature throughout recorded history, was the unqualified acceptance of the Industrial Revolution which created the very possibility of modern socialism.'[27] And socialists found many who were willing to listen; both amongst the working classes and amongst more well-heeled intellectuals like Karl Marx and Friedrich Engels. The latter famously declared that as capitalism and its liberal handmaiden had demolished the old world, so too would liberalism and capitalism be sublimated by transitioning to a far higher form of society.

Liberals responded to these threats in a variety of ways. Some followed Herbert Spencer and the Lochner era US Supreme Court by simply rejecting every argument for economic redistribution or, more radically still worker control of the economy. In so doing, many liberals would make their peace with forms of conservatism which were often wary of the disintegrationist impact of capitalism and libertine permissiveness but were committed to the order induced by respect for private property. But others like Mill or Keynes chose to pivot left instead, holding that there was no essential reason liberals needed to remain committed to the most gloves-off forms of capitalism. Perhaps they needn't even be committed to capitalism at all. What decided the debate between these liberal siblings in the mid-20th century wasn't intellectual competition, but geopolitical and economic factors. The Great Depression and the emergence of staunch competitors like communism on the left and fascism on the right compelled massive state action such as the New Deal and growing tolerance for unionisation and labour movements in general.[28] This shift climaxed in the joint Soviet/Anglo defeat of Nazism in the Second World War, which discredited the authoritarian right for a while and massively increased the prestige of democratic socialism and (sadly) authoritarian communism. A combination of these pressures led administrators and politicians in liberal states to introduce expansive welfare states which, for all their flaws, came closer than perhaps any others to creating societies genuinely committed to liberty, equality, and solidarity for all. In this, socialist thought and hope played not a little role.[29] As Olaf Palme, prime

---

27 Hobsbawm, *The Age of Revolution*, p. 241.
28 On this history see Piketty, *Capital and Ideology*.
29 I take this point from Moyn, *Liberalism Against Itself*.

minister of Sweden during its social democratic heyday put it, they had 'come further in realising socialism than the countries that usually call themselves socialist'.[30] This was rolled back with the ascendancy of neoliberalism.

What is neoliberalism?

Neoliberalism is also infamously hard to define, not least because in many spaces it has become a venomously pejorative term. Consequently many of those associated with neoliberalism have tended to reject the label. Von Mises and Hayek preferred to call themselves classical liberals, while plenty of other neoliberal advocates became variously aligned with flavours of right-libertarianism.[31] Nonetheless, the term has become wildly popular for good reasons I hope to make clear. Milton Friedman wrote a short paper *Neo-Liberalism and Its Prospects* in 1951. In it he describes the project of neo-liberalism in brief:

> Neo-liberalism would accept the nineteenth century liberal emphasis on the fundamental importance of the individual, but it would substitute for the nineteenth century goal of laissez-faire as a means to this end, the goal of the competitive order. It would seek to use competition among producers to protect consumers from exploitation, competition among employers to protect workers and owners of property, and competition among consumers to protect the enterprises themselves. The state would police the system, establish conditions favourable to competition and prevent monopoly, provide a stable monetary framework, and relieve acute misery and distress. Citizens would be protected against the state by the existence of a free private market; and against one another by the preservation of competition.[32]

Centre-right commentator Matthew Continetti discusses how Trumpists set themselves against 'neoliberalism, the set of public beliefs and practices that, since the Ronald Reagan era, have privileged the market over the state

---

30 Quoted in Kjell Ostberg, *The Rise and Fall of Swedish Social Democracy* (Verso Press, 2024), p. 210.
31 On this history see Matt Zwolinski and John Tomasi, *The Individualists: Radicals, Reactionaries, and the Struggle for the Soul of Libertarianism* (Princeton University Press, 2022).
32 Milton Friedman. 'Neo-liberalism And Its Prospects,' *Farmand/Human Events*, 17 February 1951.

and the individual over the community.'[33] This has echoes of Hayek's well-known distinction between a society committed to collectivism and one committed to individualism – often taken to be one of the foundational dualisms of neoliberal thought. As Hayek summarises this political posture:

> There is one aspect of the change in moral values brought about by the advance of collectivism which at the present time provides food for thought. It is that the virtues which are held less in esteem, and which consequently become rarer are precisely those on which Anglo-Saxons justly prided themselves and in which they were generally recognized to excel. The virtues those people possessed…were independence and self-reliance, individual initiative and local responsibility, the successful reliance on voluntary activist, noninterference with one's neighbour and tolerance of the different and queer, respect for custom and tradition, and a healthy suspicion of power and authority. Almost all the traditions and institutions in which democratic moral genius has found its most characteristic expression, and which in turn have moulded the national character and the whole moral climate of England and America, are those which the progress of collectivism and its inherently centralistic tendencies are progressively destroying.[34]

Interestingly this distinction between (neo)liberal market individualism and different species of collectivism is insisted upon forcefully by Hayek at some points and blurred in others. Throughout *The Constitution of Liberty* he takes a more nuanced perspective, acknowledging the need for state institutions and social traditions to establish the conditions for market society. Indeed Hayek even chastises believers in pure laissez faire for endorsing anarchism rather than classical liberal ordered liberty.[35] Alongside Hayek's preference for authoritarian liberalism over socialist democracy and his willingness to experiment with radical forms of market decentralisation through encasing them from political pressures, this has led even some libertarians to acknowledge that Hayek was more willing to entertain rationalistic

33 Matthew Continetti, *The Right: The Hundred Year War for American Conservatism* (Basic Books, 2022), p. 377.
34 F.A. Hayek, *The Road to Serfdom: The Definitive Edition* (University of Chicago Press, 2007), p. 219.
35 F.A. Hayek, *The Constitution of Liberty: The Definitive Edition* (University of Chicago Press, 2011).

and statist interventions than his reputation would suggest. This included occasionally arguing for certain modest redistributionist policies, though more pre-eminent are Hayek's insistence on the importance of law to maintain order and respect for property rights.[36]

Much like the classical liberal antecedent upon which it is built, many neoliberal thinkers often intentionally or unintentionally vacillated between a descriptive and a normative account of the world as they sought to naturalise their preference for the acquisitive ethic by suggesting it lay in individual's inherent desire to pursue their self-interest. This often took the form of projecting back into human nature and practises many of the characteristics preferred by neoliberals. But this tendency was not universal. Unlike many of the classical liberal thinkers, figures like Hayek often expressed an awareness that their views may be conceived as sufficiently unnatural as to require a long process of development to obtain. At times this was even a point of triumphalist pride amongst influences on neoliberalism like Von Mises, who stressed that private property and markets were not natural but instead an epochal historical achievement since 'private ownership of the means of production coincides with the history of the development of mankind from an animal-like condition to the highest reaches of modern civilization.'[37]

This point about neoliberalism relying heavily on the state and international institutions has been central to the definitions of critics across the spectrum. In his book *Tyranny Inc,* the idiosyncratic conservative Sohrab Ahmari defines neoliberalism as 'ultimately a theory and practice aimed not just at liberating markets from politics but at turning politics itself into a tool of the marketplace and of neutralising any political claims that don't fit the logic and needs of capitalism.' Ahmari goes on to stress how neoliberal practice has required a powerful set of state actors, ranging from the courts to politicians, to establish itself even in the face of popular resistance.[38] Wendy Brown defines neoliberalism as a 'normative order of

36 See Matt Zwolinski, 'What's Right About Social Justice?' *Learn Liberty,* 17 December 2012, https://www.learnliberty.org/videos/whats-right-about-social-justice/.

37 Mises, *Liberalism*, p. 60. On the point about naturalisation see Gary Becker's work arguing that people approach marriage from an economistic standpoint in Gary Becker. 'A Theory of Marriage,' in *Economics and the Family: Marriage, Children and Human Capital,* ed. Theodor W. Schultz (Chicago Press, 1974).

38 Sohrab Ahmari, *Tyranny, Inc: How Private Power Crushed American Liberty – and What to Do About It,* Uncorrected Proofs (Forum Books, 2023), p.164.

reason developed over three decades into a widely and deeply disseminated governing rationality' which 'transmogrifies every human domain and endeavour, along with humans themselves, according to a specific image of the economic. All conduct is economic conduct; all spheres of existence are farmed and measured by economic terms and metrics, even then those spheres are not directly monetized.'[39] Quinn Slobodian draws on the example of Karl Polyani to 'conceive of the neoliberal project as "a simultaneous roll-back and roll-out of state functions." Neoliberals wanted the state to back welfarist functions while simultaneously being more pro-active in encasing the market created from political and especially democratic pressures.' Indeed, Slobodian points out how for the neoliberals even the state was not sufficient-international legal institutions were needed to truly make the world safe for capitalism.[40]

Of these definitions my own draws most heavily on Wendy Brown, with some alterations: neoliberalism is a governing ideology which holds that economic efficiency specifically and human flourishing generally is best obtained by the establishment of a possessive and acquisitive market ethic across social norms, institutions and individuals. More specifically we can say neoliberalism has three emblematic commitments:[41]

1. Neoliberals are committed to a mixed social ontology. Classical liberals were methodologically committed to an atomistically individualist social ontology to complement their normative possessive individualism. By contrast neoliberals recognise the need for state institutions to play a role in establishing market relations even if they will characterise other statist functions as artificial or a derivation from spontaneous order.

2. Neoliberals are normatively committed to a possessive and acquisitive ethic. It is possessive in stressing that individuals have rights to own themselves, their labour and property, but may choose to legitimately alienate those rights under market conditions. It is acquisitive in holding that individual and aggregate utility will be increased through individuals pursuing self-interested acquisition in capitalist markets.[42]

39 Wendy Brown, *Undoing the Demos: Neoliberalism's Stealth Revolution* (Zone Books, 2015), pp. 9-10.
40 Quinn Slobodian, *Globalists: The End of Empire and the Birth of Neoliberalism* (Harvard University Press, 2018), p. 6.
41 My account here is deeply influenced by Macpherson, *The Political Theory of Possessive Individualism*.
42 I say capitalist markets to distinguish between the neoliberal and the Millsean market socialist position I will describe later.

3. Neoliberals are committed to practical process of the establishment and expansion of market institutions and norms into different spheres of life. This can be carried out directly through marketisation, but in practice neoliberals have also accepted and endorsed statist, international legal, and cultural projects of expansion. The obverse of this process is neoliberals' insistence that the market be insulated from all forms of political pressure, and that the state withdraw from spheres of life (even those where it has long played a role) to make way for marketisation.[43]

These commitments are of course idealised and are conceived and applied more or less stringently by various neoliberal thinkers and regimes. It is the latter that interests me more right now because after several decades of hegemony neoliberalism appears to be faltering under assault from the right.

The end of the neoliberal and conservative counter-offensive?

As indicated before, during the heyday of the welfare state many liberals might have found the prospect of neoliberalism's emergence surprising. A combination of Keynesian economics, anti-communist Cold War, and a powerful, if moderate, labour movement seemed to portend the end of ideology, delivering high economic growth, comparable levels of equality, and a degree of political stability. In many respects this view, still popular amongst some on the centre left, is nostalgic: anti-colonialism and imperialism ensured that the era of the Cold War was defined by plenty of hot conflicts, demands for racial, gender, and sexual equality increased, and many social democrats and socialists were discontented with how much was still to be achieved. Nevertheless it wouldn't have been irrational for mid-century welfarist liberals to assume these problems could be managed and even overcome without shifting to neoliberalism.

The shift could not have occurred without neoliberals aligning themselves or being coopted by other factions on the political right. The ideological opening was available since many Cold War liberal intellectuals had a strangely lukewarm view of the welfare states being constructed by liberal politicians, and wished for a return to a more muscular form of capitalism than those politicians were willing to countenance.[44] But far more important were changing material conditions in the 1960s and 1970s. In the United States the Johnson administration opened its tenure by crushing

---

43 On the point about cultural and moral change, see Brown, *Undoing the Demos*.
44 See Moyn, *Liberalism Against Itself.*

Barry Goldwater in the 1964 election. But the shine quickly wore off as the United States became mired in the Vietnam war and Johnson's pro-Civil Rights policies seemed to abet social chaos rather than order. This opened the door for candidates like Richard Nixon to promise a return to law and order which was amenable to the more statist dimensions of neoliberalism. In the 1970s inflation and unemployment brought the Keynesian consensus into crisis, as evidenced by Hayek and Milton Friedman winning the Nobel Prize in close succession. After 1980 Ronald Reagan integrated anti-welfarist neoliberals into a three-legged-stool coalition that included Christian social conservatives and militant anti-communists, forming a winning combination that took the Republican Party to victory in three successive elections. Reagan's domestic and international policies reflected the neoliberal impulses quite well; from slashing taxes for the wealthy and cracking down on unions to mass criminalisation and muscular anti-communism abroad. Just as importantly, Reagan's electoral success had the hegemonic effect of transitioning the opposition Democratic Party towards neoliberalism. By 1996 it was Bill Clinton, in his State of the Union Address, who declared the era of big government was over.

In the UK Margaret Thatcher pursued a parallel program on a smaller scale. Interestingly she often characterised neoliberalism less as a natural outlook than one which needed to be internalised by state power. As she put it in a revealing *Sunday Times* interview if one wanted to 'change the approach you really are after the heart and soul of the nation. Economics are the method; the object is to change the heart and soul.'[45] To change sufficiently the soul of a post-Beveridge nation, Thatcher broke the back of British unions with great skill, privatised state institutions, and deregulated the finance market, while insisting society didn't really exist and individuals and families must learn to take care of themselves. Much like in the US this enacted a hegemonic shift in the orientation of the opposition, such that near the end of her life Thatcher declared Tony Blair was her greatest accomplishment, since she'd persuaded the once socialist Labour opposition to change their minds. The consequences of the neoliberal shift for liberalism have been dire. Skyrocketing inequality has led to deepening elite capture of state institutions, and the widespread perception that governments serve the rich.[46] Conservatives and progressives alike foreground how the

---

45 Margaret Thatcher, 'Interview for the Sunday Times,' *Sunday Times*, 3 May 1981.
46 See Piketty, *Capital and Ideology.*

spread of neoliberal norms into the lifeworld have corroded communal ties and spread a competitive ethos across society. One consequence of this is a ruling class unique in history that repeatedly blames the poor for their own failure while exonerating the self-made rich of any significant social responsibility or even *noblesse oblige* to the lower orders.[47] The anger provoked by this has since been directed against not just neoliberalism but liberalism more generally and has mainly benefited self-described illiberal democrats like Victor Orban and post-modern conservatives like Trump. Unless we liberals redeem ourselves, it is quite possible we will see an end to our creed. This is where a return to the progressive and inspirational ideals of Mill becomes crucial.

John Stuart Mill, socialist

In those days I had seen little further than the old school of political economists into the possibilities of fundamental improvement in social arrangements. Private property, as now understood, and inheritance, appeared to me, as to them, the dernier mot of legislation: and I looked no further than to mitigating the inequalities consequent on these institutions, by getting rid of primogeniture and entails. The notion that it was possible to go further than this in removing the injustice—for injustice it is, whether admitting of a complete remedy or not—involved in the fact that some are born to riches and the vast majority to poverty, I then reckoned chimerical, and only hoped that by universal education, leading to voluntary restraint on population, the portion of the poor might be made more tolerable. In short, I was a democrat, but not the least of a Socialist. We were now much less democrats than I had been, because so long as education continues to be so wretchedly imperfect, we dreaded the ignorance and especially the selfishness and brutality of the mass: but our ideal of ultimate improvement went far beyond Democracy and would class us decidedly under the general designation of Socialists.[48]

John Stuart Mill has serious claim to being the most quintessential and iconographic liberal thinker. That such a definitive liberal also proudly identified as a socialist in his *Autobiography,* and wrote sympathetically

---

47 See Michael Sandel, *The Tyranny of Merit: What's Become of the Common Good?* (Farar, Straus, and Giroux, 2020).

48 John Stuart Mill, *Autobiography of John Stuart Mill* (Compass Circle, 2019).

about struggles for equality and an end to capitalist domination, should tell us a great deal about the direction a principled liberalism should move in. Helen McCabe reminds us, in her definitive work *John Stuart Mill: Socialist,* that for a long time the socialist dimensions of Mill's thought tended to be invisiblised or treated as a source of embarrassment.[49] Otherwise adept commentators like Geoffrey Scarre fall into the invisibilisation camp. Scarre largely takes for granted that Mill's commitments to liberty seamlessly mapped onto his support for capitalism. He argues that provided that 'markets are avoided in manufacture or supply, Mill believes that everyone will benefit from the existence of capitalist free markets.'[50] On the other front, John Gray, writing during his neoliberal phase, fell into the embarrassment camp. Writing in *Liberalism,* Gray chastises Mill for effectively completing the 'rupture in the development of the liberal tradition begun by Bentham and James Mill and created a system of thought which legitimated the interventionist and statist tendencies which grew even stronger in the latter half of the nineteenth century.' Gray chides Mill for his 'attitudes to trade unions, to nationalism, and to socialist experimentation' since they are a 'decisive breach in the intellectual fabric of the liberal tradition.'[51]

Both the invisibilisation and embarrassment approaches are intellectually unsatisfying. They treat Mill's socialism anomalously, or else as an immediate criticism, rather than trying to understand how and why he connected it integrally to his liberalism. Mill was of course profoundly committed to personal liberty; but for reasons quite different from those like the neoliberals who conceive of liberty as possessive individualism and an acquisitive ethic. His endorsement of liberty flowed from an idiosyncratic utilitarianism which combined a consequentialist concern for the happiness of all, where each count as one and no more than one, with a liberal commitment to individual rights. The fusion came in part from Mill's conviction that allowing each individual maximal personal liberty, subject to the harm principle, would enable them to best pursue individual happiness and so increase aggregate utility overall. But it also flowed from Mill's commitment that it was the development and expression of the self which is of great and primary importance to individuals. This was nowhere better expressed than in *On Liberty,* where Mill claimed that we are not

---

49   McCabe. *John Stuart Mill.*
50   Geoffrey Scarre, *Mill's On Liberty,* (Continuum Press, 2007), p. 113.
51   Gray, *Liberalism,* p. 30.

machines designed to do work prescribed to us but a 'tree, which requires to grow and develop itself on all sides, according to the tendency of the inward forces which make it a living thing'.[52]

In his ambivalent but generally positive evaluation, C.B. Macpherson refers to Mill as offering one of the first accounts of a developmental liberalism focused on the growth of human capacities rather than the acquisitive ethic common to possessive individualism.[53] This commitment to a developmental ethic is linked to Mill's broader egalitarianism and his firm rejection of the competitive and hierarchical culture which emerged with capitalism. Such a profoundly anti-social society runs afoul Mill's egalitarianism in denying the poor opportunities for development while engendering domineering concentrations of power in the rich. Mill had deep reservations about this. As Claeys reminds us '…Mill was committed to much greater egalitarianism than anything Bentham envisioned. The "great end of social improvement," he suggested, should be a "state of society combining the greatest personal freedom with that just distribution of the fruits of labour which the present laws of property do not even propose to aim at."'[54] Culturally, acquisitive individualism was to be rejected for corroding the solidaristic ties with others which were vital to one's self-development. Mill was very much committed to a normative expressive individualism. As McCabe reminds us, such an individualism was inherently other-oriented in its recognition of our integration with humanity as a whole and was marked by a sensitivity to the social prerequisites for development.[55] Capitalism, by contrast, was predicated on an anti-social competitive individualism which produced great harm.

Mill laid out his mature arguments for socialism the way he typically did, through a careful examination of its strengths and weaknesses. In *Socialism* he adopts an almost proto-Rawlsian language to describe great poverty, and that poverty very little connected to desert as the 'first grand failure in the existing arrangements of society. The second is human misconduct; crime, vice, and folly' – the blame for which largely lies with poverty, a lack of work, and bad education.[56] Mill notes how previous reformers largely stopped at observing

52 John Stuart Mill, *On Liberty and Other Essays* (Oxford University Press, 1991), p. 66.
53 C.B. Macpherson, *The Rise and Fall of Economic Justice and Other Essays* (Oxford University Press, 2013),
54 Gregor Claeys, *John Stuart Mill: A Very Short Introduction* (Oxford University Press, 2022), p. 57.
55 McCabe, *John Stuart Mill*, pp. 183-195.
56 John Stuart Mill, *Socialism* (East India Publishing Company, 2020), pp. 22-23.

these social problems. Later in *Socialism,* Mill points out how they are often explained away by meritocratic and naturalising rhetoric which blame the poor for their lot or suggest their situation is immutable. This in turn reinforces a vicious and anti-social competitive order which produces many evils. None of this is acceptable to Mill, his revulsion towards these modes of argumentation and the principles they embody is one of the major catalysts in prompting his shift to supporting the far-sighted doctrines of the socialists.

> At this point, in the enumeration of the evils of society, the mere levellers of former times usually stopped; but their more far-sighted successors, the present Socialists, go farther. In their eyes the very foundation of human life as at present constituted, the very principle on which the production and reparation of all material products is now carried on, is essentially vicious and anti-social. It is the principle of individualism, competition, each one for himself and against all the rest. It is grounded of opposition of interests, not harmony of interests, and under it everyone is required to find his place by a struggle, by pushing others back or being pushed back by them. Socialists consider this system of private war (as it may be termed) between everyone and everyone, especially fatal in an economical point of view and in a moral. Morally considered, its evils are obvious. It is the parent of envy, hatred, and all uncharitableness; it makes everyone the natural enemy of all others who cross his path...[57]

Mill's liberal socialism – an idea whose time has come?

Socialism is often regarded monolithically by critics. This is uncharitable, and it is far more clarifying to emulate Ryan's approach to liberalism by speaking of socialisms plural. Mill had a robust knowledge of contemporary schools of socialist thought in his time, though most of these were of a pre-Marxist and utopian flavour.[58] Generally he had a dim intellectual view of most of these doctrines, except the Saint Simonians, with whom he debated respectfully and learned much from. Mill was also deeply wary of command-and-control economic authoritarianism, and prophetically warned this could be the future of socialism if steps weren't taken to avoid it. He wanted to combine socialist

---

57 Mill, *Socialism*, pp. 22-23.
58 Mill was aware of Marx's existence, and even commended a speech he gave on the working class and war. See McCabe, *John Stuart Mill*, p. 97 and Claeys, *John Stuart Mill*, p. 101.

commitments to economic equality with the benefits of markets. Provisionally I argue this crystalised into a liberal socialism which had four central features:

1. A commitment to a market socialism where the major firms were worker cooperatives and capitalists were largely discarded.

2. A welfare state which, while unimpressive by contemporary standards, would have been regarded as robust in the 19th century. As McCabe indicates, the Millian state was to provide a range of public utilities including, street lighting, sewers, public baths, public health initiatives, communication networks, roads, canals, and railways, the transportation and printing of money, the provision of schools (though not a state monopoly on education), the funding of endeavours of public benefit such as geographical exploration and research in the arts and sciences, including endowments for the learned class.[59] Updated for our times, Elizabeth Anderson is no doubt correct to claim that 'given Mill's thorough-going positivism about property rights, and his willingness to rewrite property rules to liberate and empower workers, there is little ground for thinking that he would have resisted the social democratic innovation.'[60] We can imagine a modern Millian welfare state would be expansively generous.

3. Representative democracy with universal suffrage, including for women, qualified by epistocratic restrictions.[61] These restrictions were contingent upon the level of development in the society and could be removed with the extension of education and political maturation.

4. A strong commitment to liberal rights, constrained only by the harm principle. These liberal rights would include rights to personal property, but not private ownership of the means of production by capitalists.

Taken together, Mill's liberal socialist vision constitutes an inspiring alternative to the forms of neoliberalism which are currently facing a crisis of legitimation. And it can do so while renewing and even deepening liberal principles of liberty, equality, and solidarity for all. Unlike neoliberalism Mill's liberal socialism is robustly committed to equality, particularly the equal

---

59 McCabe, *John Stuart Mill*, p. 206.

60 Elizabeth Anderson, *Hijacked: How Neoliberalism Turned The Work Ethic Against Workers And How Workers Can Take It Back* (Cambridge University Press, 2023), p. 187.

61 On the point about women see John Stuart Mill, *On The Subjection of Women*, reprinted in *John Stuart Mill's 'The Subjection of Women': His Contemporary and Modern Critics*, by Richard Vandewetering and Lesley Jacobs (Caravan Books, 1999).

growth of an individual's capacities in cooperation with others. Recovering these political threads would enable Millsian liberal socialism to be of service to our contemporary conditions. Mill's synthesis of markets and community could provide an effective counter to the yawning inequalities produced by neoliberal policies. Mill's generous validation of co-operation and community provides a powerful foil against an anti-social society and an aloof ruling elite who ask precarious citizens to internalise a sense of responsibility for their own domination and subordination.[62] Mill's liberal socialism is also both robustly democratic and participatory while being respectful of liberal rights. It could answer neoliberalism's habitual suspicions of democracy. In place of technocratic governance cloaking elite capture,[63] Mill postulates a political economy where localised industrial forms predominate over centralised monoliths. Given these striking advantages there is a compelling case to be made that Mill's liberal socialism, or something like it, is an idea whose time has come. Liberals have been on the backfoot for almost a decade now. We are unlikely to see liberalism sustain itself unless we do better than neoliberalism. Liberal socialism deserves a shot.

Bibliography

Ahmari, Sohrab. *Tyranny, Inc: How Private Power Crushed American Liberty- and What to Do About It*. Uncorrected Proofs. Forum Books, 2023.

Anderson, Elizabeth. *Hijacked: How Neoliberalism Turned The Work Ethic Against Workers And How Workers Can Take It Back*. Cambridge University Press, 2023.

— *Private Government: How Employers Rule Our Lives (and Why We Don't Talk About It)*. Princeton University Press, 2017.

Becker, Gary. 'A Theory of Marriage.' In *Economics and the Family: Marriage, Children and Human Capital*. Edited by Theodor W. Schultz. University of Chicago Press, 1974.

Brown, Wendy. *Undoing the Demos: Neoliberalism's Stealth Revolution*. Zone Books, 2015.

Burke, Edmund. *Reflections on the Revolution in France*. Oxford University Press, 2009.

Claeys, Gregory. *John Stuart Mill: A Very Short Introduction*. Oxford University Press, 2022.

---

62 See Sandel, *The Tyranny of Merit*.
63 See Piketty, *Capital and Ideology*.

Continetti, Matthew. *The Right: The Hundred Year War for American Conservatism*. Basic Books, 2022.

Deneen, Patrick. *Why Liberalism Failed*. Yale University Press, 2018.

Fawcett, Edmund. *Liberalism: The Life of An Idea*. 2nd ed. Princeton University Press, 2018.

Friedman, Milton. 'Neo-liberalism And Its Prospects.' *Farmand/Human Events*, 17 February 1951.

Gray, John. *Liberalism*. 2nd ed. University of Minnesota Press, 1995.

— *The New Leviathans: Thoughts After Liberalism*. Farar, Strauss and Giroux, 2023.

Gregg, Samuel. 'First Things and the Market Economy: A Reply to R.R Reno.' *Public Discourse*, 20 September 2017.

Hayek, F.A. *The Constitution of Liberty: The Definitive Edition*. University of Chicago Press, 2011.

— *The Road to Serfdom: The Definitive Edition*. The University of Chicago Press, 2007.

— 'Why I Am Not a Conservative.' Foundation for Economic Education, 2016. https://fee.org/resources/why-i-am-not-a-conservative/ [Accessed 7/10/2024].

Hobsbawm, Eric. *The Age of Revolution 1789-1848*. Vintage Books, 1996.

Kirk, Russell. *The Conservative Mind: From Burke to Eliot*. Regnery Press, 2016.

Lefebvre, Alexandre. *Liberalism as a Way of Life*. Princeton University Press, 2024.

Locke, John. *Two Treatise of Government*. Edited by Peter Laslett. Cambridge University Press, 1988.

Losurdo, Domenico. *Liberalism: A Counter-History*. Verso Books, 2014.

Macpherson, C.B. *The Political Theory of Possessive Individualism: Hobbes to Locke*. Oxford University Press, 1962.

— *The Rise and Fall of Economic Justice and Other Essays*. Oxford University Press, 2013.

McCabe, Helen. *John Stuart Mill: Socialist*. Queens-McGill University Press, 2021.

McManus, Matthew. T. *The Political Right and Equality: Turning Back the Tide of Egalitarian Modernity*. Routledge, 2023.

— *The Political Theory of Liberal Socialism*. Routledge, 2025.

Mill, John Stuart. *Autobiography*. Compass Circle, 2019.

— *On Liberty and Other Essays*. Oxford University Press, 1991.

— *Principles of Political Economy with Chapters on Socialism.* Edited by Jonathan Riley. Oxford University Press, 2008. https://oll.libertyfund. org/titles/mill-principles-of-political-economy-ashley-ed.

— *Socialism.* East India Publishing Company, 2020.

— *The Subjection of Women.* Reprinted in *John Stuart Mill´s The Subjection of Women: His Contemporary and Modern Critics.* By Richard Vandewetering and Lesley Jacobs. Caravan Books, 1999.

— *Three Essays on Religion: Nature, The Utility of Religion, Theism.* Prometheus Books, 1998.

Mises, Ludwig von. *Liberalism.* Ludwig von Mises Institute, 2018.

Moyn, Samuel. *Liberalism Against Itself: Cold War Intellectuals and the Making of Our Times.* Yale University Press, 2023.

Nietzsche, Friedrich. *Twilight of the Idols and The Antichrist.* Penguin Books 1990.

Nussbaum, Martha. *The Cosmopolitan Tradition: A Noble But Flawed Ideal.* The Belknap Press of Harvard University Press, 2019.

Ostberg, Kjell. *The Rise and Fall of Swedish Social Democracy.* Verso Press, 2024.

Piketty, Thomas. *Capital and Ideology.* Translated by Arthur Goldhammer. The Belknap Press of Harvard University Press, 2020.

Pinker, Steven. *Enlightenment Now: The Case for Reason, Science, Humanism and Progress.* Penguin Books, 2018.

Ryan, Alan. *The Making of Modern Liberalism.* Princeton University Press, 2012.

— *The Philosophy of John Stuart Mill.* MacMillan Press, 1987.

Sandel, Michael. *The Tyranny of Merit: What's Become of the Common Good?* Farar, Straus and Giroux, 2020.

Scarre, Geoffrey. *Mill's On Liberty.* Continuum Press, 2007.

Slobodian, Quinn. *Globalists: The End of Empire and the Birth of Neoliberalism.* Harvard University Press, 2018.

Tawney, R.H. *Religion and the Rise of Capitalism: A Historical Study.* Angelico Press, 2021.

Thatcher, Margaret. 'Interview.' *Sunday Times*, 3 May 1981.

Zwolinski, Matt. 'What's Right About Social Justice?' *Learn Liberty*, 17 December 2012. https://www.learnliberty.org/videos/whats-right-about-social-justice/.

Zwolinski, Matt, and John Tomasi. *The Individualists: Radicals, Reactionaries, and the Struggle for the Soul of Libertarianism.* Princeton University Press, 2022.

9

Liberalism and the Environmental Crisis

Edward Robinson

Liberalism once did a work of emancipation. But it is so influenced by an inheritance of absolute claims that it invented the myth of 'The Individual' set over in dualistic separation against that which is called 'The Social'. It obscured the fact that these words are names for traits and capacities of human beings in the concrete. It transformed that which they actually name into entities by themselves. It thereby obscured, indeed, prevented recognition of the fact that actual realization of these traits and capabilities depends on the specific conditions under which human beings are born and in which they grow up.[1]

Take Kitchener's maximum [on army estimates for rifles], square it, multiply that result by two; and when you are in sight of that, double it again for good luck.[2]

Dialectical thinking has been out of fashion in the Anglosphere for a century and I am not proposing a resuscitation attempt here. I do, however, want to posit that we have come to a very dialectical-looking impasse, one which political liberals, especially, ought to take serious note. One does not have to subscribe to the full-throated Hegelianism of say *Scientific Logic* (1812) to note that we appear to be in an intellectual and sociological bind of almost unimaginable tightness. The rivers of reason that have borne us to this estuary do not seem to offer up any obvious solutions on their own. By contrast, the common sense of the Western culture in which we are embedded – especially in any sort of liberal clothing – now appears to pull hard in opposite directions. We can barely imagine our way

---

1   John Dewey, *Problems of Men* (New York Philosophical Library, 1946), pp. 18-9.
2   Lloyd George in Hugh Purcell, *Lloyd George* (Haus Publishing, 2006), p. 41.

out of the bind, let alone act with any sort of decisiveness. It is in this context that Adorno (or Fred Jameson's[3]) smart-arse Marxian joke, that it is easier to imagine the end of the world than the end of capitalism, can only elicit a smile. At one minute to midnight, the stopped clock may well be finally showing the correct time. What am I talking about?

Liberalism for me, in all its forms, remains a product of the pursuit of reason over divinely justified authority. I think this is uncontroversial. Married to a rising class of industrialists and European nationalists in the 18th and 19th centuries, it became a political movement that placed bourgeois leaders at the helm of European and North American chancelleries and (in some cases) on thrones.[4] At its best – and in the eyes of its sympathisers – liberalism is a byword for civilisation. Civilised values are liberal values, etc. We have all read the pamphlets and the speeches connecting the Liberal cause (capital L) to some great universal and intergenerational goals peace, the nation state, anticlericalism, voting reform, freedom from arbitrary taxes, even imperialism – but most often (as the title of the collection refers) the cause is simply Freedom (provided the last Jesuit has been despatched). But liberalism has also been connected to the scientific method, to universalism in philosophy and to rationalism (as opposed to romanticism[5]). Herein lies the dialectic of 'liberal common sense' in antithesis to the understood problem of generalised environmental breakdown. Liberal political sociology (coming from rational choice theory) *knows* that voter-citizens will not, in today's cultural context, *choose* policies that make them materially worse-off unless these can be compensated for by policies that make them better off in non-material ways. As Mill would understand, they remain utility maximisers. In addition to this, liberal science (the natural philosophy of old), *knows*, that the surrounding environment – which has always been the flooding, violent and capricious parent of romanticism – is now quite probably moving from one state to another and is, as such, even more violent and unpredictable than it has been at any other period of time in human existence. Rationalism has, in many senses, undergirded both these insights. Non-liberal theories like utilitarianism might find themselves

3   The jury seems to be out on the provenance.
4   Given that the most common justification given for the continued existence of the British monarchy seems to be 'tourism' I think we are now safe in considering Charles III to be a thoroughly bourgeois monarch.
5   That Hegel saw it as his lifework to try to reconcile romanticism with rationalism is not something I can get into here.

less constrained but these (thanks very largely to the work of John Stuart Mill himself) no longer enjoy culturally dominant status. To restate the dialectical bind (as analytically as I can) I add a third component, that of electoral constraint: (1) we *know* we cannot win free elections by offering things that voters do not want or cannot reasonably be expected to want, e.g. lower material living standards; less food; intermittent access to energy. (2) we *know* that civilisation as we understand it cannot survive if current trends in greenhouse gas emissions and biodiversity loss continue. (3) we *know* that the actions available to us as individuals are highly unlikely to be anywhere near sufficient to change the culture or ethics underpinning our civilization in the time allowed (that is, in around 20-30 years maximum and – realistically – in more like 5-10 years[6]).

'Reasonableness' is thus at odds with itself. Reasonable actions on one dimension of knowledge[7] carry within themselves the seeds of their own contraction on another, to adapt Marx. Or, to adapt Kipling, 'If you can keep your head when all about you are losing theirs – *you have seriously misjudged the gravity of the situation.*' This is why non-liberals of all persuasions (from ethno-nationalists to Californian yogis, to what remains of communists) think that there can be no resources within liberalism to avoid or survive climate change. My response to them is that the disenchantment of the world that liberalism has been so successful in promulgating itself internationally has now also undercut its ability to act wholesale. Not enough people (I wager) now believe enough in magical justifications for authority (either those of a god-emperor or those of a proletarian dictatorship) to spring us out of the dialectic to which liberalism has brought us. And I am unconvinced by most sociologically-inspired routes out, which suggest that there is some rising class somewhere (gen-Z?) that will benefit from aggressive climate action of the kind required *and* that is about to seize the cultural leadership; or that China is simply the answer by default – as the new superpower.[8] There may be a 'world soul' out there able to save us. If not, we are stuck in

---

6   This is on the understanding that we are almost certainly already in breach of the 1.5 degree UN temperature target and now looking to avoid more like 2-3 degrees of average warming by the end of the century.

7   'Knowledge' here stands in for whatever you think best sums up the received ideas of the political elite.

8   Of course, that leaves a chaotic and violent disentangling of the civilisation that liberalism has built – a second sacking of Rome – but that would hardly constitute a liberal future and so I leave it aside.

the prison of our intellectual and social history. We can act only as liberals. But what if we acted as radicals? What if we used the resources of our own tradition and culture to understand our own behaviour. In undertaking such an analysis, I am not proposing some Heideggerian move back to a pre-liberal Being but, on a much less ambitious plain, to allow us better to pinpoint our coordinates, and the route we have taken to reach them. In what follows, I want to draw on three recent contributions to the discussion of environmental policy. I write as a radical who thinks, like Keynes and Dewey, that liberalism happens to be only one of the rivers flowing from the enlightenment, with versions of Hegalisanism and Marxism as the others. One of the authors I want to discuss writes in a tradition very close to a post-Marxist position. Another examines environmental history from the perspective of a moral philosopher, and the third seeks to return us to a more classical economic understanding of asset management, taking aim at both neoclassical and Keynesian approaches to postwar economic policy, arguing that they have prioritised short-term consumption over a responsible and farsighted culture of asset investment (or at least asset protection) and deferred gratification. All of these approaches strengthen me in a view that radicals need to be a long way from intellectually-dead, election-orientated centrism if they are even to understand the position we are in in relation to nature, let alone to act with confidence. I will leave aside possible neo-conservative or neo-fascist approaches to responding to climate breakdown, although we may – before long – need to be prepared very seriously to engage with them on a political level.

Stoll, Christophers and Helm: paths into the forest

Capitalism, nature and technology are concepts with contested histories, which (luckily for me) there is insufficient space here to define. But I want to draw on three recently published books to explore how they might help us pinpoint our coordinates.[9] The first theme is an exploration of the kind of capitalism we see at large in the world today, and which, I think, is more fully culturally embedded in the UK than perhaps any other country in the world outside the US. Mark Stoll's latest book *Profit: An Environmental History*[10]

---

9   I like the terminology of coordinates as it suggests that we find our position by taking bearings off (to us in our current position) relatively fixed marks, without thinking for a minute that those marks are not themselves in motion.
10   Mark Stoll, *Profit: An Environmental History* (Polity Press, 2023).

sweeps through economic history from the Bronze Age to the coronavirus with the aim of explaining 'how capitalism changed the environment and how the environment shaped capitalism.'[11] But as a historian of religious ideas about nature, Stoll brings a more nuanced approach to the shift from an austere productivism to a consumption-led version of capitalism than one often reads in, for example, materialist-inspired texts that focus only on changes in modes of production or extraction, rather than intellectual climate. One of the most germane to this chapter concerns the work of the British economist William Stanley Jevons.

Jevons published *The Coal Question: An Enquiry Concerning the Progress of the Nation and the Probable Exhaustion of Our Coal Mines* in 1866.[12] Stoll argues that it was the first work of its kind to argue that industrial capitalism's very success at exploiting nature was undercutting the ability of future generations to benefit from progress. 'We are now in the morning of our national prosperity, approaching noon...we have to make the momentous choice between brief greatness and longer continued mediocrity,'[13] Jevons wrote. *The Coal Question* was also the first explication of the now famous 'Jevons paradox', that greater efficiency in the exploitation of a commodity generally leads to more demand for that commodity and, consequently, speeds up the pressure on natural resources rather than relieving it. The book horrified parliament and a commission of inquiry was set up. Jevons was looking – much like the IPCC today – at a long horizon, stretching to 1970. British coal production in fact peaked in 1913, considerably earlier than Jevons had imagined and at less than half its expected peak. But was there anything special about Jevons as an economist? Like John Stuart Mill and Adam Smith, he began life as a classical economist and, therefore, as one who viewed land (and natural resources) as finite inputs into the economy. But as Stoll highlights, he was also a born and bred Unitarian who believed firmly in individual conscience and the moral obligation of bequeathing an inheritance to posterity. *The Coal Question* – like many of Jevons's later books – was not unusual for its time in being a work of moral philosophy. In fact, the motivation for writing the book probably sprang more out of

11 Stoll, *Profit*, p. 9.
12 William Stanley. Jevons, *The Coal Question: An Enquiry Concerning the Progress of the Nation and the Probable Exhaustion of Our Coal* 2nd ed. (Macmillan, 1866), https://oll.libertyfund.org/titles/jevons-the-coal-question [Accessed 11/11/2024].
13 Quoted in Stoll, *Profit*, p.119.

a desire to promote social action than from concern about Great Britain's economic leadership.

> The whole structure of our wealth and refined civilisation is built upon a basis of ignorance and pauperism and vice. But we are now under a fearful responsibility that, in the full fruition of the wealth and power which free trade and the lavish use of our resources are conferring upon us, we should not omit any practicable remedy. If we allow this period to pass without far more extensive and systematic exertions than we are now making, *we shall suffer just retribution*.[14]

While we know that there was a lot of moralism around in the mid-Victorian period, it is unusual now for us to be reading this sort of thing from an economist primarily – in this case – concerned with energy efficiency. And that Jevons was able to spark a political debate should give us pause to wonder why it has been that his moral ideas (and ideas like them), which the later proponents of welfare economics built on, have been so out of fashion since the 1970s. Mark Stoll's core interest and expertise as an environmental historian, but also as a historian of religion, is on how social and moral norms have influenced capitalism, technology and nature. In this sense, Jevons is an interesting character to pick on, as he is at once both a classical economist, with all the moral foundation and wider generational concern of Smith, Mill and David Ricardo, but also one of the English founders of the marginal revolution that took place in economics in the mid-19th century and which sought to translate 'political economy', with all its historicism and moral baggage, into a science with mathematical foundations.[15] It is possible that Jevons did as much as anyone, therefore, to shift economics away from moral idioms and interest in distribution and outcomes. Joan Robinson put the shift from classical to neoclassical economics amusingly in her famous *Open letter from a Keynesian to a Marxist*, although it is Alfred Marshall

---

14   Quoted in Stoll, *Profit*, p.124 [emphasis my own].

15   Jevons' first famous book, *A General Mathematical Theory of Political Economy* (1862) was actually published a few years before *The Coal Question*. For a short extract see Jevons in *The Journal of the Royal Statistical Society, London*, vol. XXIX (June 1866): pp. 282-87, Section F of the British Association, 1862, Marxist Archive, https://www.marxists.org/reference/subject/economics/jevons/mathem.htm [Accessed 11/11/2024].

rather than Jevons who comes in for most of the blame for marginalism. Robinson is worth quoting at length:

> [David] Ricardo existed at a particular point when English history was going round a corner so sharply that the progressive and the reactionary positions changed places in a generation. He was just at the corner where the capitalists were about to supersede the old landed aristocracy as the effective ruling class. Ricardo was on the progressive side. His chief pre-occupation was to show that landlords were parasites on society. In doing so he was to some extent the champion of the capitalists. They were part of the productive forces as against the parasites. He was pro-capitalist as against the landlords more than he was pro-worker as against capitalists (with the Iron Law of Wages, it was just too bad for the workers, whatever happened).
>
> Ricardo was followed by two able and well-trained pupils – Marx and Marshall. Meanwhile English history had gone right round the corner, and landlords were not any longer the question. Now it was capitalists. Marx turned Ricardo's argument round this way: Capitalists are very much like landlords. And Marshall turned it round the other way: Landlords are very much like capitalists. Just round the corner in English history you see two bicycles of the very same make – one being ridden off to the left and the other to the right.
>
> [But] Marshall did something much more effective than changing the answer. He changed the question. For Ricardo the Theory of Value was a means of studying the distribution of total output between wages, rent and profit, each considered as a whole. This is a big question. Marshall turned the meaning of Value into a little question: Why does an egg cost more than a cup of tea?[16]

I am not qualified to get into a discussion on the precise relationship between Jevons' and Marshall's work. Marshall was slightly younger and took Jevons' work very seriously. What is interesting is that, in light of Stoll's remarks on Jevons' Unitarian Christianity, both understood themselves to be providing mathematical, non-moral foundations for economies. That is to say, moral

---

16   Mike Beggs, 'Joan Robinson's "Open letter from a Keynesian to a Marxist"', *Jacobin*, https://jacobin.com/2011/07/joan-robinsons-open-letter-from-a-keynesian-to-a-marxist-2 [Accessed 24/10/2024].

philosophy and historicism were not to the fore in their work and nor were questions of value or distribution (which does not mean they were not interested in them, as they both very much were). It is well-known that between 1935 and 1975 the neoclassical variant of economics was practically defunct among policymakers (even though it continued to enjoy a strong following in economics departments, especially in the US). It took the proselytising genius of Milton Friedman and his followers at the University of Chicago to bring neoclassical economics back into political vogue (helped by a large dose of inflation in many Western economies).

But, strangely perhaps, the oil-addicted 1970s was also the decade in which the international environmental movement took on its modern form and the Club of Rome published its very Jevons-inspired book *The Limits to Growth*.[17] Questions that concerned the classicals – land use, distribution, the fate of future generations – came back in a way that had never really concerned even the Keynesians (apart from in a few languid essays about grandchildren by the master[18]). But the newfound interest in and concern about nature took place – in government circles anyway – in an atmosphere absolutely dominated by the idiom of neoclassical economics.[19] In much the same way that Marshall had tried to explain why an egg costs more than a cup of tea, environmental economists now sought to put a price on the degree to which polluters were free riding on environmental services. In parallel to these discussions of negative externalities and carbon prices, neoclassical economics was also being used to design markets that could be used to incentivise individuals (in reality, large financial players) to shift from carbon-emitting to clean sources of energy generation. In this regard, the UK led the way internationally, harnessing the fact that it had been the first major economy to privatise most of its electricity sector in the 1980s, 1990s and 2000s and to 'unbundle' its power sector players (which had

17   See Donella Meadows et al. *The Limits of Growth A Report for the Club of Rome's Project on the Predicament of Mankind* (Universe Books, 1972).

18   Keynes is perhaps most famous for saying that 'in the long run we are all dead'. He meant this as an attack on neoclassicals for promoting the idea of waiting for markets to correct themselves while people suffered the horrible effects of unemployment. But it is, perhaps, fair to suggest that Keynes's work is often geared towards the idea of action in the here-and-now, with his central idea of 'animal spirits' coming from outside the neoclassical school.

19   Richard Nixon and Margaret Thatcher, as conservatives never tire of reminding us, were among the first national leaders (or opposition leaders) to show an interest in environmental policy in a global sense.

previously been vertically integrated) over the same period, even going so far as to privatise the high voltage electricity transmission lines that had first been built by a Conservative government in the 1920s.

It is only by zipping forward a quarter of a century to today that we can really see the capacity of this economic idiom to deliver policies that are even more urgent than they were a decade ago. But we may also see how we have managed to become so tightly constrained by the very idiom that Western liberalism has assumed since the 1970s, and for which Jevons did so much to lay the groundwork. Here again we are introduced to the perverse intricacies of dialectic. The commodifying scientific method which so inspired Jevons now tells us that we *must* change our economies in precisely the way he might have envisioned in *The Coal Question*. Our method of reasoning has to a large degree come full circle. But enough on Jevons. I want now to turn to a much more tangible examination of why neo-classically inspired markets for energy have locked us yet further into what I am suggesting looks a lot like a dialectic. And in shifting the focus, the second of Joan Robinson's riders of the classical bicycle heaves back into view.

Brett Christophers: energy is not a commodity

Marx's understanding of the relationship between capitalism and nature has been the subject of a much-discussed new work.[20] But here is not the place. Instead, I alight on two of his much better known views: (1) that capitalist relations will eventually come to be the fetter on the very technologies they have helped to incubate, grow and generalise and (2) that competition tends to monopoly (a situation in which rents can be charged), owing to the fact that technology ('machines') tends to push profit rates down in the long run (the tendency of the rate of profit to fall).[21] It is from this stepping-off point that Brett Christophers' book *The Price is Wrong*,[22] begins its granular

---

20 Maya Goodfellow, 'A greener Marx? Kohei Saito on connecting communism with the climate crisis', *The Guardian*, 28 February 2023, https://www. theguardian.com/environment/2023/feb/28/a-greener-marx-kohei-saito-on-connecting-communism-with-the-climate-crisis [Accessed 29/6/2024].

21 Inordinate pages of scholarly journals have been dedicated to defending or attempting to refute this Marxian claim which, since the financial crisis of 2008 and the 'secular stagnation' that has set in since, appears to have risen from the dead to haunt business liberals.

22 Christophers is presently an economic geographer and political economist at Uppsala University, Sweden.

investigations of the international energy sector. A particular focus is the track-record of global electricity markets to incentivise the substitution of clean power generation for fossil fuel-based generation.[23]

The central thesis of Christophers' book is that despite (but to some degree because of) the epic falls in the cost of generating a kWh of renewable energy,[24] the profitability of renewable electricity continues to be far lower than that of fossil fuels. This lack of attractiveness to investment funds and other asset managers explains why, despite impressive growth in installed capacity, renewables investment continues to lag behind where it needs to be if governments are to hit the targets set out in the Paris Agreement of 2015.[25] This is the reason why renewables are very unlikely ever to be able to match carbon-intensive technologies without substantial government subsidies in the form of direct grants or guaranteed prices.[26] Over eleven very detailed chapters, Christophers explains why he thinks that this lack of relative profitability cannot be overcome by two of the most common solutions proffered by environmentalists: the reform of planning laws to speed up project timeframes and; reductions in the cost of capital. It is precisely the lack of profitability inherent in intermittent renewables (reliant on the 'free gifts' of wind and sun) that disallows the second option. Furthermore, while planning reform can no doubt help speed up projects, the fact that the cheapest land for electricity generation is distant from the centres of energy demand will always mean that network costs and project land costs will tend to move inversely. 'Should they not foresee profitability, in short, capitalists do not invest.'[27]

This would not matter so much for climate change if it were not for two critical aspects of the political economy: the fact that privatisation, competition and spot markets are the chosen methods of decarbonisation; and the fact that all renewable energy generators today need to compete

---

23 Bretton Christophers, *The Price is Wrong: Why Capitalism Won't Save the Planet* (Verso, 2024).

24 The price of PV modules in the US dropped by around 85 per cent 2010-20. See Christophers, *The Price is Wrong*, p. 123.

25 The scale of the investment needed in renewables in Europe and North America becomes even more stark if China's huge contribution to installed capacity is accounted for.

26 The latter are delivered in the UK via the *Contracts for Difference* scheme set up by the UKs 2010-2015 Coalition government.

27 Christophers, *The Price is Wrong*, p. 136.

with the sunk costs of an already existing fossil fuel infrastructure. This infrastructure allows the fossil fuel supply chain to enjoy the rents generated by its ownership of oil and gas reserves but also to sweat its assets. Most of these are now sunk costs – that is, non-recoverable costs, the debt on which has now been paid off. As Christophers summarises, 'there is no OPEC for electricity'. Nor are there previously state-owned assets that can be acquired at low cost and used either to make markets (in the case of some, older, gas generation) or generate income that looks suspiciously like rents (like the network fees charged by National Grid).[28] And there is a further aspect of spot markets that weighs on the bankability of renewables projects but much less so on those of fossil fuel projects, natural gas especially. As Christophers explains:

> When spot market electricity prices fall, so also, in [liberalised] countries like the UK, do gas prices. In fact, the former fall precisely because the latter fall. The significance of this is that gas – the fuel – is, of course, a gas-fired plant's principal operating cost. Accordingly, banks that finance gas-fired plants can afford to be much more relaxed about price volatility… [Essentially], the use of merit order dispatch and the status of gas as the predominant source of the last unit of dispatched power combine in such a way as to afford a certain symmetry of revenue and cost dynamics for gas-fired generating plants. In the terminology of finance, there is an inherent *hedge*…renewables plants enjoy no such hedge because, of course, there are no fuel costs. The principal cost of running a solar or wind farm in the years following its construction is the cost of servicing the debt raised to finance that construction, and that cost is typically fixed: it remains the same whether the electricity price is £20 per MWh or £200.[29]

Put together, this poses a series of acute challenges for the proponents of marketisation in the electricity sector and would seem to lock us further

---

28 National Grid's operating profit margins in 2022 differed between business segments, with electricity (transmission and system operator) at 19% and gas at 36% in 2021/22. Over the last five years, most recent filings show National Grid plc paid its international shareholders nearly £9 billion (£8,874,000,000) through dividends and buyback schemes. See 'National Grid: Ownership and Key Financial Indicators, *Common Wealth*, January 2023, https://www.common-wealth.org/publications/national-grid-ownership [Accessed 29/10/2024].

29 Christophers, *The Price is Wrong*, pp. 179-180.

into the liberal dialectic we have found ourselves in, namely, the belief that rational markets and the profit motive can save us from the very dangers which they themselves have created. While it is true that renewable power plants can make margins on generating in times of high gas prices, this does not always translate into profits, for the simple reason that gas prices are often higher precisely because renewable generation is reduced and as noted, their fixed costs remain the same. As the then CFO (now CEO) of RWE, Dr Markus Krebber, was reported to have told an earnings call in 2021: '[The] expectation that you can earn excess returns significantly above your cost of capital for decades to come is totally unreasonable.'[30] If these returns are sitting in the 5-8% range, on average, they would represent, probably, under half of what the typical fossil fuel project would be expected to return over the same timeframe. Towards the end of his book, Christophers alights on the work of Karl Polanyi to help explain how liberalism may have got too deep into the woods. Electricity is, in essence, what Polanyi would have called a fictitious commodity (Bentham would have called it a fictitious entity). The difference between a *real* and a *fictitious* entity, according to Christophers' reading of Polanyi is that fictitious entities require particular types of markets to be set up: 'Props, rules, regulations and norms must be fashioned and applied. These serve to make it appear like what exists is a real market, featuring real prices and actors earning real profits. But this is always a fiction…prices and profits in such cases are always as much a matter of external institutional intervention as of supply and demand, and all market actors are party to the collective fiction.'[31]

Dieter Helm on the stewardship of assets

It is to this collective fiction that Sir Dieter Helm also turns his attention in his latest book *Legacy*,[32] arguing that the marketisation and commodification of what are, essentially, public goods has been a mistake. But Helm's analysis is much wider than Christophers', examining a whole range of public goods and natural assets and attempting to offer political, economic solutions.

---

30 'Offshore wind no longer a game with big returns, says RWE, S&P Global: https://www.spglobal.com/marketintelligence/en/news-insights/latest-news-headlines/offshore-wind-no-longer-a-game-with-big-returns-says-rwe-63192180 - quoted by Christophers, *The Price is Wrong*, p. 212.

31 Christophers, *The Price is Wrong*, p. 362.

32 Dieter Helm, *Legacy: How to Build the Sustainable Economy* (Cambridge University Press, 2023).

Helm is very well-known in the world of energy and environment policy in the UK. A Fellow of New College, Oxford, he has tracked the path of the UK's energy policies and market design in a series of books since the 1970s. He was chair of the government's Cost of Energy Review in 2017 and is rightly credited with popularising the idea of Natural Capital, as chair of the Natural Capital Commission from 2015. But, like Christophers, he sees the role of markets in delivering zero marginal costs as highly constrained. There is also a Jevons'-like moral tone to his latest book, as he takes aim both at the neoclassicals and – especially – at the Keynesians for consistently prioritising consumption today over investment in and protection of capital assets. In fact, following one of his mentors, John Hicks, he states that we are now effectively operating on a 'consumption standard'; with politicians unwilling or unable to persuade us to vote for the higher taxes that our expectations for civilisation require of us: 'the political trick is to treat consumption as the target, and then use macroeconomic instruments to meet it in money (rather than in real) terms.'[33]

Helm would like to see us recognise public goods for what they are, while protecting and enhancing our assets for the betterment of the next generation. Importantly, though, he thinks we should move to seeing our assets – including those represented – as being embedded in a system. Of course, the natural capital he is now famous for popularising is the bedrock of this system and this explains why the kinds of regulation common for fictitious commodities are inadequate in an era of climatic change: 'Resilience gets discussed in the silos of each system, with each system's regulator. Who simulates the impact on all the systems of a series of shocks that might happen? Suppose there is a cyber-attack on the electricity grid? How is this taken into account by the water sector and the water regulator?'[34] Helm locates the driving forces behind the marketisation of public goods in the shift towards a consumption today ethic that post-classical economics has fostered. 'Since we are not prepared to vote for the taxes to pay for these public goods, the second best is to introduce user charges and create licences as property rights. Privatisation is part of this second-best approach, and it has accelerated this shift to user charges.'[35] The final three chapters of Helm's book set out political, regulatory and even constitutional ideas for coming

33 Helm, *Legacy*, p. 141.
34 Helm, *Legacy*, p. 126.
35 Helm, *Legacy*, p. 130.

to terms with his prescriptions and making them a reality. They are one of the best attempts I have read to engage properly with the serious situation we are in, from within the culturally-dominant liberal idiom – they could even be described as forming part of a new radical centre.

Conclusion

Mark Stoll, Brett Christophers and Dieter Helm offer the kind of hard looks at reality that liberals need to engage with if they are even to understand the position they are in (and then act decisively). The paths I have charted out of the woods of neoclassicism seem radically at odds with mainstream thinking in Europe, the US and possibly even China.[36] As Helm puts it, 'we need to work out how consumption can fall back to the sustainable level without triggering a major recession.'[37] Alongside this reduction in consumption, we need higher taxes and greater state intervention to foster and secure additional public resources. Where will these resources be directed? As far as I can tell, they need to go (in the UK alone) to building the vast majority of the decarbonised electricity system that British governments are committed to by 2035. It remains underreported just how colossal an engineering undertaking this will be. In the words of engineering firm AtkinsRéalis:

> Our new 2023 analysis is based on a need to deliver 187GW of new generating capacity by 2035, for a total energy system of 260GW. This is to balance supply and demand of an increasingly electrified economy, as laid out in the Government's most recent net zero scenarios. The build rate required between 2023 and 2035 has now increased to 15.5GW/year.[38]

That sum (15.5 GW/year, every year) is enormous, given that (not unimpressive) post-2010 build rates stand at 4-6 GW per year. Looking at these numbers and considering the longer-term history of capitalism (and the

---

36   A contemporary re-statement of this mainstream position, can be found in Larry Fink's op-ed in the *Financial Times*: 'Infrastructure plus pragmatism is the recipe for G7 growth' 28 June 2024, https://www.ft.com/content/1be2aba3-0089-4745-aed3-c4f22707bf43 [Accessed 29/6/2024].

37   Helm, *Legacy*, p. 134.

38   Sarah Long et al., 'Countdown to 2035: can we meet net zero energy system targets?' (January 2024), https://www.atkinsrealis.com/~/media/Files/A/atkinsrealis/download-centre/en/whitepaper/enz-countdown-to-2035-can-we-meet-net-zero-energy-system-targets-whitepaper.pdf [Accessed 28/6/2024].

more recent history of power sector markets), I remain convinced that liberals are stuck in a kind of tortuous mental dialectic, and that moving through it is more likely to be the result of actions taken on the spur of the moment, rather than the result of intellectual clarity or intentional paradigm shifts. But that shouldn't stop us from trying. Quotes from two different kinds of 20th century radical head this chapter. Both, I think, re-thought liberalism for a new world. Of the two, we need to heed Dewey's call not to allow the categories of enlightenment rationalism to calcify into intellectual straightjackets. From Lloyd George, we need to learn how politicians can seize decisive control of an industrial agenda, in part, by not being overawed by experts. But while we mustn't shrink from new ideas (or from re-embracing old ones) neither should we underestimate the difficulty of breaking out of inherited habits of mind. In contemplating our position in relation to nature, there may not have been such a dialectical bind for Jevons, intellectual child of Adam Smith and John Stuart Mill, as there is for us, now the intellectual great-grandchildren of Jevons.

Bibliography

Beggs, Mike. 'Joan Robinson's "Open letter from a Keynesian to a Marxist."' *Jacobin*. https://jacobin.com/2011/07/joan-robinsons-open-letter-from-a-keynesian-to-a-marxist-2 [Accessed 24/10/2024].

Christophers, Bretton. *The Price is Wrong: Why Capitalism Won't Save the Planet*. Verso, 2024.

Common Wealth. 'National Grid: Ownership and Key Financial Indicators, January 2023.' https://www.common-wealth.org/publications/national-grid-ownership [Accessed 29/10/2024].

Dewey, John. *Problems of Men*. New York Philosophical Library, 1946.

Fink, Larry. 'Infrastructure plus pragmatism is the recipe for G7 growth.' *Financial Times*, 28 June 2024. https://www.ft.com/content/1be2aba3-0089-4745-aed3-c4f22707bf43 [Accessed 29/6/2024].

Goodfellow, Maya. 'A greener Marx? Kohei Saito on connecting communism with the climate crisis.' *The Guardian*, 28 February 2023. https://www.theguardian.com/environment/2023/feb/28/a-greener-marx-kohei-saito-on-connecting-communism-with-the-climate-crisis [Accessed 29/6/2024].

Hegel, G.W.F. *Hegel's Logic: Being Part One of The Encyclopaedia of the Philosophical Sciences (1830)*. 3rd ed. Translated by William Wallace.

Oxford University Press.

Helm, Dieter. *Legacy: How to Build the Sustainable Economy.* Cambridge University Press, 2023.

Jevons, William Stanley. *The Coal Question: An Enquiry Concerning the Progress of the Nation and the Probable Exhaustion of Our Coal.* 2nd ed. revised. Macmillan, 1866. https://oll.libertyfund.org/titles/jevons-the-coal-question [Accessed 11/11/2024].

— *The Journal of the Royal Statistical Society, London,* vol. XXIX (June 1866): pp. 282-87. Section F of the British Association, 1862. Marxist Archive: https://www.marxists.org/reference/subject/economics/jevons/mathem.htm [Accessed 11/11/2024].

Long, Sarah, et al. *Countdown to 2035: can we meet net zero energy system targets?*, January 2024. https://www.atkinsrealis.com/~/media/Files/A/atkinsrealis/download-centre/en/whitepaper/enz-countdown-to-2035-can-we-meet-net-zero-energy-system-targets-whitepaper.pdf [Accessed 28/6/2024].

Meadows, Donella, et al. *The Limits of Growth A Report for the Club of Rome's Project on the Predicament of Mankind.* Universe Books, 1972.

Purcell, Hugh. *Lloyd George.* Haus Publishing, 2006.

S&P Global. 'Offshore wind no longer a game with big returns, says RWE.' https://www.spglobal.com/marketintelligence/en/news-insights/latest-news-headlines/offshore-wind-no-longer-a-game-with-big-returns-says-rwe-63192180 [Accessed 29/10/2024].

Stoll, Mark. *Profit: An Environmental History*. Polity Press, 2023.

10

Ending the UK Housing Crisis

Denis Robertson Sullivan

The great liberal politician and thinker William Beveridge identified squalor from bad or no housing as one of the 'five giants' to be slain in the struggle for postwar reconstruction, and by implication, a key roadblock in the path towards a liberal society.[1] Liberals believe the state should foster conditions in which individuals can fulfil their potential and while the current state of housing scarcity persists, that aim will not be reached. The Centre for Cities has reported that Britain has a shortage of 4.3 million homes and the problem has its roots in the 1940s. The road to ending housing need is littered with self-interest, political fear and cowardice. These failures of political judgement have been amplified by poor financial incentives. Those with the money to build houses have been repeatedly risk averse. Why has no government, no matter what its stripe, found solutions? Local authorities, housing associations, house builders and developers are not vocal or tenacious enough about tackling the appalling shortage of housing that blights all the nations of the UK. All are deeply involved in housing, but their interests are not coterminous, so they do not seek common ground or common solutions, but fiercely defend their own positions. These are often opposing forces when it comes to house building. Solving the housing shortage is always seen as someone else's problem, but it is not. We, the taxpayer, carry the costs of not building the necessary affordable homes. The cost of failure in housing policy is met in indirect ways, through strained public services, higher housing subsidies, and avoidable homelessness. Liberals Stephen Ross MP[2] and Lord (Donald) Wade[3] drew

---

1   William Beveridge, *Social Insurance and Allied Services Report, CMD 6404* (HM Government, 1942).
2   HC Deb 18 February 1977, vol. 926 cols. 896-995, https://api.parliament.uk/historic-hansard/volumes/5C/926 [Accessed 7/11/2024].
3   HL Deb 15 July 1977, vol. 385 cols. 1126-79, https://tinyurl.com/23x43hhr [Accessed 7/11/2024].

support from across parliament to put into law the Housing (Homeless Persons) Act 1977,[4] which established throughout the United Kingdom duties on local authorities to help homeless people and those threatened with homelessness. Subsequent housing and homelessness legislation has built on this foundation. At the time this was groundbreaking and, while it has been built upon, more legislation may be needed because the scourge of homelessness is not yet ended. If anything, many of the great social advances of the last century are steadily going into reverse. Liberals must find the solutions that others fear to implement or risk a deeply unequal and illiberal future.

In this chapter I offer some alternatives to such a grim outcome. To avoid a return to Edwardian levels of housing insecurity it will be necessary to reinvigorate both national and local government. We must invest in the tools and resources we already have, particularly housing associations, to address Britain's housing crisis at the roots. At the centre of the discussion there will be a stern repudiation of Margaret Thatcher's vision of an owner-occupier democracy. I defend the view that the goal of housing policy should not be universal owner-occupancy, but [the promotion of] a variety of renting and ownership models that meet the needs of diverse local communities. To realise this commitment to ensure genuine choice in housing, we will have challenge vested interests and both encourage and compel private capital to play a greater role in meeting housing need.

The failures of owner-occupying democracy

Before considering policy prescriptions in some detail, it is first necessary to understand the sources of our current predicament. A now little known Scottish intellectual and Conservative politician named Noel Skelton (1880-1935) first proposed universal home ownership. As James Vitali summarises Skelton's argument: democratic societies in particular require a broad base of property owners to endure. Diffusing property ownership, he [Skelton] argued, would stabilise the relationship between capitalism and democracy, and improve the character and moral qualities of citizens.[5] He called his vision the property-owning democracy. His ideas were taken up by post-

---

4   Housing (Homeless Persons) Act 1977, c. 48, https://www.legislation.gov.uk/ukpga/1977/48/contents/enacted [Accessed 7/11/2024].

5   James Vitali, *The Property Owning Democracy* (Policy Exchange 2023), https://tinyurl.com/3ef5pt8m [Accessed 6/11/2024].

Second World War Conservative Party leaders and they appeared to be the intellectual basis of Mrs Thatcher's dream of an owner-occupying democracy. In its initial stages, the strategy of right to buy appeared to have succeeded in realising Skelton's vision. In the ten years from the passage of the right to buy legislation to Mrs Thatcher's resignation, owner occupation in Britain rose from 55% to 67% of housing tenure. In 2003 the figure stood at a high of 70.9%.[6] But since then, owner occupancy has declined markedly. The latest figure is 65%.[7] Within these numbers it should be observed that 1,313,000 council houses were sold in England and Wales between 1980 and 1990.[8] The policy of right to buy continues in England and Northern Ireland but has been abolished in Scotland and Wales. Given our present conditions of housing scarcity, why should it continue anywhere in the UK? Social housing was sold but not replaced like for like, so the need for it increased. Over the last forty years, Conservative governments have believed that the state should only intervene when there is market failure. But since the right to buy was introduced there has been a growing failure to provide enough affordable housing whether to buy or rent. The market has not come to our rescue and yet governments have refused to act.

Who will build the necessary housing? Local government is frequently hampered from building affordable housing. Housing Associations are not obliged to be developers nor build houses. House builders and developers want guaranteed returns before they will lay a brick. They will never build a wide enough range of houses because there is no such thing as a low-cost house. All house building is expensive because of the ways we have chosen to do it. What Mrs Thatcher's efforts showed is that we will never achieve an owner-occupying democracy, and politicians who espouse this view are deeply misguided. Her successor as prime minister, John Major, listed the sale of council houses and low taxes as examples of the huge amount

6   Brian Lund, *Understanding Housing* (Policy Press, 2017), p. 132.

7   See 'Housing Statistics for Scotland, 2022-23,' Scottish Government, 27 February 2024, https://tinyurl.com/3vrh7npa [Accessed 6/11/2024]. See also 'Dwelling Stock Estimates by Year and Tenure,' Welsh Government, September 2023, https://tinyurl.com/3csmr4ye [Accessed 06/11/2024] and *Subnational Estimates of Dwellings and Households by Tenure – England 2021*, Office for National Statistics, 27 February 2023, https://tinyurl.com/33nv3m4m [Accessed 6/11/2024].

8   Official Housing and Construction Statistics, cited in David Butler and Gareth Butler, *Twentieth-Century British Political Facts 1900-2000* (Palgrave Macmillan, 2005).

achieved by Margaret Thatcher,[9] but, as a former local authority chair of housing, he was aware that a large minority, the poorest, were excluded from benefitting from such policies.[10]

Is there a model that could generate a fully owner-occupying democracy? To achieve this, housing would need to be within the grasp of those at work or earning. The lowest rate of pay in the UK is the government's national minimum wage and national living wage. Crudely, we are looking at earnings in the order of £20,000 a year. Mortgage terms used to be 25 years, but it is not uncommon to see 40 years being offered. Most lenders now will allow 4.5 to 5.5 as a multiplier when calculating maximum borrowing. People on those low rates of pay could perhaps find mortgages of £110,000. But the average house price is of the order of £280,000 (2024 figures) and prices below this average will not be anywhere low enough. So, there is no possibility of anyone earning such rates of pay ever being able to buy a house. It is a mirage or a cruel flight of fancy to keep suggesting that Britain will ever be an owner-occupying democracy.

If we want to make housing within the reach of all, then the government's national minimum wage and national living wage would have to go up to a level that made local house purchases feasible. This would certainly mean a differential living wage across the devolved nations and regions. Whilst a differential rate of a 'London and the rest' divide might be conceivable, raising it anywhere near enough to make house buying possible for the lowest earners seems remote. The minute housing became widely affordable, is the same moment developers and house builders would push up house prices. Worse still, there is a conspiracy of silence about the material benefits that accrue to owner-occupiers in conditions of scarcity. Houses have not only provided homes, but they also have become lucrative investment opportunities. This has drastically exacerbated social inequality, with owners becoming wealthy 'haves' while everyone else (precarious renters) becoming the 'have nots'. It is nothing short of an Orwellian nightmare to perpetrate the lie that owner occupation is good for everyone, and renting is bad.

Renting has always existed and was a perfectly acceptable form of providing a home for families. It is common in Europe, often the chief

---

9   Thomas McMeeking, *The Political Leadership of Prime Minister John Major: A Reassessment Using the Greenstein Model* (Springer International Publishing, 2020), p. 182.
10   John Major, *John Major The Autobiography* (Harper Collins, 1999), p. 204.

means of providing homes. But when Mrs Thatcher acted as a disrupter to the housing market, somehow renting became something poor people did and those who could bought their homes. House values outstripping inflation meant that housing not only became a means of providing a home for your family, it became an investment opportunity, creating wealth most people never had before. Therefore, the benefits of home ownership became magnified by a relentless outstripping of house prices by inflation. With this huge double benefit to be accrued by owning a home, the social divide in our society got wider.[11] The least vocal, least likely to vote, became the least able to find homes. They became second-class citizens, but of course we do not publicly acknowledge this, so there is a conspiracy of silence on the matter of the creation of an under-class.

We should not leave the matter of affordability without considering the most inequitable feature of the British housing landscape, namely the feudal practice of leasehold. While the situation differs in Scotland, leaseholders in England and Wales have been subject to long and expensive contracts, trapping people in often badly maintained properties with no means of adequate redress. We must give leaseholders the right to buy out leases at say five times the annual lease. We should set up local tribunals to arbitrate in cases where leasehold fees have been hiked. Above all, the government should set an absolute ending date for leases, say fifteen years. In the meantime, if flats or properties are found to be unsafe, the burden of repair should fall on the landlord, not those buying their homes in such buildings.

Abolition of feudal leasehold took place in Scotland in the early 2000s,[12] carried out by the first Lib Dem-Labour coalition, in whose formation and policy agenda negotiation I played an active part. Plans to abolish leaseholds in England and Wales were dropped in 2023. If we could do it in Scotland, there is no reason why it should not happen everywhere in the UK. Yet, legislation in the final days of the 2019-24 Conservative government, and the reforms proposed by the 2024 Labour government, only tinker with leaseholds,[13] when abolition is needed.

11   Housing benefit is paid to a majority of social renters. This is a population which not only suffers from a precarious housing situation but also suffers from failing or failed social and economic networks of support and becomes adversely differentially exposed to injury, violence, and death.
12   Abolition of Feudal Tenure etc (Scotland) Act 2000, plus legislation in 2003 and 2004, https://www.legislation.gov.uk/asp/2000/5 [Accessed 7/11/2024].
13   See King's Speech 2024, draft Leasehold and Commonhold Reform Bill, UK Parliament, 17 July 2024, https://tinyurl.com/4upy8k5b [Accessed 7/11/2024].

Market failure

If we wish to improve the present housing landscape, we must confront the hard truth, namely that markets alone cannot solve our present crisis. Tinkering with demand is not a solution. The current housing deficit demonstrates that British capitalism has failed housing. Government consensus over the last 50 years is to let the market provide solutions. The wholesale outsourcing and privatisation of state services is a testament to this philosophy. In accord with this view governments have limited their intervention to when there is a market failure. However, the current chronic and acute need for affordable housing shows there is a market failure. Not enough houses are being built, never mind affordable ones.

Private builders do not build social housing to sell. They build them when obliged to do so by local planning requirements. The only people who build social housing are local authorities and housing associations and they are not building enough. A vile and pernicious byproduct of rising housing need is homelessness. No part of the housing market appears to be functioning properly to meet the needs of our society. After half a century we can say emphatically that Mrs Thatcher's strategy for an owner-occupying democracy has not been achieved. Capitalism has not worked to solve the housing crisis. There therefore needs to be significant government intervention to ensure the acute and chronic housing shortage is resolved. Until that happens, the current crisis will continue indefinitely, maybe forever.

Role of housing associations

There is no one legal definition that covers what a housing association is. Broadly speaking they are defined as non-profit organisations in receipt of public money whose primary purpose is to meet housing need. But there is considerable diversity in their aims and activities. Given that housing associations are major providers of housing in the UK, it remains surprising that there is no common model for their operation. There appears to be no clear guidance or instruction to housing associations as to their role in responding to their tenants' needs. They certainly have not been told explicitly that they have a role in ending homelessness and building affordable homes. Why the lack of standardisation? If there was a common housing association model, then we could all have the assurance that the best use of public money was being made. As currently constituted, they suffer from being too narrowly focused and are highly risk averse. Too few of them are developers. Almost exclusively, only housing associations that are also developers build additional housing. Why is this important? Because housing associations could build more social housing. We desperately need them to be developers. All associations need to be part of the solution to providing affordable rented homes. It would seem obvious that organisations providing homes at social rents should also have a role in building such homes, but apparently not. The plethora of different legal entities only makes for confusion, not clarity or consistency of approach. We must ensure that everyone is focussed on helping to solve the chronic and acute housing need.

One of the great conundrums found between housing associations is why some associations manage to build homes with much less Housing Association Grant (HAG). The government HAG subvention figure across the UK varies widely, with little logic. There is an imperative to ensure the minimum amount of HAG money is used to build houses. There needs to be much greater sharing of best practice and learning. We need to discover why some housing associations only require 10% subvention, whereas other require 50%. Many housing associations hold substantial reserves. Why do housing association need any reserves beyond a few months' cash flow? Few housing associations become bankrupt and those that do are rescued. Where is the government guidance on reserve policy to prevent money being squirrelled away needlessly? There is definitely unused cash that could easily be released to build more houses rather than languish in banks. We might consider that if a social rented property reached a point where it paid off all the money borrowed on it (including the HAG and the upgrades and improvements) then ownership would transfer to any existing tenant. It is not hard to imagine the difficulties that such a proposal would throw up. The question is, would such a property, even free, at this point in its life, be an attractive proposition? So much of today's housing seems to have been built to a price roughly equated to the life of the house. Would anyone in a high-rise flat ever contemplate assuming ownership with the unfortunate history of that type of construction?

In noting the key role of housing associations in tackling the housing shortage, we should consider the wider role of affordable rented homes in building stable, safe and pleasant communities. We now recognise that housing policy is not only about building houses but generating homes in places where everyone can flourish. There is widespread recognition that infrastructure needs are essential to sustaining thriving communities. The present writer is a strong proponent of the ideals underlying the '15 minute' city, with its guiding principles of proximity, diversity, density and ubiquity, which aim to fulfil the basic social functions of living, working, supplying, caring, learning and enjoying. We should also ensure that existing social infrastructures are more fully utilised, making development not only more sustainable but also less homogenous. We must also be mindful of housing quality. The UK governments should immediately introduce housing regulations that insist that all new houses are properly insulated and built to be net carbon neutral or to produce zero emissions. By so doing, we would extend the life of all housing types. This would have the immediate added advantage of making them cheaper to run and socially responsible. It should be intrinsic to development that consideration must also be given to connectivity to reduce excessive car use. Where possible, we should return to building 'garden cities' but updating that concept to embed '15 minute' principles.

The role of local authorities

Government should not only allow, but encourage and incentivise local authorities to be social house builders, even if it is to be through arm's length legal entities. Many local authorities wish to be active in remedying the problem of housing shortage. Any restrictions and shackles preventing them from doing so should be removed. The government needs to enable and encourage local authorities to become lenders of last resort, if the banks and building societies and other sources of money and investment fail to come through for potential homebuyers. This used to happen, and many people took their first steps into home ownership with development corporation or local authority mortgages.[14] It should happen again.

The first call on publicly owned land, (excluding land in public use like schools, hospitals, parks and sports or playing fields), should be for social housing purposes. The land and its value should be used to allow borrowing to build more houses. These houses could be for sale and the sale money received used to build more houses. We should allow the houses that are built to be shared equity, mid-market rent or social rent properties (or a mixture of these elements), while always seeking to avoid monocultures or limited house types.

---

14 Housing Act 1985, s. 435, https://www.legislation.gov.uk/ukpga/1985/68/section/435 [Accessed 7/11/2024].

Local authorities must vigorously enforce on developers the statutory time periods for building to take place before planning consent expires: three years in Scotland,[15] three in England[16] and five in Wales.[17] Provision could be made within this policy to allow the developer to indicate the timescale for completion as well as starting. This will avoid building sites lying empty for years with little or no work on them. If the land is not then built on, there should be public purchase of that land at its current value, not its potential or enhanced value. This would drive down land costs. A reform of the land compensation acts could do this. A commission should be set up to ensure that land banking is not used to circumvent these last two suggestions. There should also be a publicly owned bank, like the UK Infrastructure Bank, to provide finance for house building, so that want of finance would not frustrate grants of planning permission. Alongside these measures, local authorities should identify empty properties for council tax purposes. They should also use this information (or if there were confidentiality issues) to conduct separate surveys of empty properties in their areas. On this basis, they could advise owners that unless the properties are repaired and lived in within a year, the local authority would compulsorily purchase the property. If no owner were found, then after five years, the properties should become the property of the local authority without charge or further liability offered to its previous owner.

City centre regeneration

The above policy proposals are suggestive of the widespread re-use of existing land and housing stock, but we could go much further to meet social needs. We now have the common blight of large former retail shops, often many storeys high, lying empty not for years but for decades. They give the already sad high streets a very neglected air. Why not give local authorities, in partnership with housing associations, the power to step in and buy the properties at a valuation reflecting their current state and not their value arising from public investment? Why not redevelop them for mixed tenures, bought, shared equity, full rent, mid-market rent and social rent properties?

---

15 Town and Country Planning (Scotland) Act 1997, s. 58, https://www. legislation.gov.uk/ukpga/1997/8/section/58 [Accessed 7/11/20234].
16 Town and Country Planning Act 1990, s. 91, https://www.legislation.gov.uk/ ukpga/1990/8/section/91 [Accessed 7/11/2024].
17 Town and Country Planning Act 1990, s. 91.

Manchester city centre, I believe, had only 400 people living in its city centre in the 1960s and now has over 60,000 with a view of growing it to 100,000. There are invariably lots of pre-existing infrastructure to support such growth. Some smaller buildings in city centres would lend themselves to becoming primary schools. We could knock down adjacent dilapidated properties to create playgrounds and green spaces. We must think the unthinkable if the issue of housing supply is ever to be fully resolved. For example, resurrecting the prefabrication of housing off-site, as in other countries. Some of the more innovative work being done by a number of enterprises would allow a dramatic reduction of house completion times. Why not a government call for proposals with timing and costs to build various size houses off site and then proposed installation costs? Let us look anew at what has been done that has actually addressed the issue of housing shortage and has been popular.

Issues of finance and investment

In the last 50 years we have seen the transfer of public money from building houses (a national asset) to supporting people. HAG creates houses, supporting people is part of annual revenue expenditure. Worse still, this public money frequently ends up in landlords' pockets while condemning individuals and families to temporary accommodation. Why this situation has occurred is difficult to fathom. It has crept up on all of us without a proper public debate about the sensible use of public money. There is plenty of money in Britain, but house building does not seem to attract enough of it. Banks are risk averse, yet they are part and parcel of every community where they are allowed to trade and make profits. More pressure needs to be applied to banks to lend for house building, especially social housing, where repayment is virtually guaranteed by the government, albeit indirectly.

Pension funds are in a similar position since they hold a large swathe of the country's savings. They too should be encouraged to see the long-term investment opportunity of social renting, especially mid-market rented properties. House builders themselves are notoriously risk averse. Hence their reluctance to build on brownfield or marginal land. But brownfield sites are often eyesores in towns and depress the community in which they are situated. Special subventions should be made offering direct government support to encourage building on such sites. Where current subventions exist, then clearly, they do not offer enough of an incentive, so they should be reviewed with the intention of increasing the level of support that ensures the house building we all need.

As already noted, builders and developers will only build where they can see a certainty of return. Clearly, we have another market failure, namely the proper development of brownfield sites. The government needs to intervene directly to correct this. It needs to offer generous concessions to house builders to get them to build on such land with exemptions for local restrictions. We should look carefully at what other incentives might be required to kick-start much needed development, especially in our older cities formerly based around heavy industries. To encourage the building of affordable homes, the Scottish government has a charitable bond programme with a private provider. Why can this not be done throughout the UK? Could not housing associations and local authorities cooperate to raise bonds to build houses? Why doesn't the government encourage and support this form of raising finance? Most of the above is dealing with what the government already spends. A truly radical idea would be to raise a corporate social housing tax on businesses above a certain size where there is a need for local housing in the areas where they trade. The tax should be spent building homes only in those specific areas. The opportunities for such a tax must exist in successful places like central London.

The problem of social rent

What bedevils any meaningful discussion on housing and especially social housing is the lack of generally accepted definitions. In particular, there is no guidance about how to arrive at a social rent. John Stuart Mill wrote that: 'It is at once evident that rent is the effect of a monopoly; though the monopoly is a natural one, which may be regulated, which may even be held as a trust for the community generally, but which cannot be prevented from existing.'[18] Even if we were to find a consistent definition of social rent, arriving at an agreement on mid-market rent proves almost impossible to find. There is no equation to guide us. If you cannot measure it, how do you improve or adapt it to circumstances? Ambiguity might arise from ignorance, but it is also politically convenient. If social rent is not well defined, then there is lots of wiggle room concerning its calculation. And

18   John Stuart Mill, *The Principles of Political Economy*, Book 2, Chapter 16, https://cooperative-individualism.org/mill-john-stuart_on-rent-1848.htm [Accessed 7/11/2024].

there is nothing politicians like better than wiggle room. Until we have a shared definition in this area, uncertainty will abound to the benefit of political expediency, but to the manifest detriment of social tenants. A major step forward would be for the government to give guidance on the variables to be considered when arriving at a social rent. This methodology could then be applied across the UK. Once agreement has been reached, it will be possible for the first time to make a proper assessment of the validity of the wide range of social rents currently being charged. Such agreement should also allow the HAG within those social rents to be recovered and re-used to build new houses.

Homelessness

HAG is an expensive intervention to allow social housing to be built to alleviate the chronic and acute housing situation we have, but it is not the only cost to the government. Governments also have to contend with the blight of homelessness. Legislation in each of the four nations of the UK defines both homelessness and the threat of homelessness. These definitions serve as a basis for determining the cases in which local housing authorities have duties to act. The European Federation of National Organisations Working with the Homeless (FEANTSA) advocates for a broad understanding which encompasses rooflessness, houselessness and inadequate and insecure housing. FEANTSA has developed ETHOS (the European Typology on Homelessness and Housing Exclusion) in order to provide a common framework through which to discuss homelessness. It attempts to cover all living situations which amount to homelessness or housing exclusion:

- Rooflessness (people living rough and people in emergency accommodation).
- Houselessness (people in accommodation for the homeless, in women's shelters, in accommodation for migrants, people due to be released from institutions and people receiving long-term support due to homelessness).
- Living in insecure housing (people living in insecure tenancies, under threat of eviction or violence).
- Living in inadequate housing (living in unfit housing, non-conventional dwellings or in situations of extreme overcrowding).[19]

19 'Working Together to End Homelessness in Europe,' FEANTSA, https://tinyurl.com/38y478mx [Accessed 7/11/2024].

In 2022-23, across the UK, local housing authorities decided 353,558 applicant households (including single-person households) met the statutory criteria of homelessness or being at risk of homelessness. This was an increase of 250% over ten years previously. In Scotland, the total was 32,242, an increase of 4%;[20] in Wales, 12,537, an increase of 109%;[21] Northern Ireland, 10,349, a decrease of 1%;[22] and England, 298,430, an increase of 457%.[23] Numbers of rough sleepers are more difficult to ascertain, because data is gathered through irregular or partial counts at different times. With this said, in 2023 in Scotland 1,500 rough sleepers were counted;[24] in Wales in 2023, 167;[25] in Northern Ireland in 2022, 38;[26] and in England in 2023, 3,069.[27] The homeless are disproportionately represented in the prison population. They often experience poorer health than the general population, particularly poorer mental health, resulting in greater demands being placed on the NHS and social work services. Accommodating people in sometimes ruinously expensive short-term accommodation represents a huge cost. If there are children living in such circumstances, their education is often disrupted. This leads to downstream consequences for them and society.

There are of course the hidden homeless, those who are homeless but often do not seek help from the local authority or housing associations because they fear that little or no help would be forthcoming, or what help

20 'Homelessness in Scotland, 2022-23,' Scottish Government, 29 August 2023, https://tinyurl.com/ym93t5kt [Accessed 7/11/2024].
21 Homelessness in Wales 2022-2023, Welsh Government, September 2023, https://tinyurl.com/45nbpyxf [Accessed 7/11/20224].
22 Northern Ireland Homelessness Bulletin January-June 2023, Department for Communities, September 2023: https://tinyurl.com/2s426jea [Accessed 7/11/2024].
23 'Statutory homelessness in England: financial year 2022-2023,' Department for Levelling up, Housing and Communities, 6 November 2023, https://tinyurl.com/76bj7cwn [Accessed 7/11/2024].
24 'Homelessness in Scotland 2022-23.'
25 'Homeless accommodation provision and rough sleeping: August 2023,' Welsh Government, 26 October 2023, https://tinyurl.com/2f5semk7 [Accessed 7/11/2024].
26 '2022 Rough Sleeping Count/Estimates,' in Ending Homelessness Together: Homelessness Strategy 2022-27, Northern Ireland Housing Executive, 2022, https://tinyurl.com/yc67jyhm [Accessed 7/11/2024].
27 2893 people estimated to be sleeping rough on a single night in June 2023- 'Support for people sleeping rough in England, June 2023,' Department for Levelling Up, Housing and Communities, 13 October 2023, https://tinyurl.com/yc487jby [Accessed 7/11/2024].

they would offer would be scarcely better than what they were surviving on already. Counting this group is exceedingly difficult – see above. The suggested figures for them vary widely, perhaps because they think there would be no use trying to seek help, because they hear constantly of the housing crisis and perhaps already know people in similar situations as themselves who could not find proper and adequate solutions. Few in this category ever imagine that they will be able to buy their own homes. The sheer extent of the precarity experienced by the homeless is difficult for those of us living in secure accommodation and with settled lives, to appreciate fully.[28] Given the dynamic nature of homelessness, accurate estimates of prevalence are difficult to capture. The Europeans have made a valiant effort at seeking an adequate and all-embracing definition, but it has proved elusive. Because it is difficult does not mean it should not be pursued. More work needs to be done here. Under the current regime, the hidden homeless are hopeless.

Homelessness, both hidden and visual, is very damaging to the individual or families, with economic consequences for the entire community. Throughout this chapter, I have argued for choice, not simply a policy focus on owner-occupation, which can be an impediment to stable employment. A range of rental options must be available nationwide to allow people choice. Even if we could do everything advocated in this essay, there would always be a need for some proportion of housing to rent. If cities like Paris can set percentages for rented accommodation and owner occupation, then why not let national and regional areas adopt the same idea? Within the rented sector, the range must be such that the entire population in a locality can live in decent houses.

Summing up

I have demonstrated that there is market failure and policy failure in providing housing. There is therefore an obligation to intervene. So, the question is not should governments be involved, but how? I have suggested a few routes they might travel to end this desperate situation. Mrs Thatcher did not create even the foundations of an owner-occupying democracy. Rather, she wilfully damaged social housing that could have contributed to easing the current housing crisis, so ensuring there would be no owner-

---

28　Simon Community Northern Ireland has commissioned work in this area, 2024.

occupying democracy. As in so many areas, politicians have failed, because they are trapped, perhaps willingly, in a political system based on worn out assumptions. If there is not to be universal home ownership, then there also needs to be a clear policy for providing the necessary kinds of homes to rent to ensure that all can have a home. This chapter has endeavoured to suggest how we might spread wealth and opportunity across our entire society, often with highly controversial solutions, but unless we are prepared to accept the current sticking plaster approach has failed, we will not make progress. We need to think the unthinkable on the way to a solution. Housing associations have done a decent job to date, but I hope I have demonstrated that they too need more guidance on how they might offer more help to end the housing crisis. We need to be prepared to make more demands of them and give them the power to respond positively.

Banks and pension funds must be encouraged or forced to invest in social housing much much more than they do. Each of the four nations has (or has had) an ending homelessness strategy. It should be possible to revive or reinvigorate these strategies with more emphasis in setting timetables and targets, with annual publication of progress. If we could harness that goodwill and desire, then what is needed thereafter is our politicians at every level of government to give more weight to the housing crisis and the problems it creates.

Where is the new Nye Bevan (whose responsibilities as minister of health included housing) to deliver that new NHS – National Housing Strategy? Liberals must be the ones to do it. In the confusion and fog of controversy, we must march towards the sound of gunfire,[29] towards, that is, ending homelessness and meeting the housing shortage. To do so, we must face down the forces who oppose us. We will get the job done.

Bibliography

Beveridge, William. *Social Insurance and Allied Services Report,* CMD 6404. HM Government, 1942.

Butler, David, and Gareth Butler. *Twentieth-Century British Political Facts 1900-2000*. Palgrave Macmillan, 2005.

Department for Levelling Up, Housing and Communities. 'Statutory homelessness in England: financial year 2022-2023.' 6 November 2023.

---

29 For the origin of the phrase, see Jo Grimond, Leader's speech, 1963, British Political Speech Archive, https://tinyurl.com/2yk8ekr4 [Accessed 28/11/2024].

https://www.gov.uk/government/statistics/statutory-homelessness-in-england-financial-year-2022-23/ [Accessed 7/11/2024].

— 'Support for people sleeping rough in England, June 2023.' 13 October 2023. https://www.gov.uk/government/publications/support-for-people-sleeping-rough-in-england-june-2023/support-for-people-sleeping-rough-in-england-june-2023 [Accessed 7/11/2024].

FEANTSA. 'ETHOS Typology on Homelessness and Housing Exclusion.' https://www.feantsa.org/en/toolkit/2005/04/01/ethos-typology-on-homelessness-and-housing-exclusion [Accessed 7/11/2024].

Grimond, Jo. 'Leader's Speech 1963.' British Political Speech Archive. http://www.britishpoliticalspeech.org/speech-archive.htm?speech=36 [Accessed 28/11/2024].

HC Deb 18 February 1977, vol. 926, cols. 896-995. https://api.parliament.uk/historic-hansard/volumes/5C/926 [Accessed 7/11/2024].

HL Deb 15 July 1977, vol. 385, cols. 1126-79. https://hansard.parliament.uk/Lords/1977-07-15/debates/d95993db-64cf-4995-b0c0-a7d58325230c/Housing(HomelessPersons)Bill [Accessed 7/11/2024].

'King's Speech 2024.' https://www.gov.uk/government/speeches/the-kings-speech-2024 [Accessed 07/11/2024].

Lund, Brian. *Understanding Housing.* Policy Press, 2017.

Major, John. *John Major The Autobiography.* Harper Collins, 1999.

McMeeking, Thomas. *The Political Leadership of Prime Minister John Major: A Reassessment Using the Greenstein Model.* Springer International Publishing, 2020.

Mill, John Stuart. *The Principles of Political Economy,* Book 2, Chapter 16. https://cooperative-individualism.org/mill-john-stuart_on-rent-1848.htm [Accessed 7/11/2024].

Northern Ireland Department for Communities. *Northern Ireland Homelessness Bulletin January-June 2023*, June 2023. https://www.communities-ni.gov.uk/publications/northern-ireland-homelessness-bulletin-january-june-2023 [Accessed 7/11/2024].

Northern Ireland Housing Executive. '2022 Rough Sleeping Count/Estimates.' In *Ending Homelessness Together: Homelessness Strategy 2022-27, Year 1 Annual Progress Report,* 2022. https://www.nihe.gov.uk/search/redirect-file?aliasPath=%2FDocuments%2FHomeless-Strategy-Reports-2022-2027%2FYear-1-Annual-Progress-Report-2022-2023-(PDF-1-3-M [Accessed 7/11/2024].

Office for National Statistics. *Subnational Estimates of Dwellings and Households by Tenure: England 2021.* https://backup.ons.gov.uk/wp-content/uploads/sites/3/2023/02/Subnational-estimates-of-dwellings-and-households-by-tenure-England-2021.pdf [Accessed 6/11/2024].

Scottish Government. 'Homelessness in Scotland: 2022-23.' https://www.gov.scot/publications/homelessness-in-scotland-2022-23/ [Accessed 7/11/2024].

— 'Housing Statistics for Scotland, 2022-23.' https://www.gov.scot/news/housing-statistics-for-scotland-2022-23/ [Accessed 6/11/2024].

Vitali, James. *The Property Owning Democracy.* Policy Exchange, 2023. https://policyexchange.org.uk/wp-content/uploads/The-Property-Owning-Democracy.pdf [Accessed 6/11/2024].

Welsh Government. 'Dwelling Stock Estimates by Year and Tenure.' September 2023. https://statswales.gov.wales/Catalogue/Housing/Dwelling-Stock-Estimates/dwellingstockestimates-by-year-tenure [Accessed 6/11/2024].

— 'Homeless accommodation provision and rough sleeping, August 2023.' 26 October 2023. https://www.gov.wales/homelessness-accommodation-provision-and-rough-sleeping-august-2023 [Accessed 7/11/2024].

— *Homelessness in Wales 2022-2023.* September 2023. https://www.gov.wales/sites/default/files/statistics-and-research/2023-08/homelessness-april-2022-march-2023-603.pdf [Accessed 7/11/20224].

11

Liberalism and Economic Democracy

Stuart White

Historically there is a current within the liberal tradition in the UK that has had a strong commitment to democratising the workplace and the wider economy. In the 19th century, John Stuart Mill expressed support for schemes of profit-sharing, co-ownership and workers' co-ops. The Liberal Party in the post-war era explored proposals for profit-sharing and codetermination. In the context of the New Lefts of the 1960s and after, some radical liberals, such as those connected to the Union of Liberal Students, declared support for forms of libertarian socialism. John Pardoe, a candidate for the Liberal Party leadership in the 1970s, advocated what he termed a 'post-capitalist' vision of the economy. The confrontation between capitalism and socialism was a central feature of 20th century politics in the UK. Liberal radicalism on the economy was a response to this confrontation. Liberals were under pressure to offer an alternative to capitalism-as-usual and to authoritarian forms of socialism, and also to post-war social democracy. With the triumph of neo-liberalism, however, this radicalism has withered. Contemporary challenges – rising inequality, oligarchic tendencies in politics, climate emergency – now make it urgent to revisit it.[1]

This chapter will therefore set out some key proposals for a contemporary radical liberal agenda for economic democracy, drawing on the ideas I explore in more depth in a forthcoming book, *The Wealth of Freedom*. Central to this agenda are universal basic income; codetermination in corporate governance and the encouragement of worker co-ops; a promotive stance towards trade unionism; and the building of a democratically managed collective investment fund or citizens' wealth fund. In addition to sketching this reform agenda, however, I also wish to raise questions about

---

1 Stuart White, '"Revolutionary Liberalism"? The Philosophy and Politics of Ownership in the Post-War Liberal Party,' *British Politics* vol. 4, no. 2 (2009): pp. 164–187.

political strategy. In concluding – and noting my own current membership of the Green Party of England and Wales – I argue that liberals cannot hope to attain such a vision through a centrist politics that presents itself as a moderate alternative to left and right. Liberal socialism implies not only a *policy agenda* but a distinctive way of *doing politics*. It requires challenging structural inequalities through oppositional popular campaigns and social movements that go well beyond any particular party.

Freedom as non-domination

Freedom is often viewed as the core value of liberalism. But what kind of freedom? The political philosopher Philip Pettit has recently argued that freedom is best understood as the status of 'non-domination'.[2] The core intuition behind this conception of freedom is captured in Jean-Jacques Rousseau's observation that 'the worst thing that can happen to one in the relations between man and man is to find oneself at the mercy of another'.[3] To be unfree is precisely to be 'at the mercy of another'. It is to be in a position, that is, where another party has the power to interfere in your choices at their discretion, a power which you are not able to control so that it tracks your interests. In this sense, to be unfree is to be *dominated*. Freedom, by contrast, consists in the status of not being dominated – of having a status so that another is not empowered to interfere in your choices at their discretion.

For Pettit, non-domination is a specifically *republican* understanding of freedom distinct from, and in opposition to, a *liberal* conception of freedom as non-interference.[4] For the liberal, as Pettit defines liberalism, one is free when nobody interferes in one's choices. This differs from the idea of freedom as non-domination in two ways. First, one can be dominated without experiencing actual interference. If someone has the power to interfere, should they so choose, on terms they decide, then this makes one dominated, and so unfree, even if the powerholder chooses not to interfere. Their power to interfere, as they wish, means that you must always act with their blessing, with a fear of future interference and, perhaps, with an eye

2   See Philip Pettit, *Republicanism: A Theory of Freedom and Government* (Oxford University Press, 1997).

3   Jean-Jacques Rousseau, *Discourse on the Origin of Inequality*, trans. Franklin Philip (Oxford University Press, 1999), p. 70.

4   See Quentin Skinner, *Liberty before Liberalism* (Cambridge University Press, 1998).

on behaving well, by their standards, so as to forestall possible interference. Second, one can experience interference that is not an expression of domination. For example, a red traffic light constitutes interference. But if the traffic light is there as a result of a political process that you have an equal share in and is there for a reason you can understand and endorse, then the interference is not the expression of anyone's power to dominate you. In Pettit's view this interference, because it is not an expression of domination, does not diminish your freedom. While I think Pettit is right to emphasise the importance of freedom understood as non-domination, I think he is mistaken to set up an opposition between republicanism and liberalism around this point.[5]

Take, as an example, Mill's discussion in *On Liberty*, perhaps the canonical liberal text on freedom. In setting out his so-called 'harm principle' Mill is concerned to establish a clear rule for when the democratic state may interfere with individual choice: only when this is necessary to stop people doing things that harm others. However, while the harm principle is a principle to regulate interference this does not mean Mill's concern is only, or even primarily, with interference as distinct from domination. The reason he puts this principle forward is precisely because he is concerned with the underlying unlimited power of interference of the democratic state. The worry, in part, is that people will be nervously looking over their shoulders, afraid that a state with such unlimited power *might* intervene in and penalise their choices, e.g. because a moralistic majority disapproves of what a minority is doing. The harm principle is intended to lift this state of uncertainty, of fear, assuring the individual that they are safe to act however they wish, to initiate 'experiments in living' as they see fit, so long as their actions do not threaten the basic interests of others. This is not to say that Mill's principle is adequate to its objective – but the point is that it is aimed at a problem of domination.

Turning to the workplace and wider economy, while right-wing liberals have seen freedom of contract as sufficient for workers' freedom, socialists and left liberals have pointed out ways in which the background structures

---

5   I also depart from Pettit in not seeing non-domination as freedom to the exclusion of non-interference (or, indeed, conceptions of liberty as the power self-development); and in not seeing social justice as adequately captured by the achievement of non-domination alone. I develop these points in my forthcoming book *The Wealth of Freedom*.

of capitalism expose workers to risks of domination by employers. Here, for example, is Leonard Hobhouse in his 1911 book, *Liberalism*, discussing why laissez-faire is not the basis for working-class freedom:

> Here was the owner of a mill employing five hundred hands. Here was an operative possessed of no alternative means of subsistence seeking employment. Suppose them to bargain as to terms. If the bargain failed, the employer lost one man and had four hundred and ninety-nine to keep his mill going. At worst he might for a day or two, until another operative appeared, have a little difficulty in working a single machine. During the same days the operative might have nothing to eat and might see his children going hungry. Where was the effective liberty in such an arrangement?[6]

The power of the employer in making the employment contract carries over into the terms of the contract itself. Indeed, even when workers have a stronger bargaining position than depicted in Hobhouse's example, the standard capitalist enterprise gives employers power over workers in a number of key areas: in the allocation of tasks between people and directions related to task performance; in determining conditions in the workplace; and in making product and investment choices.[7] Arguably, one major reason why liberals since Mill have been so concerned to democratise the firm is to address the power inequalities that risk domination. There is also a concern that where one class in society controls investment, this gives it a significant, uncontrolled power over others, another source of class domination.

Universal basic income

How might a liberal economics address these risks of domination and so secure freedom? One proposal that is highly relevant to preventing domination in the economy is that for universal basic income (UBI): an income paid to all residents as a periodic cash grant with no conditions in terms of means, work history, or willingness to work. The vulnerability

6   Leonard T. Hobhouse, *Liberalism* (Oxford University Press, 1911:1945), pp. 83-84.

7   See Nien-hê Hsieh, 'Rawlsian Justice and Workplace Republicanism,' *Social Theory and Practice* vol. 31 no. 1, (2005): p. 122. See also Elizabeth Anderson, *Private Government: How Employers Rule Our Lives (and Why We Don't Talk about It)* (Princeton University Press, 2017).

of wage workers to domination by employers is grounded in the fact that most wage workers have to get a job to make ends meet, and in their *basic needs dependency* on employers. This is the point emphasised in the passage from Hobhouse's *Liberalism* above. Payment of a UBI, the argument goes, reduces the extent to which workers are dependent on employers for an income sufficient to satisfy basic needs. The UBI makes it more feasible for workers to refuse job offers or to walk away from jobs and this, so the argument runs, will change the power dynamics at work. Employers will use their power in ways that are more sensitive to workers' wants and needs, diminishing workplace domination. Feminists point out that UBI can also enhance women's financial independence from men in traditionally gendered households and thereby make women better protected from domination in the household.[8] The radical unconditionality of UBI also makes people on low incomes less subject to the power of state bureaucrats who, in conventional welfare systems, often stand in judgment of welfare claimants' continued eligibility for support. In this way, UBI looks like it may be a very productive policy in terms of addressing risks of domination across a range of situations.[9]

Focusing on the labour market, critics might counter that setting a UBI at a level sufficiently high to allow for withdrawal from employment is not feasible in the near future. This will diminish the policy's impact on power relations between workers and employers. I suspect this is correct, but I don't think it tells against UBI as a direction of travel. In picturing a feasible direction of travel, Stewart Lansley helpfully distinguishes between a *guaranteed income floor* and a *guaranteed minimum income*.[10] The former

8   Carole Pateman, 'Democratizing Citizenship: Some Advantages of a Basic Income,' *Politics & Society* vol. 32, no. 1 (2004): pp. 89-105.

9   The argument that the means-tested option is more politically feasible is that the immediate, headline cost of the scheme is lower if the state only needs to cover, roughly speaking, the difference between actual incomes and the guaranteed income threshold. UBI supporters will rightly insist that the true, net cost of a UBI needn't be any different once we factor in the way taxes work to recoup the costs of the upfront UBI payments. But this formal equivalence may underestimate the political challenge of winning support for a policy that channels more income through the tax-transfer system.

10   Stewart Lansley, 'Reforming Benefits: Introducing a Guaranteed Income Floor', in *The Return of the State: Restructuring Britain for the Common Good*, ed. Patrick Allen, Suzanne J. Konzelmann, and Jan Toporowski (Agenda Publishing, 2021), pp. 189-197.

ensures everyone some cash as a UBI, but might be set initially at a level well below that needed to satisfy a standard set of basic needs. The latter ensures everyone an income at a basic needs level – a 'minimum' in that sense. However, this minimum income guarantee might initially be means-tested. Putting the two ideas together: everyone would receive some income as a UBI, and those whose incomes are still below the minimum income threshold would get additional transfers to top up their income to the threshold (which would be phased out as earnings and asset income increase). While this is far from ideal – because of the use of means-testing – it may be more feasible in the short- to medium-run than trying to introduce a UBI at a minimum income threshold. As long as the work conditionality element of the current system is removed or seriously scaled back, such a means-tested guaranteed minimum income would have some of the benefits of a high UBI. Studies of the Mincome experiment in Canada in the 1980s suggest that an income transfer scheme of this kind had significant benefits in terms of better health and increased worker bargaining power.[11] Having set up a scheme with this structure, liberals could then seek over time to raise the guaranteed income floor so that it gradually approaches the minimum income guarantee level, slowly phasing out the means-tested element of the scheme. Some of the funds for the guaranteed income floor could come from a Citizens' Wealth Fund which we will consider below.

Codetermination

Another criticism of UBI as the only or main response to the risk of domination is that by itself it does not directly address the underlying legal structure of authority within a firm. For this reason it seems advisable to combine UBI with direct reform of workplace and corporate governance. This brings us onto some very familiar liberal terrain, that of codetermination and related ideas. In a historical review of post-war Liberal Party policy, I argued that liberals developed an ideal of the firm in the 20th century based on profit-sharing and power-sharing.[12] Profit-sharing, in an historic liberal view, makes a distinction between the cost of capital, and of the pure profit

11   See Evelyn Forget, 'The Town with No Poverty: The Health Effects of a Canadian Guaranteed Income Field Experiment,' *Canadian Public Policy*, vol. 37, no.3 (2011): pp. 283-305. See also David Calnitksy, 'The Employer Response to the Guaranteed Annual Income,' *Socio-Economic Review*, vol. 18, no. 2 (2020): pp. 493-517.
12   White, 'Revolutionary Liberalism,' pp. 164–187.

which is left after deducting all costs from revenues. Liberals held that pure profit should be shared between labour and capital. One interesting variant of this idea, which featured briefly in liberal discussions in the 1960s, is to invest labour's profit share in buying firms' assets so that in time workers become co-owners of firms. (One can imagine schemes of this sort working at the level of individual firms, or across all firms in an industry, or across the entire national economy.)

Alongside proposals for profit-sharing, liberals also supported a restructuring of decision-making structures within firms. Rather than firms being wholly under the authority of representatives of share-holders – shareholder sovereignty – liberals generally argued for labour to have a guaranteed share in governance. Much attention was focused on codetermination arrangements of the kind in other European nations such as the Federal Republic of Germany. Under these arrangements, workplaces are governed through works councils which include representatives of employers and workers' elected representatives. The board responsible for setting overall policy for the firm also consists of representatives of capital owners and workers. Codetermination thus means that the worker has a say in decisions that set the terms of interference in their working life and is thereby more able to ensure that the terms of interference track their wants and needs. This addresses the risk of domination. One gets a hint, at least, of this idea in the language of the 1962 report of the Liberal Party's Industrial Affairs Committee which proposed reform of corporate governance towards codetermination: 'Just as there is a difference between a citizen and a mere subject, so there is a difference between an employee who is simply hired by his company and one who shares, officially and formally, in the ultimate power to determine the company's aims and call its directors to account'.[13] Codetermination has its critics, however. In the German model, workers usually do not have equal representation to capital-owners on firms' governing boards.[14] One review of research into codetermination suggests that there are only 'sparse' non-monetary gains to workers.[15]

---

13   White, 'Revolutionary Liberalism', p. 172.
14   Tom O'Shea, 'Socialist Republicanism', *Political Theory* vol. 48, no. 5 (2020): pp. 548-572.
15   See Simon Jäger, Shakked Noy, Benjamin Schoefer, 'The German Model of Industrial Relations: Balancing Flexibility and Collective Action', *Journal of Economic Perspectives* vol. 36, no. 4 (Fall 2022): pp. 53–80.

In reply, we may note that some of the evidence marshalled in this study does indicate some improvement in terms of job satisfaction and modest but positive effects on working conditions. In addition, existing forms of codetermination are not the only models we can adopt. More radical and apparently worker-empowering possibilities are available. Thomas Piketty has recently proposed a form of codetermination which caps the percentage share of voting rights of shareholders.[16] Isabelle Ferreras has proposed a model of 'bicameralism' which gives owners and workers independent assemblies of representation in firms' governance, with each 'chamber' of the firm's legislature having veto power over the other.[17] In some contexts at least, such as public services, it will also be crucial to include service users in the system of representation as a guard against producer or state domination of service users.[18] Some argue that we ought to go further than codetermination and aim for labour-managed firms or worker co-operatives. There is a long history of liberals, including party leaders such as Jo Grimond and Paddy Ashdown, arguing that the ideal is an economy in which 'labour hires capital' rather than capital hiring labour.[19] Although worker co-ops may not be appropriate in all areas of the economy, they should have a place in addressing workplace domination. Public investment and procurement policy might be used to support the growth of the cooperative sector, such as in the context of a Green New Deal, and as is the case in community wealth-building initiatives.[20] Insofar as a lack of assets acts as a break on the formation of co-ops, there may also be a long-run role here for a citizens' inheritance scheme to ensure that every person starts their working life with a reasonable endowment of capital.[21]

---

16 Thomas Piketty, *Capital and Ideology*, trans. Arthur Goldhammer (Harvard University Press, 2019), pp. 973-974.

17 Isabelle Ferreras, 'Democratizing the Corporation: The Bicameral Firm as a Real Utopia,' *Politics & Society* vol. 51, no. 2 (2023): pp. 188-224.

18 See O'Shea, 'Socialist Republicanism,' pp. 48-572.

19 White, 'Revolutionary Liberalism,' pp. 164–187.

20 See Green New Deal Group (UK), *The Green New Deal: A Bill to Make it Happen*, 2019, https://tinyurl.com/yr3f2e5w and Joe Guinan and Martin O'Neill, *The Case for Community Wealth-Building* (Polity, 2020).

21 See Dane Clouston, 'Spreading Individual Wealth,' *New Outlook* vol. 14, no. 9/10 (1974): pp. 17–19. See also Bruce Ackerman, and Anne Alstott, *The Stakeholder Society* (Yale University Press, 1999) and White, 'Revolutionary Liberalism.'

Trade unions and associative democracy

Alongside UBI and codetermination, trade unions and collective bargaining over wages and conditions offer another important response to the risks of workplace domination. UBI and codetermination are sometimes put forward as alternatives to trade unionism. Alternatively, strong trade unionism is sometimes put forward as an alternative to UBI or to codetermination. But the three are more plausibly seen as complementary parts of an economic ecosystem that offers robust protection against domination. UBI offers a degree of exit power from jobs which means that the individual worker is not reliant solely on trade unions for protection against domination. Codetermination arrangements can be used to support collaborative working with employers, leaving unions free to function in a more contestatory role.[22] The significance of trade unions, however, is not simply to address power inequalities within the individual workplace or firm. In a capitalist society, strong and encompassing unions shift the wider balance of power.

Capitalist democracies are always, in Aristotle's terms, a 'mixed constitution', combining elements of democracy and oligarchy. Capital can and does exercise enormous influence through the resources it offers politicians and bureaucrats, through its ability to influence media narratives, and not least through the private control of investment. Trade unions offer a corrective to all of this, pushing the general balance of the mixed constitution in a more democratic direction. Trade unions can be important here in the resources they mobilise to support political parties which counter the claims of capital. They can help support people to vote. They can support alternative media and offer an alternative source of information and political judgment to a media that is otherwise dominated by oligarchic perspectives. They can promote wider recruitment of the political elite, giving legislatures and governments more cognitive diversity. In these and other ways, unions help to limit class domination in the wider political system. Many have argued that contemporary politics in capitalist democracies has become more oligarchic in recent decades. The decline of unions is a contributory factor to this.[23]

22 Tom Malleson, *After Occupy: Economic Democracy for the 21st Century* (Oxford University Press, 2014).
23 Martin O'Neill and Stuart White, 'Trade Unions and Political Equality,' in *Philosophical Foundations of Labour Law,* ed. Hugh Collins, Gillian Lester and Virginia Mantouvalou (Oxford University Press, 2018), pp. 252-268.

It is crucial to see that this decline was not inevitable. A key insight, developed by associative democrats, is that levels and patterns of trade union organisation reflect political decisions about the legal rules within which people form secondary associations (such as trade unions).[24] For example, if a state allows unions to form but subjects them to the standard requirements of the law, a lot of basic trade union activity, such as strike action, will become effectively illegal.[25] This then discourages union formation. Or imagine that the state requires employers to recognise and bargain with unions if this is supported by more than 50% of workers in a workplace secret ballot (the model established in UK legislation). Much will then depend on the rules about how union representatives and employers can respectively access the workplace to campaign on the issue. These rules can readily be skewed to advantage employers and make unionisation more difficult, an issue that has recently been highlighted in the efforts of the GMB union to unionise workers at the Amazon warehouse in Coventry.[26]

Given the contribution that trade unions can make to limiting class domination at the level of the firm and more widely, liberals should support what I have elsewhere termed as a promotive stance towards trade unionism.[27] This means deliberately setting the rules around trade union formation and action to encourage and empower them. Some right-wing liberals might argue that strong unions create divisions between 'insiders' and 'outsiders': privileged, unionised insider workers against disadvantaged, non-unionised outsiders. Where pay setting arrangements reflect the power of the insiders, this can lock the outsiders into unemployment or push them into jobs that are much worse than the insiders in terms of pay and conditions. This cautionary point underscores, however, precisely why we should support a deliberately promotive stance so as to achieve extensive, encompassing union membership and to help ensure that all groups of workers have access to unions. Indeed, we should consider

24 See Joshua Cohen and Joel Rogers, *Associations and Democracy* (Verso, 1995) and Paul Hirst, *Associative Democracy: New Forms of Economic and Social Governance* (Polity, 1994).

25 G.D.H. Cole, *Guild Socialism Re-Stated* (Allen and Unwin, 1920), p. 140.

26 Richard Partington and Heather Stewart, 'Amazon Workers in Coventry Lose Union Recognition Ballot by Handful of Votes', *The Guardian*, 17 June 2024, https://tinyurl.com/4uu8pxm9 [Accessed 9/10/2024].

27 O'Neill and White, 'Trade Unions and Political Equality', pp. 252-268.

how to move this approach outside of the sector of formal employment to cover the self-employed, unpaid care workers, migrant labour and the unemployed.[28] In many richer capitalist nations deindustrialisation since the 1970s has produced a reduction in trade union coverage and strength. We are paying a high price for this in terms of oligarchic power and, arguably, in the growth of far-right politics. It is time to push back against this and to attack the roots of the far-right through the promotion of trade unionism and related forms of popular association. We do not need state action to make a start on this but, as explained, state policy can make a big difference to the success of our efforts.

Citizens' wealth funds

In 1989, the economist James Meade published *Agathotopia*, a presentation of his vision of a 'liberal socialist' economy.[29] It represented a statement of a view that he had developed over a long intellectual career since the 1930s during which he was, at various points, a student of John Maynard Keynes and an advisor to the Labour, Social Democratic, and Liberal parties. At the centre of his liberal socialist vision was the idea of public ownership. But this was public ownership with a difference. Post-war public ownership typically involved the UK state taking over the control of specific firms and industries and paying compensation for the nationalised assets. Meade's proposal was to develop a publicly-owned asset fund spread across the economy.[30] The state would not seek to control or run specific firms. It would get a return on its widely spread investments.

In *Agathotopia* – the good place – this return would be used to pay a social dividend – a form of UBI (of which Meade was also a long-standing supporter). Let's refer to this as a proposal for a citizens' wealth fund (CWF). Meade's support for a CWF impacted on debates in and around the Liberal Party in the 1980s. Meade envisaged the CWF being built up from firms issuing new shares each year as a small fraction of their existing capital stock.

28 See Iris Marion Young, 'Social Groups in Associative Democracy', in *Associations and Democracy*, ed. Joshua Cohen and Joel Rogers (Verso, 1995), pp. 207-213. See also Judy Fudge, 'Labour as a "Fictive Commodity": Radically Reconceptualizing Labour Law', in *The Idea of Labour Law*, ed. Guy Davidov and Brian Langille (Oxford University Press, 2011), pp. 120-136.

29 James Meade, *Agathotopia: The Economics of Partnership* (University of Aberdeen, 1989).

30 O'Neill and White, 'Trade Unions and Political Equality', pp. 252-268.

The idea was briefly policy of the Social Democratic Party in the run up to the 1987 general election. Paddy Ashdown, the first leader of the Liberal Democrats, revived a version of it in his 1989 book, *Citizens' Britain*.[31] If the idea seems utopian, consider the state of Alaska which provides all of its residents with an annual dividend paid out of the return on a collectively owned investment fund, the Alaska Permanent Fund. Indeed, as Angela Cummine points out in her important book, *Citizens' Wealth*, many nation states have sovereign wealth funds. Cummine argues that the governance of these funds should be democratised and that there is a strong case for distributing some part of the returns on the funds as a social dividend.[32] Stewart Lansley has considered how we might establish a citizens' wealth fund in the UK.[33] Transferring some existing public assets into such a fund and new taxes on corporate profits and on wealth are among the funding options he outlines.

At the time of writing, a new Labour government is proposing a national wealth fund to support its green investment objectives. This does not appear to be a CWF, but there is perhaps an opportunity here for radical liberals to try to develop the policy in that direction.[34] One reason for developing a CWF is that it offers a way to reshape the underlying distributional dynamics of the economy in a positive way. When it starts paying out a social dividend this will not be, initially, anywhere close to what is necessary to meet a standard set of basic needs. But, as Lansley suggests, it can contribute to the guaranteed income floor we discussed above. It can help provide a modest UBI which the rest of the tax-transfer system builds on. As the CWF builds up over time, this UBI can be gradually increased. In this way the CWF can support the project of establishing a UBI to help prevent domination. A second reason for supporting a CWF is that it can help in establishing

31 See Paddy Ashdown, *Citizens' Britain: A Radical Agenda for the 1990s* (Fourth Estate, 1989), pp. 128-129.
32 See Angela Cummine, *Citizens' Wealth: Why (and How) Sovereign Wealth Funds Should be Managed by the People for the People* (Yale University Press, 2016).
33 Stewart Lansley, 'The People's Stake: Inequality and "Asset Redistribution", in *The Return of the State: Restructuring Britain for the Common Good*, ed. Patrick Allen, Suzanne J. Konzelmann, and Jan Toporowski (Agenda Publishing, 2021), pp. 167-175.
34 Steven Schifferes and Stewart Lansley, 'Sell-offs and tax cuts stripped the UK of vital assets. A national wealth fund could turn the tide,' *The Conversation*, 28 June 2024, https://tinyurl.com/yccjbsjt [Accessed 8/10/2024].

more democratic control over investment. Remember, one source of class power in a capitalist society is the control that capital-owners exercise over investment. Democratic publics have to make policy under the shadow of the threat of disinvestment. A CWF, however, might offer a basis for a public investment policy that, while not oblivious to commercial considerations, does take into account wider social values such as environmental protection and social cohesion.

Conclusion: towards a politics of liberal socialism

Imagine an economy that has developed institutions along the lines we have just sketched. Every citizen has a right to a guaranteed minimum income, without work condition, much of which is paid in the form of a UBI. Some of this UBI is funded out of returns on a sizeable CWF, accounting, as Meade envisaged, for some 50% of asset ownership. Individual firms take a plurality of forms. Some are workers co-ops, whose formation is assisted by community wealth-building programmes and by a background scheme of citizens' inheritance, which guarantees every citizen a capital sum at the start of their working life. Other firms are sites of codetermination. Strong unions are available to all employees. Although I have not had space to discuss this aspect, we should assume that universal public services are also part of the picture. A further discussion would also need to consider how this kind of economy could be built in the context of something like a Green New Deal, helping societies address global climate justice. Sounds great to me. But what is the *politics* of building such an economy?

Historically, liberalism has been strong on philosophy and on policy. That is, it has lots of interest to say about core values ('philosophy'). It has also been strong on policy, in proposing ways of advancing these core values. Reflecting this, my discussion above offers – albeit in a very preliminary way – an opening account of a core value (freedom as non-domination) followed by some ambitious institutional prescription (UBI, codetermination, a promotive stance towards trade unions, developing a CWF). This might suggest a view of politics as a kind of moralism mixed with technocracy. Is politics just stating your values and rationally explaining why a given policy is a good way to advance them? If this is one's view of politics, however, then I think it is unlikely to be very effective.

What is missing here is a recognition of structural inequality in contemporary societies and the need to organise with others to challenge and overcome these inequalities. My challenge to liberals – and particularly to those in the Liberal Democrat Party – is whether their model of politics really acknowledges this. A politics adequate to the policy ideas sketched above must be rooted in, and engaged with, social movements that have the capacity and energy to support elected governments that are enacting major reforms. Without this supportive context, politicians will lack the ambition and confidence necessary to take on powerful interests. Absent this social movement support and radical liberal policy proposals, like those I have outlined, risk becoming a kind of 'Sunday best', worn with a certain pride on the right occasion, but largely divorced from the messy reality of weekday, working politics.

Speaking as a former Labour, and now Green Party, member, this perspective does not sit easily with what I perceive as a default setting in liberal/liberal democratic politics – to offer liberalism as a centrist alternative to left and right – rather than one of the radical democratic left. Within British liberalism's history perhaps the Land Campaign of the early 20th century gives some pointer to what is needed. Seeking resources to fund a new welfare state, liberals, notably David Lloyd George as chancellor of the exchequer, looked to the assets of the landed aristocracy as a source of tax revenue. Lloyd George initiated moves to assess land values as a first step to taxing them. In combination with the momentous constitutional reforms to the House of Lords of this period, one can perhaps see here a kind of left populism in which the 'people' were constructed, and appealed to by liberals, as a political constituency in opposition to the aristocratic elite.

Can radical liberals build a left populism for today? What kind of political strategies and alliances, within and well beyond the Liberal Democrat Party will be necessary to bring serious reforms into the frame?

Bibliography

Ackerman, Bruce, and Anne Alstott. *The Stakeholder Society*. Yale University Press, 1999.

Anderson, Elizabeth. *Private Government: How Employers Rule Our Lives (and Why We Don't Talk about It)*. Princeton University Press, 2017.

Ashdown, Paddy. *Citizens' Britain: A Radical Agenda for the 1990s*. Fourth Estate, 1989.

Calnitksy, David. 'The Employer Response to the Guaranteed Annual Income.' *Socio-Economic Review* vol. 18, no. 2 (2020): pp. 493-517.

Clouston, Dane. 'Spreading Individual Wealth.' *New Outlook* vol. 14, no. 9/10 (1974): pp. 17–19.

Cohen, Joshua, and Joel Rogers. *Associations and Democracy.* Verso, 1995.

Cole, G.D.H. *Guild Socialism Re-Stated.* Allen and Unwin, 1920.

Cummine, Angela. *Citizens' Wealth: Why (and How) Sovereign Wealth Funds Should be Managed by the People for the People.* Yale University Press, 2016.

Davala, Sarath, Renan Jhabvala, Souma K. Mehta, and Guy Standing. *Basic Income: A Transformative Policy for India.* Bloomsbury, 2015. https://www.bloomsburycollections.com/monograph?docid=b-9781472593061 [Accessed 9/10/2024].

Ferreras, Isabelle. 'Democratizing the Corporation: The Bicameral Firm as a Real Utopia.' *Politics & Society* vol. 51, no. 2 (2023): pp. 188-224.

Forget, Evelyn. 'The Town with No Poverty: The Health Effects of a Canadian Guaranteed Income Field Experiment.' *Canadian Public Policy* vol. 37, no. 3 (2011): pp. 283-305.

Fudge, Judy. 'Labour as a "Fictive Commodity": Radically Reconceptualizing Labour Law.' In *The Idea of Labour Law.* Edited by Guy Davidov and Brian Langille. Oxford University Press, 2011.

Green New Deal Group (UK), *The Green New Deal – A Bill to Make it Happen*, 2019. https://greennewdealgroup.org/the-green-new-deal-a-bill-to-make-it-happen/ [Accessed 9/10/2024].

Guinan, Joe, and Martin O'Neill. *The Case for Community Wealth-Building.* Polity, 2020.

Hirst, Paul. *Associative Democracy: New Forms of Economic and Social Governance.* Polity, 1994.

Hobhouse, Leonard T. *Liberalism.* Oxford University Press, 1945:1911.

Hsieh, Nien-hê. 'Rawlsian Justice and Workplace Republicanism.' *Social Theory and Practice* vol. 31, no. 1 (2005): pp. 115-142.

Jäger, Simon, Shakked Noy, and Benjamin Schoefer. 'The German Model of Industrial Relations: Balancing Flexibility and Collective Action.' *Journal of Economic Perspectives* vol. 36, no. 4 (Fall 2022): pp. 53-80.

Lansley, Stewart. 'The People's Stake: Inequality and "Asset Redistribution".' In *The Return of the State: Restructuring Britain for the Common Good.* Edited by Patrick Allen, Suzanne Konzelmann and Jan Toporowski. Agenda Publishing 2021.

—   'Reforming Benefits: Introducing a Guaranteed Income Floor.' In *The*

Return of the State: Restructuring Britain for the Common Good. Edited by Patrick Allen, Suzanne J. Konzelmann, and Jan Toporowski. Agenda Publishing, 2021.

Malleson, Tom. *After Occupy: Economic Democracy for the 21st Century.* Oxford University Press, 2014.

Meade, James. *Agathotopia: The Economics of Partnership.* University of Aberdeen, 1989.

Mill, John Stuart. *'On Liberty' and Other Writings.* Edited by Stefan Collini. Cambridge University Press, 2012.

O'Neill, Martin, and Stuart White. 'Trade Unions and Political Equality.' In *Philosophical Foundations of Labour Law.* Edited by Hugh Collins, Gillian Lester and Virginia Mantouvalou. Oxford University Press, 2018.

O'Shea, Tom. 'Socialist Republicanism.' *Political Theory* vol. 48, no. 5 (2020): pp. 548-572.

Pateman, Carole. 'Democratizing Citizenship: Some Advantages of a Basic Income.' *Politics & Society* vol. 32, no. 1 (2004): pp. 89-105.

Partington, Richard, and Heather Stewart. 'Amazon Workers in Coventry Lose Union Recognition Ballot by Handful of Votes.' *The Guardian,* 17 June 2024. https://www.theguardian.com/technology/article/2024/jul/17/amazon-workers-union-recognition-gmb-vote [Accessed 9/10/20224].

Pettit, Philip. *On the People's Terms: A Republican Theory of Democracy.* Cambridge University Press, 2012.

— *Republicanism: A Theory of Freedom and Government.* Oxford University Press, 1997.

Piketty, Thomas. *Capital and Ideology.* Translated by Arthur Goldhammer. Harvard University Press, 2019.

Raventós, Daniel. *Basic Income: The Material Conditions of Freedom.* Pluto, 2007.

Rousseau, Jean-Jacques. *Discourse on the Origin of Inequality.* Translated by Franklin Philip. Oxford University Press, 1999.

Schifferes, Steven, and Stewart Lansley. 'Sell-offs and tax cuts stripped the UK of vital assets. A national wealth fund could turn the tide.' *The Conversation,* 28 June 2024. https://www.city.ac.uk/news-and-events/news/2024/june/sell-offs-tax-cuts-national-wealth-fund [Accessed 8/10/2024].

Skinner, Quentin. *Liberty before Liberalism.* Cambridge University Press, 1998.

White, Stuart. "'Revolutionary Liberalism"? The Philosophy and Politics of Ownership in the Post-War Liberal Party.' *British Politics* vol. 4, no. 2 (2009): pp. 164–187.

— *The Wealth of Freedom: Radical Republican Political Economy.* Oxford University Press, forthcoming.

Young, Iris Marion. 'Social Groups in Associative Democracy.' In *Associations and Democracy* by Joshua Cohen and Joel Rogers. Verso, 1995.

12

Ownership for All

Paul Hindley

Austerity has proven to be a social catastrophe. Successive British governments since 2010 have advanced neoliberal policies that have entrenched social hardship. Food poverty has risen significantly since the first decade of the century. Hundreds of thousands of people have become dependent on handouts from food banks.[1,2] Child poverty has also risen as punitive welfare reforms have taken effect. Viewed in the round, reductions in public services and income transfers to Britain's poorest households have led to worsening health outcomes. A study, led by the Glasgow Centre for Population Health (GCPH) and the University of Glasgow, linked some 335,000 deaths across England, Scotland and Wales to public spending cuts between 2012 and 2019.[3] So extreme were the impacts of these policies that the UN's special rapporteur to the UK, Philip Alston, condemned Britain's austerity programme as an 'ideological project designed to cause pain and misery'.[4] Given the worsening social picture in Britain, will we see an end to austerity policies in the near future? The picture remains contested

---

1   Data from the Trussell Trust shows that between April 2023 and March 2024, 3.1 million emergency food parcels were distributed, over a million of which went to children. Trussell Trust 'End of year stats', https://www.trussell.org.uk/news-and-research/latest-stats/end-of-year-stats [Accessed 26/10/2024].
2   See Mary O'Hara, *Austerity Bites: A Journey to the Sharp End of Cuts in the UK* (Policy Press, 2014).
3   Patrick Butler, 'Over 330,000 excess deaths in Great Britain linked to austerity, finds study', *The Guardian*, 5 October 2022, https://www.theguardian.com/business/2022/oct/05/over-330000-excess-deaths-in-great-britain-linked-to-austerity-finds-study [Accessed 26/10/2024].
4   May Bulman, 'UN tears into Tory-led austerity as "ideological project causing pain and misery" in devastating report on UK poverty crisis,' *The Independent*, 22 May 2019, https://www.independent.co.uk/news/uk/home-news/un-poverty-austerity-uk-universal-credit-report-philip-alston-a8924576.html [Accessed 26/10/2024].

and uncertain. While Britain's young Labour government has signalled its aversion to further fiscal consolidation it has, at the time of writing, yet to fully abandon an austerity mindset. Chancellor Rachel Reeves has demanded spending reductions in key government departments, including in working-age welfare.[5]

Despite Britain's rapidly deteriorating social fabric, the progressive left has so far failed to produce a workable, socially just, alternative to neoliberal austerity. The great social liberal, William Beveridge, pioneered the development of the British welfare state that lay at the heart of post-war social democracy. The principle of universal social insurance was a great advance on the patchwork of municipal and private insurance schemes which preceded it. It established minimum social protection as a right. But Beveridge was a man of his time, who sought to address the giant social evils of the 1940s. Our society is neither as predictably class bound or as culturally homogeneous. Contemporary radical liberals should seek to build upon the achievements of the Beveridge welfare state, but in doing so, offer a distinctive alternative to the austerity and social hardship of neo-liberalism. Even if it were thought desirable, it is impossible to return to the world of statist social democracy that informed the post-war consensus. The trade union movement has been diminished. The traditional working-class political culture of democratic socialism is lacking its former strength.[6] The international Bretton Woods system that sustained post-war Keynesianism is dead and buried, so too are the majority of its policy assumptions.[7] The Washington consensus of the 1980s and 1990s has consigned talk of even modest social democracy to the margins, joined by proletarian revolutions and communist utopias. If so, what's left for the Left? Are progressives doomed to follow the route of minimal change and soulless political triangulation offered by some third way?[8] Are forms of progressive politics

5   Eleni Courea, 'Cabinet ministers contest chancellor's planned cuts to their departments,' *The Guardian*, 16 October 2024, https://www.theguardian.com/uk-news/2024/oct/16/rachel-reeves-tax-rises-spending-cuts-budget [Accessed 26/10/2024].

6   Sidney Webb, 'Historic,' in *Fabian Essays in Socialism* (The Ball Publishing Co., 1911), pp. 4-55.

7   David Harvey, *A Brief History of Neoliberalism* (Oxford University Press, 2007), pp. 10-13.

8   Anthony Giddens, *The Third Way: The Renewal of Social Democracy* (Polity Press, 2000).

to become nothing more than a Mary Poppins' palliative, offering a spoon full of sugar to help the bitter neoliberal medicine go down? The answer is no. Solutions to our present social injustices and avoidable hardships are not found in a fantastical resuscitation of social democracy or in empty centrism, but in the reinvigoration of a radical form of liberalism, one which firmly extends democracy into the economic sphere.

The bare bones of this approach can be found in neglected traditions of property and asset redistribution advocated by the liberal left in the early part of the last century. In 1938, the British Liberal Party adopted an economic platform under the slogan of 'Ownership for All' that aimed to break up concentrations of economic power and spread ownership more widely across society.[9] 'The true remedy for the concentration of property and the evils to which it has led is to spread private ownership as widely as possible.'[10] This was the approach of radical liberals towards the harsh inequalities of ownership in the mid-20th century. The Ownership for All approach was intended to gradually lead to what a later generation of political theorists would call a property-owning democracy. That is, a society in which a minimum level of capital is guaranteed to all citizens, achieved through a fairer distribution of productive assets. As James Meade defined its structure:

> Let us suppose that by the wave of some magic wand... the ownership of property could be equally distributed over all the citizens in the community... Imagine a world in which no citizen owns an excessively large or an unduly small proportion of the total of private property. Each citizen will now be receiving a large part of his income from property. For we are assuming that for society as a whole the proportion of income which accrues from earnings has been greatly reduced by automation.[11]

Meade's property-owning democracy was later adopted by the American social liberal philosopher, John Rawls, as one of two models he believed would satisfy his two principles of justice (the other being liberal socialism).[12]

---

9   Peter Sloman, *The Liberal Party and the Economy, 1929-1964* (Oxford University Press, 2015), pp. 123-124.

10   Elliott Dodds, *Ownership for All* (Liberal Publication Department, 1953), p. 3.

11   James E. Meade, *Efficiency, Equality and the Ownership of Property* (Routledge, 2012), p. 40.

12   John Rawls, *Justice as Fairness: A Restatement* (The Belknap Press of the Harvard University Press, 2003), p. 138.

Rawls contrasts a property-owning democracy with the welfare state capitalism that had become the hallmark of 20th century centre-left labour movements.[13] According to Rawls, a property-owning democracy works to 'disperse the ownership of wealth and capital, and thus to prevent a small part of society from controlling the economy, and indirectly, political life as well'.[14] This would be achieved by 'ensuring the widespread ownership of productive assets' with the aim being to 'put all citizens in a position to manage their own affairs on a footing of a suitable degree of social and economic equality'.[15] Radical liberalism in the realm of the economy stands for both individual economic freedom and social justice, for both an open market economy and the universal redistribution of wealth and assets. True economic liberalism is any approach that advocates for guaranteed capital and asset ownership for all. Therefore, in practice, a radical liberal political economy would represent universal capitalism for the people, alongside the economic means for everyone to participate in the market economy and wider society. Radical liberalism emphasises a bottom-up approach that focuses on placing wealth and asset ownership directly into the hands of individuals. While there would still be the need for the state to facilitate the provision of healthcare, education and other essential public services, the radical liberal state would also be obliged to universalise access to capital and asset ownership. Rather than adopting the social democratic aim of collective equality and social justice as ends in themselves, radical liberalism sees equality and social justice as the means to facilitate the maximum individual freedom. Put another way, whereas social democrats strive for collectivistic means in an effort to secure egalitarian social outcomes, radical liberals adopt egalitarian means in an effort to achieve individualised outcomes.

Radical liberalism and welfare economics

Compared to its ideological competitors, radical liberalism represents a distinctive alternative to both contemporary neoliberalism and traditional Fabian social democracy. While neoliberals affirm the importance of individual ownership of capital as a means of enhancing freedom and dignity, they are largely fatalistic concerning the character of its social

---

13   Rawls, *Justice as Fairness*, pp. 139-140.
14   Rawls, *Justice as Fairness*, p. 139.
15   Rawls, *Justice as Fairness*, p. 139.

distribution. In contrast, while social democrats are attentive to matters of wealth distribution, they are suspicious of private ownership, preferring mediating institutions and cash-transfers as a means of remedying inequality. In a refutation of both approaches, radical liberals concern themselves both with the virtues of private ownership and the importance of just distribution. When applied macro-economically, these preferences are intended to guarantee a much more egalitarian society, where the ownership of basic capital (and the property ownership that would naturally result from it) would be structurally embedded. By combining private ownership with a wide dispersal of wealth, radical liberals seek to inaugurate a new set of social conditions which are fundamentally hostile to the dehumanising dynamics of class-power. Why would anyone accept a job with minimal pay and harsh working conditions, if they had an alternative source of guaranteed income? That is the promise of a radical liberal economy, true economic freedom and the building of a genuine property-owning democracy.

In terms of political economy, enacting this form of radical liberalism would not only represent an alternative to contemporary British capitalism, but an alternative to all forms of capitalism yet advanced at the level of the nation state. By ensuring that everyone is an asset-owning capitalist, as a fundamental human right, it represents an egalitarian model of politics which far surpasses the ambitions of most postwar European socialist and social democratic parties. What is being described here is a capitalist democracy, or rather a democracy of capitalists. It is worth dwelling for a moment on the democratic dimension of such a settlement. If a democracy is a regime which values the voice and dignity of individual citizens, the proposals of Meade and Rawls attempt to secure its fundamental material basis. Everyone would have a right to capital[16] through a basic income or other measures like a universal inheritance. But one should not dismiss the contribution of social democracy too hastily. Any policy of universal ownership should continue to exist alongside a comprehensive social security system that would provide support for vulnerable groups. In addition, there would still need to be strong, decent and universal public services in areas like housing and education. In this way, radical liberals should not strive just to restore

---

16   The term 'right to capital', which is used throughout this chapter, is taken from Stuart White, "'Revolutionary liberalism"? The philosophy and politics of ownership in the post-war Liberal party,' in *British Politics* vol. 4, no. 2 (2009): pp. 164-187.

the traditional welfare state that has been savaged by years of austerity, but also to build a radical welfare society.[17]

Abolishing the precariat

Both neoliberal and socialist forms of economics thrive on class-based competition. Neoliberalism favours wealthy corporate managers and executives, while traditional democratic socialism favours the working class. Radical liberalism seeks to bridge that divide. Karl Marx and Friedrich Engels in the 1840s developed the concept of the proletariat to describe the class of urban labourers that had emerged under industrial capitalism.[18] They stated that the proletariat would inevitably, through class-based revolution, overthrow the bourgeoisie, the ruling class under the capitalist mode of production.[19] In the 1940s, the British Liberal Party was committed to 'abolish the proletariat and make all men owners' through the diffusion of private property throughout society.[20] Radical liberalism therefore sought to invert the class dynamics of Marxism by transforming the working-class into the owners of property. However, the nature of capitalism has changed radically since the mid-20th century. The rise of neoliberalism in the 1980s, de-industrialisation, globalisation and our modern service-based economy have together produced a new social class, the precariat.[21] Guy Standing describes being a member of the precariat as:

> …not just a matter of having insecure employment, of being in jobs of limited duration and with minimal labour protection, although all this is widespread. It is being in a status that offers no sense of career, no sense of secure occupational identity and few, if any, entitlements to the state and enterprise benefits that several generations of those who saw themselves as belonging to the industrial proletariat or the salariat had come to expect as their due.[22]

---

17 A radical liberal approach to workplace democracy is discussed in other chapters of this volume and falls outside the scope of this chapter.
18 Karl Marx and Friedrich Engels, *The Communist Manifesto* (Penguin Books, 2004), pp. 3, 11-13.
19 Marx and Engels, *The Communist Manifesto,* pp. 20, 51-52.
20 R.J. Cruikshank, *The Liberal Party* (Collins, 1948), p. 48.
21 Guy Standing, *The Precariat: The New Dangerous Class* (Bloomsbury Publishing, 2011), pp. 9-11.
22 Standing, *The Precariat,* p. 41.

This has led to some members of the precariat being 'capable of veering to the extreme right or extreme left politically and backing populist demagoguery that plays on their fears or phobias'.[23] This should concern liberals and progressives of all kinds. In a world of rising extreme right-wing populism, from Donald Trump in America to Vladimir Putin in Russia, and a range of fellow travellers across Europe, radical liberals must address the precarity and alienation that is fuelling (in part) the rise of such extremist politics. Precarity gravely inhibits an individual's capacity to maximise their personal freedom to the full, to exercise their rights as citizens effectively and to realise the fullest extent of their personal individuality. Any economy that allows a whole social class to languish in economic precarity can never be truly liberal. It can only at best be partially liberal. Therefore, the ultimate aim of a modern radical liberal economy is the abolition of the precariat, by providing all citizens with basic economic security; ensuring that everyone becomes the owners of property and fundamental capital and that they receive a degree of income and wealth divorced from wage labour.

A rather lazy socialist critique could be levelled at this approach by characterising universal ownership proposals as nothing more than a reheated version of Margaret Thatcher's shareholders' democracy. Nothing could be further from the truth, however. A radical liberal economy is one steeped in social justice, equitable distribution and universality of essential services. Thatcherism, despite its populist rhetoric, was fundamentally oligarchic in both instinct and practice. Neoliberalism represents capitalist ownership for the few, radical liberalism represents guaranteed universal capitalist ownership for everyone. It is no dictatorship of the bourgeoisie. It would be more accurate to describe it as a democracy of universal capital and asset owners, through which, true emancipation for the working classes would be realised. Equally, a right-libertarian could critique the radical liberal approach to welfare as merely an exercise in socialist apologism. While it is certainly true that a radical liberal economy would include far more state intervention than any right-libertarian could reasonably tolerate, it does not represent top-down Fabianism or any such state-socialist equivalent. It assumes as axiomatic a bottom-up approach to political economy. It is a mode of politics which believes in placing wealth, power, opportunity and ownership into the hands of as many people as possible. What more dynamic marketplace could there be?

23 Standing, *The Precariat,* p. 6.

Repairing the safety net

Having given a broad outline of the radical liberal approach to welfare, in this section, I outline urgent policy action that needs to be taken in order to repair the social safety net. The culture of welfare reform and austerity has led to a welfare state notable for its glaring gaps in provision and its increasingly punitive character. In such a system, claimants face ever higher levels of scrutiny and means testing. In the short-term, the welfare cuts of the previous Conservative government (in power from 2010-2024) need to be reversed entirely if we wish to make a dent in the rising tide of social need. There is mounting evidence that shows the detrimental impact of the two-child benefit cap. Under this policy, families in receipt of child benefit, universal credit or child tax credit can only claim welfare support for up to two children. This has increased child poverty. Anti-child poverty campaigners, including the former Labour Prime Minister Gordon Brown,[24] have called for the two-child benefit cap to be scrapped. Doing so would lift 250,000 children out of child poverty.[25] Another contentious welfare reform policy from the previous government is the so-called bedroom tax – a policy that abolished the spare room subsidy component of housing benefit support. This has meant that if recipients of housing benefit have a spare room, they are liable to receive less housing benefit or universal credit. The bedroom tax has been a cruel policy that has put thousands at risk of being left homeless. The restoration of the spare room subsidy would strengthen the social safety net markedly.

Overall, Britain's welfare regime has become both draconian and inhumane. One of the most egregious examples of this can be seen in a sanctioning regime attached to Universal Credit and Jobseeker's Allowance. Here, a claimant can risk losing their entitlement to welfare from between one to six months if they fail to meet the terms of their claimant contract. Such penalties leave individuals at risk of food insecurity and destitution. Research has demonstrated that those welfare claimants who are subject to benefit sanctioning 'may face avoidable crises relating to worsening mental and physical health, poverty, hardship, unmanageable debt, insecurity or

---

24 Basit Mahmood, 'Gordon Brown reiterates call for two-child benefit limit to be scrapped,' *Left Foot Forward*, 19 May 2024, https://leftfootforward. org/2024/05/gordon-brown-reiterates-call-for-two-child-benefit-limit-to-be-scrapped/ [Accessed 27/10/2024].
25 Mahmood, 'Gordon Brown.'

eviction'.[26] The welfare sanctions regime is vicious and must be abolished. While these measures only represent policy repairs to a fraction of the welfare safety net impacted by austerity, if implemented, they would have an immediate impact in mitigating levels of poverty. However, merely repairing the holes left by austerity is not sufficient. A new and transformed welfare state is needed, one that universalises economic participation as a fundamental human right and an article of citizenship.

The right to capital

The mark of a true capitalist[27] is being able to gain wealth divorced from work. A capitalist has a right to capital. The problem with the contemporary capitalist economy is that there are not enough capitalists i.e. the owners of capital and productive assets. As G.K. Chesterton remarked 'Too much capitalism does not mean too many capitalists, but too few capitalists.'[28] Capitalist elitism (as embodied under contemporary neoliberalism) needs to be replaced by the capitalist democracy that would result from a radical liberal economy. In a true democracy, every citizen should be in receipt of economic fairness and every citizen should have the ability to participate in the operation of the market economy, should they wish to. One final way to facilitate a right to capital is to ensure a wider distribution of share ownership. This should be achieved by giving all employees of publicly listed companies greater access to share equity, by making those companies issue new shares to their employees alongside their pre-existing wages.

But we could go much further through the implementation of a universal basic income (UBI).[29] The object of such a policy is to lift everyone above the poverty line. In its first instance, a UBI should provide all adults in the UK with at least £100 a week, as an absolute minimum. I am not going to pretend that this would be cheap, it would not be. It would be very expensive and it is these perceived high costs associated which are its greatest stumbling

---

26 Sharon Wright et al., 'Why benefit sanctions are both ineffective and harmful,' LSE, 7 September 2018, https://blogs.lse.ac.uk/politicsandpolicy/benefit-sanctions-are-harmful-and-ineffective/ [Accessed 27/10/2024].

27 The term 'capitalist' dates back to the late 17th century and referred to 'a person who possess and invests in capital assets'. It therefore predates the term 'capitalism' that emerged in the early 19th century. See Matthew Eagleton-Pierce, *Neoliberalism: The Key Concepts* (Routledge, 2016), p. 10.

28 G.K. Chesterton, *Superstition of Divorce* (Chatto & Windus, 1920), p. 1.

29 See Guy Standing, *Basic Income: And How We Can Make It Happen* (Pelican Books, 2017).

block. However, not all of the money put into a UBI will be new public spending – much of the pre-existing social security budget would be rolled into it. However, it is important to emphasise that some additional social security provision would still be needed. Universality is essential for any social welfare policy to gain support and acceptance across society. When advocates of universal basic income are asked 'why should a millionaire receive a universal basic income' by concerned citizens and political opponents alike, they should respond simply that a 'millionaire shouldn't receive it'. However, instead of implementing a divisive and bureaucratic means test, UBI advocates should explain that such income would be taxed back from wealthier citizens. Like many other pre-existing social security benefits, UBI would be treated as part of an individual's taxable income. In accordance with this view, the tax system should be designed so that the top 10% of earners would have all of their UBI taxed back in full.

Should it prove to be politically or financially impossible to implement a universal basic income in the terms just described, then radical liberals should instead strive for the implementation of a guaranteed basic income (GBI).[30] GBI differs from a UBI in the sense that it is not a universal payment handed to everyone. Instead, it is an unconditional payment given to the poorest members of society. This would certainly be easier and more cost effective to implement than a UBI. Its major drawback, however, is related to its narrow focus. Like the old means-tested benefits it would seek to replace, GBI would still leave recipients open to stigma and societal pressure. Hopefully, over time, it would evolve into a UBI as the scheme is gradually expanded to include more and more citizens. While a UBI is, in my view, preferable, a GBI is still a serviceable policy with which to fight deep poverty. In striving for the implementation of a full UBI, radical liberals should not make the perfect the enemy of the good.

Another promising policy in advancing the democratisation of capital is that of a universal inheritance.[31] This is a block capital grant of at least

30   The term guaranteed basic income is used to describe the limited, more targeted, basic income policy of the Liberal Democrats that the party adopted in 2023. Hannah Davenport, 'Liberal Democrats vote for a Guaranteed Basic Income,' *Left Foot Forward*, 18 March 2023, https://leftfootforward.org/2023/03/liberal-democrats-vote-for-a-guaranteed-basic-income/ [Accessed 27/10/2024].

31   Also referred to as a citizens' inheritance. See Stuart White, 'Beginning the world: Liberalism and citizens' inheritance,' in *The Wolves in the Forest: Tackling Inequality in the 21st Century*, ed. Paul Hindley and Gordon Lishman (Social Liberal Forum, 2019).

£10,000 given to all citizens when they reach their early to mid-20s, usually when they reach the age of 25. In 2018, two progressive think tanks, the Institute for Public Policy Research (IPPR)[32] and the Resolution Foundation[33] proposed the introduction of a universal inheritance.[34] The French left-wing economist, Thomas Piketty, has been even more radical in his proposals. He has proposed giving all 25-year-olds a universal inheritance of €120,000 (almost equivalent to £100,000).[35]

One way of funding a universal inheritance is through restructuring inheritance tax. Such an approach is intended to redistribute wealth from the asset-rich older generation to the asset-poor younger generation. In our own society, dominated as it is by the socially deleterious impacts of inflated asset prices, the policy is certainly an attractive one. While £10,000 is a modest amount in comparison with Piketty's proposals, it may be possible to increase the payment over time for future cohorts. A universal inheritance would be a vital tool in the facilitation of intergenerational justice and establishing the right to capital. A third approach, not incompatible with the other two, would be the establishment of a national dividend, paid for through taxation on the country's natural resources. In the United States, Alaska's Permanent Fund pays out an annual social dividend payment to all Alaskan citizens, as their share of the state's annual oil revenue. In 2024, the annual Permanent Fund Dividend amounted to $1,702 (approximately £1,300) for all Alaskan citizens, up from $1,312 (approximately £1,000) in the previous year.[36]

A fourth policy which should naturally commend itself to radical liberals is that of a national wealth fund. Britain's Labour government has already launched a National Wealth Fund to invest in green industries.[37] James

32 Carys Roberts and Mathew Lawrence, *Our Common Wealth: A Citizens' Wealth Fund for the UK* (Institute for Public Policy Research, 2018).

33 George Bangham, *The New Wealth of our Nation: The Case for a Citizen's Inheritance* (Resolution Foundation, 2018).

34 Bangham, *The New Wealth of our Nation*, pp. 5, 29.

35 Thomas Piketty, 'Inheritance for all,' interview by Nikolaos Gavalakis, *IPS*, 31 March 2020, https://www.ips-journal.eu/interviews/inheritance-for-all-4207/ [Accessed 27/10/2024].

36 'Permanent Fund Dividend,' Alaska Department of Revenue, https://pfd.alaska.gov/ [Accessed 27/10/2024].

37 Jim Pickard et al, 'New £7bn National Wealth Fund to start green investment immediately,' *The Financial Times*, 9 July 2024, https://www.ft.com/content/f9134dde-3b10-4022-8899-b012f3b15cbd [Accessed 27/10/2024].

Meade envisioned a sovereign wealth fund, (a citizens' share ownership unit trust) which could be capitalised through the equity generated by a 10% public share of private companies over a given size.[38] Once a sovereign wealth fund has been sufficiently capitalised, politicians will have to decide what to do with the immense wealth accumulated. The global arm of Norway's sovereign wealth fund, the Government Pension Fund Global, is the world's largest sovereign wealth fund, currently valued at over $1.6 trillion (approximately £1.2 trillion).[39] The Norwegian fund invests in companies: it currently owns 1.5% of all the world's stocks covering almost 9,000 companies[40] and acts as a national savings fund for the people of Norway.

The obvious drawback of both the Norwegian and Alaskan funds is that they are both capitalised primarily through oil and gas revenues. Radical liberals should therefore pursue a much greener approach. One option for the UK to consider would be to establish a GB Energy permanent fund. This could be done by merging the National Wealth Fund and Great British Energy. GB Energy[41] could use a large portion of the wealth generated from green energy sales, if the revenue was large enough, to deliver an annual social dividend to all the adults in the UK. These dividend payments would represent their share of their national green energy wealth. The GB Energy permanent fund could also invest in green industries as the National Wealth Fund is already structured to do. A GB Energy permanent fund would do for green energy revenues what the Norwegian and Alaskan funds do for oil and gas revenues. Transforming GB Energy and the National Wealth Fund into a GB energy permanent fund would embed both policy approaches as an integral part of Britain's political culture and make it more difficult for Conservative politicians to abolish and privatise it in the future. Imagine the emancipatory potential that would be delivered through the provision of a universal basic income, a universal inheritance and regular social dividend payments for all citizens. Guaranteed wealth for all, the means to abolish poverty and with it the abolition of the numerous social and societal ills it

---

38   Meade's 'Citizens' Share Ownership Unit Trust' is discussed by Paddy Ashdown in *Citizens' Britain: A Radical Agenda for the 1990s* (Fourth Estate, 1989), pp. 130.

39   'The Fund,' Norges Bank Investment Management, https://www.nbim.no/ [Accessed 27/10/2024].

40   Norges Bank, 'The Fund.'

41   Great British Energy will be a new, publicly owned, clean energy company working with the Department for Energy Security and Net Zero.

generates, would give everyone real genuine economic freedom: freedom from poverty, from social hardship and from social injustice. It would open up hitherto unimaginable, unrealised opportunities for people from the poorest backgrounds, giving everybody, especially the poorest and most vulnerable, the means to realise their full potential.

Taxing wealth more than work

Any discussion about the welfare system (or about public spending in general) is incomplete without a discussion about the nature of the tax system. Too much of the burden of taxation in Britain still falls upon income earners. As radical liberals, we have long held the view that taxes should fall predominantly on those who gain wealth through the receipt of unearned income – those who benefit financially from the cumulation of financial assets such as housing property, land, inheritance and stocks and shares etc. John Stuart Mill spoke out against the accumulation of unearned income resulting from the rent seeking of landowners.[42] The taxation of asset-based wealth must take priority in any radical liberal vision of the economy. There is an urgent need to reform and increase capital gains tax. Why should wealth accrued through capital gains be taxed less than wealth accrued through waged employment? Such an arrangement is both illiberal and immoral.

Here again we should return to the issue of inheritance. It was a Liberal government that first introduced inheritance tax in the form of estate duties in 1894. Despite right-wing conservative agitations to abolish the tax, inheritance tax is one of the most egalitarian forms of taxation as it directly mitigates concentrations of wealth and assets. No liberal society could ever be achieved if wealth and asset ownership was concentrated in the hands of an elite few. If a property-owning democracy is to be achieved, radical liberals need to strive for a radical redistribution of inherited wealth. At the time of writing, inheritance tax stood at 40% on all inherited wealth and assets above the value of £325,000. This amount should be increased to 50% with the threshold being lowered to £200,000. A higher rate of inheritance tax should be introduced on all inherited wealth and assets above £1.8 million which should be taxed at 99%. With such a system of inheritance tax, no one would be able to inherit more than £1 million in wealth and assets, before having almost all of their additional inherited

42 Helen McCabe, *John Stuart Mill, Socialist* (McGill-Queen's University Press, 2021), pp. 72, 240.

wealth taken in tax revenue by the state. It is reasonable that the £200,000 and £1.8 million figure should be raised (to say, £325,000 and £2.5 million respectively, for example) if someone chooses to distribute their wealth and property to their immediate family members and dependants or chooses to donate a large portion of their wealth to charity. This would encourage the holders of larger estates to voluntarily share their wealth and assets more equitably.

Radical liberals since the late 19th century have championed the taxation of land ownership. Land value taxation was pioneered by the American social reformer Henry George.[43] It has inspired British radical liberals ever since. In the 'People's Budget' of the Liberal Chancellor David Lloyd George in 1909, land taxes were introduced, but only lasted for a few years.[44] While I reject the view of single taxers that land value taxation should represent the only form of taxation, I nevertheless believe that the introduction of a land value tax is vital in the construction of a more egalitarian tax system. Land continues to be an important commodity, even in the international economy of the 21st century. Land ownership continues to be a source of great unearned income and radical liberals should seek to tap that source in order to redistribute the proceeds to achieve a fairer society.

Finally, a discussion about taxing wealth more than work would be incomplete without considering the societal implications of both automation and artificial intelligence (AI). Both technologies are already beginning to reshape the world of work. Several neoliberal think tanks, such as the Tony Blair Institute for Global Change, have advocated for the use of AI in the delivery of public services.[45] Such new technologies are at the forefront of the so-called Fourth Industrial Revolution. They have the potential not just to make work easier, but to make the need to employ physical human workers less necessary. A machine, be it physical equipment, a piece of AI software or a combination of the two, does not require the payment of a wage, it will not fall sick, it will not need to take rest breaks or be required to sleep for several hours, and it will not threaten to go on strike. Yes, there will be the initial costs of installing such technology and there will be continual

---

43   Henry George, *Progress and Poverty* (The Modern Library, 1879).
44   Chris Cook, *A Short History of the Liberal Party* (Palgrave Macmillan, 2010), p. 47.
45   Alexander Iosad et al, *Governing in the Age of AI: A New Model to Transform the State* (Tony Blair Institute for Global Change, 2024).

maintenance costs throughout, however in the medium term these costs would pale into insignificance compared to the cost of employing a number of human workers to facilitate the same tasks.

In its initial phase the rollout of automation and artificial intelligence will not result in extreme job scarcity. For the foreseeable future, we still require human intelligence to design such machines and to develop AI software. We still need humans to extract the resources and raw materials needed to manufacture such technologies and we still need human oversight to direct the process. It is possible, over time, that many of these functions could be performed by machines meaning that the human component would be kept to an absolute minimum. These technologies will enhance the productivity of the companies that deploy them and potentially earn those same companies significant amounts of wealth. Policymakers need to consider carefully how to regulate artificial intelligence alongside the best way to rollout intensive automation to maximise its social benefits. They should consider too the best way of structuring company law to guarantee that profits are shared equitably between owners, management and the workforce. If social inequalities prove particularly extreme, radical liberals should support an automation tax, the additional revenue generated should be redistributed throughout society either in the form of a regular social dividend payment (similar to the Alaska Permanent Fund) or through the provision of a universal basic income, whichever is more financially viable.

Conclusion: freedom from precarity as real liberalism

The current political economy in Britain is that of a capitalist economy, not an economy of capitalists, let alone a democracy of capitalists. A radical liberal economy would end the exclusivity and elitism of contemporary neoliberal capitalism by replacing it with genuine egalitarian capitalism for all citizens. Its mission would be to abolish the precariat, to abolish economic insecurity, economic precarity and social injustice. No one should lack the basic means to achieve their personal development and maximise their talents to the full. No one should be at the mercy of social hardship or the exploitative practices of unscrupulous employers. No one should be allowed to languish in poverty due to a lack of access to fundamental capital and asset ownership. It is the aim of a radical liberal economy to solve this by empowering each and every individual within the realm of the economy by ensuring the equitable distribution of capital and assets. Only through universalising access to fundamental capital and asset ownership will the precariat be vanquished. And in so doing, radical liberals would create a true property-owning democracy of capital owners, a society of empowered individuals emancipated from the chains of economic precarity. If progressives desire a radical alternative to neoliberalism, they need not look any further than the economics of radical liberalism.

Bibliography

Alaska Department of Revenue. 'Permanent Fund Dividend.' https://pfd. alaska.gov/ [Accessed 27/10/2024].

Ashdown, Paddy. *Citizens' Britain: A Radical Agenda for the 1990s*. Fourth Estate, 1989.

Bangham, George. *The New Wealth of our Nation: The Case for a Citizen's Inheritance*. Resolution Foundation, 2018.

Bulman, May. 'UN tears into Tory-led austerity as "ideological project causing pain and misery" in devastating report on UK poverty crisis.' *The Independent*, 22 May 2019. https://www.independent.co.uk/news/uk/ home-news/un-poverty-austerity-uk-universal-credit-report-philip-alston-a8924576.html [Accessed 26/10/2024].

Butler, Patrick. 'Over 330,000 excess deaths in Great Britain linked to austerity, finds study.' *The Guardian*, 5 October 2022. https://www. theguardian.com/business/2022/oct/05/over-330000-excess-deaths-in-great-britain-linked-to-austerity-finds-study [Accessed 26/10/2024].

Chesterton, G.K. *The Superstition of Divorce*. Chatto & Windus, 1920.

Cook, Chris. *A Short History of the Liberal Party*. Palgrave Macmillan, 2010.

Courea, Eleni. 'Cabinet ministers contest chancellor's planned cuts to their departments.' *The Guardian*, 16 October 2024. https://www.theguardian. com/uk-news/2024/oct/16/rachel-reeves-tax-rises-spending-cuts-budget [Accessed 26/10/2024].

Cruikshank, R.J. *The Liberal Party*. Collins, 1948.

Davenport, Hannah. 'Liberal Democrats vote for a Guaranteed Basic Income.' *Left Foot Forward*, 18 March 2023. https://leftfootforward.org/2023/03/ liberal-democrats-vote-for-a-guaranteed-basic-income/ [Accessed 27/10/2024].

Dodds, Elliott. *Ownership for All*. Liberal Publication Department, 1953.

Eagleton-Pierce, Matthew. *Neoliberalism: The Key Concepts*. Routledge, 2016.

George, Henry. *Progress and Poverty*. The Modern Library, 1879.

Giddens, Anthony. *The Third Way: The Renewal of Social Democracy*. Polity Press, 2000.

Harvey, David. *A Brief History of Neoliberalism*. Oxford University Press, 2011.

Iosad, Alexander, et al. *Governing in the Age of AI: A New Model to Transform the State*. Tony Blair Institute for Global Change, 2024.

Mahmood, Basit. 'Gordon Brown reiterates call for two-child benefit limit to be scrapped.' *Left Foot Forward*, 19 May 2024. https://leftfootforward. org/2024/05/gordon-brown-reiterates-call-for-two-child-benefit-limit-to-be-scrapped/ [Accessed 27/10/2024].

Marx, Karl, and Friedrich Engels. *The Communist Manifesto*. Penguin Books, 2004.

McCabe, Helen. *John Stuart Mill, Socialist*. McGill-Queen's University Press, 2021.

Meade, James E. *Efficiency, Equality and the Ownership of Property*. Routledge, 2012.

Norges Bank Investment Management. 'The Fund.' https://www.nbim.no/ [Accessed 27/10/2024].

O'Hara, Mary. *Austerity Bites: A Journey to the Sharp End of Cuts in the UK*. Policy Press, 2014.

Pickard, Jim, et al. 'New £7bn National Wealth Fund to start green investment "immediately."' *The Financial Times*, 9 July 2024. https://www.ft.com/content/f9134dde-3b10-4022-8899-b012f3b15cbd [Accessed 27/10/2024].

Piketty, Thomas. 'Inheritance for all.' *IPS*, 31 March 2020. https://www.ips-journal.eu/interviews/inheritance-for-all-4207/ [Accessed 27/10/2024].

Rawls, John. *Justice as Fairness: A Restatement*. The Belknap Press of the Harvard University Press, 2003.

Roberts, Carys, and Mathew Lawrence. *Our Common Wealth: A Citizens' Wealth Fund for the UK*. Institute for Public Policy Research, 2018.

Sloman, Peter. *The Liberal Party and the Economy, 1929-1964*. Oxford University Press, 2015.

Standing, Guy. *Basic Income: And How We Can Make It Happen*. Pelican Books, 2017.

— *The Precariat: The New Dangerous Class*. Bloomsbury Publishing, 2011.

Trussell Trust. 'End of year stats.' https://www.trussell.org.uk/news-and-research/latest-stats/end-of-year-stats [Accessed 26/10/2024].

Webb, Sidney. 'Historic.' In *Fabian Essays in Socialism* by George Bernard Shaw, et al. The Ball Publishing Co., 1911.

White, Stuart, 'Beginning the world: Liberalism and citizens' inheritance.' In *The Wolves in the Forest: Tackling Inequality in the 21st Century* by Paul Hindley and Gordon Lishman. Social Liberal Forum, 2019.

— Revolutionary Liberalism? The philosophy and politics of ownership in the post-war Liberal party.' *British Politics* vol. 4, no. 2 (2009): pp. 164-187.

Wright, Sharon, et al. 'Why benefit sanctions are both ineffective and harmful.' London School of Economics. https://blogs.lse.ac.uk/politicsandpolicy/benefit-sanctions-are-harmful-and-ineffective/ [Accessed 27/10/2024].

13

Community, Diversity and Nonconformity

Gordon Lishman

This chapter addresses some current challenges around the issues of community and conformity in the context of modern liberalism. I start by setting out my stall with the principles I apply in this essay. Liberalism starts with the assertion of the unique value of each precious, distinctive, individual person. Everyone has the right and duty to be themselves. Each has their own conscience and their own morality, their sense of what is right and what is wrong. This commitment to conscience has an important corollary. An individual cannot and must not be subsumed into a category or group. Individual identity is more important than identification solely with one or more groups. Group identities – sex, race, nation, class, sexuality, ability, creed, and others – are part of a person's identity; they do not define or limit the person. Putting someone into a category does not imply a right to direct or diminish the person. The ultimate obscenity is to reduce a person to an object who can be led, manipulated, directed and discarded. Leaders may guide and help – even lead – but they cannot impose or demand the right to be followed. This commitment to autonomy leads quite naturally to the view that human improvement should be an exercise in persuasion. Liberalism hopes, helps and encourages, but does not demand, that a person develops and learns throughout their life to find and fulfil their potential to lead their good life and pursue happiness in their own way.

Liberalism is not about having one's own way; it is about having a way which is one's own. What applies to individuals also applies to society. People develop in the context of communities. Social and political life should require the active consent of everyone who participates. People have the right and duty to make their own choices which are respected by others. They will have a fuller life if they choose to take and share responsibility for moulding and changing their political, social, and physical environments. Communities can be loving, supporting, encouraging, and sharing. They can also be closed, restrictive and dominating, stultifying and harmful to someone's unique identity and potential. Harm is done to the victims of closed communities, sometimes with the passive consent of the victims. Society should challenge that oppression and sometimes the state should intervene to limit its effects and to support and enable a person to be free and find themself as an autonomous person. The state should use its powers to challenge the structural causes of subordination and closed thinking, including patriarchy, groupthink, and propaganda against 'otherness'.

This brings us to another central aspect of liberalism; freedom needs humane and equitable social and economic structures in order to flourish. The life chances of individuals and groups are diminished by deprivation, powerlessness, poverty of aspiration, and economic systems which benefit the privileged and limit equal access to goods and opportunities. An enabling state is a necessary counter to that structural inequality. In all these positions and reflexes there is arguably a single political doctrine, namely a commitment to social and political pluralism. According to this view, there is no one route to the best society or system. The good society is one in which policies, options, models, arguments and systems of government compete in an open marketplace of ideas to convince and persuade. The result is improvement, compromise and positive consent. Pluralism enriches all by the fact of shared participation in the crafting of better outcomes. This sense of politics as inclusive and open-ended practice has radical implications for liberalism, as an identifiable 'ism'. For liberalism ideas are more important than ideologies. Freedom of thought is more important than freedom of speech. Ideology is useful because ideas are connected, and systems of ideas are necessary to help construct coherent societies. However, analysis of contemporary conditions can become outdated and untrue and an ideology which is closed to reality and new ideas can be oppressive and murderous. To counter the deep dangers of closed ideologies, liberals habitually insist that liberalism is never achieved or completed. The marketplace of ideas can never be closed. People in all their complexity, restless individuality and inventiveness can never settle into bovine contentment – nor would we wish it. Isaiah Berlin quoted Kant that 'out of the crooked timber of humanity' arise better social and moral conditions.[1] There isn't a single, clear route to Nirvana.

1   Emmanuel Kant paraphrased in Isaiah Berlin's essay on 'Two Concepts of Liberty' in *Four Essays on Liberty* (Oxford University Press, 1969), p. 170.

The pitfalls of identity

Kindness is what matters, all along, at any age – kindness, the ruling principle of nowhere.[2]

Fifty years ago, I helped run a campaign on gay rights. It succeeded partly because we concentrated on what happened when a person suffered from specific acts of discrimination, how that person felt, and how they were prevented from being themselves and living their own life. The campaign helped a group because we created some understanding of what happened to a person. The outcome benefitted the wider community. It worked because it led to a fellow feeling with a person who was threatened or diminished. Populist and authoritarian politics thrives on the dichotomy of 'us' and 'them'. It is an easy matter to make 'them' the scapegoats for everything that feels wrong. It says that everything would be so much better if 'they' weren't here, or if they would simply keep out of our way and try to be invisible. This narrative says that 'they' are all the same as each other and are identified by a single feature of themselves: their sex, colour, political belief, race, nationality, age, or disability. On the opposite side of the political axis, one finds a stern policing of the in-group: 'we are all identified by a feature of who we are'; our Britishness, whiteness, class, religion, ideology. When we were setting up what is now the UK Equalities & Human Rights Commission, I argued that we should have started from the human rights of every individual and only secondarily address group discrimination. Members of a community can be discriminated against because they are part of a distinct group, but the primary injury is to the person who suffers. We lose sight of that reality when too much of the emphasis is on the group. It makes it easy for the populists and racists when we accept their categories and the way in which they frame the public debate. That's the trap of identity politics.

Just look at the small boats crisis in the United Kingdom and the plight of thousands at the United States southern border. Desperate people, refugees from horror, persecution and threats to their lives, are being made into symbols of groups who can then be presented as a danger. For those who create that false narrative, it's about demonising people who

---

2 Jan Morris, 'Trieste and the Meaning of Nowhere,' quoted in Jay Parini 's *British Writers: Supplement X*, ed. Ian Scott-Kilvert and Jay Parini (Scribner, 2004), p. 187.

are already victims and using them as surrogates for wider issues about race, religion, employment, terrorism or 'wasteful' state spending. In the UK general election campaign of 2024, there was competition about who would be best at excluding people. When you accept the argument that the issue is who is best at practising inhumanity, you have already lost the wider battle.

Liberals are not immune from putting people into categories and behaving as if that determined voting behaviour. That's what 'demographic targeting' means. It involves campaigning as if all one sort or category of people can be put into the same electoral box and will respond to the same electoral arguments or sectional promises. The challenge is to appeal beyond those boxes. Throughout the democratic world, we see the old political categorisations breaking down because most people are no longer part of a large, recognisable class with shared life experience and shared interests. Traditional parties of the centre-left or centre-right no longer reflect the big communities to which they have traditionally appealed. This leaves the path open to parties whose appeal is to a single shared aspect of identity which excludes and demonises others. The true alternative to sectional politics is a party which appeals across divides and is about shared citizenship and responsibility, shared ways of meeting shared needs – a shared social contract, if you like. Crucially, such an inclusive perspective involves open communities which are helped to find their own ways to work together, compromise and address real problems. The challenge for liberals in facing our future is whether we can create a different narrative from that which puts people into opposing, competing, mutually excluding categories. Instead, we must build a story about unity founded in diversity, difference and learning about each other. Both history and economics give good support to the case for that approach.

Pluralism, federalism and the middle ground

What then are the specifics of liberal pluralism? The idea is the opposite of that oxymoron 'liberal purity'. The latter position defines our liberalism as a creed only open to all those who subscribe to a set canon of beliefs. Of course, some ideas are illiberal in themselves, but there are very many people who share some of our beliefs and we should happily work with them to achieve specific outcomes. It would be inconsistent for liberals to argue for an open, democratic society where ideas, policies and actions are developed in open debate, while simultaneously defining liberal beliefs as an exclusive creed. In the UK, that generous approach is necessary today to an extent that hasn't applied for a century. With the fracturing of the traditional two-party system, there is an opportunity to build a new broad-based liberal party, one which appeals beyond the duration of a single manifesto and a narrow definition of 'target markets'. The liberal vision is about the way in which our whole society works and not just about a short-term vision of being in office.

Self-confident liberalism is where we start. We know what we want to achieve and how liberal politics should work. We achieve results by working with others where we agree and making compromises that take us forward. That's why the middle ground of politics is important. The middle ground is where deals are made, compromises are reached, and consensus created about what to do next. Important, long-term change is built on agreement between the wide range of inter-locking decision-making layers in society. The changes made by the Jenkins social reforms of the 1960s and those of the Thatcher era were not simply based on parliamentary majorities; they reflected changes in attitudes and underlying trends of a sort which have occurred throughout history. One of those periods of change is facing us now. We can choose to aim for a leading role for liberalism or we can settle back into, and play the games of, a party system which is obviously on its last legs.

Pluralism and political parties

Some of the liberals I most respect have forged their liberalism in conjunction with their religious beliefs, in one god and one religious system. Their liberalism has been integrated with their religion and both their liberalism and their faith have been fortified by that requirement to think and feel. I have seen and respected it in Catholics, Nonconformists Muslims and Anglicans in my party over the years. Liberalism exists and draws its force from the inter-action between different beliefs and priorities, circumstances and contexts. In each person, it finds its way and emerges as people think, combine and learn from the different elements of their lives. Pluralism is important within parties as well as between them. Tony Greaves and I wrote a booklet in 1987 about the sort of political party of which we wanted to be part. It was called *Democrats or Drones*? The choice reflected a view of how parties work. We said:

What do we mean when we say our Party is a pluralist party? Firstly, we mean that we do not, as a Party, accept the authority of one person or leader or Central Committee, on matters of policy and direction. Secondly, we welcome within our Party, as within society, the sight of people 'organising for power' because that is an essential part of our definition of a free and liberal society… In liberalism, there is no 'One Party' or single text. There is a broad sweep of common ideas on common foundations, but within which different groups have different priorities and different degrees of urgency. Thirdly, as we preach open government, federalism and part-icipation, so we seek to practise it within our Party. We cannot divorce our Party structures and practice from our ideals. This means keeping open a variety of channels of communication and means of access: it leads to diversity, initiatives developing at all levels, and bottom-up structures.[3]

Naturally and rightly, liberals see issues of the possession and application of power as a decisive element in the way societies work. Historically, plural and tolerant societies have been those where power is shared, whether by constitution, geography, the existence of countervailing forces or just tradition. Spain in pre-Reconquista days, Sicily, India, Belgium, Finland, Nigeria, South Africa and Canada are examples – certainly all less than perfect, but much better than the alternatives for the people who live (or lived) there. It was the vision of Nelson Mandela and Mahatma Gandhi. There is an obvious overlap between that list and one of the most important of liberal practical principles, which is federalism. As M.E. Hawkesworth and Maurice Kogan have noted; '[Federalism]…has worked well as a principle to combine diverse interests into one polity and at the same time produce some of the most stable and long-lasting political systems.'[4] It's certainly striking that federal states which share power amongst different regions or states are amongst the most stable democracies. They have their separatist challenges, but it's rare that they succeed and, even when they do, it doesn't usually provoke civil war. Federalism is a crucial barrier to centralisation and autocracy. It may be the most important constraint on Donald Trump as it was to Jair Bolsonaro and still is to Narendra Modi. Northern Ireland

---

3   Tony Greaves and Gordon Lishman, *Democrats or Drones?* (Hebden Bridge, 1987), p. 6.
4   M.E. Hawkesworth and Maurice Kogan, eds., *Encyclopaedia of Government and Politics*, vol. 1 (Routledge, 1992), p. 349.

and Bosnia-Herzogovina still have some way to go, but in both cases power-sharing by legislation provides a necessary starting point. Constitution and law can only go some way to achieving a long-term result and they may collapse as in Lebanon. The success of federalism can depend on social attitudes, the interpretation of history, the appeal of the unscrupulous or power-hungry and outside forces, but, as in Palestine, the development of federal structures may be a necessary first step towards developing a pluralistic and stable form of nationhood.

Closed and open communities

I live in a community where people responded to the distorted logic and caricatures of the European Union by voting for Brexit. It's not very surprising following the decades of failure to communicate a different reality. It's also a place where every day public attitudes have shifted immensely and for the better over the last twenty years on issues around race and gay freedom. There is some liberal failure to value and respect people with less formal education and fewer life chances. It isn't sufficient to show occasional and condescending sympathy with the poor benighted underclass. A 'liberal elitist' cast of mind doesn't only exist amongst those who use it as an insult. In the petty arguments between parties in a more or less free society, we lose sight of the threats to the whole system of liberal democratic, open government. We need to work together across parties and states to protect the most fundamental freedoms of our societies.

Liberals believe in an open society in which people interact and are open to new ideas and engagement with others. We do not feel at home where a state, a religion, an ideology, or an idea of class uses its dominant power to restrict freedom, access to new ideas and information, or the right to challenge and be different. The growth of inward-looking communities, referring to their group's norms and values to understand everything, is a threat to a free and open society. Such groups create their own moralities, insulated from the rest of the world and sometimes from reality. One unexpected and unintended consequence of the internet is the echo chambers where every member supports and learns the prejudices of other members, free from unwelcome facts, analysis and challenge. They harm each other and stunt moral and personal growth. They may also act on their prejudices in ways which cause direct harm to others. That creates challenges for education, already harmed and undermined in many countries by control of curricula to reinforce government and majority norms and prejudices. The concept of a 'liberal education' has never been more important. It is becoming ever more difficult to differentiate between alternative facts and analysis, sometimes presented with spurious authority.

The concept of 'consent to be indoctrinated' is a difficult one for liberals, although less so when the victim is a child who doesn't have the power actively to consent or to discriminate between options. It needs to be addressed throughout life but is most important when young people are learning to navigate their way through a world of multiplying choices. The emphasis on learning facts and skills is insignificant compared with the central importance of enabling active, autonomous citizens who have the power and ability to make the choices that are right for them. The sources of hate and misinformation are difficult to control in a globalised world. The answer involves liberal societies and liberal governments investing much more and better in countering arguments and calling out those who are misguided or deliberately malevolent. Difficult as it is for a liberal to write these words, it may also have to include regulation. To paraphrase Martin Luther King, regulation cannot change a heart, but it can restrain the heartless from spreading poison and creating divisions between people. Another answer, difficult to implement by liberals with other ways of spending their time, is to engage consistently as an overt liberal, with liberal arguments aimed at the ordinary citizens who can be influenced. It is easy to retreat into groups of like-minded and (more or less) tolerant liberals, but that cedes the ground to the intolerant and prejudiced in the battle to influence the mass of ordinary people. If we make a stand, we suffer from the keyboard warriors and we are unlikely to convert many of them. But we can influence the millions of people who read but don't engage – partly by making it clear that there are alternative, liberal visions of a better world.

Conforming, nonconforming, and nonconformism

The preambles to the UK Liberal Party and Liberal Democrat constitutions read, 'none shall be enslaved by poverty, ignorance or conformity'. However, conforming has its advantages. Every community and society has its working rules and norms for getting by. Politeness oils the wheels of social interaction. It's unhelpful to flout those conventions unless there's clear and sufficient reason. The problem comes when shared norms of behaviour are insisted upon, informally policed, or legislated. 'Common decency' applied to politicians in their professional lives is a useful concept. It is reasonable to expect honourable members to behave honourably. When applied, say, to breastfeeding in public, expressions of gay affection, or wearing a burqa, it is oppressive and wrong. The first principle of community politics is 'start from where people are' rather than where you are. If you simply reject or scorn someone's opinion, that's unlikely to engage their heart or brain with a different perspective.

Enslavement by conformity can apply in liberal communities as in others. At its worst, it can look like contempt for the honestly held views and feelings of others. I like and feel at home with my liberal prejudices, but I shouldn't expect or insist that others share them. One of my least favourite forms of conformity is when liberals insist on other liberals conforming with their opinions and norms. There are of course boundaries to what is acceptable in a liberal party and liberal debate, but they are set widely. Challenging a liberal dogma (a contradiction in terms if ever I heard one) is welcome even if, in my opinion, the challenge is wrong. That particularly applies when debate is fouled and foiled by the attribution of motives. At the very least, it is not acceptable amongst liberals to refuse to engage with another liberal (or anyone else) without accepting their right to explain motives or even to have different ones from their interlocutor. One phrase which raises my hackles is 'What you really mean is…' A good rule of debate is to respect what people say about their own motives and intentions rather than refusing to engage because you have defined what they 'really mean'.

'Wokeism' is an interesting example of the working of liberal prejudices. In fact, the concept is a deliberate and fundamentally dishonest trap. The way the trap works is to create a caricature of liberal belief by finding occasional and outlandish examples. That provokes liberals to argue back and defend those examples. This is then taken as evidence – proof even – of liberal adherence to an extreme caricature. In reality, our opinions are not defined at all by these extreme examples. Why do liberals insist on fighting those battles on our opponents' terms rather than asserting core liberal beliefs? Historically, liberalism has often been a response to insistence on conformity with religious beliefs and dogma. The refusal to conform with a belief system that is oppressive to people with different beliefs isn't liberal in itself; it can be adherence to a different sort of conformity which can be oppressive. Salem was a nonconformist society. Religious or nationalist beliefs can arise from closed or conformist opposition from the point of view of different religions or nationalities. Nonconformism can simply be saying, 'my morality and conformity, not yours'.

Reason, rationalism and rationalisation

Liberals like to appeal to reason. It's certainly better than unreason. On the other hand, thinking is more than reasoning logically. Thinking includes feelings, sensations and openness to others' thinking and feelings as well as the narrow path of logic. Difficult medical diagnosis is an example of where reason needs to be applied, but along with all the other senses. In politics as well as medicine, reason is a better tool than a crutch. Great breakthroughs in scientific thinking emerge from a moment of inspiration or insight or luck which sets reasoning onto a new course. Think of Einstein or Newton or Darwin or Fleming. Liberals sometimes use reason as a battering ram rather than as a means of persuasion and can be affronted and unsympathetic when someone else doesn't share their premises, logical process, and (to them obvious) outcomes. Even if someone is wrong, you are more likely to persuade them if you start from their thinking rather than imposing your own. It's easy to confuse reason with rationalisation.

The internet and Wikipedia encourage people to look for arguments which support their current conclusions. I am disappointed when people only refer to books and writers with whom they agree. Those writers consider and dismiss any alternative approaches; it might be better to read the original or at least check it. I prefer the occasional writer like Amartya Sen on Rawls, who is respectful and thoughtful in their disagreement. I have learned from Marx, despite agreeing with Popper's central argument against Marxism.[5] Along with views on diagnosis, I learned from my father about Ockham's razor, the philosophical principle that, when faced with apparently equal choices, go for the simplest.[6] Of course, complicated problems sometimes need complicated solutions, but even then, it's a good idea to refer back to core principles when making policy choices. Morality is a crucial part of political choice. Portentously Lord Shaftesbury once opined that, 'What is morally wrong can never be politically right.'[7] If 'Blairism' in government meant anything at all

5   See for instance, Karl Popper, *The Open Society and Its Enemies, vol. 2: Hegel and Marx* (Routledge, 2002).

6   Interestingly, Karl Popper denies the validity of Ockham's Razor on the basis that there is no objective criterion for logical simplicity.

7   Quoted in John Beeson, *John Wesley and the American Frontier* (Xulon Press, 2007), p. 184.

(a questionable assumption), it was about finding technical and politically acceptable answers to big problems. We are fortunate that Gordon Brown was there to give some grounding in ideas and direction. The civil service can work out the technicalities and they are good at it. What they need is clear political direction and goals and that's what ministers are for.

Liberalism in politics: concluding thoughts

I speak the truth not so much as I would, but as much as I dare, and a dare a little more as I get older.[8]

I wrote above about closed communities. Their growth has been assisted by the decline of civic culture. At its best civic cultures offer open, vibrant centres of belonging in which people engage with each other in a host of different overlapping activities, from church groups, unions and political parties to women's groups, bowling leagues and town hall meetings. The Lancashire village in which I grew up felt very much like that. In building the idea of liberal community politics in the 1970s, we built on that experience with ideas about community engagement, campaigns and participation. Unfortunately, that period coincided with the precipitous shrinking of civic culture and many of the organisations that sustained it. Robert Putnam has been the US chronicler of that deterioration.[9]

The decline of party-political loyalties and membership meant that there simply weren't the people to engage in those debates. And that's even if there had been the clarity about differences of policy to spark and sustain important discussions. Nowadays, when the divisions are becoming much clearer – even if the structure of parties doesn't well reflect them – we don't have the fora and institutions for constructive engagement, even if modern styles of debate, honed on Facebook, allowed it. Schools are discouraged and even prevented from serious debate and discussion. Class boundaries have been breaking down. Much of the growth in the self-identifying working class in the UK has come from people to whom the phrase could not reasonably be applied on any objective grounds. When we have built new estates, even new towns, there has been a crushing failure to invest

---

8   Michel de Montaigne, 'Of Conscience,' in *The Essays of Michael Seigneur de Montaigne*, trans. Charles Cotton (Alex Murray & Son, 1870), p. 490.
9   See in particular Robert Putnam, *Bowling Alone: The Collapse and Revival of American Community* (Simon & Schuster, 2001).

in community development, community institutions and community engagement. There have been a few successes, but more failures. The UK's present Labour government is set massively to increase the number of new homes including, if the secretary of state is to be believed, much social housing. I see little sign of parallel investment in community building, community cohesion, community power and participation. There seems even less commitment to investing in making old houses fit for living in.

The most fundamental fact about politics is this: politics isn't about political systems, governments, parties and elections. Those things are all means to an end. The true definition of politics is about how people and communities decide things: priorities, spending, and mutual help; how to construct the society in which we live; how to share the responsibility for looking after fellow citizens when they need it; how to create new citizens, aware of their world and how to mould and live in it; how to address the challenges of climate change and so on. No party possesses the answer to all these challenges, and few are fully honest about the choices that have to be addressed. To paraphrase Thomas Jefferson, 'An enlightened citizenry is indispensable for the proper functioning of a republic.'[10] Enlightenment in that context is partly about education. It's also about engagement and people learning the habits and techniques of influencing government and decisions about all the things that affect their lives. Politicians have retreated from engagement for bad reasons and good; at the same time people have imbibed a contempt for democratic politicians and democratic decision-making in a way that makes politicians more fearful and less willing to engage. The 2024 UK general election showed the unwillingness even to try to explain the financial implications of high debt, an ageing population, public services on the verge of collapse, and, of course, Brexit.

It follows that our politics are not defined by what happens in Westminster or even in local councils although we certainly need councils to have more power and resources to make their own decisions with their own populations. This perspective might provide a basis for new forms of political engagement and the sharing of responsibility for decisions and priorities. The answer for liberals is a dual approach, working both inside and outside the institutions of mainstream politics. Trust in politics and

---

10 Jefferson never actually used these words, although they are an accurate summation of his views concerning the relation between education, democracy and citizenship.

politicians is built when they work with people on everyday matters, share their daily experience and work together to achieve results. Leaflets can be a way for a politician to engage personally and honestly with people; that is not the same as the relentless delivery of nationally drafted and approved marketing messages.

Tip O'Neill,[11] a former Speaker of the US House of Representatives, was closely associated with the phrase: 'All politics is local'.[12] He was a good local representative, thoroughly embedded in his Boston community. He was also the Speaker who saw through Congress the landmark Johnson legislation on civil rights and the war on poverty. I prefer to re-phrase the aphorism as: 'All politics is about relationships.' It's about the feeling that this person is one of us and the politician feeling the same. It's about language and respect and honesty and relaxed, everyday engagement. That comes from being there and listening and laughing and joining in. Of course, a politician can't do that with everybody all the time, but, if such engagement is honest, people can feel it. It will be an interesting challenge for a new Liberal Democrat generation of MPs. An example I hear quite frequently is on the West Coast Mainline. I chat to the people opposite and, quite often they come from Westmorland. I say, 'I know your MP'. The response is often the same: they smile and say, 'Oh, our Tim'.[13] That's the gold standard!

Bibliography

Beeson, John. *John Wesley and the American Frontier.* Xulon Press, 2007.

Berlin, Issiah. *Four Essays on Liberty.* Oxford University Press, 1969.

Greaves, Tony, and Gordon Lishman. *Democrats or Drones?* Hebden Bridge, 1987.

Hawkesworth, M.E., and Maurice Kogan, eds. *Encyclopaedia of Government and Politics* vol. 1. Routledge, 1992.

Montaigne, Michel de. *The Essays of Michael Seigneur de Montaigne.* Translated by Charles Cotton. Alex Murray & Son, 1870.

Parini, Jay. *British Writers: Supplement X.* Edited by Ian Scott-Kilvert and

---

11   Thomas Phillip 'Tip' O'Neill Jr. was an American Democratic Party politician from Massachusetts who served as the 47th Speaker of the United States House of Representatives from 1977 to 1987.

12   The precise phrase goes back as at least as far as 1932.

13   Timothy James Farron (born 27 May 1970), a British politician who served as leader of the UK Liberal Democrats, 2015–2017. He is the member of parliament for Westmorland and Lonsdale and has been an MP continuously since May 2005.

Jay Parini. Scribner, 2004.

Popper, Karl. *The Open Society and Its Enemies, Vol. 2: Hegel and Marx.* Routledge, 2002.

Putnam, Robert. *Bowling Alone: The Collapse and Revival of American Community.* Simon & Schuster, 2001.

14

In Defence of OWL:
The Crisis of Civil Liberty

Bob Marshall-Andrews

In 2007, during one of several parliamentary rebellions on the subject of civil liberty I was summoned to the office of the chief whip Hilary Armstrong for a severe warning on dissident behaviour which transpired to be a half-hearted caution. I used the opportunity to tell the chief whip that further attacks on civil liberties or freedom of speech would, inevitably, lose us, the Labour Party, the next election. She disagreed. Memorably she said to me 'Bob, people in my constituency do not give a fuck about civil liberties.' There are two immediately alarming things about that statement. Firstly, that it could be true and, secondly, that she obviously believed it was. But her simple and robust assertion contained a wider and disturbing truth. It is that people do not 'give a fuck' about obtaining or retaining something they believe immutably to be theirs.

In Britain it is generally assumed that our civil liberty is not a benign gift, or a bundle of rights obtained by struggle and retained by vigilance. It is our defining characteristic as a nation. It is *Our Way of Life* (OWL). Implicit in this simple mantra are centuries of brawny self-confidence. We famously do not have a written constitution and while subscribing to the European Convention we have never possessed our own detailed charter of rights. No statute since Magna Carta has codified or informed the British as to the extent of their liberties. Many statutes and edicts tell us what we legally cannot do. None define what we can. The self-evident truths of the American constitution are, for us, not spelled out or amended. They are assumed as the cornerstone of our democracy.

And, in reality it is impossible to divorce democracy from civil liberty. Civil liberty is the handmaiden of democracy, and, in turn, democracy is the foundation of the rule of law without which freedom cannot exist. Yet the study of democracy or civil liberty is curiously absent from the British national curriculum unlike in most European democracies. There is an implicit assumption that fundamental freedoms and principles affecting freedom of speech, physical liberty, association and protest are absorbed with our mothers' milk. 'Rule, Britannia!' informs us that we will never be slaves but is silent as to the means by which servitude is to be avoided. Ruling the waves may see off foreign tyrants but provides scant protection from the authoritarian within. Asked about the source of his or her freedoms the puzzled British citizen is likely to invoke the plebiscite as the primary bulwark. That, at least, forms a common weal and general knowledge. But asked about the meaning and value of parliamentary democracy few British citizens would, or could, cite 'control of the executive' or the 'balance of powers'. The Victorian biblical tomes from Walter Bageot[1] and A.V. Dicey[2] grace few bookshelves and achieve even fewer hits on social media. However, the puzzled but thoughtful citizen is likely to assert that the power to change governments is, in itself, a guarantee of liberty – 'If one lot abuses trust and power we can throw them out before they can do much damage.' Also a new, libertarian, reforming administration has the power to rectify wrongs at the behest of the electorate which it serves. This is of course fundamentally true but contains obvious flaws.

The last 20 years have seen in Britain, a steady and consistent erosion in our civil liberty despite, in that time, enduring eight general elections. Repeated general elections have done nothing to reverse or control this process. Indeed, it is unhappily the case that the electoral process has been used by successive populist administrations to ensure that it continues. We are dangerously close to a political and social derangement in which the citizen exposed to and manipulated by social and mass media directly colludes with government in the restriction of his or her liberty. How this has come about and how we can redress it is the subject of this short essay.

Labour governments 1997-2010

It all began with the Labour government of 1997 with its massive parliamentary majority, of which I was a part. In 13 years, the New Labour government passed more criminal justice legislation than became law

---

1   Walter Bagehot (1826-1877) was a 'conservative liberal' journalist and theorist of the English constitution. His work emphasises the virtues of common law, custom, and institutional evolution.
2   Albert Venn Dicey (1835-1922) was a jurist and political theorist whose work is often treated as part of Britain's unwritten constitution.

in the whole of the 19th century, a formidable achievement. In 2009, a Liberal Democrat home affairs spokesman estimated the figure to be upwards of 3,000.[3] As to the number of new criminal offences that have been created, there is a continuing debate. Certainly, it is more than 500. Yet more impressive are the number of new sentences and the rules, regulations, strictures and statutory exhortations that have been applied to the sentencing process. The result is a judicial nightmare. The prisons are massively overcrowded with prisoners who by common consent should not be serving anything like the sentences to which they have been subjected as a result of the statutory straitjacket that now confines judges. As a result of the same legislation, those same experienced judges (still by common consent the finest such cadre in the world) are now enjoined to recite meaningless mantras calculated to baffle defendants and enflame victims and their families. How did we arrive at this dreadful state? How had a party that prided itself upon its civil libertarian credentials become one of the most authoritarian regimes in British history, certainly since that of Lord Liverpool[4] in the middle of the 19th century? The answer is an interesting reflection on party politics. Amazingly, until the 1970s, law and order, crime and punishment did not appear as a political issue in the election manifestos of any of the major parties. The reason for this (now startling) omission was simple. There was a political consensus that human wickedness was a matter for theology and not for politics. Certainly, the conditions and circumstances which gave way to human venality were something for the political arena. Education, housing, health and the general physical and mental wellbeing of the subject could, self-apparently, affect the propensity towards crime. This simple truth dates back to Lord Shaftesbury and beyond. However, crime and punishment itself was not perceived to be part of the political arena and neither side thought to blame the other for rising crime rates or, indeed,

---

3   See Nigel Morris, 'More than 3,600 new offences under Labour', *The Independent*, 4 September 2008, https://www.independent.co.uk/news/uk/home-news/more-than-3-600-new-offences-under-labour-918053.html [Accessed 6/7/2024].

4   Robert Banks Jenkinson, 2nd Earl of Liverpool (1770-1828) served as Conservative prime minister from 1812-1827. During the first part of his premiership, he introduced a series of socially repressive measures in the aftermath of the Napoleonic wars. These included the banning of mass meetings, the suspension of *habeas corpus*, press censorship, particularly those publications which offered a platform for radical political opinions.

achieve accolades for their fall. All this changed in the course of the 1970s. The Labour Party had always been (indeed, prided itself on being) the party of civil liberty. This stemmed from a history and tradition of trade union emancipation mixed with the softer liberal tendencies of the Bloomsbury intellectuals and Shavian literature.

In the 1970s the Tories perceived this as a wonderful political opportunity. It was, they realised, a short step to allege that understanding and compassion for the sinner was, in fact, approbation for the sin. Thus, in the manifestos of the 1970s the Tories launched their onslaught on law and order.[5] Being 'soft on crime' was one of many albatrosses suspended around the emaciated neck of the Labour Party. It had a deadly political effect. It coincided with a number of other developments. The popular press embraced the whole concept of criminal behaviour as a political issue and, at the same time, sociology was becoming a science as opposed to an enjoyable pastime.

The result was particularly bad for Labour in working class areas and taken together with the sale of countless council houses, formed a Tory bridge into the working class. Those in charge of the New Labour Project knew this very well. It, therefore, became a part of the Project itself to ambush and then outflank the Tories on issues of law and order, crime and punishment. The method employed was to blame lawlessness on liberties, thereby perpetuating an ancient totalitarian myth that the more liberty human beings enjoy, the more wicked they become. It was a particularly easy message to filter through the pages of *The Sun*. Thus, New Labour embarked upon an extraordinary onslaught of authoritarian legislation challenging some of the most revered and cherished institutions of British society, from jury trial to the rights of an individual to maintain silence in the face of accusation by the state. In doing so it ignored a profound political truth, that you can never reduce human wickedness by a reduction in civil liberty.

---

5   See for instance Keith Joseph's speech at Luton, on 3rd October 1974: 'It was not long ago that we thought that utopia was within reach. What has happened to all this optimism? Has it really crumbled under the weight of rising crime?' In fact, crime was falling. 'Has it really crumbled under the weight of rising crime, social decay and the decline of traditional values? Have we really become a nation of hooligans and vandals, bullies and child-batterers, criminals and inadequates? Our loud talk about the community overlies the fact that we have no community.' Quoted in Vernon Bogdanor, *Sir Keith Joseph and the Market Economy*, https://www.gresham.ac.uk/watch-now/sir-keith-joseph-and-market-economy [Accessed 6/7/2024].

Totalitarian regimes may reduce crime rates, but this is achieved only by the transfer of delinquency from the citizen to the state. To this should be added the personality of New Labour itself embodied in successive home secretaries, and particularly David Blunkett. Blunkett's withering contempt for liberals and liberty should not be seen as an aberration. He faithfully and zealously represented the character of his government and its architects. It is a role that has been enthusiastically adopted by successive Tory home secretaries, including Suella Braverman, whose vituperative language has set a previously unsurpassed level of unpleasantness and bile. In part, of course, it is aimed at the leadership of a dying Tory party, but it goes well beyond personal political calculation and manifests itself in a messianic zeal aimed at any activity which threatens OWL. There has been no greater self-appointed custodian of OWL than the former home secretary. In her mind those who threaten OWL fall into a remarkably diverse and eclectic array of organisations from impoverished immigrants in rubber boats to noisy middle class members of Extinction Rebellion. There is a legitimate, but unspoken, suspicion that a child of immigrants herself may not have grasped that an essential part of OWL includes the humane treatment of asylum seekers and noisy, disruptive protest. The long-term effects of this political development have been infinitely more serious than the legislation itself. The change in British politics and British society has been insidious. Successive governments, far from repealing repressive legislation, have entered into a populist competition to restrict activities they characterise as extremist, anti-social or unpleasant but which contain the bedrock of civil freedoms.

International developments

Coincidentally, these developments occurred and mirrored two connected international phenomena. First, there has been the lurch toward populist, right wing parties and governments from Trump to Berlusconi. Right wing populist parties are, of course, naturally authoritarian, basing their success on the demonisation of immigrants, vulnerable minorities and disruptive protestors who interrupt and interfere with ordinary lives. They are abetted by a toxic right wing media whose financial existence relies on a mass circulation among an increasingly aggressive, largely working class electorate. The universal, international growth of this dangerous political trend has been the subject of much analysis and speculation outside the remit of this essay. But it undoubtedly stems from gradually increasing impoverishment caused by technology and also globalised labour which has removed both opportunity and, in the West, a sense of historic entitlement. The nature of this creeping deprivation, from the American mid-west to the old industrial areas of Europe, does not beget solidarity. Unlike the depressions of the 1930s or the class struggles of the 1970s, there is an absence of concerted protest manifest in marches and assembly. Technology and globalisation are difficult targets against which to unite, indeed their effects tend to be divisive. As a result there is declining sympathy with dissent and protest and the liberties on which they depend. In turn this encourages and permits the rise in repressive legislation aimed at protest supporting more abstract causes such as climate change. To this may be added an increasingly influential social media devoid of moral compass and, if anything, more toxic than the established media with which they effectively compete. More recently London and other cities have seen massive demonstrations focused on the devastation of climate change, Black emancipation and the military conduct of Israel in the occupied territories of Palestine. Again, government ministers have publicly declared that these marches are the concerted work of extremist groups, (in the case of Palestine, hate marches) dedicated to enflaming racism. Unelected and unknown commissioners or 'tsars' have declared that vast areas of our cities have been rendered no go areas to minorities and citizens. Anyone who has attended these demonstrations knows this to be despicable nonsense. It is also clear that these deliberate falsehoods are employed for the political ends of the ministers responsible, acting in collaboration with an increasingly extreme right wing press.

There are repeated demands for further legislation to curb protest with greater police power to enforce it. The process then becomes toxic and farcical. Senior police officers are placed under pressure to explain why they have not taken steps to deal with a non-existent problem, namely a peaceful demonstration, falsely designated as a hate march. The officers respond quite reasonably that they apply the law as it exists. This is translated into a demand for unspecified changes in the law itself. It results in increasingly draconian statutes such as the Police, Crime Security and Courts Act 2022 and the Public Order Act 2023. At the time of writing, there will be a general election within months. Populist manifestos will be full of the threat of extremism to Our Way of Life. The party manifestos may well compete on the stern measures needed to stamp out this cancer within. The tragic irony does not require emphasis. The Reform Party will no doubt place the blame for extremism expressly or implicitly on immigrants, thus upping the bidding war with the right-wing rump of the party from which they have sprung. The threat to liberal progressive government therefore occurred on a global stage. It is brilliantly analysed by Ferdinand Mount in his learned and accessible work *Big Caesars and Little Caesars*. The erosion of civil liberty was in part an inevitable consequence. In Britain it continued a political, dialectical process which began in 1997. The second phenomenon has been the growth of terrorism, the eruption of violent political and religious movements and causes, existing outside democratic control and dedicated to its destruction. Terrorism, migration and dissent provided the essential and classic means by which liberty is constrained, namely fear.

Fear

Since 1997 fear has become an increasing and carefully nurtured aspect of British life. It is a savage irony that the national level of general trepidation and mutual distrust has, by a deliberate process, been increased in inverse proportion to the quantum of real risk. All of this has been assiduously and deliberately cultivated by government both by statute and behaviour. By the end of his period of office, Blair's transport around his own capital was wholly unlike that of any previous prime minister. In order for him to progress the 150 yards from Downing Street to Westminster (a rare but necessary journey) one bullet-proofed limousine and four black windowed armoured Range Rovers were pressed into service. On one occasion I wandered innocently into the underground private road which runs the length of the Palace of Westminster. I was fortunately, physically restrained by a police officer in black fatigues before I was reduced to pulp by the first Range Rover accelerating with wailing sirens through the mother of parliaments. 'Who's that then?' I said to the paramilitary officer, gently backing away from his sub-machine gun. 'Can't tell you', he said without a hint of irony.

None of this is original. The political nightmares created by George Orwell and Aldous Huxley were predicated entirely on the creation of meaningless fear in order to promote and popularise totalitarian government. Kafka's short story *The Burrow* concerns a small animal so terrified that he frantically digs himself deeper and deeper. There is no cause for his fear other than the certainty that only a terrible danger would have caused him to dig with such frenetic anxiety. The deeper the burrow the more the fear is reinforced. The prevailing fears employed by governments are of course terrorism and domestic crime, in particular, abusive anti-social behaviour. Both are real enough. Fundamentalist terrorism is an ugly and deadly threat and abusive behaviour is a curse of our age. Neither, however, required the avalanche of repressive and authoritarian responses that have been passed in their name.

Repressive legislation which restricts or curtails liberty falls into three categories. The first creates or expands existing criminal conduct. Brand new offences are created or amplified by new definition. Not all new offences are repressive and many simply rebrand old delinquent behaviour with new terminology to meet supposed popular demand. Upskirting is a good example, replacing indecent assault (which it undoubtedly is). More serious is the creation of terrorist offences which we will describe later. The second category concerns increases in punitive powers. The most obvious is the power of arrest and detention with or without trial. This may, or may not be linked to the first category. The creation of new offences obviously involves new sanctions. This may have a compounding effect if the new offences are simply a rebranding exercise with an increase in punitive sanctions. If, for instance, a public order offence is rebranded as terrorism the effect is to render the citizen at increased risk of arrest and punishment for precisely the same activity. The third category is the erosion of safeguards against conviction. This may affect the detection process, charging and ultimate trial. It involves, among others, the right to silence, the right to disclosure and, most important the right to trial by jury, famously described by Lord Devlin as the 'lamp that shows that freedom lives'.[6]

Terrorism

In the first category, the creation of new offences, by far the most important and most dangerous is terrorism as defined and refined by the Terrorism Acts of 2000 to 2006. Throughout the 19th century, the rules of statutory construction were clear. Criminal statutes should be precise both as to conduct and intention. The citizen should know when he or she had

---

6   See *Regina v. Connor and another* (Appellants) (On Appeal from the Court of Appeal (Criminal Division)). *Regina v. Mirza* (Appellant) (On Appeal from the Court of Appeal (Criminal Division)) (Conjoined Appeals), https://publications. parliament.uk/pa/ld200304/ldjudgmt/jd040122/conn-1.htm [Accessed 5/10/2024].

transgressed. As important, magistrates, judges and juries should be in no doubt as to the delinquent acts and necessary intention of those they tried. Criminal intent was a normal requirement, either direct intent or (more rarely) recklessness. Crimes committed by conduct alone (absolute offences), were extremely rare and were viewed as the hallmark of totalitarian states. Since 1997 these noble principles have come under increasing strain.

The extent of dangers to come could be read into the very first section of the first new Terrorist Act passed by the New Labour government in the year 2000. That section enshrined the new interpretation and definition of terrorism as including the 'use or threat of action made for the purpose of advancing a political, religious or ideological cause'. The action included 'any action which creates a serious risk to the health and safety of the public or a section of the public or is designed seriously to interfere with or disrupt an electronic system'.[7] Thus the threat of any serious damage or hacking for an ideological purpose was endowed immediately with terrorist status. This was, and remains, ominous. To prosecute those who commit criminal damage during the course of a demonstration on, say, climate change may represent a reasonable use of the criminal process. To prosecute such actions as terrorism offends law, language and common sense.

Other aspects of this legislation bordered on farce. One of the terrorist offences created by the bill criminalised the possession of a vast range of educational literature which would include (I told a surprised Commons) Baden Powell's manual *Scouting for Boys*. Section 57 of the act created an offence to possess *any article* giving rise to a suspicion that it was for a purpose connected to the preparation or instigation of an act of terrorism. Large parts of Baden Powell's famous work, the official bible of the largest male youth movement on earth, is dedicated to survival in hostile terrain. Techniques such as the creation of bivouac and camouflage would undoubtedly assist the potential terrorist or insurgent in many parts of the world to which the extra territorial reach of the legislation was directed. Furthermore, under the act, it is for the suspected citizen to prove that the offending article was *not for a terrorist purpose*. The legislation had the inevitable and expected result. In the years that followed, hundreds of dedicated and committed young people, protesting against the effects of globalisation and the environmental

---

7   See the summary definition of terrorism provided by the Crown Prosecution Service for England and Wales, https://www.cps.gov.uk/crime-info/terrorism [Accessed 6/7/2024].

degradation of their planet, were duly corralled, 'kettled,' searched and made subject to random forfeitures and finally arrested *as terrorists*. Perfectly innocent photographers, such as my friend and colleague, Austin Mitchell MP, were subject to harassment, forfeiture and confiscation. And coach loads of perfectly innocent demonstrators were imprisoned for hours in their vehicles as potential terrorist subjects. The effect has been, simultaneously, to alienate hundreds and thousands of respectable young citizens and to debase the coinage of terrorist activity to the point of dangerous legal farce.

Subsequent acts contained more flagrant attempts to create new and unenforceable offences while dispensing with criminal intent. The Terrorism Bill 2006 created a serious offence: to *glorify* terrorism. This phrase, and the section itself, again bore the unmistakable hallmark of the prime minister. Glorification, as I subsequently observed in the debate, 'may be a magnificent word in music of Handel and the pen of Blake or Milton. It has absolutely no place in criminal jurisprudence. We do not do Beatitudes at the Old Bailey. We do criminal justice based on statutes.'[8] The section, however, was not simply floridly religious, it was positively and seriously dangerous. The danger lay in the absence of any element of intent. Thus, any statement which glorified terrorism *as perceived by the listener* became a terrorist offence (and ipso facto under the bill the subject of a 90-day imprisonment, detention without charge). The definition of domestic and international terrorism was so wide that any expression of opinion, during debates, academic studies, journalistic writing or otherwise, that, say, the ANC in South Africa had fought a noble campaign against an oppressive apartheid regime, would have rendered the speaker immediately liable to a criminal offence (for which he had no defence). Similarly, Cherie Blair's public comment in 2002, that young Palestinians could be hopelessly driven to be bombers, would have amounted to a crime.

It is worth recording however that these provisions caused a substantial parliamentary rebellion both in the Commons and in the Lords. On the crucial issue of intention, the government's commons majority was reduced to one. Memorably the junior minister promoting the bill at the dispatch box, Angela Eagle, being informed of the numbers on the division quite audibly said 'Oh fuck' which suitably described the hopelessness of the

---

8   See HC Deb 15 February 2006, vol. 442, col. 1456, https://publications. parliament.uk/pa/cm200506/cmhansrd/vo060215/debtext/60215-15.htm [Accessed 6/7/2024].

government position and *glorification* was consigned back to the Albert Hall where it belongs. The importance of the passage lies not in the defeat (which was rare and welcome) but in the willingness of government to dispense with the normal, ancient limits of criminal behaviour in favour of perceived, populist appeal. The act also created a new criminal offence of inducing religious hatred in another and so far, so good. Inducing hatred of anyone else, for whatever reason, is undesirable human behaviour and might easily be criminal if it is intended to cause violence or social unrest. The bill, however, required no such intention, the crime was committed if the offensive act was reckless or careless. Thus the unintentional creation of racial hatred in some (unspecified) third party, however dysfunctional, bigoted or irrational that third party might be, became a serious criminal offence. This would include comedies or sketches debunking or vilifying religious orthodoxy or holding it up to ridicule. Not surprisingly, this attracted the excited attention of the celebrity circuit. Luvvies are not natural libertarians but the prospect, as one of them put it to me succinctly, 'of being banged up for having a pop at the Prophet' caused an outbreak of angst in Notting Hill. And, of course, they had a perfectly good point. Since the Age of Reason, we have always set our collective face against the protection of faith by statute. After two hundred years of religious intolerance, (which led to nothing but bigotry and death), we came to understand perfectly well that one cannot protect the faith without protecting the fundamentalist and the bigot who lies within it. And indeed, legislation passed ostensibly to protect religion has precisely the reverse effect because the people who are protected most are those who come close to committing the offences we are attempting to place on the statute book. A loathing of bigotry and those that preach it would render me liable under the very legislation that was passed to protect religious susceptibilities. We would not create a tolerant society but a legislative and cultural bear pit.

On a whipped vote the government, on the first division, suffered a humiliating defeat by ten votes. The second vote (the more important of the two) represented a glorious own goal by the chief whip. Having suffered a loss by ten votes and, not wishing the prime minister to be seen in another defeated lobby, she advised Blair to stay in his room or return to Downing Street. In the event the government lost by just one vote. Had the prime minister voted, this dangerous and unpleasant piece of legislation would have made its way to the statute books. As we have seen the primary drive towards authoritarian government is populist. You take an existing threat to public safety or comfort, exaggerate it, stimulate demand for draconian action, present legislation to meet it, stigmatise opponents for befriending terrorists/fanatics/troublemakers, pass the legislation and take credit for the reduction in a non-existent danger. One of the more egregious examples is the new statutory offence of 'public nuisance'. This is simply the old common law offence famously employed against noisy brothels and, more importantly, environmental damage. It is a savage irony that the new offence is now regularly used against climate change protestors.

The truth is that many of these new offences and the increased punishments which they entail are totally unnecessary. Many simply replicate existing sanctions while others are practically unenforceable. This does not stop strangulated cries in parliament to the effect that 'we have given the police the powers, why don't they use them.' The obvious answer is that the crimes and behaviour claimed to be rife in parliamentary ranting and debates simply do not exist on the ground. The massive hate marches, darkly alleged to conceal terrorist behaviour do not exist. If they did then existing police powers, statutory of common law, are more than adequate to deal effectively with such offences. The truth is that the police and prosecuting authorities have not asked for more or greater powers of prosecution and punishment and do not want them. The political purpose of passing them through parliament is a synthetic populist response calculated to present an iron fisted answer to a non-existent threat invoked by the rabid elements of the media. There are excellent examples of this process, some serious, some bizarre. In 2009 in the death throes of the government, Gordon Brown enjoying his brief period in office decreed that yet another Terrorism Act should increase the maximum period of detention without trial from 28 to 90 days. The sole reason given for this suicidal attempt at populist government was that the prosecuting authorities and the security services required time to decrypt digital messages cunningly concealed by terror networks. No examples were given to parliament of this problem which ministers justified by the usual reliance on state security. The bill limped into the House of Lords where it met its nemesis in the redoubtable form of Eliza Manningham Buller, the formidable ex head of MI5. In a devastating short speech she revealed that she had never known extra detention time to be necessary for encryption of secret communication and indeed that the 28-day period had only been employed *once* for entirely different purposes. The bill collapsed, which was inevitable, but left the unanswered question, why did the government persist with an authoritarian measure on a basis that was completely false? The answer can only be that Gordon Brown, by no means the most hard line of New Labour ministers, had been persuaded by party spin doctors that long periods of incarceration without trial would be attractive to an electorate in the coming election.

Judicial oversight and jury trial: reason for hope

The third and most serious category of repressive legislation is that which limits or abolishes judicial review and the rights concerning, arrest, process and trial. In this category, in the last thirty years we have seen repeated attempts by government to legislate against judicial review. Provisions inserted in individual criminal statutes to circumscribe the powers of judicial scrutiny have been consistently rejected by parliament. In this respect the contribution of the House of Lords has been immense. Those who would rush to reform the second chamber, and to see its replacement by an elected body, would do well to consider this role. There can be little doubt that an upper house, comprised of elected members inevitably tied to party machines and party whips, would lack both the power and inclination to confront and defeat abuse of government power. The most striking example lies in the battle over jury trial which we will consider next. As to the judiciary, senior judges have defied the contemptible headlines of the pusillanimous press (*Enemies of the People* – Daily Mail) to strike down political corruption. Given Boris Johnson's notorious attempt to prorogue parliament, (an act which involved lying to the Sovereign), Brenda Hale, the Head of the Supreme Court, in twenty coruscating minutes, delivered a unanimous verdict which eviscerated the government's case. Vengeful attempts to restrict judicial review were thereafter largely rejected by the parliament whose very existence the judiciary had guaranteed.

Finally, to jury trial which has been a persistent target of government and is likely to become so again. Pressure against it comes from two sides. First the Treasury who perceive it to be an expensive indulgence compared to summary justice and sentencing from magistrates (very cheap) and professional judges. Frequent and illiterate comparisons are made with the French inquisitorial system with its heavy reliance on *juges d'instruction* at the expense of lay juries. This ignores the fact that the inquisitorial system contains its own checks and balances against the state's power completely absent from the common law jury system. To emulate the inquisitorial system by simply removing juries is like removing the wheels from a car and claiming that you have created a boat. The second aversion to juries is more serious and more sinister. It comes from the view that juries cannot be controlled by the government. It is this brawny, bloody-minded independence that lies behind Lord Devlin's famous dictum: 'The first object of any tyrant in Whitehall would be to make parliament utterly subservient to his will; and the next to overthrow or diminish the right to trial by jury, for no tyrant could afford to leave a subject's freedom in the hands of twelve of his countrymen.'[9]

Given its central importance it is worth recording in some detail the attempt to abolish the right to elect jury trial in 1998 by the New Labour government and its home secretary Jack Straw. It came in the form of the Mode of Trial Bill. This short piece of legislation proposed that defendants in the vast majority of indictable cases should lose the right to elect trial by jury which would lie instead in the gift of individual magistrates. It was widely anticipated that magistrates would retain an increasing number of trials to themselves; that they would gradually assume a more judicial role and, thus, within a short period, jury trial would be reduced to a limited number of the most serious and venal offences. Although barely ten clauses long the importance of this bill could not be over stated. Had it become law it would have marked the end of eight centuries of trial by jury.

There was, however, a problem for the government which arose from class deference and the wonderful concept of the *Respectable Defendant*. The government apprehended, rightly that a limited number of defendants in criminal cases possessed reputations so immaculate and pure that any conviction, however minor, would blight their entire lives. The respectable professional person who, in a moment of absent mindedness, leaves WH Smiths with an unpaid copy of Martin Amis' new novel would, if convicted, lose far more than the sentence imposed. Their reputation and professional careers would likely be ruined. This group of people required, so the government perceived, a special form of protection. The act, therefore, required that magistrates, in deciding whether jury trial was appropriate, expressly had to consider the reputation of the defendant and the likely damage a conviction would do to their way of life.

9   Quoted in John Hostettle, *The Criminal Jury Old and New: Jury Power from Early Times to the Present Day* (Waterside Press, 2004), p. 141.

The reputation clause provided obvious ground for criticism that the government was creating a two-tier system of justice. There was a right for those who possessed a reputation and none for those who did not. Thus, in losing your reputation by a criminal conviction you also lost in perpetuity the likelihood that you would achieve jury trial for future offences. The obvious class basis of this distinction touched a chord with many of my Labour colleagues who might otherwise have been indifferent to the trial process. There was a spirited debate on the subject. When the House divided the Labour majority was reduced to 53. It was a significant moment. In parliamentary terms a majority of 53 is perfectly normal but for a government which had swept to power with a majority of three times that size, it represented, effectively, a serious defeat. The whips were furious. The effect of this vote was far reaching. The House of Lords defeated the bill. The government was then faced with a dilemma. It either attempted to force the act through using its parliamentary leverage by the Parliament Act or it retreated and redrafted the bill. What the Home Office and the home secretary did was bizarre. The bill was reproduced with the reputation clause surgically removed. Indeed, it was not only removed but magistrates were now specifically told that they *could not* consider reputation. This opened up a merry riposte. Those of us who were totally opposed were now able confidently to ask what would happen to the elderly, absent minded professional of immaculate reputation who walks out of WH Smith with an unpurchased Martin Amis novel. Were they to run the risk of the total loss of their lifestyle, their friends and their reputation, without the safeguard of jury trial which has been enjoyed by such professionals (and everyone else) for 800 years? The government's majority did not improve, the House of Lords stood firm and the bill disappeared into the parliamentary quicksand never to be seen again.

So, jury trial remains after 800 years and juries still acquit defendants who they perceive have been unjustly prosecuted or persecuted by the state, whatever the law. They are therefore a bulwark against not only bad prosecution but bad law; for juries to act in this way is rare but it is fundamental to our liberties (and OWL). Examples of this fierce and unbendable independence date back to Bushel's case in 1670, tried in the Old Bailey. In this famous trial the defendants were the Quaker dissidents William Penn and William Mead. Bushel was the foreman of the jury. Penn and Mead had no defence in law to the offences of unlawful assembly, with which they were charged. The judge duly directed the jury to convict which they steadfastly refused to do. Unable to sentence Penn and Mead the judge imprisoned Bushel and his jury. After a night in the cells Bushel was summoned before the judge who asked whether the jury had come to their senses and would convict. Bushel replied that they had not and would not do so. Days passed before the appeal court ordered their immediate release establishing the jury's right to act according to conscience. Penn and Mead made the journey to puritan America where Penn founded the state of Pennsylvania.

Four centuries later, Clive Ponting, a senior civil servant, also stood in the same court charged with offences under the Official Secrets Act which he had broken to reveal government secrecy and lying over the sinking of the Argentinean battleship, the *Belgrano*. He had no defence. However venal the behaviour of the government the act required silence from those who had signed it. The judge directed the jury that they should return a verdict of guilty. After a short retirement the foreman delivered a unanimous verdict 'not guilty'. Ponting lost his pension but retained his liberty. Forty years on, Katherine Gun, a middle ranking civil servant also broke the Official Secrets Act to reveal government secrecy and lies in the build up to the Iraq war. She had no defence in law. Her barrister, the formidable Ben Emerson KC, made demands for wide disclosure from the prosecution. Rather than comply and face a jury the prosecution dropped the case. In 2021, a protest took place in Bristol at the Colston Hall, a large public arena donated to the city by Edward Colston as thanks for the use of Bristol docks to conduct his main business, namely slavery. Four of the protestors removed Colson's substantial statue. They rolled it down the road and dumped it in the river. It was subsequently retrieved, somewhat dented. The four protestors were charged with causing criminal damage and tried at the Bristol Crown Court. They had no defence in law. Whatever the participation of Colston in the enslavement, violent punishment and deaths of thousands of slaves, his statue commemorating his works was property to which the act applied. The jury found all four not guilty. Had they been tried two years later they would probably have been charged under the new Public Nuisance Offences, the brainchild of Suella Braverman to which they would have had no defence. There can be no serious doubt that the jury would have returned precisely the same verdict. Bushel's case achieved welcome and emphatic topicality on the 22 April 2024. This involved a despicable attempt by the attorney general to bring contempt proceedings against a 69-year-old social worker who, at the trial of climate change protestors, held up a placard reminding jurors of their right to act according to their conscience. Relying on Bushel the judge threw out the government case with costs.

These cases show the jury system at its incomparable and irreplaceable best. Its value cannot be overstated, which is why it attracts the unremitting hostility of the authoritarian establishment. And it is much more than a part of the legal system. It involves the citizen directly in the process of criminal justice and as such is the true reflection of the people's character and mores. The spirit of William Bushel and William Penn lives on, brave, irreverent and bloody minded. It is, where necessary, rudely nonconformist and possessed of a deep underlying sense of fairness and justice whatever the laws bullied onto the statute book by humourless and vituperative government. This is the true embodiment and manifestation of OWL. Home secretaries should learn it.

Bibliography

Bogdanor Vernon. *Sir Keith Joseph and the Market Economy.* https://www.gresham.ac.uk/watch-now/sir-keith-joseph-and-market-economy [Accessed 6/7/2024].

Crown Prosecution Service. 'Terrorism.' https://www.cps.gov.uk/crime-info/terrorism [Accessed 6/7/2024].

Devlin, Patrick. *The Enforcement of Morals.* Oxford University Press, 1965.

— *Trial By Jury.* Oxford University Press, 1956.

HC Deb 15 February 2006, vol. 442, col. 1456. https://publications.parliament.uk/pa/cm200506/cmhansrd/vo060215/debtext/60215-15.htm [Accessed 6/7/2024].

Hostettle, John. *The Criminal Jury Old and New: Jury Power from Early Times to the Present Day.* Waterside Press, 2004.

Morris, Nigel. 'More than 3,600 new offences under Labour'. *The Independent*, 4 September 2008. https://www.independent.co.uk/news/uk/home-news/more-than-3-600-new-offences-under-labour-918053.html [Accessed 6/7/2024].

Mount, Ferdinand. *Big Caesars and Little Caesars: How They Rise and How They Fall – from Julius Caesar to Boris Johnson.* Bloomsbury, 2023.

15

Prison Policy in an Age of Crisis

Andrea Coomber and Noor Khan

When we speak of freedom, we rarely speak of prisons. People sentenced to a term of imprisonment lose their liberty as punishment but also lose very many other freedoms that we all too often take for granted. To a large extent, their lives are controlled by the state – what prison they are in, who they share a cell with, when they can shower or exercise or access fresh air, if or when they can see or speak to loved ones, if or when they can access education, work or therapy. Lives with limited choices. And lived beyond the oversight of the public and the press, with all the vulnerabilities and potential for impunity that that brings. To deny people their liberty in this way is an awesome responsibility of the state. And Britain's prisons are failing. The crisis is a result of disastrous government policies, political shortsightedness, inefficiency, and decision-making based on sentiment and point-scoring rather than evidence and data. The cliff-edge on which the prison system now finds itself was not approached at speed, but one that we slowly but surely trudged towards, even as those of us who work in and around prisons raised every flag and sounded every available alarm.

To trace the history of crime and prisons in this country, we could go back a decade to austerity measures enacted under the most recent government; back centuries to the opening of Milbank prison in the 18th century;[1] or even further back to the use of prison as a precursor to public punishment or trial. Each of these would illuminate Britain's unique relationship with crime, punishment and imprisonment, but would also need a doctorate level thesis to do it justice. Going back three decades will allow us to trace a meaningful trajectory.

---

1   See UK Parliament, 'Early prisons and imprisonment,' https://tinyurl.com/uvzwa27p [Accessed 27/6/2024].

In 1993, the then home secretary, Michael Howard declared that 'prison works'.[2] His statement was intended to combat defeatism around a perceived rise in crime, and subsequently delivered a raft of measures designed to increase the use of prison. Under his leadership, the Conservative government adopted a tough line on penal policy, including a lowered threshold for prison sentences, an increase both in time served and the number of crimes carrying longer sentences, and it made use of recall to custody easier and more common. This toughening of sentencing was adopted and sustained by successive governments of all colours. In 1991 there were only 43,000 people in prison,[3] by 2007 this number had shot up to 80,000.[4] One factor was the introduction by the Blair Labour government of Schedule 21 of the Criminal Justice Act 2003, which introduced mandatory minimum terms for murder. This distorted proportionality in sentencing with the effect of driving up sentence lengths for other offences.

Blair's government further entrenched the mantra of tough sentencing with the introduction of anti-social behaviour orders (ASBOs) criminalising children and people with mental health problems, and the appalling indeterminate sentence of imprisonment for public protection (IPP) introduced in 2005.[5] The IPP sentence saw more than 8,000 people imprisoned with a minimum jail tariff, but no maximum, for a range of crimes.[6] Those on an IPP sentence were placed on licence indefinitely after release, meaning they could be recalled to prison for administrative breaches, and often are. It has resulted in untold suffering for people in prison, their families and children – the uncertainty and endlessness of the sentence has resulted directly in self-harm and suicide; the indirect costs to their sense of self cannot be known. Lord Brown of Eaton-upon-Heyward has described the

2   From a speech given by Michael Howard at the Conservative Party Conference in 1993, quoted in *Dictionary of Prisons and Punishment*, ed. Jamie Bennett and Yvonne Jewkes (Routledge, 2013), p. 227.

3   Quoted in Ian Cummins, 'Strangeways 25 years after the riot: are British prisons better?', The Conversation, 1 April 2015, https://tinyurl.com/38hcxkn7 [Accessed 27/6/2024].

4   See 2007 figure in UK Government Justice Data, 'Public protection: Justice in Numbers', https://tinyurl.com/33tj29f6 [Accessed 24/6/2024].

5   A useful summary of these sentences can be found in 'Sentences of Imprisonment for Public Protection', House of Lords Library, https://tinyurl.com/yuvrcr92 [Accessed 24/6/2024].

6   See 'The indeterminate sentence of Imprisonment for Public Protection (IPP)', The Prison Reform Trust, https://tinyurl.com/2b5m7k79 [Accessed 24/6/2024].

IPP sentence as 'the greatest single stain on our criminal justice system'.[7] And so it remains.

In 2012, Chris Grayling came into post as justice secretary and over the next few years did away with anything that had previously worked well in probation. Grayling introduced a part-privatisation of the service, severely reduced legal aid, promoted longer sentences, massively reduced cost per prisoner in prisons across the country, and made huge cuts in numbers of frontline prison staff while also offering early retirement to experienced staff working in the system. In a matter of years our prisons, which already had no shortage of issues, were now faced with a crippled probation service unable to rehabilitate or resettle people, deteriorating conditions, woefully impoverished regimes due to lack of funding, insufficient officer numbers and a dearth of sufficiently experienced staff to deal adequately with the rising prison population.

Later years saw further similar measures, as well as attempts by other justice secretaries to reform the system in ways that ultimately led to increasing levels of bureaucracy and less power in the hands of those working in prisons. Alongside this, the Coalition government instituted the biggest cuts to state spending since the Second World War. At no point was there a serious attempt to match these cuts with a reduction in demand for prison places, or in the size of the criminal justice system generally.

By 2020, capitalising on the public sentiment and political points to be gained through tough on crime rhetoric, Boris Johnson's government introduced even more punitive sentencing. People were sent to prison for longer and longer, while previous austerity and benchmarking measures meant that costs and prison conditions were still at the bare minimum. This was then followed by a once in a lifetime global event that prisons were little equipped to deal with. In the grips of the pandemic, prisons that were already working with no funding and a lack of staff, found the only way to deal with Covid was to keep prisoners locked up for as long as possible. Unfortunately, once enacted, this regime was difficult to reverse. Across the country in the years since Covid, prisons have failed to return to pre-pandemic levels of work, education, training or time out of cell. Ultimately, policy decisions by a series of governments and ministers – both red and blue - created hundreds

---

7   Jamie Grierson, 'Indefinite sentences "the greatest single stain on justice system"', *The Guardian*, 3 December 2020, https://tinyurl.com/5hhct7n8 [Accessed 24/6/2024].

if not thousands of new offences, prioritised punishment over rehabilitation, made sentences longer, and put more and more people in prison.

In 2024, we find ourselves with the largest prison population in Western Europe, with the Ministry of Justice's (MoJ) own weekly figures consistently showing the prison population either near or above 88,000.[8] Not only is this the highest number ever recorded, but it has grown at a frightening rate, with weekly figures as low as 77,859 as recently as April 2021. Official projections suggest the number of people in prison could rise to as high as 114,800 by March 2028, which would represent an increase of 47% in only seven years.[9] This is an untenable state of affairs. The spaces to accommodate all these people simply do not exist.

With little irony, alongside publishing projections expecting almost 30,000 more people in the prison system, the latest MoJ figures show that over 70% of all prisons are at or over capacity. For example, Leeds prison is meant to hold 641 men, yet holds an additional 461 men at the time of writing. Wandsworth – a prison now notorious for failings that led to a high-profile escape – has 1,517 men crammed into a building made for 964. The system is bursting at the seams. The number of people in prison on remand – awaiting trial or sentence – is also at its highest level for at least 50 years.[10] Most of these will be acquitted at trial or sentenced to less time than they have served. It is perhaps little wonder that we have the highest rates of suicide in the prison estate. As for women's prisons, a report published in February 2023 on Eastwood Park jail found that in six months, around a third of the women had self-harmed, 86% said they were experiencing mental ill-health, and there had been two self-inflicted deaths since 2019. The inspectorate said the prison was 'failing in its most basic duty – to keep the women safe'.[11]

However, it is not just prisons, probation is also in crisis. Probation services are overburdened and under-resourced, with numbers of people

8   See 'Prison Reform Trust response to the Justice Committee's inquiry on the future prison population and estate capacity,' Prison Reform Trust, October 2023, https://tinyurl.com/ky9p2vde[Accessed 24/6/2024].

9   'It's time for a grown-up debate about prison overcrowding,' Howard League for Penal Reform Blog, 11 March 2024, https://tinyurl.com/y9tevemu [Accessed 24/6/2024].

10   Helen Pidd, 'Two-thirds of prisons officially overcrowded in England and Wales,' The Guardian, 15 October 2023, https://tinyurl.com/mw8rafkr [Accessed 24/6/2024].

11   Sammy Jenkins, 'HMP Eastwood Park: women held in bloodstained cells,' BBC News, 3 February 2023, https://tinyurl.com/4ph5hvrj [Accessed 24/6/2024].

in probation continuing to grow, all while funding decreases. Following the changes made by Grayling, privatisation in 2014 decimated what was previously working well. Where the service had been based in, and catered to, local communities through a network of probation trusts, the part-privatisation did away with those crucial local connections and instead handed contracts to private companies with little expertise, who in turn did not adequately train staff or fund services. Although the change was reversed, the service has been unable to return to its previous community-based model. Unsurprisingly, given the state of these services, reoffending after release is worryingly high, and Ministry of Justice figures show average rates of proven reoffending for adults within a year of release at almost 32%.[12] These rates vary further according to offence types and time frames, with short sentences of less than six months seeing reoffending rates of a staggering 57%.[13]

Underlying these problems, the crux of almost every issue in our system is simply this: we are sending too many people to prison. This has serious consequences for safety and decency in prisons, and severely curtails the ability of the prison system to do much more than lock people in their cells all day. Far from supporting rehabilitation and reintegration, very many of our prisons are places of despair. Reports of the chief inspector of prisons over the first half of 2024, for example, are a consistently depressing read. At Wandsworth prison, inspectors expressed serious concern about severe overcrowding, alongside failings in security, vermin, drug use, violence and self-harm. In Peterborough prison, inspectors described overcrowding, and the churn of men stuck in cycles of reoffending and recall to prison, as well as drug use, staffing shortages, and people being released into homelessness due to inadequate provision of services. Lewes prison was found to be overcrowded and rundown, with men out of cell for less than an hour a day; and increasing violence, high drug use, and rising self-harm. Week after week, inspectors publish official reports documenting the dreadful state in which people are kept in prison. Certain themes crop up almost every time – staff shortages, violence, dreadful living conditions, and little access to work, education or training. Someone in prison self-harms at least once every seven minutes, which is perhaps unsurprising given that most are locked up in dire conditions, often for up to 23 hours a day.

---

12 See for instance, Ministry of Justice, 'Proven reoffending statistics: January to March 2021,' https://tinyurl.com/444xra2h [Accessed 24/6/2024].

13 Ministry of Justice, 'Proven reoffending statistics.'

Writing about the effects of these numbers, chief inspector of prisons, Charlie Taylor, has warned that the consequences spill over into every aspect of prison life. More prisoners crammed into prisons means purposeful activity, namely time out of cell, education, work and training, becomes even more rare while deprivation and violence become more common. Prisons become less safe and the numbers of deaths, self-harm and assaults all increase. And, having spent months or years locked up with no recourse to rehabilitation, people are then released having been given none of the support needed to resettle successfully.[14]

Nonetheless, the system continues to cram more people inside because addressing overcrowding would mean acknowledging the difficult truth that no political party wants to broach: that crime is primarily the by-product of social failure. There is next to no evidence that prison in any way addresses or lessens crime, indeed the opposite is true. Rather than invest to solve and address the unmet needs of society and its vulnerable people, governments of both colours have sought to punish and imprison their way out of a mental health crisis, a drug addiction crisis, and now the cost-of-living crisis. This is even though crime, including violent crime, has been decreasing for the past 30 years across the Western world.[15]

Rather than engage with the widely understood drivers of crime, it is easier to engage in cheap talk about a law-and-order crisis. And we are reaping the seeds of this now, because across the system – but particularly in the courts, in probation and in prisons – there is a crisis of the gravest order. The challenges faced are immediate but also likely to be far-reaching. Only a fundamental review of the pipeline between courts and custody, and a sweeping reassessment of what the system's priorities should be, is going to steer us from a future doomed to decades of sclerotic, failing justice and prisons that continue to damage people and moulder at the fabric of society.

Instead, the order of the day is shortsighted solutions and unrealistic proposals. In 2020, the government signed off £4bn to build 20,000 prison spaces by 2025.[16] When only 3,400 places had been built by 2023, this

14 Andy Gregory, 'Chief prisons inspector: Overcrowding is a ticking time bomb,' *The Independent*, 25 December 2023, https://tinyurl.com/mrtyx88k [Accessed 24/6/2024].
15 See Manuel Eisner, 'Why violent crime is plummeting in the rich world,' *New Scientist*, 4 February 2015, https://tinyurl.com/55b3n29f[Accessed 24/6/2024].
16 See Gill Richards and Nick Davies, 'Performance Tracker 2023: Prisons,' The Institute for Government, 30 October 2023, https://tinyurl.com/5n8upzwp [Accessed 24/6/2024].

was pushed to 2030. In 2022, the government implemented 'Operation Safeguard',[17] allowing the emergency use of police cells to hold people in areas where prisons were full. In 2023, with prison building taking too long, they announced the building of 'rapid deployment cells'[18] essentially demountable cells – to meet the urgent demands of the rising prison population. Then, there came an announcement that due to capacity problems, the government would be renting prison cells abroad, likely in Estonia.[19] Later the same year, they implemented the End of Custody Supervised License (ECSL) scheme to move some lower-level offenders out of prison on to licence up to 18 days before their automatic release date to ease pressure on prisons.[20] This was then extended up to 60 days in March of 2024 and then 70 days in May. Shockingly, the pressure on prisons still has not abated.

Upon its election in July, among the Labour government's first challenges was the fact that 'we have too many people in prison', to quote the prime minister.[21] The urgency of the population pressures led to the introduction of SDS40, which reduces the time served in prison by many people on standard determinate sentences, from 50% of their sentence to 40%. This measure will see around 5,000 people released over a matter of months to relieve pressure on prisons, though every one of these people will be added to the workload of a probation officer.[22] Despite these measures, the pressure on prisons has not abated.

However, these are facts and figures describing the prison system, they do not tell the human story of what is happening inside. Reading statistics, inspection reports or articles on prison policy, it's easy to forget that behind each fact or figure there is, on any given day, one of the 88,000 individuals who have had their liberty stripped by the state, whose families and friends

17   Peter Dawson, 'Operation Safeguard – what does it tell us?', Prison Reform Trust, Blog, 2 December 2022, https://tinyurl.com/4p3m35mt [Accessed 24/6/2024].
18   Ministry of Justice, 'Further rollout of Rapid Deployment Cells to boost prison places,' Press release, 24 June 2023, https://tinyurl.com/kabn2x8d [Accessed 24/6/2024].
19   Ministry of Justice, 'Foreign prison rental to ensure public protection,' Press release, 3 October 2023, https://tinyurl.com/4baj4jf6 [Accessed 24/6/2024].
20   HL Deb, 'End of Custody Supervised Licence Scheme: Extension,' 13 May 2024, vol. 838, https://tinyurl.com/389z4tj7 [Accessed 24/6/2024].
21   Paul Seddon and Sam Francis, 'We have too many prisoners, says new PM Starmer,' BBC News, https://tinyurl.com/mvxzd68j [Accessed 4/12/2024].
22   See 'Addressing Prison Capacity Pressure,' House of Lords Library, https://tinyurl.com/5n7a399a [Accessed 5/12/2024].

now live with their absence. Hidden from view, people in prison are easy targets for both the public and politicians' fears and projections. But too infrequently, politicians speak of who is in prison. Care leavers make up 2% of the general population, but 31% of women and 24% of men in prison. People from abusive households make up 14% of the population, but 41% of prisons. Less than 1% of people in England have been permanently excluded from school,[23] yet they comprise 42% of people in prison.[24] Only 4% of the general population have been homeless or in temporary accommodation, compared to 15% of people in prisons.[25] We also incarcerate far too many people with mental health problems, sometimes masked by struggles with drugs and alcohol.

Prisons are a closed space, and due to their inaccessibility, it has become too easy for the public and politicians alike to project the worst of their fears and shift social problems and difficult people out of sight and out of mind. Prisons are a form of social exile, with huge financial, but also social costs. Their closed nature also means increased vulnerability to violations of human rights and fundamental freedoms. Beyond challenges of accessing affordable legal representation, it is very difficult to raise concerns when to complain would mean biting the hand that feeds you. Many of the chief inspector's reports and accounts from people who contact us at the Howard League speak of breaches of rights, for example from poor prison conditions, use of excessive force or overuse of segregation. Dealing with crime is not straightforward and it is much easier to tell people that they will be safe if we just lock more people up. Implicit in this are the beliefs that a prison sentence works to reduce crime, that people in prison deserve to be there, and that we are safer as a result. Unfortunately, there is little evidence to support these beliefs and much data to refute them.

Prison is the most severe criminal justice sanction and should therefore be reserved for the most serious offences and people who present most risk to

23 'Spring term 2022/23: Suspensions and permanent exclusions in England,' Department of Education, 18 April 2024, https://tinyurl.com/25keka8y [Accessed 27/6/2024].
24 See Sally Coates, 'Unlocking Potential A review of education in prison,' Ministry of Justice, May 2016, https://tinyurl.com/4846pz38 [Accessed 27/6/2024].
25 Kim Williams et al., 'Accommodation, homelessness and reoffending of prisoners: Results from the Surveying Prisoner Crime Reduction (SPCR) survey,' Research Summary, Ministry of Justice, March 2012, https://tinyurl. com/2vez52wt [Accessed 27/6/2024].

the public. This could not be further from the current reality. Recent figures show that 36%[26] of people in prison under immediate custodial sentence have committed non-violent offences, while for women this figure is even higher at 47%.[27] At the time of writing, there were 16,196 people held on remand, or 18% of the total prison population, a significant proportion of which will go on to be acquitted or receive a non-custodial sentence.

For those people who do go on to be sentenced, there are swathes of evidence to show that both long sentences and short sentences are not working. A Ministry of Justice briefing from 2023 acknowledges that there is little evidence that short sentences are effective, and highlights that they are associated with higher reoffending than community orders or suspended sentences.[28] In fact, the briefing adds that short sentences may serve to give people access to criminal networks and negative associations that they would otherwise not have. Essentially, short sentences make people more likely to reoffend, are more dangerous for the communities' people to return to and could be increasing criminality.

On long sentences, research from the Sentencing Council reveals that increasing sentence length is not linked to a reduction in reoffending, but that rehabilitative interventions could be.[29] And yet, rather than increasing the education, work and training available in prisons, or funding better resources adequately to rehabilitate the population, more and more people continue to be crammed into prisons for more and more time. And it is not just the length of sentences that is increasing, but also the frequency. In 2023, 56% of sentences were for four years or more compared with 36% in 2008;[30] while the average custodial sentence length has consistently risen over the last 10 years from 14.5 months in 2012 to 22.6 months in 2022. Addressing

---

26 See 'New factsheets showing detailed breakdown of use of imprisonment for women in each police force area,' Prison Reform Trust, 14 May 2024, https://tinyurl.com/w35n8fs4 [Accessed 27/6/2024].

27 Quoted in Rajeev Syal, 'MoJ postpones plans to reduce female prison population,' *The Guardian*, 2 May 2018, https://tinyurl.com/3h96hhs3 [Accessed 27/6/2024].

28 'Sentencing Bill Factsheet: Short Sentences,' Ministry of Justice Policy Paper 5 December 2023, https://tinyurl.com/mruz26ub [Accessed 5/12/2024].

29 Jay Gormley et al., *The Effectiveness of Sentencing Options on Reoffending* (The Sentencing Council, 2022).

30 See Jacqueline Beard, 'Sentencing Bill 2023-24,' Research Briefing, House of Commons Library, 4 December 2023, https://tinyurl.com/5ejzsvdt [Accessed 27/6/2024].

these trends, the Justice Committee, in a report on public opinion and understanding of sentencing explained that increased sentence lengths are a result of government-led inflation in response to a hardening of public opinion towards serious crime.[31]

The failure of sentencing law and policy over successive governments was highlighted in a landmark paper prepared by the Howard League for the five most senior retired judges in England and Wales in September 2024. Citing the huge financial and human costs of overuse of imprisonment, *Sentence inflation: a judicial critique* described the status quo as unsustainable.[32] It called for both a reversal of the trend of longer sentences, and exploration of accelerated routes out of prison for those already serving them.

This is the situation in which we find ourselves, and how we got here. But where can we go from here? The election of the new Labour government has shown encouraging signs to those working in the sector and focussing on criminal justice. In his first press conference following the election, Prime Minister Keir Starmer raised the need to 'be clear about the way in which we use prisons'.[33] Significantly, Starmer appointed James Timpson OBE to the role of prisons minister. For over 20 years, his company Timpson's has actively recruited staff from prisons, with James Timpson becoming a stalwart of the prison reform sector.

Immediately, in response to overflowing prisons, the government was forced into the early release of thousands of prisoners, and prison capacity is likely to absorb ministers' energies for the foreseeable future. Having a prime minister willing to speak about prisons, and a prisons minister who knows them well have led to a renewed sense of hope in the prison sector that this government will, finally, understand and be willing to address meaningfully the well-evidenced truth that prison does not work. This will require significant political courage; it remains to be seen whether this government is sufficiently courageous.

Having been at the forefront of prison reform in England and Wales for over 160 years, the Howard League has seen firsthand the decline in prisons and probations in recent decades. We have consistently called for

31 See 'Public Opinion and Understanding of Sentencing, House of Commons,' House of Commons Justice Committee, 25 October 2023, https://tinyurl.com/4s2h894y[Accessed 4/12/2024].

32 'Sentence Inflation: A Judicial Critique,' Howard League for Penal Reform, September 2024, https://tinyurl.com/2tytb29w [Accessed 4/12/2024].

33 Seddon and Francis, 'We have too many prisoners.'

an urgent decrease in the prison population in order for people to be able to serve productive, safe sentences that are able to successfully rehabilitate and reintegrate. Our overriding ambition is to move the dial on punishment away from cruelty and towards building a more humane and effective response to crime that provides justice and helps to lower levels of reoffending. However, these longer-term changes can only be addressed on the back of significant policy changes that address the huge cohorts of people who do not need to be held in our prisons, which can be achieved by prioritising the following short-term solutions.

Short term solutions

Automatic early release: In September 2024, the newly elected Labour government implemented the SDS40 early release scheme in which Standard Determinate Sentences saw a reduction in time served from 50% of the sentence to 40%.[34] The Howard League had long been advocating for this change as a short-term measure to address prison capacity. Alongside this change, we also advocate for changes brought in via the Police, Crime, Sentencing and Courts Act (2022), which increased the requisite custodial portion of a sentence for certain offences to two-thirds, to be reversed.

Sentencing practice and policy: The government has committed to holding a sentencing review early in its term. Its terms of reference and its composition are unknown at the time of writing, but any review should consider the purpose, realities, and costs (both human and financial) of ever longer sentences. To address those already serving very long sentences, the government should firstly, take urgent and decisive action to release safely all IPPs and two-strike prisoners who are over-tariff, with suitable support in the community upon release. Next it should review the determinate sentences of all prisoners serving longer than 10 years at the half-way stage and then at regular intervals, resulting in earlier release on licence or sentence reduction. It should also require a regular review of the minimum terms for people serving indeterminate sentences. The provision that releases those prisoners who must serve two-thirds of their sentences must be reinstated and reduced to one-half.

Beyond this, the government should review the needs and risk levels of older prisoners upon reaching a certain age, followed by a managed move to

34 'Addressing Prison Capacity Pressure,' House of Lords Library.

a more appropriate secure location if required. Those who are very elderly, dying or suffering dementia should be removed from the prison estate. It is not just the sentences of the elderly and frail that need to be examined but those who committed offences at a younger age too. Given all that is known about maturity, people who committed their index offence before they turn 25 should receive a regular sentence review or expedited parole eligibility.

Finally, the new Labour government should significantly increase the size and number of the open (Category D) prison estate to facilitate return to work, education and family community for those serving long sentences. As part of a new approach to open prisons, life-sentenced prisoners should be allowed to apply to move to open prison years earlier than the current three years before release. Next, we turn to re-release and supervision.

Re-release and supervision: Changes to release and supervision policy could facilitate a reduction in the prison population in the short term. The government should abolish the use of recall for sentences of 12 months or less. Recall is disruptive to rehabilitation, and time constraints mean that there often is no meaningful opportunity for re-release before the sentence end date. In addition, Post Sentence Supervision (PSS), a mandatory period of 12 months' supervision in the community post-release for sentences of up to 12 months, should also be abolished (assuming some short prison sentences would continue to be served even with a presumption against them). PSS was introduced via the Offender Rehabilitation Act 2015 as part of the part-privatisation of the probation service, and is a needless hangover of this period, and of legislation which has since been reversed. This move would lessen pressure on the probation service, enabling it to focus on supervising those who pose most risk.

It is also vital that there should be a rapid review of administrative recalls and guidance. The best outcome would be to abolish recall for administrative breaches entirely. Alternatively, any recall for administrative breach should be fixed term and set at 14 days, as opposed to a standard recall which requires review by the parole board prior to release. However, we welcome the expansion of the use of Home Detention Curfew (HDC) for sentences of more than four years, as contained in the Victims and Prisoners Act. To ensure this is a meaningful change, the resourcing and administration of HDC should be improved. Executive release by the secretary of state for justice under the Release following Risk Assessed Recall (RARR) review process is a more time- and cost-effective method of release than parole. Yet figures suggest that use of RARR has declined significantly from more than 1,500 releases in 2017 when the scheme was introduced, to just 20 in the first five months of 2023.[35] This trend should be reversed.

Use of remand: Turning to remand, a review of the use of remand and reducing the remand population is urgently needed, and the new government should explore mechanisms which facilitate a presumption in favour of bail (particularly for children, women and people experiencing mental health crises), reserving the use of remand for those who pose the most risk to the public. The practice of remand for own protection (or own welfare as in the case of children) should be halted through reforms to the Bail Act, as suggested in the draft Mental Health Bill published by the last government. Where restrictions and monitoring are required for public safety, policymakers should explore and invest in alternatives to remand such as community monitoring requirement.

Next, in-order to reduce the population of those already in custody on remand, custody time limits (CTL) should be adhered to for people awaiting trial. Time spent on remand should not exceed the likely length of any eventual custodial sentence. Timely and properly resourced sentencing should also be prioritised for convicted people awaiting sentencing (where CTLs do not apply). This would include the provision of timely pre-sentence reports and sufficient judicial capacity to ensure that judges are able to sentence people as soon as they are able. Policymakers should also seek to improve data collection to understand better the composition of the remand population, the reasons for remanding to custody, and the length of time people are being held – the government does not currently routinely collect this data.

Unfortunately, as set out in this chapter, the time has passed for sticking plasters and emergency measures. After decades of mismanagement, the challenges to our system are too deeply entrenched to be solved through short-term measures – a total reset is needed. This reset will need to include a comprehensive, independent review of sentencing; a review of the management of people in prison, including their sentence progression,

35   See 'Prisoners' Release,' HC Deb, 1 May 2024, cW, https://tinyurl.com/u928t5cj [Accessed 4/12/2024].

routes out of custody, release and reintegration; and a renewed focus on humanising the prison experience. Ultimately, the policy changes set out above will not provide the total reset that is needed in the criminal justice system – but they will give the new government enough space to be able to review and enact the longer-term changes that need implementing.

With numbers projected to rise to over 114,800 by 2028,[36] the Howard League's work over the next five years will focus on the acute crisis in prisons – and we hope that the new government will do the same. We recognise that law is the product of power; and that it criminalises and punishes some behaviours, people and groups more than others. This undermines the legitimacy of our entire criminal justice system and demands challenge in the interests of fairness and equality. We understand that our current systems of punishment are often unjust, cruel and counter-productive; and that they make our communities less rather than more safe. We want to see a reduction in the use of punishment, specifically a very significant reduction in the use of prison and much better conditions and opportunities for those who remain there.

We believe the answers to crime lie not in the criminal justice system, but in a more fair and equitable society, one investing in education, housing, employment and health. We believe in evidence-informed policy, but also in values beyond simply retribution. We believe that everyone is better than their worst moment or decision, in second chances and in the ability of people to change. We know that excessive punishment harms individuals but also the fabric of society. Michael Howard was wrong – prison might work as an easy sell on the doorstep, but it does not cut crime or keep communities safe. To do that, this country must reduce the numbers of people in prison, drastically and urgently.

Bibliography

Beard, Jacqueline. 'Sentencing Bill 2023-24' Research Briefing. House of Commons Library, 4 December 2023. https://researchbriefings.files. parliament.uk/documents/CBP-9907/CBP-9907.pdf [Accessed 27/6/2024].

Coates, Sally. 'Unlocking Potential A review of education in prison.' Ministry of Justice, May 2016. https://assets.publishing.service.gov.uk/media/5a7 f537 eed915d74e33f5bf5/education-review-report.pdf [Accessed 27/6/2024].

---

36 'Prison Population Projections 2023 to 2028, England and Wales,' Ministry of Justice and ONS, https://tinyurl.com/4dwampbc [Accessed 27/6/2024].

Cummins, Ian. 'Strangeways 25 years after the riot: are British prisons better?' The Conversation, 1 April 2015. https://theconversation.com/ strangeways-25-years-after-the-riot-are-british-prisons-better-39482 [Accessed 27/6/2024].

Dawson, Peter. 'Operation Safeguard – what does it tell us?' Prison Reform Trust, Blog, 2 December 2022. https://prisonreformtrust.org.uk/blog-operation-safeguard-what-does-it-tell-us/ [Accessed 24/6/2024].

Department of Education. 'Spring term 2022/23: Suspensions and permanent exclusions in England,' 18 April 2024. https://explore-education-statistics. service.gov.uk/find-statistics/suspensions-and-permanent-exclusions-in-england/2022-23-spring-term [Accessed 27/6/2024].

Eisner, Manuel. 'Why violent crime is plummeting in the rich world.' New Scientist, 4 February 2015. https://www.newscientist.com/article/ mg22530073-200-why-violent-crime-is-plummeting-in-the-rich-world/ [Accessed 24 June, 2024].

Gormley, Jay, et al. The Effectiveness of Sentencing Options on Re-offending. The Sentencing Council, 2022.

Gregory, Andy. 'Chief prisons inspector: Overcrowding is a ticking time bomb.' The Independent, 25 December 2023. https://www.independent. co.uk/news/uk/home-news/prison-overcrowding-charlie-taylor-chief-inspector-b2459658.html [Accessed 24/6/2024].

Grierson, James. 'Indefinite sentences "the greatest single stain on justice system."' The Guardian, 3 December 2020. https://www.theguardian. com/law/2020/dec/03/indefinite-sentences-the-greatest-single-stain-on-justice-system [Accessed 24/6/2024].

HC Deb, 1 May 2024, cW. 'Prisoners' Release.' https://www.theyworkforyou. com/wrans/?id=2024-04-23.23202.h [Accessed 4/12/2024].

House of Commons Justice Committee. 'Public Opinion and Understanding of Sentencing.' 25 October 2023. https://committees.parliament.uk/ publications/41844/documents/207521/default/ [Accessed 24/6/2024].

HL Deb, 13 May 2024. vol. 838, col. 417. 'End of Custody Supervised Licence Scheme: Extension.' https://hansard.parliament.uk/lords/2024-05-13/ debates/89A27B63-AC6C-4043-BAB8-98A3467BF555/EndOf CustodySupervisedLicenceSchemeExtension [Accessed 24/6/2024].

House of Lords Library. 'Addressing Prison Capacity Pressure.' https:// lordslibrary.parliament.uk/addressing-prison-capacity-pressure/ [Accessed 5/12/2024].

— 'Sentences of Imprisonment for Public Protection.' https://lordslibrary. parliament.uk/sentences-of-imprisonment-for-public-protection/ [Accessed 24/6/2024].

Howard League for Penal Reform. 'It's time for a grown-up debate about prison overcrowding.' Blog, 11 March 2024. https://howardleague.org/ blog/its-time-for-a-grown-up-debate-about-prison-overcrowding/ [Accessed 24/6/2024].

— 'Sentence Inflation: A Judicial Critique.' September 2024. https:// howardleague.org/wp-content/uploads /2024/09/Sentencing-inflation- a-judicial-critique_September-2024.pdf [Accessed 4/12/2024].

Howard, Michael. Quoted in *Dictionary of Prisons and Punishment*. Edited by Jamie Bennett and Yvonne Jewkes. Routledge, 2013.

Jenkins, Sammy. 'HMP Eastwood Park: women held in bloodstained cells.' BBC News, 3 February 2023. https://www.bbc.co.uk/news/uk-england- bristol-64498520 [Accessed 24/6/2024].

Ministry of Justice. 'Foreign prison rental to ensure public protection.' Press release, 3 October 2023. https://www.gov.uk/government/news/foreign- prison-rental-to-ensure-public-protection [Accessed 24/6/2024].

— 'Further rollout of Rapid Deployment Cells to boost prison places.' Press release, 24 June 2023. https://www.gov.uk/government/news/further- rollout-of-rapid-deployment-cells-to-boost-prison-places [Accessed 24/6/2024].

— 'Proven reoffending statistics: January to March 2021.' https://www. gov.uk/government/statistics/proven-reoffending-statistics-january- to-march-2021/proven-reoffending-statistics-january-to-march-2021 [Accessed 24/6/2024].

— 'Sentencing Bill Factsheet: Short Sentences.' Policy Paper 5 December 2023. https://www.gov.uk/government/publications/sentencing-bill- 2023/sentencing-bill-factsheet-short-sentences [Accessed 5/12/2024].

Ministry of Justice and ONS. 'Prison Population Projections 2023 to 2028, England and Wales.' https://assets.publishing.service. gov.uk/media/65df5123b8da630f42c86271/Prison_Population_ Projections_2023_to_2028.pdf [Accessed 27/6/2024].

Pidd, Helen. 'Two-thirds of prisons officially overcrowded in England and Wales.' *The Guardian*, 15 October 2023. https://www.theguardian. com/society/2023/oct/15/two-thirds-prisons-officially-overcrowded- england-wales [Accessed 24/6/2024].

Prison Reform Trust. 'The indeterminate sentence of Imprisonment for Public Protection (IPP).' https://prisonreformtrust.org.uk/wp-content/uploads/2021/11/IPP_sentences_the_facts.pdf [Accessed 24/6/2024].

— 'New factsheets showing detailed breakdown of use of imprisonment for women in each police force area.' 14 May 2024. https://prisonreformtrust.org.uk/new-factsheets-showing-detailed-breakdown-of-use-of-imprisonment-for-women-in-each-police-force-area/ [Accessed 27/6/2024].

— 'Prison Reform Trust response to the Justice Committee's inquiry on the future prison population and estate capacity.' October 2023. https://prisonreformtrust.org.uk/wp-content/uploads/2023/11/Justice-Committee-Future-of-prison-population-and-estate-capacity-PRT-written-evidence.pdf [Accessed 27/6/2024].

Richards, Gill, and Nick Davies. 'Performance Tracker 2023: Prisons.' The Institute for Government. https://www.instituteforgovernment.org.uk/publication/performance-tracker-2023/prisons [Accessed 24/6/2024].

Seddon, Paul, and Sam Francis. 'We have too many prisoners, says new PM Starmer.' BBC News. https://www.bbc.co.uk/news/articles/c16jpkzz9g3o [Accessed 4/12/2024].

Syal, Rajeev. 'MoJ postpones plans to reduce female prison population.' The Guardian, 2 May 2018. https://www.theguardian.com/society/2018/may/02/moj-postpones-plans-on-reducing-female-prison-population-strategy-non-violent-offences#[Accessed 27/6/2024].

UK Government Justice Data. 'Public protection: Justice in Numbers.' https://data.justice.gov.uk/justice-in-numbers/jin-public-protection [Accessed 24/6/2024].

UK Parliament. 'Early prisons and imprisonment.' https://www.parliament.uk/about/living-heritage/transformingsociety/laworder/policeprisons/overview/earlyprisons/ [Accessed 27/6/2024].

Williams, Kim, et al. 'Accommodation, homelessness and reoffending of prisoners: Results from the Surveying Prisoner Crime Reduction (SPCR) survey,' Research Summary. Ministry of Justice, March 2012. https://assets.publishing.service.gov.uk/media/5a757ec340f0b6397f35edf3/homelessness-reoffending-prisoners.pdf [Accessed 27/6/2024].

16

Immigration as a Liberal Issue

Vince Cable

Immigration is a central and often bitterly divisive issue throughout the Western world. The issues are complex, reflecting different motives for migration, different characteristics of migrants and the different categories of migrants as defined by host countries. That complexity makes it difficult, and perhaps foolish, to approach immigration in terms of 'good' versus 'bad'. But politicians feel under pressure to act on immigration levels, and specifically against 'illegal' immigration, with rhetoric and policies which are often hostile and draconian. We have seen evidence of this hostile environment in Donald Trump's political use of irregular US-Mexican border crossings, the British government's preoccupation with 'small boats' and the rise of anti-immigration populism throughout Europe. The question I pose is whether it is possible to frame the arguments in terms of liberal principles.

There are two main strands in liberal thinking which apply. One is the economically liberal belief in the efficacy of free markets, which include labour markets. The other strand is a culturally liberal openness of mind and tolerance of diversity. They are not the same and may conflict. Moreover, they are both constrained by the boundaries of the nation state within which politics operates. There are universal principles around the rights of refugees and politically specific or regional agreements to permit free movement, as in the EU or within empires. But it has very rarely been seriously suggested that there is a universal right to migrate. And there are few advocates of 'open borders' anywhere. Even the politically obscure libertarian movement is divided on the issue.[1] In practice, national governments regard defence of their borders as a fundamental duty. Liberal principles must fit around that constraint.

---

1   Vipul Naik, 'Open Borders and the Libertarian Priority List: Part 1,' Open Borders: The Case, https://openborders.info/blog/open-borders-and-the-libertarian-priority-list-part-1/ [Accessed 16/11/2024].

For that reason, the issue of immigration does not map well onto the usual left-right dialectic within which we normally frame political debate. Parties which self-identify as right-wing might be expected to embrace a more liberal approach to immigration along with a belief in free or freer trade and capital movements. Hein de Haas argues that 'you cannot have an open liberal market economy and want less immigration at the same time. It just doesn't work.'[2] He also notes that the political excitement generated by migration is wildly disproportionate to its actual importance; the share of migrants in the world of all kinds has been stable at around 3% for the last 60 years. But politicians committed in principle to the open, liberal market economy have found it difficult to sustain the belief in practice. At times when the process of globalisation was largely uncontroversial, ruling parties of the right were, indeed, part of a broad, business-led consensus in favour of relatively liberal immigration policies. And there are occasions when parties of the right have taken a stand, though more for humanitarian than economic reasons: as with Angela Merkel and Syrian refugees and the Heath government in the UK in relation to Asians from East Africa. But, for the most part, parties of the right have identified with popular anxieties around immigration as a threat to national sovereignty and identity.

By contrast, parties of the left have most frequently found themselves defending immigration from a culturally liberal standpoint. There has, however, often been a contrary argument from organised labour that immigrants undercut wages and conditions and from some social democrats, recently in Denmark, that a successful welfare state requires strong social cohesion involving an exclusiveness which immigrants can undermine.[3] A deeper problem is that the left-right distinction simply breaks down amid the 'politics of identity'.[4] [5] The 'politics of the soil', with its link to ideas of racial purity, can appeal to people across the traditional spectrum.[6] The French anti-immigrant National Front of Marine Le Pen has sunk some of its deepest roots in areas formerly represented by the Communist Party. The same is true of the fringes of German politics where the Alternative for

2   Hein de Haas, *How Migration Really Works – A Factual Guide to the Most Divisive Issue in Politics* (Penguin Viking, 2023).
3   David Goodhart, 'Too Diverse?', *Prospect* issue 95 (February 2004).
4   Vincent Cable, *The World's New Fissures: Identities in Crisis* (Demos, 1994).
5   Vincent Cable, *Multiple Identites: Living with the New Politics of Identity* (Demos, 2005).
6   Michael Ignatieff, *Blood and Belonging* (BBC/Chatto, 1993).

Germany (AfD), often described as extreme right, overlaps in immigration policies with the extreme left party of Sara Wagenknecht. In East Asia, the idea of diluting national and racial identity through large scale immigration, even in the face of demographic collapse, is as much anathema to Chinese Communists as to conservative Japanese Liberal Democrats. In the UK, which I discuss here, the post-war politician most successful in capturing, through virulent and overtly racist rhetoric, an anti-immigrant strand in public opinion was Enoch Powell: a genuine and intellectually coherent economic liberal.[7] This fact illustrates, with great vividness, the deep ambiguities experienced by liberals when they are confronted with the complexities of immigration policy.

A very brief history of UK immigration policy

If we go far enough back in time Britain is a country of immigrants who have settled and married the locals. My paternal family seems to have moved from Flemish France to East Anglia, centuries ago, though whether they were religious refugees or economic migrants is unclear. My maternal family proudly but improbably claimed direct descent from a Baron Pinkney, a genocidal Norman. Most British people can claim an exotic foreign heritage.

In the formative years of British democracy, immigration was not however a political issue in the modern sense, not least because Britain was a country of emigration- to America and the Dominions. The experience of migrants in rapidly growing British cities was mainly from across the Irish Sea when the island of Ireland was still part of the UK. There was a history of non-white immigration from black escaped or freed slaves and Asian seamen, but they were few and largely assimilated into the host population.[8]

The first attempt to define the limits of immigration in law was in the form of the 1905 Aliens Act which was a response to a wave of Jewish immigration: refugees from pogroms in Tsarist Russia. An estimated 150,000 came to the UK over a 20-year period and there was strong anti-immigrant feeling, encouraged by campaigners aiming to stop 'Britain becoming the dumping ground for the scum of Europe'.[9] The debate on the act in

---

7   Patrick Cosgrave, *The Lives of Enoch Powell* (Bodley Head, 1989).
8   Ron Ramdin, *Reimagining Britain: 500 Years of Black and Asian History* (Pluto Press, 1999).
9   Alison Bashford et al., *The Alien Invasion: The Origins of the Aliens Act, 1905* (Heineman, 1972).

parliament was the occasion for Winston Churchill to cross the floor from the Conservatives to the Liberals and his speech was a classic statement of cultural and economic liberalism: 'The Bill would commend itself to those who like patriotism at the expense of others and admire Imperialism on the Russian model. It is expected to appeal to insular prejudice against foreigners, to racial prejudice against Jews and to labour prejudice against competition.'[10] The rejection of ethnic minorities on racial grounds also took other forms, as in the 1919 riots in sea-ports – Liverpool, South Wales, Glasgow – against Asian seamen, mainly British subjects, allegedly taking jobs from demobilised soldiers.[11]

The 1948 British Nationality Act clarified the distinction between British citizens and subjects but one of its consequences, unappreciated at the time, was that Commonwealth citizens still retained the right to settle in the UK. It soon became clear that there were practical consequences in the form of unrestricted economic migration from – black – British subjects in the Caribbean and – Asian – Commonwealth citizens from the sub-continent attracted by strong labour demand in the years of post-war recovery. Commencing with Windrush in 1948, Caribbean migrants came mainly to work in public services – the NHS and public transport – and settled in the big cities, especially London and Birmingham. The South Asian migrants were attracted to the Yorkshire and Lancashire textile towns and other centres, where there was a demand for factory workers willing to undertake difficult work for low pay: the Black Country in the West Midlands; Southall in London.

Net immigration of non-white Commonwealth citizens rose rapidly in the late 1950's and reached 60,000 in 1960 and 140,000 in 1961.[12] The new arrivals faced discrimination in the housing and job markets and from the police. There was growing backlash from the host population against what were called 'coloured immigrants', culminating in race riots in Notting Hill and Nottingham. The clamour for restrictions on Commonwealth migrants reached its peak with the big numbers in 1961 (partly caused by anticipation of expected controls). The 1962 Commonwealth Immigration Act gave

10 Martin Gilbert, *Churchill: a Life* (Henry Holt, 1991), p. 165.
11 Jacqueline Jenkinson, *The 1919 Race Riots in Britain* (Edinburgh University PhD, 1987).
12 Dhananjayan Sriskandarajah, 'Outsiders on the Inside,' in *Social Justice: Building a fairer Britain*, ed. Nick Pearce and Will Paxton (Institute for Public Policy Research, Politicos, 2005).

powers to curb immigration and Commonwealth citizens were relegated to the same status as non-Commonwealth citizens (though Irish immigration was left untouched).[13] Whilst the Act effectively blocked new workers, it allowed families to be united through settlement in the UK. Britain set its face against the European 'gast-arbeiter' model and saw integration as best achieved through family units. The numbers of dependants, around 50,000 a year, did however provide the trigger for perhaps the most important and divisive political pronouncement on immigration in the 20th century: Enoch Powell's 'rivers of blood' speech in April 1968.[14]

Powell's central claim was that continued family migration from groups with relatively high birth rates would radically transform Britain's ethnic mix. According to this analysis, Britain was 'heaping the fuel on its own funeral pyre'. Powell predicted that by 2000 there would be 5 to 7 million people of non-white immigrant descent: up to 1 in 10 of the population. His projections proved to be broadly accurate; in 2001, in England, there were 4.4 million people of non-white descent, 8.7%: 5.2% self-identifying as Asian, 2.6% black and 0.75% mixed race or 'other'. By 2021 the total (for the whole UK) was 8.2 million, 12.2% of the population: 6.3% Asian, 3.0% black and 2.9% mixed race or other. Where Powell proved to be totally wrong was his prediction of widespread conflict and violence: 'Like the Roman, I see the River Tiber foaming with blood.' He wanted families united, through deportation back to their countries of origin; used deliberately insulting language as in 'coloured, Negro and picanninies'; and whipped up fear of when 'the black man will have the whip hand'. There were strikes and marches in his support and he undoubtedly had a significant following.

Powell's speech created the combustible material to ignite the next fire. The tinder was made up of the British subjects of Asian origin living in East Africa. In Kenya there were approximately 140,000 excluding the 30,000, mainly Ismailis, who had become Kenyan nationals.[15] The author's extended family of in-laws were among them. The Kenyatta administration declared its intention to replace non-Kenyan Asians by Kenyans and an exodus of British Asians began in mid-1968 which accelerated when there were rumours that

13   Randall Hansen, *Citizenship and Immigration in Post-war Britain* (Oxford University Press, 2000).

14   Shirin Hirsch, *In the Shadow of Enoch Powell* (Manchester University Press, 2018).

15   Vincent Cable, *Whither Kenyan Emigrants?* Young Fabian Pamphlet 18 (The Fabian Society, 1968).

the UK would close off the exit route. In a climate of panic, further inflamed by the Powell speech, emergency legislation, the 1968 Immigration Act, was steered through parliament by the then home secretary, James Callaghan, as part of the Labour government of Harold Wilson. It removed the right to live in the UK from millions of British overseas subjects. These included most Hong Kongers and many others who did not have a family connection to the UK (through a parent or grandfather). Those Kenyan Asians who did not beat the ban went to India or Canada but of those who did, and settled in Leicester or London, the nucleus was created for what became a highly successful, upwardly mobile, minority group.

Three years later the East African crisis erupted again when President Idi Amin threatened to expel all the 'British' Asians. This time the (Conservative) government did not panic, accepted its obligation to take any Ugandan Asians who were expelled and organised a resettlement scheme. It also passed legislation to confirm entitlement to settle based on close family connection. Within a decade, a consistent set of criteria for immigration – the right to settle in the UK – had been established and legislated. (Britain also joined the European Union in 1973 though no one at the time seems to have appreciated the significance of the commitment to free movement). In the three decades of the 70s, 80s and 90s there was a broad consensus around the fundamentals of immigration policy, though there were disagreements around implementation and around detail, issues like bogus marriages and the appropriate response to illegal overstayers.

Those decades also saw the virtual decline of the numbers issue. In the 1970s especially, net immigration was negative. Gross immigration rarely exceeded 50,000 and was exceeded by British emigrants (though this was not very reassuring to those who shared the Powell race-based view, that is now called Great Replacement Theory). The emphasis of policy shifted from immigration to integration of the ethnic minorities. Racial discrimination and incitement to racial violence had been outlawed but individuals suffered more subtle forms of injury and insult and poor relations with the police. White extremist groups had only modest support but enough to cause fear and alarm. The years 1980/81 saw a succession of inner-city riots often triggered by friction between black youths and the police: St Pauls (Bristol), Chapeltown (Leeds), Moss Side (Manchester), Toxteth (Liverpool), Handsworth (Birmingham) and Brixton (London). Deeper problems like joblessness, bad housing and poor social amenities also lay behind the frustrations. And these continued with a repetition of riots in 1985 in Handsworth, Brixton and Broadwater Farm in Tottenham.

In 1989/2001 there were also riots involving Asian and white residents in Oldham, Burnley and Bradford involving some of the same social issues, but also the differences arising from the parallel lives of Muslim communities originating mainly in traditional Pakistan society. Moreover, the emergence of a decidedly multicultural Britain, was a challenge for many people of a broadly liberal disposition, since it appeared to involve accepting cultures which were deeply illiberal around such issues as the role of women and of freedom of expression. But, reassuringly, concentration in ghettos has since been breaking down. Censuses show a consistent trend for every ethnic group to disperse, with the biggest population growth in suburbs and small towns.

From the mid-1990s net immigration rose rapidly and was typically over 100,000 p.a. by the end of the century. The migration flows were then accelerated by the decision of the Blair government in 2002 to remove any restrictions on future arrivals from the eight accession countries to the EU. The decision was partly economic – the UK economy was growing strongly – and partly geopolitical to show support for EU expansion to the East (the UK was copied by Sweden and Ireland though others dragged their heels, with Germany not lifting restrictions until 2012). Government forecasts of annual inflows of 5,000 to 13,000 proved to be wildly inaccurate; 130,000 arrived in the two years 2004/5 and 112,000 in 2007 with overall net migration figures of close to 300,000, and it was this level of immigration, which led to a decade-long debate on the economic and social impact of mass immigration. Even with the chilling effect of the financial crisis on labour markets, there was just over 250,000 net immigration in 2010 and the new Conservative-led Coalition sought to reduce the figure to the Conservative's net migration target of under 100,000. Despite attempts to reduce the numbers, using every – non-EU – channel subject to visa controls, the overall net immigration figure in 2015 was over 300,000: then, a record level. That was the backdrop to the EU referendum in 2016 in which high immigration levels were a central issue.

The consequence of Brexit has been that, as of 1 January 2021, free movement from the EU ceased. All entry for work purposes became subject to a points-based visa regime. It is not easy to chart the impact of the new regime since the Covid pandemic massively disrupted flows initially – from around 300,000 net in 2018, to 100,000 in 2020 followed by a surge in net migration in 2022 to the extraordinary level of 745,000. Included in the total have been officially approved inflows of refugees from Hong Kong and Ukraine and unofficial entries from refugees in small boats. One plausible figure for a new equilibrium net immigration level is 250,000 to 300,000[16] which, given the recent political history of immigration, and Brexit, is extraordinarily high. The new regime is now probably the most liberal of any advanced economy and on a par with traditionally immigration-friendly countries like Canada or Australia.[17]

How has this unusual outcome been achieved? The upsurge in immigration has been almost exclusively a non-EU phenomenon and in 2022 European net migration was negative. The new skilled work visa has proved relatively easy to obtain. The salary threshold designed to exclude unskilled workers – £25,000 – proved to be a weak deterrent with gaps in the hospitality sector caused by EU personnel leaving being filled from non-EU countries. The cap has been removed altogether for PhD students, and workers in the NHS and social care. In social care, especially, immigrant staff now make up a high proportion of staff. In addition, overseas students can stay to work for two years after graduation in any job – though the rules were tightened in 2024 to prevent overseas students bringing dependants. Numbers of overseas students (net) are estimated at around 250,000 though the vast majority return in due course so the equilibrium level for them should be close to zero: a controversial area of policy debate to which I return below.

Looked at as a whole, it seems that despite the negative rhetoric around immigration, the implicit assumption of government policy is that a liberal approach to immigration for work and study is good for the British economy. I now look at that assumption.

The economics of immigration

The OECD has supported a positive view towards immigration and its impact on the economy. They note that immigrants tend to be net-economic

---

16   Tessa Hall et al., 'Why are the Latest Net Immigration Figures not a Reliable Guide to Future Trends,' The Migration Observatory, https://migration observatory.ox.ac.uk/resources/reports/why-are-the-latest-net-migration-figures-not-a-reliable-guide-to-future-trends/ [Accessed 17/11/2024].
17   Jonathan Portes, 'What to Make of the Latest ONS Migration Statistics,' UK in a Changing Europe, https://ukandeu.ac.uk/what-to-make-of-the-latest-ons-migration-statistics/ [Accessed 16/11/2024].

contributors and that in general, 'immigrants are not taking up more benefits than the native-born'.[18] How far is this positive view economically justified?

The economic impact of immigration on the host country will depend on the make-up of the migrants and the conditions in the host economy. There is no clearly predictable outcome and the evidence from experience is ambiguous. Immigrants add to demand through additional spending, though the impact on Gross Domestic Product (GDP), or inflation, will then depend on the amount of spare capacity. Immigrant workers who augment the labour force will add to production directly but that does not apply to dependants or to refugees who are not able to work. Immigration typically adds to GDP – and the growth of GDP – by the simple fact of creating a bigger economy but the more valid measure is GDP per head which is more difficult to predict. Alan Manning, formerly Chair of the UK Migration Advisory Panel, comments that 'the impact of well-chosen migration policy on growth was very small unless measured as GDP, which is the wrong measure'.[19] What is more relevant is whether immigration adds to overall living standards in the host country which is achieved by raising productivity.

Most of the big international studies of the link between growth and migration tend to converge on a positive conclusion. An IMF study concludes: 'migration to advanced economies improves economic growth and productivity'.[20] [21] But they also agree that the effects are small. One study of 22 OECD countries over 20 years concluded that 'a 50% increase in registrations of foreign-born workers leads to a 10% increase in productivity growth'.[22] A survey covering the period 1950-2010 said: 'the broad conclusion

18   OECD, 'Economic Impact of Migration,' https://www.oecd.org/en/topics/sub-issues/economic-impact-of-migration.html [Accessed 5/12/2024].

19   Alan Manning, 'The Link Between Growth and Migration: Unpacking the Confusion,' London School of Economics Blog, https://blogs.lse.ac.uk/politicsandpolicy/the-link-between-growth-and-immigration-unpicking-the-confusion/ [Accessed 16/11/2024].

20   Philip Engler et al., 'Migration to Advanced Countries Can Raise Growth,' International Monetary Fund Blog, https://www.imf.org/en/Blogs/Articles/2020/06/19/blog-weo-chapter4-migration-to-advanced-economies-can-raise-growth [Accessed 16/11/2024].

21   International Monetary Fund, 'Chapter 4 The Macroeconomic Effects of Global Migration,' in *World Economic Outlook,* April 2020 (International Monetary Fund, 2020).

22   'OECD Migration Policy Debates May 2014', based on Ekrame Boubtane, Jean-Christophe Dumont, *Immigration and Growth in OECD Countries 1986-2006* (Sorbonne, 2013).

is that an increase in the net migration rate increases the rate of growth of output per worker slightly.'[23]

But some analysts question the faintness of the praise. Jonathan Portes has argued that in the UK the benefits to the economy from migration of improved productivity have been underestimated and are strongly positive.[24] [25] There are migrants who can make a significant contribution since they are successful entrepreneurs or have a unique technical or scientific attribute which enables them to contribute through innovation. Even if migrants are working in low paid and relatively unskilled jobs, they may free up opportunities for others to take up higher paid and more productive roles. It is the different mix of skills and the complementary role of migrant workers which, in a functioning market economy, raises overall productivity. Those who object to immigration will sometimes argue that it discourages firms from investing in equipment to raise productivity. But some occupations, as with social care and hospitality or picking soft fruit, don't lend themselves to automation, though, if efficiently organised, can aid the overall performance of the economy.

In practice much of the economic debate around migration relates to the impact on the labour market and particularly on the wages of workers in the host country. Anti-immigrant protests in Britain from the anti-refugee protests in the early days of the 20th century have coalesced around groups of workers arguing that wages and conditions are being undercut by immigrant workers. The UK Migration Advisory Committee in 2018 commissioned a review of the extensive academic literature on labour markets assessing the impact of the high levels of net migration to the UK.[26] The main conclusion was that there was little or no measurable impact on British wages (probably because the migrants were in complementary, not competitive roles). The was some evidence however of negative impacts on workers with low

23 Stephen Bruno, in *Handbook of the Economics of International Migration: vol. 1*, ed. Barry Chiswick and Paul W. Miller (North Holland, 2015).
24 Jonathan Portes, 'The Economics of Migration,' *Contexts* vol. 18, no. 2 (2019): pp. 12-17.
25 Jonathan Portes, 'The Economic Impacts of Migration to the UK,' CEPR, https://cepr.org/voxeu/columns/economic-impacts-immigration-uk [Accessed 17/11/2024].
26 Madelaine Sumption and Carlos Vargas-Silva, 'The Labour Market Effects of Immigration,' The Migration Observatory, https://migrationobservatory.ox.ac.uk/resources/briefings/the-labour-market-effects-of-immigration/ [Accessed 17/11/2024].

education levels who were competing directly with immigrants for jobs. And the impact depended on the economic cycle: positive in periods of upswing and labour shortage; negative during recession.

There is one sense in which immigration may have a negative impact which also resonates with critical public opinion. Where there is a fixed supply of public services – doctors' surgeries and NHS waiting lists; school places and class sizes; bus queues; availability of social housing – an additional source of demand from immigrants and their dependants will detract from the quality of services available for the host population, especially when highly concentrated in some geographical areas. If the effects are felt more generally, immigration can potentially contribute to a breakdown in the social contract whereby services which the host population has paid for in tax or insurance contributions is having to be shared with newly arrived foreigners. Milton Friedman is said to have commented: 'You cannot simultaneously have free immigration and a welfare state.'[27] That has also been the basis of the harsh approach to benefit entitlements employed by the Social Democratic Danish government for example.

A major offsetting factor is the tax paid by immigrant workers. Highly skilled and highly paid immigrants will make substantial net contributions to the exchequer. That is especially the case if immigrants are of a younger age profile than the host population and therefore likely to be tax contributors for longer and less demanding of services like health for which demand grows with age. Furthermore, some immigrants, like social care workers and nurses, which have seen the biggest increase in UK work visas since the post-Brexit regime came into force, are propping up overstretched public services, The alternative – to fix the shortage of these occupations – might well require a substantial increase in salaries and in taxation to pay for them. The Migration Observatory has tried to estimate for the UK the net fiscal effect and concludes that there is a 'small net cost' overall.[28] But there is a wide variety of estimates based on different groups of migrants and different methodologies. A review of evidence regarding EU migrants concludes that

---

27 Sam Bowman, 'Milton Friedman's Objections to Immigration,' Adam Smith Institute, https://www.adamsmith.org/blog/economics/milton-friedman-s-objection-to-immigration [Accessed 17/11/2024].

28 Carlos Vargas-Silva et al., 'The Fiscal Impacts of Immigration in the UK,' The Migration Observatory, https://migrationobservatory.ox.ac.uk/resources/briefings/the-fiscal-impact-of-immigration-in-the-uk/ [Accessed, 17/11/2024].

'there is a positive impact on public finances'.[29] [30] Jonathan Portes echoes the position of the Office of Budget Responsibility and the Treasury that more immigration is good for the budget and for reducing government debt.[31]

There is one sector in which increased demand from immigrants appears to have an unambiguously negative effect and that is on the market for housing. Housing supply is often constrained by regulation designed to protect amenity in the places where new arrivals want to live because there are jobs nearby. The host population is then affected negatively by rising rents or mortgage payments (though older owner occupiers who have paid their mortgage loans benefit from capital appreciation). Britain may be uniquely negligent in meeting increasing housing demand but one study across the 'Anglosphere' showed that growth in housing starts over a thirty-year period was consistently well below the growth in the working age population.[32]

But to offset that negative there is one sector in which there are substantial net benefits for the UK and other host countries: overseas students. These (temporary) immigrants pay large, uncapped fees cross-subsidising domestic students and make very little call on public services (though that depends in part on whether they bring dependants). If they then work for some time in graduate-level employment they may contribute unique skills especially in sciences.[33] Yet a narrow focus on immigrant numbers has led to their being subject to controls. And the preoccupation with numbers comes from political fears that this is what the public cares about. I therefore turn to the issue of public attitudes.

Public attitudes

Policy is determined by politicians and politicians are heavily (though not exclusively) influenced by public opinion or what they believe public opinion

29 Johnny Runge, *Review of the Evidence on Economic Impacts of EU Migration*, ESRC Briefing (NIESR, 2019).

30 Christian Dustmann and Tommaso Frattini, 'The Fiscal Effects of Immigration to the UK,' *Economic Journal* vol. 24, issue 580 (2014).

31 Jonathan Portes, 'Has Higher Immigration Saved the Chancellor Again,' UK in a Changing Europe, https://ukandeu.ac.uk/has-higher-immigration-saved-the-chancellor-again/ [Accessed 17/11/2024].

32 'Immigration is surging, with big economic consequences,' *The Economist*, 30 April, 2024, https://www.economist.com/finance-and-economics/2024/04/30/immigration-is-surging-with-big-economic-consequences [Accessed 17/11/2024].

33 London Economics, *The Costs and Benefits of International Higher Education Students to the UK Economy*, report for the Higher Education Policy Institute, Universities UK, Kaplan International Pathways (London Economics, 2023).

to be. Unsurprisingly public attitudes to immigration vary over time and in different places, within and between countries. Several factors consistently emerge. First, the public seriously and consistently over-estimate the scale of immigration. An ODI (Oversees Development Institute) study of the UK, suggested that the (average) public estimate of the share of the foreign-born population was wrong by a factor of two – 27% rather than 14% with non-EU migrants estimated to be 21% rather than 9%.[34] [35]

Second, there are big short-term fluctuations reflecting the salience of the issue in public debate. Although the British Conservatives, in government and out, have been preoccupied by the immigration issue, the share of Conservative voters judging immigration to be one of the most important issues facing the country has fluctuated between 10% and 70% in a decade. The numbers exceeded 50% only briefly at the EU referendum, when all voters, including Labour and Liberal Democrat, put the issue at the top of their concerns. The share of Conservative voters expressing concern about immigration then fell from 70% to under 10% during the pandemic, before returning to almost 50% in mid-2024 with 'small boats' being a big controversy.[36] Labour supporters tracked the same fluctuations, but were typically 10% to 20% less concerned. The gap widened to 40% in 2024.

Third, hostility to immigration has markedly declined over time, despite (or perhaps because of) the significantly increased population of immigrant origin. There is some indication that hostility to non-white immigrants grows in proportion to distance and inversely proportional to the amount of actual interaction. The British Election Study showed that over the five decades from the mid-60s until the period around the referendum, the proportion agreeing that 'there was too much immigration' remained consistently high – over 70% – though it had gradually declined from almost 90%. Then, quite suddenly in historical terms, after the referendum, the share fell to under 50%. Surveys by IPSOS asking the same question showed the same trend but at a lower level of hostility (falling to 40%).

34 Helen Dempster and Karen Hargreaves, *Understanding Public Attitudes Towards Refugees and Migrants,* Working Paper 512 (ODI/Chatham House, 2017).
35 ODI, *Hearts and Minds: How Europeans Think and Feel about Immigration* (ODI, 2019).
36 John Burn-Murdoch, 'The Great Immigration Miscalculation', *Financial Times*, 15 December 2023, https://www.ft.com/content/a4540259-463e-4aa3-ac3b-912ac0819807 [Accessed 17/11/2024].

Using a different methodology, the European Social Survey tracked the same sharp decline in negative perceptions of immigration in the UK with a fall over the last decade in the proportion of those who judged immigration to be excessive, from around 50% to 20%.[37] The same survey has shown that the proportion who consider that immigration has made Britain a better place to live rose from 30% in 2002 to 50% in 2022. Other European countries saw a similar trend with Ireland and Portugal the most positive and France the least.[38] Other surveys confirm the trend. British Futures found that the proportion who see immigration as damaging to the UK fell from 54% in 2012 to 20% in 2022, and the proportion who believe that immigrant skills are beneficial rose from 24% to 50%.[39] Finally, Britain is now best in class when it comes to positive attitudes to immigration. A World Values Survey shows that in 2022 70% of Britons believed that immigration strengthens society through diversity and Britain was the least likely country for immigrants to be blamed for crime.[40] Just 5% objected to the idea of living next to a migrant family.

What general conclusions can be taken about public attitudes which are relevant to policy? An ODI study pointed to the ambiguities in public attitudes: many people feeling positive about immigration but wanting less; with a large 'conflicted middle' who could easily sway in different directions.[41] Also there was a more positive approach to some forms of immigration than others, with a preference for skilled people and a more negative feeling about asylum seekers.[42]

But while the public is negative it is also ahead of the government in liberal thinking on how to treat refugees: 75% support refugee protection; only a third support 'deterrent' policies for asylum seekers; and over 80%

---

37 'Britain is the best place in Europe to be an immigrant,' *The Economist*, 21 March, 2024, https://www.economist.com/leaders/2024/03/21/britain-is-the-best-place-in-europe-to-be-an-immigrant [Accessed 17/11/2024].

38 Christa Rottensteiner and Claire Kumar, 'As UK public attitudes toward migration are increasingly positive, it's time for more balanced and evidence-based narratives,' UN Migration – United Kingdom, https://unitedkingdom.iom.int/news/uk-public-attitudes-toward-migration-are-increasingly-positive-its-time-more-balanced-and-evidence-based-narratives [Accessed 17/11/2024].

39 Ipsos/British Future Trends, *Attitudes Towards Migration* (IPSOS, 2022).

40 C. Haerpfer et al., eds, '2022 World Values Survey,' JD Systems Institute & WVSA Secretariat. doi:10.14281/18241.24, https://www.worldvaluessurvey.org/WVSDocumentationWV7.jsp.

41 Amy Leach et al., *Public Attitudes to Immigration and Immigrants* (ODI, 2020).

42 Dempster and Hargreaves, *Understanding Public Attitudes*.

believe that asylum seekers should be allowed to work six months or more into their UK residence.[43]

With all the necessary qualifications, British attitudes have generally moved in a positive direction. One reason could be that the economic arguments have cut through and are also reflected in peoples' lived experiences. Another could be that, while there is still evidence of discrimination in the labour market and elsewhere in society and still a higher level of deprivation in foreign born communities, there are significant signs of success in integration, more than elsewhere in Europe. A study of hourly wages as a share of the native-born average shows that immigrant children from all backgrounds have made big advances relative to their parent's generation and in general are now at the native-born average with Indian and Chinese-origin well above it and with the most striking advance in those of Bangladeshi-origin.[44] An Institute of Fiscal Studies (IFS) study of educational progress tells the same story. The largest minority groups now do as well as their white British counterparts in GCSE Maths and English (and slightly better on PISA[45] scores). Bangladeshi children are catching up very fast. Black Caribbean, as opposed to African-origin, children remain the only outlier.[46] The positive story continues elsewhere: 60% of foreign-born adults aged 25-45 have attended university as against 46% for the host population (though they are underrepresented in elite universities). Employment levels of men (not women) shows rough equality (though there is still discriminatory pay). Many problems remain but apparently successful integration – reinforced by greater ethnic minority representation amongst government ministers – has fed through into positive public perceptions.

These findings raise the question of why such a big gap has opened between public sentiment and a government seemingly anxious to capture the public mood on immigration. A plausible argument is that, while a dwindling minority are hostile to immigration, the minority hold their

43 Steve Ballinger, 'Where is British Opinion on Refugee Protection,' British Future, https://www.britishfuture.org/where-is-public-opinion-on-refugee-protection/ [Accessed 17/11/2024].

44 John Burn-Murdoch, 'The Anglosphere has an Advantage in Immigration,' *Financial Times*, 25 April 2024, https://www.ft.com/content/c6bb7307-484c-4076-a0f3-fc2aeb0b6112 [Accessed 17/11/2024].

45 Programme for International Student Assessment.

46 Imran Rasul and Heidi Mirza, *Deaton Review of Inequalities* (Institute of Fiscal Studies, 2022).

opinions much more intensely than the majority. And that minority is influential within the Conservative Party, which has sanctions at hand such as the ability to select or deselect candidates and to change the leader. But there is also a big gap between rhetoric and reality. Policy in practice has been liberal especially, and surprisingly, since Brexit. Tough targets for net migration are set and not reached even approximately. Attention is focussed instead on refugees in small boats who make up a small proportion of immigrants (30,000 out of 1.2 million (gross) migration in the year to June 2023).

The policy debate

Brexit is not about to be reopened or major immigration laws repealed by either the Conservatives or Britain's new Labour government under Sir Keir Starmer. But that should not prevent liberals from advocating for closer ties with the European Union or for a fairer approach to immigration. There are still some important issues that need to be resolved. First, there is the operation of the work visa scheme. What matters in practice is the salary threshold which can be prohibitively high or permissively low and in the case of the former can create unnecessary cruelties as with permission to bring in foreign spouses. Business start-ups, which is an area of real economic gain from migration, often depend on founders working initially at low levels of pay, which also needs flexibility. The current system however is broadly liberal at present and reflects labour market conditions. One issue for the future is whether there should be some forward thinking about the evolving structure of the economy and employment reflecting a more strategic approach and for that to be reflected in visa applications. Second, there are rumbling arguments over overseas students for no better reason than that statistically they count as 'immigrants' even though they are temporary visitors akin to long stay tourists. The matter has been complicated by two factors. The first is that the Home Office appears to have no mechanism for counting people out and has used a discredited and inflated estimate of the percentage staying behind. Universities, colleges and schools have records of legal departures which would deflate the numbers of net student migration. There has also been an assumption of widespread visa abuse. Some undoubtedly occurred in language schools, though there is now a tightly managed system of trusted providers. In any event, it is inherently unlikely that families would pay university fees and expenses of more than £50,000 so their son and daughter could then stay illegally in irregular employment. British universities rely on overseas students for around a quarter of their income, and they are operating in a competitive international market (with the USA, Canada and Australia mainly). New restrictions like those on dependants of postgraduate students have a significant deterrent effect and undermine UK universities.

The above issues are essentially about economic benefit and cost. A third is about liberal values in a different sense: generosity to refugees seeking asylum and specifically those who have arrived by irregular means: the boat crossings from France. There is a formal distinction between legal and illegal asylum seekers which has been entrenched by the provision in the Illegal Migration Act of 2023 to prevent illegal arrivals from seeking asylum. But when there are no legal routes to apply through (as there are for Ukrainians, Hong Kongers and some other select groups) the distinction is largely academic. It is equally artificial to distinguish economic and political migrants since people fleeing the fighting in Sudan or Somalia or Yemen may well be both destitute and in fear of being persecuted. But it is reasonable in principle to say that asylum seekers from semi-democratic India, Nigeria, or Pakistan or Albania do not, prima facie, have a strong asylum case compared to those fleeing Afghanistan and Syria. However, even here, there would still be some grounds for claiming asylum on the basis of sexuality or religious persecution.

Honesty demands acknowledgment that this is a genuinely difficult issue since potential demand is vast and people are desperate given the political and economic conditions in much of Sahelian Africa and the Near East. We are not dealing with the limited flows of fugitives envisaged in Britain's open-door policy after the French Revolution or post-war international legal commitments.

Several principles should apply. First, deterrence, the Rwanda scheme proved to be inhumane, unworkable, economically prohibitive and lacked widespread public support. It was right to be scrapped by the new government. Second, a swift resolution to asylum claims is humane and reassuring to the public. The rate of asylum decisions has collapsed since the early part of the century from around 100,000 a year to under 20,000 and removals of failed asylum seekers has fallen from around 10,000 a year in 2010 to barely 2,000 in recent years. And that is partly a question of deploying resources better to clearing the backlogs involved. There is nothing wrong in principle with processing claims offshore in British dependent territories or friendly democratic states rather than using British hotels as a staging post. But Rwanda was not a good choice. Third, burying the legacy of Brexit and working alongside Europeans, especially the French, is imperative both in respect of migrant returns and people smuggling. There is a shared problem. And finally, the long-term prohibition on work for asylum seekers is economically wasteful and allows talent to atrophy.

We should reflect also on the big picture of demographic change and how it will play out over the decades to come. As noted earlier, Enoch Powell was completely wrong about the social and political consequences of immigration, but he was right about the scale of demographic transformation. With net immigration speeding up, the transformation will also accelerate. The Office for National Statistics has predicted that by as soon as 2036 Britain's population will have risen from 67 million in 2021 to almost 74 million in 2036[47] (it was 50 million in 1950). Migration will account for almost all the increase, and almost all of that from outside Europe. Powell was obsessed by stopping the growth of the non-white population, but it has grown anyway and will probably be close to 20% of the population in little over a decade. Many of us celebrate the diversity that this brings. And we also celebrate the fact that British democracy has been mature and tolerant enough to absorb, generally young, working people from abroad to sustain an otherwise ageing society. But there are problems which are not yet being faced: a chronic inability to expand the housing stock sufficiently and a decaying, inadequate infrastructure. These are problems which will not solve themselves.

Bibliography

Ballinger, Steve. 'Where is British Opinion on Refugee Protection.' British Future. https://www.britishfuture.org/where-is-public-opinion-on-refugee-protection/ [Accessed 17/11/2024].

Bashford, Alison, et al. *The Alien Invasion: The Origins of the Aliens Act, 1905*. Heineman, 1972.

Boubtane, Ekrame, and Jean-Christophe Dumont. *Immigration and Growth in OECD Countries 1986-2006*. Sorbonne, 2013.

---

47 Office for National Statistics, 'National population projections: 2021-based interim,' https://www.ons.gov.uk/peoplepopulationandcommunity/populationandmigration/populationprojections/bulletins/nationalpopulationprojections/2021basedinterim/previous/v1 [Accessed 17/11/2024].

Bowman, Sam. 'Milton Friedman's Objections to Immigration.' Adam Smith Institute. https://www.adamsmith.org/blog/economics/milton-friedman-s-objection-to-immigration [Accessed 17/11/2024].

Burn-Murdoch, John. 'The Anglosphere has an Advantage in Immigration.' *Financial Times*, 25 April 2024. https://www.ft.com/content/c6bb7307-484c-4076-a0f3-fc2aeb0b6112 [Accessed 17/11/2024].

— 'The Great Immigration Miscalculation.' *Financial Times*, 15 December 2023. https://www.ft.com/content/a4540259-463e-4aa3-ac3b-912ac0819807 [Accessed 17/11/2024].

Cable, Vincent. *Multiple Identites: Living with the new Politics of Identity.* Demos, 2005.

— *Whither Kenyan Emigrants?* Young Fabian Pamphlet 18. The Fabian Society, 1968.

— *The World's New Fissures: Identities in Crisis.* Demos, 1994.

Chiswick, Barry, and Paul W. Miller, eds. *Handbook of the Economics of International Migration: vol. 1.* North Holland, 2015.

Cosgrave, Patrick. *The Lives of Enoch Powell.* Bodley Head, 1989.

Dempster, Helen, and Karen Hargreaves. *Understanding Public Attitudes Towards Refugees and Migrants*, Working Paper 512. ODI/Chatham House, 2017.

Dustmann, Christian, and Tomasso Frattini. 'The Fiscal Effects of Immigration to the UK.' *Economic Journal* vol. 24, issue 580 (2014).

Economist, The. 'Britain is the best place in Europe to be an immigrant.' 21 March 2024. https://www.economist.com/leaders/2024/03/21/britain-is-the-best-place-in-europe-to-be-an-immigrant [Accessed 17/11/2024].

— 'Immigration is surging, with big economic consequences.' 30 April 2024. https://www.economist.com/finance-and-economics/2024/04/30/immigration-is-surging-with-big-economic-consequences [Accessed 17/11/2024].

Engler, Philip, et al. 'Migration to Advanced Countries Can Raise Growth.' International Monetary Fund Blog. https://www.imf.org/en/Blogs/Articles/2020/06/19/blog-weo-chapter4-migration-to-advanced-economies-can-raise-growth [Accessed 16/11/2024].

Gilbert, Martin. *Churchill: a Life.* Henry Holt, 1991.

Goodhart, David. 'Too Diverse?' *Prospect* issue 95 (February 2004).

Haas, Hein de. *How Migration Really Works – A Factual Guide to the Most Divisive Issue in Politics.* Penguin Viking, 2023.

Haerpfer, C., et al., eds. '2022 World Values Survey.' JD Systems Institute & WVSA Secretariat. doi:10.14281/18241.24. https://www.world valuessurvey.org/WVSDocumentationWV7.jsp.

Hall, Tessa, et al. 'Why are the Latest Net Immigration Figures not a Reliable Guide to Future Trends.' The Migration Observatory. https:// migrationobservatory.ox.ac.uk/resources/reports/why-are-the-latest-net-migration-figures-not-a-reliable-guide-to-future-trends/ [Accessed 17/11/2024].

Hansen, Randall. *Citizenship and Immigration in Post-war Britain*. Oxford University Press, 2000.

Hirsch, Shirin. *In the Shadow of Enoch Powell*. Manchester University Press, 2018.

Ignatieff, Michael. *Blood and Belonging*. BBC/Chatto, 1993.

International Monetary Fund. 'Chapter 4 The Macroeconomic Effects of Global Migration.' In *World Economic Outlook*, April 2020. International Monetary Fund, 2020.

Ipsos/British Future Trends. *Attitudes Towards Migration*. Ipsos, 2022.

Jenkinson, Jacqueline. *The 1919 Race Riots in Britain*. Edinburgh University PhD, 1987.

Leach, Amy, et al. *Public Attitudes to Immigration and Immigrants*. ODI, 2020.

London Economics. *The Costs and Benefits of International Higher Education Students to the UK Economy*. Report for the Higher Education Policy Institute, Universities UK, Kaplan International Pathways. London Economics, 2023.

Manning, Alan. 'The Link Between Growth and Migration: Unpacking the Confusion.' London School of Economics Blog. https://blogs.lse.ac.uk/politicsandpolicy/the-link-between-growth-and-immigration-unpicking-the-confusion/ [Accessed 16/11/2024].

Naik, Vipul. 'Open Borders and the Libertarian Priority List: Part 1.' Open Borders: The Case. https://openborders.info/blog/open-borders-and-the-libertarian-priority-list-part-1/ [Accessed: 16/11/2024].

ODI. *Hearts and Minds: How Europeans Think and Feel about Immigration*. ODI, 2019.

OECD, 'Economic Impact of Migration': https://www.oecd.org/en/topics/sub-issues/economic-impact-of-migration.html [Accessed 5/12/2024].

Office for National Statistics. 'National population projections: 2021-based interim.' https://www.ons.gov.uk/peoplepopulationandcommunity/

populationandmigration/populationprojections/bulletins/nation
alpopulationprojections/2021basedinterim/previous/v1 [Accessed
17/11/2024].

Portes, Jonathan. 'The Economic Impacts of Migration to the UK.' CEPR.
https://cepr.org/voxeu/columns/economic-impacts-immigration-uk
[Accessed 17/11/2024].

— 'The Economics of Migration.' *Contexts* vol. 18, no. 2 (2019): pp. 12-17.

— 'Has Higher Immigration Saved the Chancellor Again.' UK in a
Changing Europe. https://ukandeu.ac.uk/has-higher-immigration-
saved-the-chancellor-again/ [Accessed 17/11/2024].

— 'What to Make of the Latest ONS Migration Statistics.' UK in a Changing
Europe. https://ukandeu.ac.uk/what-to-make-of-the-latest-ons-
migration-statistics/ [Accessed: 16/11/2024].

Ramdin, Ron. *Reimagining Britain: 500 Years of Black and Asian History.*
Pluto Press, 1999.

Rasul, Imran, and Heidi Mirza. *Deaton Review of Inequalities.* Institute of
Fiscal Studies, 2022.

Rottensteiner, Christa, and Claire Kumar. 'As UK public attitudes toward
migration are increasingly positive, it's time for more balanced and
evidence-based narratives.' UN Migration – United Kingdom. https://
unitedkingdom.iom.int/news/uk-public-attitudes-toward-migration-
are-increasingly-positive-its-time-more-balanced-and-evidence-based-
narratives [Accessed 17/11/2024].

Runge, Johnny. *Review of the Evidence on Economic Impacts of EU Migration.*
ESRC Briefing, 2019.

Sriskandarajan, Dhananjayah. 'Outsiders on the Inside.' In *Social Justice:
Building a fairer Britain.* Edited by Nick Pearce and Will Paxton. Institute
for Public Policy Research, Politicos, 2005.

Sumption, Madelaine, and Carlos Vargas-Silva. 'The Labour Market
Effects of Immigration.' The Migration Observatory. https://
migrationobservatory.ox.ac.uk/resources/briefings/the-labour-market-
effects-of-immigration/ [Accessed 17/11/2024].

Vargas-Silva, Carlos, et al. 'The Fiscal Impacts of Immigration in the UK.'
The Migration Observatory. https://migrationobservatory.ox.ac.uk/
resources/briefings/the-fiscal-impact-of-immigration-in-the-uk/
[Accessed 17/11/2024].

17

Federalism from a Scottish Perspective

Ross Finnie

Federalism is the form of constitutional settlement generally regarded as being best suited to a state having within it regions or nations with distinct historical, religious, cultural and or linguistic identities. It has been adopted by a wide range of states, including Belgium, Germany, Switzerland, Australia, India, Pakistan, United States and Canada. One practitioner of federalism, former Canadian Prime Minister Pierre Trudeau (who governed a country comprising a diverse range of culture and language groups), observed in a joint meeting of the United States Congress that Canadian federalism is 'a brilliant prototype for moulding tomorrow's civilisation.'[1] Ever since the first premiership of William Gladstone there have been prime ministers of the UK who have been supportive of federalism, but without perhaps exuding the same level of enthusiasm as Pierre Trudeau. The history of the Scottish Liberal Party records that 'Constitutional reform of some sort (home rule or devolution within a federal framework) has been a constant thread linking the 19th, 20th and 21st centuries.'[2] Whilst substantial measures of decentralisation have been introduced in recent years, the case for federalism *per se* has gained little traction. This chapter endeavours, from a Scottish perspective, to provide some clarity as to what federalism is and what it is not. It seeks to explain why federalism is an integral element of liberal democratic politics and examines some of the key historical steps towards federalism. Finally, it reflects upon the current position and considers how federalism might be advanced.

Federalism

The terminology used in discussions about federalism can become very confusing. Federalism, con-federalism, devolution, self-government and

---

1   Pierre Trudeau, *Federalism and the French Canadians* (Macmillan, 1968), p. 179.
2   David Torrance, *A History of the Scottish Liberals and Liberal Democrats* (Edinburgh University Press, 2022), p. 3.

home rule are often used inter-changeably, implying each has the same meaning. This is not the case. Gladstone shared this sense of confusion in a letter to Lord Fermoy in 1874: 'With respect to Home Rule I have not yet heard an authoritative or binding definition of the phrase, which appears to be used by different persons in different senses.'[3] Before trying to disentangle the various definitions, it might be helpful to establish the baseline namely: the current constitutional position. The UK is a unitary state which, according to the late David M. Walker, the former Professor of Law at the University of Glasgow, consists of 'a constitutional monarchy' with a constitution which is described as 'unwritten' insofar as 'there is no comprehensive constitutional document but rather the principles and rules as to the structure of government and its powers and operation have to be gathered from various statutes, decisions of the court, books of authority, constitutional conventions, understandings and practices... the [King] in Parliament may, by statute, alter any rule as to the constitution as readily as it may alter any other part of the law. Parliament is accordingly supreme in that it may alter any law whatever...'[4] The basis of this unitary architecture can be traced back to The Treaty of Union of 1707. The treaty took the form of two identical acts of union passed by both the Scottish and English parliaments. In 1706 the Scots negotiators of union proposed a federation of Scotland, England and Wales, but this was rejected by the English negotiators.[5] Scots' support for the principles of federalism, therefore, goes back a long way. The unitary state is to be contrasted with federalism, which Walker defines as:

> A system of government of a country under which there exist simul-
> taneously a federal or central government (legislature and executive) and
> several state or provincial legislatures and governments as contrasted
> with a unitary state. Both federal and state governments derive their
> powers from the federal constitution, both are supreme in particular
> spheres, and both operate directly on the people; the state governments

3   Roy Jenkins, *Gladstone* (Macmillan, 1995), p. 378.
4   David M. Walker, *The Oxford Companion to Law* (Oxford University Press, 1980), p. 462.
5   George Lockhart of Carnwath, 'Scottish commissioner (Treaty of Union negotiator) 1706,' cited in the *National Records of Scotland, Dalhousie papers*, GD45/14/336/32, https://www.scottisharchivesforschools.org/union1707/chapter3-2.asp [Accessed 20/01/2025].

accordingly are not exercising powers by the federal government; nor are they subordinate to it…[6]

Translating that definition into a simple illustration would leave us with the following structure: A federal UK parliament and state parliaments for England, Scotland, Wales and Northern Ireland. There is one rider to that model. Given that England represents some 85% of the UK's population, federalists point out that whilst establishing a parliament for England creating asymmetrical federalism would work, the creation of parliaments for recognisable regions throughout England to create symmetrical federalism might be better. Irrespective of which model is adopted, a written federal constitution would set out the limits of the jurisdiction of the respective parliaments based on the principle of subsidiarity, no parliament would have supremacy over the other and there would be express entrenchment provisions and powers for local government.

Federalism is not to be confused with confederation, which occurs when a group of nations form an alliance or agreement to work together for a common cause, but without interfering in any way whatsoever with the respective nation's ability to govern themselves. Nor should it be confused with devolution which is the political exercise of a state legislature delegating certain powers to another body whilst retaining, at least in theory, full power over the same matters. The term 'devolved legislative and administrative powers' was therefore used correctly in the paragraph above describing the establishment of the parliaments/assemblies in Scotland, Wales and Northern Ireland. Jo Grimond, former leader of the Liberal Party, didn't much like the term devolution. He thought it 'implies that power rests at Westminster, from which centre some may be graciously "devolved". I would rather begin by assuming that power should rest with the people who entrust it to their representatives to discharge the essential tasks of government.'[7]

The term home rule, when applied to Scotland, is generally accepted to mean, and is synonymous with, the term self-government. Additionally, it is clear from common usage that home rule means self-government, in the sense of devolved government. On the other hand, the use of the term 'home rule all round' (i.e. for England, Scotland, Wales and Northern Ireland) means federalism. Gladstone and Henry Campbell-Bannerman frequently used

---

6   Walker, *The Oxford Companion to Law*, p. 1251.
7   Jo Grimond, *A Personal Manifesto* (Martin Robertson, 1983), p. 54.

the term, and a 20th century confirmation was provided by the prominent Scottish liberal, John Bannerman. As the latter observed in 1964, 'Liberals in Scotland, England and Wales have always supported the de-centralisation of executive power from Westminster to the regional areas of the United Kingdom... the Liberal road of federal home rule for the United Kingdom.'[8]

Liberal Democracy

Whilst it is important to have a definition of federalism, much greater importance is an understanding of the part federalism plays in the context of liberalism and liberal democracy more broadly. The philosophical connection between liberalism and federalism was eloquently expressed by Henry Campbell-Bannerman in *The Liberal Magazine* of January 1898:

> What do we mean by this Liberalism of which we talk?....I should say it means the acknowledgement in practical life of the truth that men are best governed who govern themselves; that the general sense of mankind, if left alone, will make for righteousness; that artificial privileges and restraints upon freedom, so far as they are not required in the interests of the community, are hurtful; and that the laws, while, of course, they cannot equalise conditions, can, at least, avoid aggravating inequalities, and ought to have for their object the securing to every man the best chance he can have of a good and useful life.[9]

The recognition that a federal form of governance accords to diversity and subsidiarity speaks to pluralism: an important principle of liberalism. As Conrad Russell put it:

> When a Liberal speaks of pluralism, he or she will probably be talking about two ideas which to a non- Liberal ear, are very clearly distinct. One of these is the attempt to control power by dispersal, a rejection of the notion of the unitary Omni competent sovereign state so beloved of Thomas Cromwell, a Russian egg model of political power, in which it is held in a series of containers, one inside the other, ranging from the

---

8   John MacDonald Bannerman, *The Memoirs of Lord Bannerman of Kildonan*, ed. John Fowler (Impulse Publications, 1972), p. 118.

9   John Wilson, *CB: A Life of Sir Henry Campbell-Bannerman* (Constable, 1973), p. 232.

United Nations at one end down to the parish council or an individual family at the other. The other thing we mean by "pluralism" is a cult of diversity, religious, geographical and cultural, in which the old Whig cry of "equality before the law" is invoked to defend the rights of the under-privileged whoever they may happen at that time to be.[10]

Federalism not only accommodates diversity and pluralism, it also entrenches the principle of subsidiarity an essential prerequisite to governance being effected at the most appropriate level. As the preamble to the Scottish Liberal Democrats' constitution states: 'We aim to dispense power, to foster diversity and to nurture creativity. We believe that the role of the state is to enable all citizens to attain these ideals, to contribute fully to their communities and to take part in the decisions that affect their lives.'[11] Two further liberal principles are engaged in creating a federal system of government: first establishing a system of federalism affords the opportunity to introduce a system of proportional representation (PR), considered by liberals as the *sine qua non* of a fair electoral system. Daniel Chandler states the case for PR very simply: 'From the perspective of political equality, proportional representation has some conspicuous advantages. The key one is that it tends to create a better match between elected representatives and the views of the population as a whole, votes translate directly into seats, and in this sense every vote counts equally, irrespective of where that vote is cast.'[12]

Secondly, a written constitution is an essential element in establishing federalism. A constitution might be thought of as an abstract legal document of little concern to the ordinary citizen. On the contrary, a constitution has the capacity to set out: from whom political power is derived; the democratic processes for exercising that power; and the means by which the people will be actively engaged in these processes. The section on liberal democracy in the *Dictionary of Liberal Thought*, underscores the importance of a written constitution. 'Liberal democracy calls for much more than a majoritarian electoral system. Liberal enthusiasm for self-determination can only be reconciled with support for a system of elections and government driven by

10	Conrad Russell, *An Intelligent Person's Guide to Liberalism* (Gerald Duckworth, 1999), p. 37.
11	Scottish Liberal Democrats, *The Constitution of the Scottish Liberal Democrats* (Scottish Liberal Democrats, 2021), p. 3.
12	Daniel Chandler, *Free and Equal: What Would a Fair Society Look Like?* (Allan Lane, 2023), p. 146.

the will of the people if there are limits to what can be done in their name; and it is vital that these limits are clear to all. A written constitution and a system of common law and/or precedent that entrenches individual rights are key features in virtually all versions of liberal democracy.'[13]

A more federal settlement

Since the intervention in 1707, noted earlier in the chapter, Scots and Scottish Liberals (now Scottish Liberal Democrats), including MPs who sat for Scottish seats like Gladstone, Asquith and Churchill but were not necessarily Scottish, have been campaigning for home rule all round: federalism. After Gladstone introduced his first Home Rule for Ireland Bill in 1886, Home rule bills for Ireland and Scotland were introduced at regular intervals in the years leading up to the two world wars, but without any success. The closest Scotland got to achieving a measure of home rule was through the Government of Scotland Bill which passed its second reading on 30 May 1913. The bill was introduced as a private members bill by William Cowan, Liberal MP for Aberdeen Eastern. Cowan's speech, moving the second reading is instructive in revealing the limited powers of the bill and its entirely devolutionary construct: '… legislation for land, for the liquor trade, for education, for housing, for fisheries, for ecclesiastical matters and for one hundred and one matters of purely local concern.' Cowan explained that monies would be transferred to the Scottish exchequer, the Scottish parliament would have powers to vary taxes and power to impose taxes on heritable property. He also highlighted an explicit limitation of the powers of the proposed Scottish parliament. 'Notwithstanding the establishment of the Scottish Parliament or anything contained in this Act, the supreme power and authority of the Parliament of the United Kingdom shall remain unaffected and undiminished over all matters and things in Scotland and every part thereof.'[14]

One of the last statements made before the outbreak of the First World War, indicating that the cause for federalism was still alive, was delivered by Winston Churchill then the Liberal MP for Dundee. In October 1913 at Lochee, a District of Dundee, 'I spoke of a federal system in the United Kingdom, in which Scotland, Ireland, and if necessary, parts of England could have separate legislative parliamentary institutions enabling them to

13 Duncan Brack and Ed Randall, eds., *Dictionary of Liberal Thought* (Politico's Publishing, 2007), p. 210.
14 See Government of Scotland Bill, HC Deb., 30 May 1913, vol. 53, cc. 479-481.

develop, in their own way, their own life according to their own ideas and needs in the same way as the great and prosperous States of the American Union and the great principalities and States of the German Empire.'[15] Understandably, there was little interest in constitutional reform in the immediate aftermath of the Second World War. When interest was renewed it was prompted not so much by federalists but more by nationalists. Plaid Cymru's Gwynfor Evans' win in the 1966 Carmarthen by-election and the Scottish National Party's Winnie Ewing's win in the 1967 Hamilton by-election helped to persuade Prime Minister Harold Wilson to establish a royal commission with a very broad remit, which allowed it to examine the present constitutional and economic relationships and to consider whether any changes were desirable. The commission was established in 1969, Lord Kilbrandon took over the chairmanship in 1972 and it finally reported in October 1973.[16] The commission considered, *inter alia*, various models of devolution, federalism and confederalism. The final report's principal recommendations were that: a majority favoured a devolved legislature for Scotland with powers broadly similar to those already under the supervision of the secretary of state for Scotland and the Lord Advocate; a smaller majority favoured legislative devolution to Wales with similar powers to Scotland; both devolved bodies were to be elected by the single transferable vote system of proportional representation; and the signatories to the report were unanimous in opposing legislative devolution in England as a whole or to any English region. A more federal solution had been rejected but the report appeared to open the door to devolved legislative parliaments elected by proportional representation.

The Kilbrandon Report was delivered too late for the Heath government to do anything with it before it fell in the February 1974 general election. Indeed, there was no progress on Kilbrandon until after the October 1974 general election which saw an increase in the nationalists representation to eleven in Scotland and three in Wales. This increase in nationalist support appeared to prompt Harold Wilson's government to publish a white paper in November 1975 *Our Changing Democracy: Devolution to Scotland and Wales*. This was followed by the introduction of a combined Scotland and Wales Bill which fell on a procedural motion in February 1977. By March,

---

15   Andrew Liddle, *Cheers, Mr Churchill! Winston in Scotland* (Birlinn, 2022), p. 106.
16   Royal Commission on the Constitution, *Royal Commission on the Constitution 1969-1973, Volume 1 Report*, Cmnd 5460 (HMSO, 1973).

the Liberal Party had entered the Lib-Lab pact raising hopes that any future legislation might be more in line with Kilbrandon. These hopes were sustained, initially, by the pact agreement which included: '... progress must be made on legislation for devolution and to this end consultation will begin on the detailed memorandum submitted by the Liberal Party... In any future debate on proportional representation for the devolved Assemblies there will be a free vote.'[17]

At the behest of the Liberals, separate bills for Scotland and Wales were introduced, but despite the terms of the agreement, their passage was to prove tortuous for Liberal members. Referendums were secured but an amendment to the clause meant the proposals had to be approved by 40% of the electorate. The Liberals secured further improvement including: enhanced financial provisions and the powers of the secretary of state to override assembly legislation were curbed. The bill fell far short of delivering a decent measure of devolution and barely touched the foothills of federalism but, on the pragmatic grounds that securing the first devolution acts was better than no acts at all, the Scotland Act 1978 and the Wales Act 1978 were passed. In the referendums the following year, the Scotland Act failed to achieve the 40% threshold while the Wales Act was heavily defeated, and both were subsequently repealed. Writing later about the Lib-Lab pact, David Steel devoted a chapter to the failure to secure devolution under the heading 'The Great Devolution Debacle'.[18] The lack of enthusiasm for the creation of devolved parliaments with appropriate powers, and the consequent rejection of the proposals in the 1979 referendums, delivered a serious blow to the federal cause. But, as the Steel Commission (considered later in this chapter) observed correctly, 'out of this apparent setback there came two seminal developments: the establishment of the first Scottish Constitutional Convention; and the assertion in the Claim of Right that sovereignty ultimately lay with the people of Scotland.'[19]

The lead up to these developments began with the formation of The Campaign for a Scottish Assembly (CSA) in 1980 by individuals who were not necessarily members of a political party but were committed to some form of home rule for Scotland. After nearly a decade of little or no

17 David Steel, *A House Divided: The Lib-Lab Pact and the Future of British Politics* (George Weidenfeld & Nicolson, 1980), pp. 93-94.
18 Steel, *A House Divided*, pp. 92-102.
19 The Steel Commission, *Moving to Federalism: A New Settlement for Scotland* (Scottish Liberal Democrats 2006), p. 13.

progress the CSA concluded that the cause of home rule would be served better by establishing a more formal convention. The CSA also appointed Sir Robert Grieve, a distinguished figure in Scottish public life, to chair a committee that, with Jim Ross as its principal draftsman, published the Claim of Right for Scotland. The Claim incorporated a sovereignty pledge derived from the Declaration of Arbroath in 1320. It stated: 'We gathered as the Scottish Constitutional Convention, do hereby acknowledge the sovereign right of the Scottish people to determine the form of Government best suited to their needs and do hereby declare and pledge that in all our actions and deliberations their interests shall be paramount.'[20] The Scottish Constitutional Convention was then established in 1989 after prominent Scottish individuals had signed the Claim of Right. Canon Kenyon Wright was appointed chair and Harry Ewing and David Steel were appointed co-chairs. The Convention was supported by a wide range of representatives of civil society, the trade unions, business and commercial organisations and all of the political parties except the Conservative Party and the SNP. The convention published a blueprint for home rule for Scotland, *Scotland's Parliament: Scotland's Right* in November 1995.

The Labour Party had been fully involved in the work of the Scottish Constitutional Convention and fully endorsed its report. Labour won the UK general election held on 1 May 1997 with a mandate to legislate for a Scottish parliament and Welsh assembly, the former to incorporate much of the convention's blueprint. The new government moved swiftly, and referendums were called for 11 September. In Scotland, there were two questions: the first on whether you agreed there should be a Scottish parliament was approved by 74% to 26%; and second was whether you agree the Scottish parliament should have tax raising powers which was approved by 63% to 37%. The Scotland Act 1998 was duly passed with its devolved powers coming into effect in the July of that year. In the same year the Welsh assembly was established, and new powers were devolved to the Northern Ireland assembly to give effect to the Good Friday Agreement. Taken together, this represented the largest ever devolution of powers from the UK parliament. The whole process from drawing up the blueprint to the passing of the act demonstrated the credibility of the constitutional convention as an effective instrument for reform. Up to this point, there had been very little consideration to any form of devolution within England, a topic of considerable interest to those

20   Iain Macwhirter, *Road to Referendum* (Cargo Publishing, 2014), p. 226.

favouring symmetrical federalism. Then the government took powers under the Regional Assemblies (Preparations) Act 2013 to hold referendums on possibly devolving limited powers to regional assemblies in North East England, North West England and Yorkshire and Humber. Unfortunately, whether justified or not, the proposals were seen as little more than a re-organisation of local government and, as a result in the first referendum held for the North East in November 2004, the proposals were rejected by 78% of the electorate. The other two referendums were cancelled and the UK government dropped its plans for any further devolution. Both the scale of the referendum defeat and the ditching of all future devolution plans threatened to stall the momentum for constitutional change raising the possibility that devolution to Scotland, Wales and Northern Ireland could become an end in itself rather than a means to a more federal end. Jim Wallace, the then leader of the Scottish Liberal Democrats, was alert to this possibility and wanted not only to strengthen the case for federalism, but also to draw lessons from the success of the Scottish Constitutional Convention, bringing public opinion behind the case for further reform. In 2005 he established a commission under the chairmanship of (now Lord) David Steel with a broad remit and with one of its stated aims being to contribute to the argument in favour of a second constitutional convention and provide any such convention with a framework on how to move towards federalism.

The work of the commission, which reported in March 2006, included studying reports on the constitutions and exercise of powers, including fiscal powers, within federal states including Australia, Canada and Germany; and unitary states including Denmark, France, Norway and the UK. Based on its extensive research and evidence gathered, the commission produced a detailed set of recommendations that could be taken forward by a second Scottish Constitutional Convention, It made two broader points of importance to the federal case: first, 'while more symmetrical systems may be desirable there is clear evidence that asymmetrical systems work too' and second, 'the key arguments for fiscal decentralisation are improving political accountability, public transparency, efficiency in the allocation of resources and decision making and stimulating economic growth'.[21] Viewed from any standpoint, the Steel Commission Report is a substantial, well-researched and intellectually cohesive piece of work which sets out with clarity an evidence-based case for federalism. Unfortunately, however,

21 The Steel Commission, *Moving to Federalism*, p. 46.

the report was perceived to be a party political document, and although it was initially well received it failed to attract endorsements from outwith liberal supporters, and with public support for independence increasing this militated against the report's findings garnering support for a second constitutional convention. The development of the devolution settlement in Scotland did, however, take another step forward in 2009 with the findings of the Commission on Scottish Devolution chaired by Professor Sir Kenneth Calman, then Chancellor of the University of Glasgow, and became known as the Calman Commission. Its recommendations formed the basis of the Scotland Act 2012, the principal provisions of which included, in particular, increased powers over income tax, control over two smaller taxes and granting borrowing powers. These measures marked the first steps in meeting the fiscal recommendations of the Steel Commission.

Whilst supportive of the Calman Commission, Scottish Liberal Democrats were concerned at the lack of any federal content in its remit and so it decided to provide further support for the case for federalism. The party appointed Sir Menzies Campbell MP to chair its Home Rule and Community Rule Commission (HRCRC). The commission reported in August 2012 and building on the Steel Commission Report set out a route map for home rule and made a wide range of recommendations including proposals to enhance the autonomy and power of local authorities and entrench the principle of partnership – working between the different tiers of government.[22] The publication of the Campbell Commission's proposals on federalism coincided with a rising tide for independence. The nationalists had won a stunning victory in the Scottish parliamentary elections of May 2011 securing an outright majority by winning 69 of the 129 seats and Alex Salmond the SNP first minister was soon lobbying the UK government for powers to hold an independence referendum. In 2013 Prime Minister David Cameron and Alex Salmond signed the Edinburgh Agreement under which Westminster would transfer the relevant powers to the Scottish parliament for a legally binding referendum to be held. Once the legislation was in place the date was set for 19 September 2014 with the question: Should Scotland be an independent country – Yes or No?

Both the Yes and No sides mounted vigorous campaigns that aroused considerable public interest and contributed to the very high turnout on the

22 Home Rule and Community Rule Commission, *Federalism: the best future for Scotland* (Scottish Liberal Democrats, 2012).

day. The No campaign, of course, included those of a federalist persuasion who found the benefits of the union relatively easy to defend but the inherent flaws less so. There was one interesting intervention that queried the absence of a federal option and two that demonstrated the need to shore up the case for the devolved settlement First, there were rumours that Alex Salmond might accept a third option on the ballot paper and this is confirmed in the following quote from the Scottish journalist Iain Macwhirter's book on the referendum 'Alex Salmond said he would welcome a second question in the referendum, specifically offering Devolution Max, a form of federalism whereby the Scottish parliament would raise the majority of the money it spends while still contributing to common UK services such as defence and foreign affairs. But this was vetoed by David Cameron who feared the SNP leader might be trying to have it both ways, placing an each-way bet on a two-horse race. Perhaps he was. But this was an opportunity missed by the Unionist parties, a curious one, because had a second question been on the ballot paper, independence would almost certainly have been defeated by a very large margin.'[23] Macwhirter's conclusion cannot be proved one way or another but, as support for independence increased, federalists were reluctant to split the No vote.

Second, Sir Menzies Campbell was still chair of the Liberal Democrats' HRCRC and it produced a second report entitled *Campbell II* in March 2014.[24] This was a very different style of report in that it sought to identify common ground amongst the pro-union camps and agree a timetable for action. The report claimed there was consensus on two issues: the Scottish parliament to be responsible for raising the tax to fund the majority of its spend; and notwithstanding the primacy of the Westminster parliament the Scottish parliament should be entrenched permanently. In addition, the secretary of state for Scotland was to convene a meeting 30 days after the referendum to secure a consensus for a further extension of powers for the Scottish parliament. 'Campbell II had clearly been discussed with figures in Labour… [Gordon] Brown emerged from his Fife fastness to give his backing to the Campbell scheme.'[25] Third, was 'The Vow' published on the front page of the Scottish tabloid newspaper the *Daily Record* two days

---

23 Macwhirter, *Road to Referendum*, p. 44.
24 Home Rule and Community Rule Commission, *Campbell II* (Scottish Liberal Democrats, 2014).
25 Macwhirter, *Road to Referendum*, p. 403.

before the referendum. The Vow took the form of a pledge that in the event of a No vote, the Scottish parliament would become permanent; new powers would be devolved; and the funding formula for Scottish expenditure would continue. It was signed by the party leaders: David Cameron (Conservative), Ed Miliband (Labour) and Nick Clegg (Liberal Democrat). The Vow was issued with polling predicting a very close result and was intended to provide assurance as to the permanence of the Scottish parliament and its funding mechanism, together with a promise of more powers. The result of the referendum was a victory for No by 55.3% to 44.7% for Yes on a turnout of 84.6%. After the referendum, Prime Minister David Cameron invited Lord Smith of Kelvin to head up a commission (known as the Smith Commission) to give effect to the Vow. The Smith Commission's recommendations formed the basis for the Scotland Act 2016. The act gave greater permanence to the Scottish parliament by requiring a referendum before it could be abolished. It also devolved further powers including management of the Crown Estates; enhanced control over social security benefits; and more control over income tax. By this further substantial devolution of powers the Vow had been fulfilled. Brexit was the next matter to take centre stage in the constitutional debate. Leaving aside the merits of the arguments as whether the UK should stay in or leave the European Union, the decision to leave was swiftly embraced by the nationalists as further ammunition in support of independence. While the UK as a whole voted by 51.9% to 48.1% to leave the EU, Scotland voted by 62.0% to 38.0% to remain. The nationalist argument has been: first, Scotland was dragged out of the EU against its will; and second, the only way to re-join is for Scotland to become independent and re-join in its own right.

The COVID-19 pandemic illustrated the extent of the powers that had been devolved with both the Scottish and Welsh governments devising their own more nuanced response to meet the particular circumstances of their respective nations. The absence of any concomitant reforms to the UK government's powers to reflect the extent of the devolution settlement left the prime minister and UK health minister uncertain as to whether they were speaking for the UK as a whole or just England, which in fact they were. The UK government and the devolved administrations played their part in tackling the pandemic but the absence of a more co-ordinated and more co-operative approach that a more federal structure could bring was sadly missing. After the pandemic was over, the only two mainstream political parties in Scotland committed to more federal forms of governance, both the Labour Party and the Liberal Democrats resumed their respective constitutional campaigns. Sir Menzies Campbell reconvened the Scottish Liberal Democrats' HRCRC and produced a further report: *Campbell III*. That report included a welcome for former Scottish Labour MP and Prime Minister 'Gordon Brown's recent work on reforming the United Kingdom is very much in line with our own thinking and we are pleased that the Labour Party are keen to pursue that agenda with a new Commission. There is an opportunity for the Liberal Democrats and Labour to work together again on this important area of reform.'[26] *Campbell III* restated the case for federalism and then laid out the steps by which it could be achieved, including preventing the UK parliament legislating in devolved areas; and creation of a UK constitutional convention. The recommendations of *Campbell III* contributed to two further developments: first at the Liberal Democrats' federal conference in Autumn 2020, where a motion was agreed entitled 'The Creation of a Federal United Kingdom'[27] which included provision for English regions to be part of the solution, and second, at their Autumn 2021 conference, the Liberal Democrats approved a motion and background paper proposing 'A Framework for England in a Federal UK'.[28]

The Labour Party's Commission on the UK's Future published its report *A New Britain: Renewing Our Democracy and Rebuilding Our Economy* in December 2022. It is understood that the report has not been adopted in full but it remains one of the most important statements on the devolution of power issued by the Labour Party. The report aims to offer: 'a fresh start – with proposals to create a virtuous circle where spreading power and opportunity more equally throughout the country – with the right power in the right places – unlocks the potential for growth and prosperity in every part of the country, and in doing so revives people's faith that we can all benefit from a responsive and accountable system of government.'[29] The recommendations, which are specifically directed towards creating a <u>significantly more</u> decentralised structure, include: replacing the House of

26 Home Rule and Community Rule Commission, *Campbell III* (Scottish Liberal Democrats, 2021), p. 3.
27 Liberal Democrats, *Autumn Conference Agenda 2020* (Liberal Democrats, 2020), pp. 24-27.
28 Liberal Democrats Federal Policy Committee, *A Framework For England in a Federal UK* (Liberal Democrats, 2021).
29 Commission on the UK's Future, *A New Britain: Renewing Our Democracy and Rebuilding our Economy* (The Labour Party, 2022), p. 2.

Lords with a democratically elected Assembly of the Nations and Regions;
a new Council of the Nations and Regions replacing the joint ministerial
committees; empowerment of towns, cities and regions; enhanced powers
and status for national/regional parliaments/assemblies; and constitutional
protection over devolved powers. The changes are to be effected by a
new constitutional statute to be enacted by the Westminster parliament
which retains its supremacy and dual function as the following extracts
demonstrate: 'Westminster remains England's Parliament so devolution
within England is mainly of executive power.'[30] 'Parliament at Westminster
is England's Parliament as well as United Kingdom's Parliament … English
Members of Parliament should be able to meet and debate English matters in
an English Grand Committee'[31] '…while continuing to uphold the supremacy
of Parliament as there is still no law which Parliament cannot change.'[32]
Labour's proposals would, if implemented, represent a substantial further
devolution of power, but the retention of Westminster's supremacy removes
a fundamental element from the creation of a federal state.

Current position

There can be no doubt that establishing the parliament in Scotland with
its devolved powers, taken together with similar devolution to Wales
and Northern Ireland (the latter under different circumstances and
arrangements) and the introduction of directly elected mayors in England,
represents the biggest constitutional and governance change to have taken
place in the history of the UK. The improvements to Scotland's constitutional
arrangements include: the parliament being more representative of
the public's political preferences through being elected by a system of
proportional representation; and ministers and members of the parliament
being much more accessible to the electors and special interest groups. The
parliament has demonstrated its ability to develop Scottish solutions to
Scottish problems passing bills designed to achieve that end such as, for
example: land reform; the cost of personal care for the elderly; the danger
to public health from smoking in public places, excessive consumption of
alcohol, child poverty and the cost of tuition fees. However, the absence of
any similar legislative devolution within England has left the UK parliament

---

30 Commission on the UK's Future, *A New Britain*, p. 69.
31 Commission on the UK's Future, *A New Britain*, p. 122.
32 Commission on the UK's Future, *A New Britain*, p. 142.

and the UK government discharging two roles simultaneously for the UK and England respectively. The anomaly of Scottish, Welsh and Northern Irish MPs actively participating in debates at Westminster on subjects that have been devolved to their respective parliament, Senedd or assembly was raised repeatedly by the Scottish Labour MP for West Lothian, Tam Dayell, during the passage of the Scotland and Welsh devolution acts and became known as the West Lothian question. The question was not effectively answered then and remains unanswered. On each occasion the question has been asked it has been considered to be a matter of procedure within Westminster and not a more fundamental question about which parliament should be responsible for discharging which powers. Indeed, the McKay Commission, established to consider the consequences of devolution, which reported in 2013, recommended a number of procedural changes to ensure the English voice was heard, but shied away from restricting the right of all MPs to vote on any matter. The Conservative government, however, pursued the West Lothian question which had now become English Votes for English Laws (EVEL). In 2015 the government used a change in standing orders to give English MPs a veto over legislation affecting only England. The change was rescinded in 2021 on the grounds that the measure had proved divisive. Regrettably, no consideration was given as to how a federal constitution would have totally resolved the EVEL/the West Lothian question.

The difficulties regarding the divisions of responsibilities are mirrored in the composition of the UK government. UK ministers are understandably drawn from the Westminster parliament, but some are still appointed as ministers of the crown with responsibility for portfolios with policy areas that have been devolved. This situation has played out in every UK general election since devolution. The media broadcast throughout the UK policy statements issued by government and opposition parties, many of which are on devolved policy areas and are, therefore, only relevant in England. The difficulties with this situation also affected inter-government relations and emerged very early in the life of the newly devolved governments. The UK was at the time a member of the European Union and meetings of EU Council of Ministers were imminent. Ministers from the devolved governments could attend council meetings as part of the UK delegation provided it was understood that only the UK minister could speak and vote at the meeting. There was no agreement however as to how the UK's policy position on any proposal might be decided, taking account of the views of the devolved administrations. The initial response was that civil servants in Whitehall write the papers and UK ministers decide. Common sense prevailed and in most subject areas *ad hoc* arrangements were put in place that allowed ministers from the devolved administrations to be involved in deciding UK policy, but there was no permanent solution. Brexit has not resolved this issue. There continue to be issues where cooperation between the administrations is required for good governance outcomes. The absence of a properly codified limits to the powers of all parliaments, including the UK parliament and a requirement for cooperation has been a source of friction from-time-to-time throughout the 25 years of devolution.

Both the UK and Scottish governments have to take their respective share of the blame for the very obvious lack of cohesion and cooperation throughout the governance of the UK. In recent years, the Scottish government has sought to push the boundaries of its legislative powers beyond their limits as in, for example the United Nations Convention on the Rights of the Child (Incorporation) Bill and the Gender Recognition Reform Bill. On appeal, the former was found by the Supreme Court to be outwith the powers of the Scotland Act and in the latter the Court of Session upheld the view that it did not comply with the provisions of the Scotland Act. The UK government has been equally guilty of overriding the devolution settlement. As part of the Brexit process the UK government altered the previously understood scope of devolved powers by the Internal Market Act 2020. For example, currently, due to a long-standing public health issue, Scotland has statutory controls over the sale and distribution of raw milk no matter where it is sourced. The Internal Market Act does not interfere with that provision, but any future similar provision would only apply to a product produced in Scotland because, under the act, if a similar product was authorised elsewhere in the UK it could be sold in Scotland thereby obviating the purpose and intent of the measure approved by the Scottish parliament. The UK government has also taken measures that have reversed the long-standing convention under which Treasury funding was sent to the Scottish government for it to allocate, but now the UK government can fund Scottish local authorities without reference to the Scottish government.

The COVID-19 pandemic showed both the best and the worst of the current governance arrangements. The best was illustrated by the UK government deploying its resources in the funding and distribution of the vaccine that brought the pandemic under control and the implementation of the furlough scheme that saved so many individuals and businesses from financial ruin. The devolved governments were able to refine their response to address specific needs as they saw fit. The worst example was to be seen in the very obvious lack of a coordinated policy response evidenced by almost daily press briefings delivered by the prime minister and the first ministers of the devolved parliaments, each attempting to justify the need for a different response to a global pandemic, underlining the need for a governance structure that facilitated cooperation as opposed to confrontation.

Can federalism be advanced?

Very real progress therefore on the devolution front, but, in spite of some serious continuing constitutional deficiencies highlighted in the immediately preceding paragraphs, little or no movement towards federalism. This lack of movement cannot be put down to an insufficiency of evidence-based reports in support of federalism. The substantive reports of the Steel and Campbell commissions might be regarded as partisan, but that is to ignore the very many other authoritative published reports by, for example, David Melding, former member of the Welsh Senedd[33] and Dr Andrew Blick, Professor of Politics and Contemporary History at King's College, London.[34] Although the Steel Commission found evidence to support the view that asymmetrical federalism (one state parliament in England) could work, the sense that a state parliament representing some 85% of the population would dominate remains. A possible solution has emerged with the introduction of directly elected mayors to the extent that, as noted earlier, the Liberal Democrat Party published *A Framework For England in a Federal UK*, which it hoped would strengthen the case for symmetrical federalism.

In Scotland, public support for the various political parties, including the nationalist parties, fluctuates but on the question of independence public opinion has remained polarised since the 2014 referendum. This means that many federalists still feel compelled to support the unionist case for fear of splitting the opposition to independence. This fear not only stifles debate on the general merits of federalism it also prevents the point being made that federalism could provide the constitutional framework for dual

---

33 David Melding, *The Reformed Union: The UK as a Federation* (Institute of Welsh Affairs, 2013).
34 Andrew Blick, *Federalism: The UK's Future* (Federal Trust for Education and Research, 2016).

loyalty i.e. being both Scottish and British for example. The possibility of a further referendum cannot be ruled out. Yet there is little evidence that federalists have considered if there is any way in which a split vote situation might be avoided. The procedure adopted by New Zealand in deciding a possible change to its voting system, whilst not entirely analogous, might be worth exploring. New Zealand held two referendums. The first in 1992 asked electors if they wanted a change Yes or No? and then asked electors to rank their preference from a list of options. The second referendum in 1993 was a choice between the existing system and the highest ranked option. A variation on that model might allow a wider range of options to be considered including federalism. The major obstacle to advancing federalism is the near reverence in which the parliament at Westminster with its constitutional position of supremacy is held by the two political parties that have dominated its membership in the post-war years. The Conservative Party has legislated for a significant measure of devolution but without any amendment to the overarching supremacy of Westminster. The Labour Party's commission on the constitution proposed a substantial increase in the scope of devolution particularly throughout England, but also made express provision for the need to retain the supremacy of Westminster. One of the means by which this supremacy of parliament could be challenged would be for federalists to campaign on a variant of Scotland's Claim of Right namely: that sovereignty ultimately lies with the people of the UK.

The details of how a federal state might be established and work in the UK are available in many of the reports that have been published, some of which have been referred to in this chapter. More attention, however, needs to be given to answering the question why? A narrative needs to be developed showing the difference changing to a federal state would make to the ordinary citizen. As a minimum, such a narrative would need to show better outcomes could be achieved by adopting a political process that: recognises the rich diversity of the nations and regions of the UK; makes every vote count; takes every decision as close to the citizen as possible; and makes cooperation and collaboration between the tiers of government the norm not the exception. This engagement with the wider public would be designed with the purpose of persuading civil society of the benefits of a federal settlement such that, based on the Scottish model, it results in civil society calling for the formation of a constitutional convention to draw up a blueprint for the delivery of federalism. As has always been the case, effective campaigning to reform the UK into a federal state will require sustained leadership. Historically, this has been provided by members of the Liberal Democrat Party and its antecedents largely on account that it was committed to the principles of diversity and subsidiarity. That will no doubt continue, but it was interesting, though slightly concerning, that the policy motion on federalism passed at the Liberal Democrat conference in 2020 contained an exhortation to 'Liberal Democrats in position of influence… to collaborate in campaigning and using their influence to build a federal United Kingdom.'[35] Leaders and activists have often been enthused to campaign if it is on a matter of principle, and in that regard Liberal Democrats have only to look at the principles engaged by federalism: diversity pluralism, subsidiarity and proportionality and the contribution federalism would make to improving the model of liberal democracy practised in the UK. If motivation is required for promoting the case for federalism throughout the UK the following quotation from a chapter advocating a state parliament for Yorkshire and the Humber by Ian MacFadyen, a Liberal Democrat ardent federalist, should suffice; 'Liberal Democrats should continue to strive for federalism to advance, reinforce and strengthen freedom, provide better government more in tune with the people than in a centralised state and to enable people, whatever their start in life, to improve life for themselves and their families and their communities.'[36]

Bibliography

Bannerman, John MacDonald. *The Memoirs of Lord Bannerman of Kildonan.* Edited by John Fowler. Impulse Publications, 1972,

Blick, Andrew. *Federalism: The UK's Future.* Federal Trust for Education and Research, 2016.

Brack, Duncan, and Ed J. Randall, ed. *Dictionary of Liberal Thought.* Politico's Publishing, 2007.

Chandler, Daniel. *Free and Equal: What Would a Fair Society Look Like?* Allen Lane, 2023.

Commission on the UK's Future. *A New Britain: Renewing Our Democracy and Rebuilding our Economy.* The Labour Party, 2022.

35 Liberal Democrats, *Autumn Conference Agenda*, p. 27.
36 Ian MacFadyen, 'A Parliament for Yorkshire and the Humber?,' in *The Yorkshire Yellow Book 2019: Essays on a Liberal future for Yorkshire and the Humber,* ed. Elizabeth Bee, Kamran Hussain, Ian MacFadyen and Michael Meadowcroft (Beecroft Publications, 2019), p. 142.

Grimond, Jo. *A Personal Manifesto*. Martin Robertson, 1983.

HC Deb 31 May 1913, vol. 53, cc. 479-481. Government of Scotland Bill.

Home Rule and Community Rule Commission. *Campbell II*. Scottish Liberal Democrats, 2012.

— *Campbell III*. Scottish Liberal Democrats, 2021.

— *Federalism: the best future for Scotland*. Scottish Liberal Democrats, 2012.

Jenkins, Roy. *Gladstone*. Macmillan, 1995.

Liberal Democrats. *Autumn Conference Agenda*. Liberal Democrats, 2020.

Liberal Democrats Federal Policy Committee. *A Framework For England in a Federal UK*. Liberal Democrats, 2021.

Liddle, Andrew. *Cheers, Mr Churchill! Winston in Scotland*. Birlinn, 2022.

Lockhart of Carnwath, George, National Records of Scotland, Dalhousie Papers. GD45/14/336/32, https://www.scottisharchivesforschools.org/union1707/chapter3-2.asp [Accessed 20/01/2025].

MacFadyen, Ian. 'A Parliament for Yorkshire and the Humber?' In *The Yorkshire Yellow Book 2019: Essays on a Liberal future for Yorkshire and the Humber*. Edited by Elizabeth Bee, Kamran Hussain, Ian MacFadyen, and Michael Meadowcroft. Beecroft Publications, 2019.

Macwhirter, Iain. *Road to Referendum*. Cargo Publishing, 2014.

Melding, David. *The Reformed Union The UK as a Federation*. Institute of Welsh Affairs, 2013.

Royal Commission on the Constitution. *Royal Commission on the Constitution 1969-1973 Volume 1 Report*, Cmnd 5460. HMSO, 1973.

Russell, Conrad. *An Intelligent Person's Guide to Liberalism*. Gerald Duckworth & Co., 1999.

Scottish Liberal Democrats. *Constitution of the Scottish Liberal Democrats*. Scottish Liberal Democrats, 2021.

Steel, David. *A House Divided: The Lib-Lab Pact and the Future of British Politics*. Weidenfeld and Nicolson, 1980.

Steel Commission. *Moving to Federalism: A New Settlement for Scotland*. Scottish Liberal Democrats, 2006.

Torrance, David. *A History of the Scottish Liberals and Liberal Democrats*. Edinburgh University Press, 2022.

Trudeau, Pierre. *Federalism and the French Canadians*. Macmillan, 1968.

Walker, David M. *The Oxford Companion to Law*. Oxford University Press, 1980.

Wilson, John. *CB A Life of Sir Henry Campbell-Bannerman*. Constable, 1973.

18

A Liberal Constitution
for an Age of Crisis

David Howarth

Countries rarely acquire new constitutions except through cataclysm. Conquest, civil war, imperial withdrawal, revolution, fiscal collapse or insuperable political deadlock, all have created crises the resolution of which included constitutional upheaval. For more than 250 years Britain escaped such catastrophes, albeit sometimes by the skin of its teeth. But in the second half of the 20th century, a combination of the disastrous economic consequences of the Second World War and the collapse of Britain's own empire created strategic and economic problems of such magnitude that fundamental constitutional change seemed to many, especially liberals, to be indispensable. Some of that change did come, in the form of joining the constitutional structure of the European Community/European Union (EU). The EU, as Vernon Bogdanor pointed out,[1] provided Britain with a new constitutional settlement involving, among other things, a codified legislative process for making EU law and courts capable of striking down (or 'disapplying') legislation incompatible with the EU treaties. That settlement gave Britain a new role in world politics, both as a leading EU power and as a 'bridge' between Europe and the USA, and, in exchange for limiting its liberty of independent legislative action in a few policy areas, provided it with increasingly open access to European markets.

The cataclysm of Brexit has generated a new crisis. In some ways the situation now is similar to that before Britain joined: international marginality, economic enfeeblement and confusion about basic values. But in other ways it is worse – imperial dissolution has reached the metropolis itself, with the prospect of Scottish independence and Irish reunification, and problems of great significance have emerged, particularly climate change, on which Britain outside any global regional formation is too small

---

1 Vernon Bogdanor, *Beyond Brexit: Towards a British Constitution* (IB Tauris, 2018), pp. vii-ix.

to have influence. Not surprisingly the question now arises again of whether major constitutional change can help Britain overcome its crisis. Thoughts turn to the standard list of possible reforms: proportional representation, democratic reform of the House of Lords, internal federalism, fixed-term parliaments, a codified constitution and so on. But these will make relatively little difference unless they contribute to the most important and obvious way of reversing Britain's decline, which is to rejoin the European Union. In assessing possible constitutional reforms, the question we must ask is will this help or hinder Britain on its path back into the EU?

One of the barriers to rejoining the EU is Britain's political and institutional instability. From the point of view of the EU, why expend great energy on negotiating with Britain if Britain's political system can generate a new prime minister every two years, each one beholden to a faction-ridden party that itself never reaches even 45% of the vote,[2] or can award an overwhelming majority to a party with less than a third of the vote and whose authority is questionable. Who can say whether a deal reached with this year's prime minister has sufficient political support to survive a general election or a referendum?

Even worse, Conservative ministers showed contempt for the rule of law, both international and domestic, and used their own lawlessness as a negotiating tactic.[3] The central problem, which British Brexiteer ministers seemed never to grasp, is that the EU itself is a creation of law. The Union has no existence outside the law and its legal system is fundamental to what it is.[4] The now common British view of its constitution as purely political,[5] with law playing no permanent part in its structure, makes Britain look deeply strange. In the EU and in its member states, politics carries on within structures and limits laid down by law. In Britain some, both on the right and on the left, see law as merely a temporary output of politics, not ultimately to be taken seriously and to be discarded if politically inconvenient. When

---

2   See Andrew Duff, *Going Back: What Britain should do to join the European Union* (European Policy Centre, 2024), p. 10.

3   Bingham Centre for the Rule of Law, *United Kingdom Internal Market Bill: A Rule of Law Analysis of Clauses 42 to 45* (British Institute for International and Comparative Law, 2020).

4   See Michel Barnier, *La Grande Illusion: Journal Secret de Brexit 2016-2020* (Gallimard, 2021), p. 198.

5   See Richard Bellamy, *Political Constitutionalism* (Cambridge University Press, 2007), pp. 37-55.

Britain's leaders were people of honour whose word its partners could trust, that strangeness was merely a tolerable quirk of doing business with Britain. But since Brexit, it is threatening to become a serious obstacle. This chapter considers the defects of Britain's current constitutional arrangements and suggests changes from a liberal perspective, but it comes back at the end to consider the extent to which its proposals would contribute to the most radical and important change of all, rejoining the EU.

The Brexit constitution

Before discussing constitutional reforms that radical liberals should be proposing, it is worth setting out the constitutional direction Britain has been taking since the 2016 referendum. The Conservative governments of Theresa May, Boris Johnson, Liz Truss and Rishi Sunak simultaneously proclaimed the sovereignty of parliament and worked to undermine parliamentary democracy and the rule of law. On parliamentary democracy, the Conservatives attempted unlawfully to prorogue parliament and started down the road of partisan interference with the right to vote.[6] They also multiplied new ministerial powers to change primary legislation with little or no parliamentary scrutiny, not only about Brexit (along the way undermining devolution) but also about strikes, subsidies, energy and other matters.[7] On the rule of law, statutes that exempt ministers from practically all legal control have become commonplace.[8]

The United Kingdom Internal Market Bill 2020 at one stage empowered ministers to ignore all law both domestic and international. The Dissolution and Calling of Parliament Act 2020 managed to attack parliamentary democracy and the rule of law simultaneously by removing the House of Commons' control over the date of elections and purporting to protect the power of the prime minister to choose the election date from judicial review.

---

6   Elections Act 2011 s. 1 and Sch. 1. See also David Howarth, 'The Politics of Public Law,' in *The Cambridge Companion to Public Law*, ed. Mark Elliott and David Feldman (Cambridge University Press, 2015).

7   See David Howarth, 'Government without discussion: Henry VIII clauses and the future of parliamentary democracy,' Statute Law Society Lecture, 14 March 2024, https://vimeo.com/showcase/statute-law-society and forthcoming in the Statute Law Review.

8   Safety of Rwanda (Asylum and Immigration) Act 2024 ss 2 and 3; Dissolution and Calling of Parliament Act 2022 s. 3.

In parallel, the Conservatives initiated a massive concentration of power into their own hands, from using financial and patronage powers to undermine the independence of the BBC, to giving themselves the right to control the policy and strategy of the Electoral Commission.[9] Conservative ultras, such as Jacob Rees-Mogg and Liz Truss, motivated either by a view of executive prerogative that might have sounded extreme in the court of Charles I, or by a desire to do anything that might obstruct Britain's rejoining the EU, go even further and speak darkly about removing the operational independence of the Bank of England, abolishing the Office for Budget Responsibility, ending the impartiality of the civil service and controlling judicial appointments.[10]

As a final, and outlandish, application of the fantasy theory of sovereignty, the Conservatives claimed that they could legislate to change aspects of the world the British state simply cannot change. The Safety of Rwanda Act 2024 purported to declare facts that were not facts and to ignore international law.[11] The Conservatives' Brexit constitution lives in a postmodern post-truth world in which all that is solid has melted into air. It deals with Britain's loss of real power by pretending to enjoy imaginary powers.

The constitutional theory that lies behind the Conservatives' Brexit constitution is an extreme form of what I have elsewhere called 'Whitehallism',[12] the view that British democracy consists of periodically electing a single party to office and then giving it unlimited power to implement its programme, a view in which parliament's only role, apart from grandstanding for the next general election, is to supply ministers with the legal and financial resources they demand. But it is Whitehallism tinged with the dangerous language of populism – 'will of the people', 'political class' and 'liberal elite'.[13] It is also

9   For the BBC, see Adam Bienkov and Patrick Howse, 'Cowed and Compliant: The BBC's Road to Appeasement,' *Byline Times*, April 2024 [Accessed 8/11/2024]. For the Electoral Commission see Elections Act 2022 s. 16.

10   See, for example, Elizabeth Truss, *Ten Years to Save the West* (Biteback, 2024), pp. 285-286.

11   Ss 2 and 5.

12   David Howarth, 'Westminster versus Whitehall: What the Brexit Debate Revealed About an Unresolved Conflict at the Heart of the British Constitution,' in *The Brexit Challenge for Ireland and the United Kingdom: Constitutions Under Pressure*, ed. Oran Doyle, Aileen McHarg, Jo Murkens (Cambridge University Press, 2021), pp. 217-238.

13   See Cas Mudde and Cristóbal Rovira Kaltwasser, *Populism: A Very Short Introduction* (Oxford University Press, 2017).

tinged with the even more dangerous doctrine that the Brexit referendum was not a political decision about a specific issue at a specific time but an unchallengeable starting point for all subsequent politics, an expression of the sovereign 'will of the people' that defines what counts subsequently as legitimate political discussion, that binds parliament and that, by defining opponents as 'traitors' or 'enemies of the people', limits who can legitimately participate in politics, a doctrine alarmingly close to the approach of the pro-Nazi legal theorist Carl Schmitt, for whom membership of a political community comes from having a common public enemy.[14]

Although resorted to by Conservative governments, Whitehallism is essentially a Labour Party theory of the constitution. Its origin is in the extra-parliamentary nature of the Labour Party and the need for the party to assert its dominance over members of parliament. We cannot expect the Starmer government to stray much from Whitehallism's basic tenets. What remains to be seen is whether the Starmer government can leave behind the language of populism. The signs are mixed. Labour ministers do not habitually denounce the 'liberal elite' but their constant references to 'working people' is potentially exclusionary; and declarations that Britain will not rejoin the EU within Starmer's lifetime,[15] while not explicitly marginalising those of a different view, seems intended to have a similar effect. But more important than the Starmer government's own initial rhetoric is the fact that its political strategy seems aimed at competing with the explicitly national populist Reform Party rather than at attracting more moderate voters. That strategy risks pulling the Starmer government into positions not very different from those of its predecessor.

Liberal basics and liberal reasons

The Brexit constitution would take Britain on a journey towards Orban – or Trump-style authoritarian illiberalism. The task of liberals, above all, is to resist authoritarian illiberalism. That resistance needs to start with asserting some liberal basics: that the political system should be built around an inclusive idea of citizenship, not around the designation and exclusion of 'public enemies'; that legislation should arise out of discussion and debate,

14 Carl Schmitt, *The Concept of the Political*, expanded ed. trans. George D. Schwab (University of Chicago Press, 2007), pp. 26-38.
15 Kiran Stacey, 'Britain will not rejoin EU in my lifetime, says Starmer,' *The Guardian*, 3 July 2024, https://tinyurl.com/55x7k4j9 [Accessed 8/11/2024].

not purely out of the political will of a majority, both because discussion generates consent and because deliberation leads to better decisions;[16] that in a democracy no separate class of 'politicians' exists since all adult citizens hold political office, namely the political office of 'elector', so that we should talk only about some people spending more time on politics than others; and that absolute political equality is impossible, if only because elected representatives do and should have more access to decision-making than people who are not elected.

Political inequality that arises out of other inequalities, especially inequalities of wealth and income, should as far as practicable be eliminated.[17] Political equality also needs protection from self-perpetuating concentrations of power within politics itself, and from the techniques authoritarians use to ensconce themselves, including electoral manipulation, abuse of the legal system and control of publicly-financed media. The most important characteristic of a radical liberal proposal for constitutional change is that it should arise directly out of liberal values and provide a basis for challenging illiberal authoritarianism. Illiberalism is on the cusp of triumphing largely because the values of liberalism are barely heard. That is why the reasons liberals give for their proposals matter as much, if not more, than their precise mechanics.

Proportional representation is the central example of a liberal proposal where reasons matter. One of the many disastrous aspects of the 2011 referendum on the alternative vote was that the main reason the 'yes' campaign gave was that AV would eliminate 'lazy' politicians who occupied 'safe' seats.[18] That reason, far from arising out of liberal values, played to and validated populism in its purest form, the view that the world divides into 'politicians' who are corrupt and 'the people' who are pure.[19] Liberals should be arguing for a proportional electoral system because it would include more

16 See Anthony King and Ivor Crewe, *The Blunders of Our Governments* (Oneworld, 2013), pp. 334-344.

17 For evidence this view is popular, see David Howarth, Theresa M Marteau, Adam P Coutts et al., 'What do the British public think of inequality in health, wealth, and power?', *Social Science and Medicine* vol. 222 (February 2019): pp. 198-206.

18 See for example Thomas Carl Lundberg and Martin Steven, 'Framing Electoral Reform in the 2011 UK Alternative Vote Referendum Campaign', *Australian Journal of Political Science* vol. 48, no. 1 (2013): pp. 15-27.

19 Mudde and Kaltwasser, *Populism*, p. 6.

political views in parliament and because it would increase political equality by eliminating not safe seats but marginal ones, seats whose voters, under the current system, enjoy disproportionate influence. And we should argue for it because it gives parliament more power and the government less power, that is, because liberals should oppose Whitehallism and embrace its opposite: the Westminster theory under which parliament, not the government, is the central institution of our democracy; under which parliament's views matter, not just the noise it makes; and under which elections are about choosing MPs who will hold governments to account and legislate well.

One can see why liberals are sometimes afraid to argue for proportional representation on properly liberal grounds that support a distinctly parliamentary democracy. A large chunk of the British electorate, presumably out of distrust of its representatives, adheres to a crude view of MPs as delegates who should vote with majority opinion in their constituencies and not think for themselves.[20] That view that might be incoherent – many MPs are elected by a minority of their electorate and so voting with their constituency's majority opinion would often require them to betray the very people who voted for them – but it is undoubtedly both widespread and incompatible with the Westminster theory. Nevertheless, it is not a majority view, and public opinion also wants parties to work together to produce policies that might not have appeared in any of their manifestos, a view incompatible with the Whitehall theory and tolerant of constructive debate.[21] More room exists for liberalism than liberals sometimes believe. The basic liberal values of citizenship, based on inclusion rather than on excluding 'enemies', and of government by discussion, should need no introduction, but the other two values, political equality and anti-populism might be less familiar and so benefit from further illustration before we turn to specific proposals for constitutional change.

Political equality

A fruitful way of thinking about equality, going beyond conventional distinctions between equality of outcome and equality of opportunity, is to look at inequality in different spheres of life and ask two things: to what degree is inequality in this sphere acceptable? And is it acceptable that

---

20 Alan Renwick, Ben Lauderdale and Meg Russell, *The Future of Democracy in the UK* (The Constitution Unit, 2023), pp. 47-49.
21 Renwick, Lauderdale and Russell, *The Future of Democracy*, p. 48.

inequality in one sphere is reinforcing inequality in another?[22] Liberals vary on the degree of economic inequality they find unacceptable. They vary far less on political inequality. They vary not at all in finding it unacceptable that economic inequality should spill over into political inequality. A fundamental problem with British politics for liberals is that it creates and reinforces precisely this form of unacceptable political inequality.

The spillover from economic to political inequality happens in the most blatant of ways, through money spent on politics. No limits exist on the size of political donations that individuals, companies or even unincorporated bodies can make. Some transparency requirements, albeit easily avoided, apply to donations to political parties but none at all apply to donations to influencer organisations such as political think-tanks. Super-rich individuals also shape politics through media ownership, not only of newspapers, whose influence endures via their websites even as their paper sales fall, and through newspapers' continuing influence on the BBC, but now also of television stations such as GB News, the regulation of which has proven feeble. British election law gives newspaper owners extraordinary privileges, exempting newspapers from all regulation of spending on elections, whether at national or constituency level.[23] If super-rich individuals want to buy a British election, the easiest way for them to do it is to buy a company that publishes newspapers.

To establish and maintain democratic political equality and to protect democratic elections should be the highest duty of the state. Economic inequality should not be allowed to leech into politics. Donations from corporate bodies and unincorporated associations should be prohibited and donations from individuals capped at a low annual level, no more than, say, 10% of average income. Donations to think-tanks should be bound by the same rules as donations to parties, including on transparency. Newspapers should lose their special privileges to spend money on influencing elections. Liberals should not be afraid to argue that equal democratic citizenship and fair elections are more important than freedom of the corporate media, and liberals should not fall into the trap into which the US has fallen, of equating spending money on politics with free speech.[24] In addition, governing parties

22   See Howarth et al., *What do the British public think*, drawing on Michael Walzer, *Spheres of justice: A defense of pluralism and equality* (Basic Books, 1983).
23   See section 85 and Sch 8A of the Political Parties, Elections and Referendums Act 2000 and section 90ZA of the Representation of the People Act 1983.
24   *Buckley v Valeo* 424 U.S. 1, 96 S. Ct. 612 (1976); *First National Bank of Boston v Bellotti* 435 U.S. 765, 98 S. Ct. 1407 (1978); *Citizens United v Federal Election*

should not be allowed to influence elections through the state. Ministers should have no power to control appointments to or the strategy and policy of the Electoral Commission. Boundary decisions – less important under proportional representation than under the current system but never unimportant – should become completely independent.

An associated issue is the relationship between the government and the BBC, which is still the most commonly consulted source for news in Britain.[25] Subversion of public broadcasters has become a common authoritarian technique for undermining the fairness of elections, whether in Hungary, Poland or Italy, and signs exist of similar moves in Britain.[26] Ministers should have no opportunity to influence the BBC's political coverage. The BBC's charter should become permanent and should guarantee independence, and ministers should lose any power to appoint BBC governors.[27]

Anti-populism

The anti-populist position that it is wrong to divide the population into 'politicians' and 'the people' has deep roots in British liberalism, not least in Mill's view that citizens should gain a 'public education' by participating in politics, especially local politics,[28] and in the community politics tradition.[29] It also draws on Mill's view that the point of that education is 'the nourishment of public spirit'.[30] But it goes further in treating the status of voter as a public office in itself, one that brings with it a moral obligation to promote the voter's view of the public interest, not just the voter's private interest. Conventional political scientists might consider this a 'republican' view of citizenship rather than a 'liberal' one.[31] But in liberal politics, as opposed to theoretical constructs of liberalism emanating from its opponents, 'republican' views of citizens' obligations have long prevailed.

Commission 558 U.S. 310, 130 S. Ct. 876 (2010).

25 Ofcom, *News Consumption in the UK 2024* (Ofcom, 2024), pp. 7-10.

26 Bienkov and Howse, 'Cowed and Compliant.'

27 For these and other suggestions for protecting the BBC, see Damian Tambini, 'Constitutionalising the BBC,' *The Political Quarterly* vol. 95, no. 1 (2024): pp. 56-63.

28 John Stuart Mill, *Considerations on Representative Government*, 2nd ed. 1861 (Cambridge University Press, 2010), pp. 274-276.

29 See Bernard Greaves & Gordon Lishman, *The Theory and Practice of Community Politics* (Association of Liberal Councillors, 1980).

30 Mill, *Considerations on Representative Government*, p. 275.

31 See Michael Lister and Emily Pia, *Citizenship in Contemporary Europe* (Edinburgh University Press, 2008), pp. 8-31.

Liberals, for example, led the 19th century campaigns against bribery in elections, campaigns that would make no sense if liberals thought that it was acceptable for voters to use their votes for purely private ends.

In reality, voters often use their votes not in the public interest but in ways that they hope will benefit themselves or their families or groups they belong to, but that is the point. When that happens, voters are falling short of standards that apply to them, just as elected representatives sometimes fall short of standards that apply to them. In truth, neither 'the people' nor 'politicians' are pure. Treating voters and candidates for office as different orders of being mischaracterises both.

Anti-populism can be further clarified by its policy consequences, which are many and various. For example, liberals should oppose the policy of successive British governments of handing over local power to single individuals. We should be creating more elected positions not fewer, so that more citizens experience the responsibilities of power,[32] and ending any linkage between devolution of power and accepting local autocracy in the shape of elected mayors. Political power should be devolved as much as practicable, but no logical connection exists between devolution and the combination of Hobbesian disdain for collective decision-making and an enthusiasm for politics as spectacle that propels the movement for elected mayors.[33]

Anti-populism also implies a campaign to lower barriers to entry into electoral politics. That includes practical measures, such as better workplace rights and more flexibility about online meetings. But we also need to eliminate the threats and abuse that discourage all except sociopaths from standing for election. Current criminal law seems not fully to reflect the seriousness of offences that undermine representative democracy, and enforcement is impeded by some police officers' lack of enthusiasm.[34] It is not illiberal to expect severer sentences and better law enforcement in defence of democracy.

Another implication is that we need to challenge prevailing orthodoxy about education. Officially, the main purpose of the English education

---

32   See Mill, *Considerations on Representative Government*, pp. 275-276.

33   For Hobbes' negative view of political assemblies, see Thomas Hobbes, *Leviathan* 1651 (Oxford University Press, 1909), pp. 96-97. For the politics of spectacle, see David Howarth, 'In the Theatre State,' *Times Literary Supplement*, issue 5632 (2011): p. 23.

34   For examples of police lack of enthusiasm see Joint Committee on Human Rights, *Democracy, Freedom of expression and freedom of association: Threats to MPs* (House of Commons, 2019).

system is to 'drive economic growth' by preparing young people for work,[35] with occasional mentions of culture and preparation for the disappointments of adult life.[36] Helping young people achieve economic independence is a reasonable goal for the education system of a democracy but even more important is helping them to become democratic citizens who will use their vote in the right spirit and with discernment.

The constitutional agenda

Having completed that preface on liberal basic values, we can turn to the details of constitutional reform. We will be thinking about institutions, but it is worth reiterating that institutions are only means to an end, or to a set of ends, or even, as in the liberal conservative doctrine of Michael Oakeshott, a means for allowing the state to avoid having any specific ends.[37] Debate about the customary list of institutional issues – proportional representation, internal federalism, reform of the House of Lords, judicial review of legislation and a codified constitution, fixed-term parliaments and indeed membership of the EU itself – is ultimately about values not mechanics.

We have already dealt with proportional representation and mentioned how it responds to basic liberal values. It is now time to look at some other items on the list.

Federalism

An elective affinity exists between liberalism and federalism. Federalism divides up state power geographically, preventing domination of the periphery by the centre and of one area by another. From a liberal point of view federalism is attractive mainly because it breaks up excessive concentrations of power, but also because it promotes democratic citizenship by maintaining the viability of relatively small political units and so making participation easier for more people. It also helps to safeguard political equality by making the acquisition of power through money more difficult, or at least more expensive. No one loves centralisation more than corporate lobbyists, since it means fewer people to influence.

---

35 See the Department for Education's 'About us' statement on its website, https://www.gov.uk/government/organisations/department-for-education/about [Accessed 1/05/2024].

36 See Nick Gibb, 'The purpose of education,' speech at the Education Reform Summit, London 9 July 2015, https://www.gov.uk/government/speeches/the-purpose-of-education [Accessed 1/5/2024].

37 Michael Oakeshott, *On Human Conduct* (Clarendon Press, 1975), pp. 108-184.

Implementing federalism is a matter of building a legal structure in which the powers of the federal units cannot be reduced by unilateral action of the centre. This is not easy to achieve in a British context. The doctrine of parliamentary legislative supremacy means that parliament can at any time dissolve all restrictions on central power,[38] a situation made worse by judicial decisions that interpret supremacy in political rather than merely legal terms.[39] Some possible solutions exist, as we will see later, but nothing is guaranteed. Federalism is also difficult to implement in Britain for political reasons. Are the federal units to be the nations of the United Kingdom, namely England, Scotland, Wales and Northern Ireland, or something else? The problem with the four-nation basis is that the federation would be enormously lopsided – the population of England is nearly five and half times greater than all the other nations together. But if we were to reduce the disparity by treating the standard regions of England as federal units we would end up annoying Scots who think of Scotland as an entity more important than a mere region and we would also annoy some inhabitants of England, for example those in Cornwall and Devon who consider Bristol to be just as distant as London, and others who would regard regional government as an unnecessary layer. The English regions option is probably not politically feasible, and so, although not entirely consonant with liberal theory, since we would not be treating citizens entirely equally, the practical answer is to take the 'four nations' option. We can leave it to England whether to institute a further level of internal federalism.

Whether England should be internally federal raises the further question of whether England should have its own parliament and its own government. The current messy compromise is that the United Kingdom parliament and government also act as the parliament and government of England. One point of view is that since few in England seem bothered by this arrangement, we should leave well alone. After all, 85% of MPs represent constituencies in England and so on issues that engage specifically English interests, English MPs cannot be outvoted. The opposite view is that at some point a situation is bound to arise in which the government of the United

38   See *R (Miller) v Secretary of State for Exiting the European Union* [2017] UKSC 5, [2018] AC 61 at [136]-[151].

39   See *Attorney General and the Advocate General for Scotland's Reference – United Nations Convention on the Rights of the Child (Incorporation) (Scotland) Bill* [2021] UKSC 42, [2021] 1 WLR 5106 at [52]. See also 2022] UKSC 31, [2022] 1 WLR 5435 at [77]-[83].

Kingdom enjoys a majority in the House of Commons solely because of support from MPs from outside England. England would then be ruled without its own electorate's consent. Proportional representation for the House of Commons would reduce the risk but not eliminate it. In addition, some argue that if liberals and progressives reject the idea of an English parliament, the far right will monopolise the proposal and an opportunity will be lost to promote a more liberal and progressive idea of Englishness.[40] The main political problem with proposing an English parliament is that, as with English regional government, no great demand for it currently exists. A consistent majority prefers the status quo to either an English parliament or regional government.[41] A risk exists that federalism as a whole might fail because of the unpopularity of a parliament for England. The practical way forward is to defer the English parliament issue until federalism has been established for Scotland, Wales and Northern Ireland.

House of Lords reform

The main problem with the long-running debate about reform of the House of Lords is that it usually proceeds backwards. Instead of asking first whether we need a second chamber and if so why, and then moving on to work out the chamber's best composition given the functions we want it to have, too many people start with their preferred composition and then make up functions that such a chamber could fulfil. This odd approach ultimately arises from the fact that the House of Lords lost its original function in 1911 and has been searching for a new one ever since. Its original function was to defend the interests of the landed aristocracy, but when the Liberal Party succeeded in passing the Parliament Act 1911, aristocratic power was all but finished, the culmination of a century-long radical liberal campaign that included repeal of the corn laws, civil service and army reform and death duties.

Denmark and Sweden, whose upper houses of parliament also originally represented the nobility or the wealthy, simply abolished them, and seem not to miss them. On the other hand, in the era following the democratic

---

40 Caroline Lucas, *Another England: How to Reclaim Our National Story* (Hutchinson, 2024), pp. 70-73.
41 Sarah Butt, John Curtice, Elizabeth Clery, eds., 'Constitutional Reform,' in *British Social Attitudes: The 39th Report* (National Centre for Social Research, 2022), p. 16.

revolutions of 1989-90 some eastern European countries, including Poland and Romania, created new second chambers.[42]

Despite the attractions of unicameralism, good liberal arguments for a second chamber do exist. They include: (1) that dividing legislative power increases the scope for genuine debate about the merits of legislation; (2) that having a second chamber chosen by a different system from the first chamber creates the possibility of more inclusive representation; and (3) that dividing legislative power reduces the risk of excessive concentrations of power. The current arrangements are supposed to fulfil the first two functions – the first in the Lords' role as a 'revising chamber' and the second in the form of the appointment of distinguished experts who would not dream of sullying themselves by competing in elections. But the House of Lords is not currently supposed to perform the third function except for a power to delay legislation for a year, which turns into a veto in the final year of a parliament, and so in practice constitutes a power to refer disagreement between the chambers to the electorate, plus an under-appreciated power to block any bill that 'extends the maximum duration of Parliament beyond five years', which is to say a bill that delays or cancels a general election.[43]

The trouble with the first argument for a second chamber, more government by discussion, is that although it might work within the confines of the current House of Lords, where the existence of dozens of non-aligned crossbenchers means that reasoned debate can make a difference, its effect on debate in the Commons is practically non-existent. When deciding how to vote on Lords' amendments, very few MPs heed what members of the Lords have said. If we are to see more rational debate in parliament as a whole, we need a different method.

As for the second argument, more inclusivity, the difficulty is not just how to square the presence of unelected (and unelectable) experts with political equality, but also how to justify the presence of these specific experts and not a different selection of experts. Legislatures can benefit from expertise without admitting into membership an unexplained subset of experts.

So that leaves the third argument, the checks and balances argument, which is the one least valued in the current arrangements. In federal systems second chambers are often charged with preventing overconcentration of

---

42 Meg Russell, *Reforming the House of Lords: Lessons from Overseas* (Oxford University Press, 2000), p. 23.
43 Parliament Act 1911 s. 2(1).

power through defending the federal units' interests and protecting the federal structure itself. If Britain is to become a federal state, it is reasonable to think about using the second chamber in that way.[44] But it would be difficult to achieve much protection through a second chamber in a very lopsided federal system in which more than four fifths of the country might be far from committed to federalism. One might try inserting a 90% majority requirement for bills that interfere with the federal units' powers, but the problem with requirements for special majorities is that they are vulnerable to attempts to circumvent them using sequences of bills that deploy the Parliament Act to chip away at them until they collapse.[45]

Second chambers do exist that are designed as checks and balances even in non-federal systems. It is noticeable, however, that non-federal second chambers rarely have full powers of veto. (Italy is one, albeit controversial, exception). Instead, second chambers have more powers over some matters than others. The upside of a veto power is that it provides a strong degree of protection, but its downside is that it can give rise to deadlock and immobility. So a sensible way forward is to distinguish between ordinary politics, in which the disadvantages of checks and balances outweigh their benefits, and fundamental politics, in which the opposite applies. In fact, oddly, that is precisely what the current British system does when it exempts from the Parliament Act bills that would extend the life of a parliament. The question is whether to expand the range of exempted bills to protect other aspects of democracy and political equality that are under threat from illiberal authoritarianism and populism. Examples might include bills that change the electoral system, bills that interfere with the independence of the Electoral Commission, bills that reduce the independence of regulators of the media and, possibly, bills that interfere with the independence of the BBC. We might add protection for the rule of law by including bills that affect the independence of the judiciary.

What should be the composition of a House whose most important function is protecting democracy? Two requirements spring to mind. First, to have sufficient legitimacy in the task of protecting democracy it should

44 Gordon Brown, *A New Britain: Renewing our Democracy and Rebuilding our Economy* (The Labour Party, 2022), p. 140.
45 This would be by an extension of the 'two step' method of using the Parliament Act to extend the life of a parliament, the effectiveness of which judges disagreed about in *R (Jackson) v Attorney General* [2005] UKHL 56; [2006] 1 AC 262 at [32] (Lord Bingham) and, in contrast, at [58]-[62] (Lord Nicholls).

itself be democratic. The current arrangements offer little protection precisely because the House of Lords accepts its own subordinate status because it is not elected. Secondly, it should be difficult, if not impossible, for a government to gain a majority in it. The question is how to achieve both at the same time. One route is to elect the upper house by the most proportional method possible, for example by a national list system. Another is to increase the probability of selecting members who belong to no party by choosing citizens randomly on the same basis as jury service. Each method has disadvantages. Even a pure form of proportionality can succumb to majority rule either directly or through coalitions, and purely random selection means that none of the members will have an incentive to do a good job to improve their chances of re-election. One possibility is to use both methods in the hope that the disadvantages of each are reduced by the other – for example a House 90% elected by a pure list system and 10% chosen by lot.

Judicial review of legislation and codification

Another old chestnut of British constitutional debate is whether Britain should adopt a written constitution. That way of framing the issue, however, contains at least two serious errors. The first, perhaps less important, is that much of the British constitution is already 'written' – it exists in acts of parliament, in the Standing Orders of the Houses of Parliament, in Erskine May, in judgments of the courts and in various codes of practice. What the British constitution is not is codified – edited into a single authoritative document that provides a common starting point for future interpretation and development.

The second error is more important. When people speak of a 'written constitution' what they usually intend is that judges should have a power to enforce it. But judicial enforcement and codification are distinct things. Some countries, notably the Netherlands, have a codified constitution that is unenforceable in the courts. And at least one country, Israel, lacks a codified constitution but its judges have given themselves a power to strike down legislation that offends against constitutional principles. The link between the two in the British debate is merely a point about implementation. How could a judicial strike-down power be protected from repeal by parliament? The doctrine of parliamentary legislative supremacy as currently recognised by the judges means that any act of parliament that gave judges a power to strike down legislation could be repealed by the simple expedient of passing another act of parliament. Some reformers hope that judges would accept that a strike-down power contained in a codified constitution which had been approved by exceptional means, for example by a referendum, was immune from repeal by a subsequent act of parliament. But it is not clear either that judges would fulfil that hope or, on the other side, that the whole laborious business of drafting a new constitution is required to persuade judges to limit parliamentary legislative supremacy. The concept of supremacy exists in the minds of judges, not on bits of paper. It might survive a codified constitution, or it might collapse even without one.

A more fundamental issue is whether a judicial power to strike down legislation is acceptable in the first place, and if so in what circumstances. The most important thing to say about that issue is that judicial power to strike down legislation is not obviously liberal. Judges are usually unelected, and in systems in which judges are elected, judges are often not very judicial. Moreover, the basic configuration of a legal dispute, in which the competing parties, and only the competing parties, put their points of view to the court, is ill-suited to decide issues about which many other people might have an interest and a view. Judicial power over legislation is consequently neither obviously democratic nor particularly inclusive. Moreover, judicial power is not the only way institutionally to protect democracy and political equality. As we have already seen, protection can also be designed into the structure of the legislature and supported by choice of electoral system. But some aspects of the constitutional system are difficult to protect except through judges. One example is the right to vote itself. It is impossible to devise a purely democratic means to decide who can vote. The decision invariably falls to those who already have the vote or to their representatives, and so automatically excludes those who do not. As Baroness Hale said in the Supreme Court:

> Parliamentarians derive their authority and legitimacy from those who elected them, in other words from the current franchise, and it is to those electors that they are accountable. They have no such relationship with the disenfranchised. Indeed, in some situations, they may have a vested interest in keeping the franchise as it is.[46]

Baroness Hale was talking about cases in which people who currently have no vote were demanding it, but her point also applies to threats to deprive

46 *R (Chester) v Secretary of State for Justice* [2013] UKSC 63, [2014] AC 271 at [89].

unpopular people of their vote, either directly or indirectly. 'Discrete and insular minorities', that is minorities with no prospect of gaining political allies, are at constant risk from combinations of their enemies.[47] That means that even a fully proportional second chamber with a right of veto might not be enough to protect them.

A second example is maintaining a federal structure in a lopsided federation. As we have already seen, protection through a federal second chamber in the British context is not straightforward. The next best solution is to give judges a power to strike down offending legislation.

Beyond these fundamentals, the case for a judicial strike-down power is less compelling. The current system for applying human rights in Britain does without it, relying on a power for judges to reinterpret, sometimes radically, offending statutory provisions, and declarations of incompatibility that merely invite parliament to pass correcting legislation. The process is one of dialogue between politics and law, without giving the final word to either. Long term refusals by British governments to move to rectify judicially declared violations of human rights have been very rare, even under recent Conservative governments and even while ministers have been making hostile noises about the European Convention on Human Rights, and leaving the precise method of rectification to the political system is beneficial in itself.[48] Dialogue is particularly valuable where an issue hinges on whether a provision constitutes a 'proportionate' response to a problem, an issue on which courts and legislatures can reasonably differ.

Admittedly, those hostile noises and the constant barrage of anti-human rights propaganda from the authoritarian populist media raise nagging doubts about whether the current arrangements, which rely on governments being committed to a civilised dialogue with the courts, could withstand assaults from a far-right government. The problem, however, is that, as events in Hungary and Poland illustrate,[49] eventually courts can be subverted themselves.[50] The question then becomes whether, for the sake

47 *United States v Carolene Products Company* 304 U.S. 144 (1938) at p. 152, footnote 4.

48 See Ministry of Justice, *Responding to Human Rights Judgments London* (Ministry of Justice, 2023).

49 See Kriszta Kovács and Kim Lane Scheppele, 'The fragility of an independent judiciary: Lessons from Hungary and Poland–and the European Union,' *Communist and Post-Communist Studies* vol. 51, issue 3 (2018): pp. 189-200.

50 See Truss, *Ten Years to Save the West*, p. 286 where a former UK prime minister proposes to make judges accountable to ministers.

of giving opposition forces more time to organise, it is worth providing the courts with additional powers of strike down, powers that would apply to all governments not just illiberal ones. For protecting the right to vote, it is worth it, since a democratic government would never attempt to undermine that right and buying time until the next election creates a chance of escaping authoritarian rule. But the balance is less clear for other rights.

We might shift the balance in favour of a strike-down power by limiting it to violations of the ECHR's absolute or unqualified rights (life, freedom from torture, freedom from slavery, liberty, no retroactive punishments), that is to the rights in which proportionality is not relevant, so that the problem of unelected judges overruling elected parliaments about the right balance between an individual interest protected by the right, and the interests of others would not arise. But a strong case exists for maintaining a dialogue system for qualified rights.

A constitutional court

Assuming that we want some strike-down powers, we can return to the question of implementation: how could we protect a strike-down power from a future parliament appealing to parliamentary legislative supremacy and repealing it? The truth is that no purely technical way of doing so exists. As long as judges themselves feel bound by the doctrine of parliamentary legislative supremacy, it will trump even a codified constitution. So, the question of how to cement a strike-down power is an empirical one: what would persuade judges to accept it? On that question little evidence exists and we should proceed with caution. We should not underestimate the reluctance of judges to take on such a responsibility. It would expose them even further to accusations of acting politically. British judges do not want to become American judges. A way forward, more in line with European than American practice, would be to establish a separate constitutional court and give it powers limited to preventing non-conforming bills being sent to the head of state for assent, a method that combines a procedure already in existence for the Scottish and Welsh parliaments with the Constitution of the French Fifth Republic before 2008.[51] One advantage of setting up a new

51 Scotland Act 1998 ss 32A and 32, Government of Wales Act 2006, s. 99; Constitution de la cinquième république française, articles 46(5), 54 and 61 (see now, in addition, art. 61-1, which extends the jurisdiction of the Conseil Constitutionnel to the constitutionality of existing laws referred to it by the ordinary courts).

body would be to protect the ordinary courts from accusations of acting politically. Another advantage would be that it would allow an argument to develop that judges were not directly challenging supremacy but merely implementing a change in the process by which a bill becomes an act.[52] Yet another advantage would be that the judges of the new court could be required to swear an oath specifically committing them to protect the powers of the court itself and to strike down bills that remove or limit its powers. One can exaggerate the potency of such oaths, but it would at least give judges inclined to maintain the court's strike-down power a publicly defensible reason for doing so.

The composition of a constitutional court and the conditions under which it could be invoked would be matters for further thought. The membership of the French Conseil Constitutionnel is more political than judicial, including, for example, all previous presidents of the Republic, but the German Federal Constitutional Court's membership is more legal than political, and the Italian Constitutional Court consists entirely of judges and legal academics, with half the court elected by the judges and half appointed by the President of the Republic. Since a British court's functions would include protecting federalism, it would make sense for several of the judges to be nominated from the federal units, which would perhaps best be achieved through nominations from their judiciaries rather than their governments.

If we establish a constitutional court with a power to prevent offending bills reaching the statute book, the question will arise of whether we should have a procedure for overriding the court's decision, the equivalent of a constitutional amendment procedure. That should depend on the subject matter of the decision. For decisions about federalism, two options exist: to allow an override by permission of the federal unit affected by the bill; or to allow an override by agreement of a majority of the federal units – in effect by agreement of three of the four parliaments. The former gives more direct protection to each parliament but is less flexible and more likely to give rise to inconsistencies between one federal unit and the others, so the latter looks preferable.

On protection of the right to vote, however, an argument exists to allow no override at all. The UK parliament should not be allowed to override, since, as Baroness Hale pointed out, all existing MPs have a vested interest,

---

52   See *R (Jackson) v Attorney-General* 2005] UKHL 56; [2006] 1 AC 262 at [24], [111] and [187].

and an override by referendum raises the question of who can vote in the referendum. Unamendable constitutional provisions are rare but not unknown. One can find them, for example, in the German constitution, the US constitution and, by judicial interpretation, in the Indian constitution. The protection of the right to vote seems sufficiently fundamental to attract the highest possible level of protection.

If judicial strike-down powers were to extend to other matters, we would need to think about override procedures appropriate to the subject matter of each. Again, a case can be made for allowing no override in cases about absolute or unqualified rights, but the degree of interpretation that courts need to carry out to apply even absolute or unqualified rights might justify at least some possibility of interpretive override, perhaps by a supermajority in both Houses. Another possibility is override by referendum, but interpretive overrides are of their nature subtle and nuanced, and so ill-suited to the oversimplifications and hallucinations of referendum campaigns. At most a referendum could be an additional requirement, after the override had completed its parliamentary passage.

Codification

That leaves the separate question of codification. Would codifying the British constitution be a good idea even if it made no difference to whether judges can strike down legislation? Possibly, although it would be an arduous undertaking and should not be seen as a substitute for substantive reform. Codification is something to attempt at the end of a process of reform not at the beginning. Its advantage at that stage is that the process of codification will bring out any contradictions between the reforms and provide an opportunity to fix them. But other sequences are not a good idea. For example, codifying existing arrangements before proposing reforms risks delaying the process of reform because of disagreement about what the current rules are. Worse still is attempting to combine codification and reform, so that no reform is considered adopted until the whole document is adopted. That might make sense from a technical point of view, since it requires designing every element simultaneously with all the others, but from a political point of view it risks bringing objectors to each individual reform together to form a majority against the whole even though each reform taken separately has majority support. Much better to bank the individual reforms and leave codification as a final tidying up exercise.

Fixed-term parliaments and the Westminster theory

The last item on the list is fixed-term parliaments. The issue might seem to be a detail on which reasonable liberals can differ, but it has a wider significance that concerns the relationship between parliament and government and whether we should be a parliamentary democracy or a quasi-presidential one.

Two distinct but connected issues arise. Who should decide when a general election happens and who should decide who should be prime minister? The current system is an unclear and unstable amalgam of the Westminster and Whitehall theories. On deciding who is prime minister the current answer is that the monarch decides, subject to a vague set of principles about making a choice after receiving advice about who could command the (undefined) 'confidence' of the House of Commons. Contrary to popular belief, appointment as prime minister is not conditional on winning a vote of confidence in the Commons. It is merely that, by convention, a prime minister who loses a vote of confidence should either resign or ask for an election. What counts as a vote of confidence and whether a government can indefinitely postpone motions of no confidence put down by the opposition is also unclear, a lack of clarity that an unscrupulous populist government could easily exploit, and did exploit in 2019. The system is based on the Westminster theory in that the confidence of the House of Commons plays a large, if undefined and informal, part. On general elections, however, the prime minister decides, subject to a five-year limit and to a vague set of rules, the Lascelles principles, that allow the monarch to refuse an election in exceptional circumstances. That is a Whitehall theory-based system.

One option is to follow through on the logic of the Whitehall theory. We could directly elect the prime minister and eliminate the possibility of parliament defying the electorate's choice by removing the House of Commons' power to vote no confidence in governments or prime ministers and by holding new general elections if prime ministers resign before the end of their term. This is already the situation for directly elected 'metro' mayors and perhaps reveals their devotees' preferred form of national government. That option, however, is illiberal: it transfers to national level a system that downgrades government by discussion and compromise, excludes large numbers of people from influence, increases the risk of corruption, and reduces politics to a spectator sport.

Assuming that the more liberal option is to move in the Westminster direction, how could it be done without creating additional risk of excessive instability? The most straightforward way of transferring the two powers to the House of Commons is to adopt and adapt some provisions of the German constitution and the current devolution arrangements. As in Germany, we should make it impossible to become prime minister without having been voted for by the House of Commons, but thereafter a motion of no confidence in the prime minister must specify a replacement.[53] The process of choosing a prime minister should be separate from the process for causing a general election. As in the devolution acts, fixed terms should be the norm, to eliminate the unfair electoral advantage non-fixed terms give to governments, and also the instability that arises from governments' incompetent attempts to benefit from their advantage. Parliament should be able to call extra elections to deal with situations of political impasse, but only to complete the fixed term then in progress, not to start a new term.[54]

One final issue is more technical, but important politically. Should the Commons need a special majority – the devolution acts specify two-thirds, as did the Fixed-term Parliaments Act 2011 – to cause an early election? The question has many complexities, but assuming that the electoral system for the Commons changes to a broadly proportional one, such as the single transferable vote, an ordinary majority would normally need more than one party to agree. That would not completely exclude the possibility of calling elections at times convenient for the governing parties and inconvenient for the opposition but restricting the effect of any new election to fulfilling the remainder of the current term would greatly reduce the incentive to use the power. Consequently, given the inconveniences that arose in 2019 out for the two-thirds rule, an ordinary majority should be enough.

Conclusion – the road back

To return to the question raised at the start of this chapter, these proposed reforms are all very well, and I hope all very liberal, but would they help or hinder a return of the United Kingdom to the EU? My answer is that they would help. Three aspects of the reforms are worth mentioning.

First, British political instability, actual and potential, is a serious obstacle to progress in negotiations, or even to starting them in earnest. The EU will want reassurance that the UK will not precipitously re-invoke Article 50 on a

---

53 Grundgesetz für die Bundesrepublik Deutschland § 67, https://www.bundestag.de/gg [Accessed 9/11/2024].
54 Scotland Act 1998, s. 3; Government of Wales Act 2006, s. 5.

political whim. Proportional representation will help to give that reassurance, reducing the risk that a pro-Brexit party could suddenly take power on a minority of the popular vote (as happened in 2015 and 2019). Under PR, a consistent majority in the electorate in favour of membership, which is what the EU will be looking for, will be able to assert itself in parliament with the same level of consistency, something the current electoral system cannot guarantee. Further reassurance would come from adopting a clear and rational system for appointing prime ministers and deciding when elections take place. In addition, an extra safeguard could be negotiated in the form of expanding the new second chamber's vetoes to include re-invoking article 50.

Secondly, although politically it would be impossible to avoid a referendum on renewed British membership, the reforms aim to create and protect a parliamentary democracy in which politics and law are in balance and in which both proceed through discussion and dialogue, not a purely political regime built on plebiscites and misinformation. The reforms would help to restore Britain's lost reputation for rational and reasonable politics and for producing honourable leaders whose word could be trusted, a reputation which Brexit very badly damaged.

Thirdly, and most importantly, proportional representation, a democratic second chamber, a constitutional court, legal guarantees for democracy and subsidiarity, and eventually a codified constitution would all help to make Britain look less strange, and more European.

Bibliography

Barnier, Michel. *La Grande Illusion: Journal Secret de Brexit 2016-2020*. Gallimard, 2021.

Bellamy, Richard. *Political Constitutionalism*. Cambridge University Press, 2007.

Bienkov, Adam, and Patrick Howse. 'Cowed and Compliant: The BBC's Road to Appeasement.' *Byline Times*, April 2024. https://bylinetimes.com/2024/03/15/bbc-road-to-appeasement/ [Accessed 9/11/2024].

Bingham Centre for the Rule of Law. *United Kingdom Internal Market Bill: A Rule of Law Analysis of Clauses 42 to 45*. British Institute for International and Comparative Law, 2020.

Bogdanor, Vernon. *Beyond Brexit: Towards a British Constitution*. IB Tauris, 2018.

Brown, Gordon. *A New Britain: Renewing our Democracy and Rebuilding our Economy.* The Labour Party, 2022.

Butt, Sarah, John Curtice, Elizabeth Clery, eds. 'Constitutional Reform.' *British Social Attitudes: the 39th Report.* National Centre for Social Research, 2022.

Department for Education. 'About us.' https://www.gov.uk/government/organisations/department-for-education/about [Accessed 1/5/2024].

Deutscher Bundestag. 'Grundgesetz für die Bundesrepublik Deutschland.' https://www.bundestag.de/gg [Accessed 9/11/2024].

Duff, Andrew. *Going Back: What Britain should do to join the European Union.* European Policy Centre, 2024.

Gibb, Nick. *Speech: The Purpose of Education.* Department for Education, 2015. https://www.gov.uk/government/speeches/the-purpose-of-education [Accessed 1/5/2024].

Greaves, Bernard, and Gordon Lishman. *The Theory and Practice of Community Politics.* Association of Liberal Councillors, 1980.

Hobbes, Thomas. *Leviathan.* Andrew Crooke, 1651.

Howarth, David. 'Government without discussion: Henry VIII clauses and the future of parliamentary democracy.' Statute Law Society Lecture, 14 March 2024. https://vimeo.com/showcase/statute-law-society.

— 'In the Theatre State.' *Times Literary Supplement,* 11 March 2011, issue 5632, p. 23.

— 'The Politics of Public Law.' In *Cambridge Companion to Public Law.* Edited by Mark Elliott and David Feldman. Cambridge University Press, 2015.

— 'Westminster versus Whitehall: What the Brexit Debate Revealed About an Unresolved Conflict at the Heart of the British Constitution.' In *The Brexit Challenge for Ireland and the United Kingdom: Constitutions Under Pressure.* Edited by Oran Doyle, Aileen McHarg and Jo Murkens. Cambridge University Press, 2021.

Howarth, David, Theresa M Marteau, Adam P Coutts, Julian L Huppert, and Pedro Ramos Pinto. 'What do the British public think of inequality in health, wealth, and power?' *Social Science and Medicine* vol. 222 (February 2019): pp. 198-206.

Joint Committee on Human Rights. *Democracy, Freedom of expression and freedom of association: Threats to MPs.* House of Commons, 2019.

King, Anthony, and Ivor Crewe. *The Blunders of Our Governments.*

Oneworld, 2013.

Kovács, Kriszta, and Kim Lane Scheppele. 'The fragility of an independent judiciary: Lessons from Hungary and Poland–and the European Union.' *Communist and Post-Communist Studies* vol. 51, no. 3 (2018): pp. 189-200.

Lister, Michael, and Emily Pia. *Citizenship in Contemporary Europe*. Edinburgh University Press, 2008.

Lucas, Caroline. *Another England: How to Reclaim Our National Story*. Hutchinson, 2024.

Lundberg, Thomas Carl, and Martin Steven. 'Framing Electoral Reform in the 2011 UK Alternative Vote Referendum Campaign.' *Australian Journal of Political Science* vol. 48, no. 1 (2013): pp. 15-27.

Mill, John Stuart. *Considerations on Representative Government*. 2nd ed. Parker, Son and Bourn, 1861.

Ministry of Justice. *Responding to Human Rights Judgments*. Ministry of Justice, 2023.

Mudde, Cas, and Cristóbal Rovira Kaltwasser. *Populism: A Very Short Introduction*. Oxford University Press, 2017.

Oakeshott, Michael. *On Human Conduct*. Clarendon Press, 1975.

Ofcom. *News Consumption in the UK 2023*. Ofcom, 2023.

Rachman, G. 'Kissinger never wanted to dial Europe.' *Financial Times*, 22 July 2009. https://www.ft.com/content/c4c1e0cd-f34a-3b49-985f-e708b247eb55 [Accessed 8/11/2024].

Renwick, Alan, Ben Lauderdale, and Meg Russell. *The Future of Democracy*. The Constitution Unit, 2023.

Russell, Meg. *Reforming the House of Lords: Lessons from Overseas*. Oxford University Press, 2000.

Schmitt, Carl. *The Concept of the Political*. Expanded edition. Translated by George D. Schwab. University of Chicago Press, 2007.

Stacey, Kiran. 'Britain will not rejoin EU in my lifetime, says Starmer.' *The Guardian*, 3 July 2024. https://www.theguardian.com/politics/article/2024/jul/03/britain-will-not-rejoin-eu-in-my-lifetime-says-starmer [Accessed 8/11/2024].

Tambini, David. 'Constitutionalising the BBC.' *The Political Quarterly* vol. 95, no. 1 (2024): pp. 56-63.

Truss, Elizabeth. *Ten Years to Save the West*. Biteback, 2024.

Walzer, Michael. *Spheres of justice: A defense of pluralism and equality*. Basic Books, 1983.

19

Liberals and War

Lawrence Freedman

D efence policy is not only about preparing for and occasionally fighting
wars. It is also about foreign policy (identifying potential allies and
adversaries), industrial and technology policy (because of the importance
of weapons procurement to both these sectors), social policy (because of
how the armed forces are recruited), and so on. How the specific questions
of defence are approached therefore reflects a much more general political
philosophy. Because liberalism has never been a unified, codified ideology
one cannot identify a single liberal approach to the issue of war and the
requirements of defence.

Liberalism contains distinct strands, which can contradict each other.
This was one of the key messages of Sir Michael Howard's *War and the Liberal
Conscience*, which drew attention to the tension between an internationalist
distaste for war and a readiness to use armed force in the name of justice.[1]
Nonetheless there are certain shared themes. In the Western liberal tradition,
attitudes to war start from the premise that this is a terrible thing that
should never be glorified. Liberals are opposed to militarism, suspicious
of movements that get youngsters dressing up in uniforms and marching
around to show their patriotic fervour, and ready to resist the imposition
of military disciplines into everyday life. Liberalism stresses the individual
over the collective and distrusts arbitrary power. A military dictatorship is
therefore the antithesis of liberalism. But despite these propositions, liberals
have, by and large, regarded military force as a legitimate instrument of
international policy under certain circumstances. Pacifism, and a belief that
security can be ensured without being prepared to engage in acts of violence,
has not been absent from the liberal tradition. It has never dominated,
however, because of the basic problem that so long as illiberal forces exist,

---

1   Michael Howard, *War and the Liberal Conscience* (Maurice Temple Smith,
1978).

often in the form of military dictatorships, they must be opposed in an effort to maintain liberal principles.

Liberal justifications for war

Historically liberals have approached defence policy pragmatically, as a matter of necessity, a consequence of living in an imperfect world, but not something to be embraced because of the opportunities to put on shows of strength. They have no desire to nurture martial virtues and demonstrate the power of the state. In line with the Western democratic theory, liberals hold that the armed forces must at all times be accountable to the civilian political leadership. They should not be allowed to choose the wars they wish – and for that matter wish not – to fight. This is one reason to be careful with Artificial Intelligence. It can facilitate better decisions, but it would be unwise to hand over decisions of life and death to algorithms.

Wars will only be fought if they have an exceptional justification, and that this should be rooted in core liberal values, which means that one way or another they will be presented as a fight against illiberalism. There was no problem, therefore, in having first militarist Germany and then Nazi Germany as the enemy in two world wars, followed by the totalitarian Soviet Union in the Cold War. Because liberalism has been a progressive creed, it has also looked for possibilities to forge a better world in which states do not find it necessary to resolve their disputes through violent means. Because wars are so self-evidently foolish, inhumane, and wasteful they really ought to be obsolete by now. At its most optimistic this strain of liberalism has looked for economic and social trends, reinforced by common sense, to turn war into a historical curiosity of no contemporary relevance. Such thoughts, which can be traced back to the 18th century enlightenment, with Kant providing an early text[2], have persisted despite continual disappointment.

Imagining a world without war

Kant's hope for a universal peace returned after the end of the Cold War, when it no longer seemed necessary to prepare for a Third World War, and the talk was of a liberal democratic globalism. In an environment of seeming liberal hegemony, many old incentives for conflict appeared to have been removed, as individuals and states shared ideas and projects, and engaged

2   See in particular Immanuel Kant, *To Perpetual Peace: A Philosophical Sketch*, trans. Ted Humphreys (Hackett Publishing, 2003).

in open trade. War had become not only nasty but also pointless. As the historian John Keegan put it, war 'may well be ceasing to commend itself to human beings as a desirable or productive, let alone rational, means of reconciling their discontents'.[3] The political scientist John Mueller took a similar view: 'like duelling and slavery, war does not appear to be one of life's necessities'. It was a 'social affliction, but in certain important respects it is also a social affectation that can be shrugged off'.[4] The most compelling presentation of the argument that war was becoming obsolescent came from the cognitive psychologist Steven Pinker in his 2011 book *The Better Angels of Our Nature*. He argued that the resort to violence in general, and not just war, was in a long and steady decline.[5] This reflected a growing conviction, at least in developed countries, 'that war is inherently immoral because of its costs to human well-being'. As with Mueller, he predicted that interstate war among developed countries would go the way of those domestic customs that had over time moved from being 'unexceptionable to immoral to unthinkable to not-thought-about'. Evidence seemed to back this up. The frequency and intensity of wars, as well as the number of violent deaths was in a steady decline. Pinker acknowledged that combinations of personalities, circumstances and chance could produce unexpected surges of death and destruction, and this could happen quite suddenly. Nonetheless, 'from where we sit on the trend line, most trends point peaceward'. Our 'better angels' of empathy, self-control, morality, were gaining the upper hand over the inner demons of instrumental violence, and domination, revenge, sadism, and ideology. This had come together as a 'civilising process'. The reasons for this were gentle commerce encouraging trusting relationships across boundaries; feminisation, as women were less belligerent than men; an expanding circle of sympathy, as more cosmopolitan societies could not dismiss the pain and feelings of others as irrelevant or demonise them as sub-human; and, lastly, the escalator of reason, allowing for an intelligent, educated critique of claims that might once have been used to justify appalling practices.

This was a very liberal analysis, reflecting traditional wariness about state power, disdain for militarism and mercantilism, and optimism about the

---

3   John Keegan, *A History of Warfare* (Knopf, 1993), p. 59.

4   John Mueller, *Retreat from Doomsday: The Obsolescence of Major War* (Basic Books, 1989), p.13.

5   Steven Pinker, *The Better Angels of our Nature: Why Violence has Declined* (Penguin Books, 2011).

possibilities of cooperative action and internationalism. The sort of social science data introduced to support this sort of optimism came with the comforting assertion, that well pre-dated Pinker's book, that democracies don't fight one another,[6] which was never completely true and, with the spread of democracy in the 1990s, turned out to be even less true than before. It confirmed what is perhaps an unfortunate rule of thumb that whenever predictions like this are made they are soon followed by an upsurge in war and violence. From the perspective of 2025, with Europe experiencing its worst war since 1945, vicious fighting in the Middle East, and regular expressions of concern about a coming confrontation between the United States and China, this confident prognosis now seems both poignant and naive.

The perennial spectre of war

When Pinker's book came out doubts were not only expressed about his methodology, but there were also references back to past claims that had turned out to be wrong. One obvious example was Norman Angell's famous dismissal on the eve of the First World War of the idea that war could ever be beneficial as 'The Great Illusion'. This idea:

> ...belongs to a stage of development out of which we have passed; that the commerce and industry of a people no longer depend upon the expansion of its political frontiers; that a nation's political and economic frontiers do not now necessarily coincide; that military power is socially and economically futile, and can have no relation to the prosperity of the people exercising it; that it is impossible for one nation to seize by force the wealth or trade of another – to enrich itself by subjugating, or imposing its will by force on another; that in short, war, even when victorious, can no longer achieve those aims for which people strive...[7]

After the war, when he was regularly cited as a false prophet, Angell insisted that his argument was that economic interdependence made such a war unwise but not impossible. There is, after all, a lot to be said for each of

6   Jack S. Levy, 'Domestic Politics and War,' in *The Origin and Prevention of Major War,* ed. Robert I. Rotberg and Theodore K. Rabb (Cambridge University Press, 1989).

7   Norman Angell, *The Great Illusion: A Study of the Relation of Military Power to National Advantage* (Cosimo Classics, 1909:2007), p. viii.

the assertions in the above quote. The economic consequences of the war were indeed dire. Perhaps if bankers, industrialists and traders had been actively consulted in the summer of 1914, which might have been expected in capitalist countries, their views would have caused governments to pause before risking so much. But they were not. Another illusion from early in the war was made by H.G. Wells, who had long been convinced that only a great conflagration would persuade the nations of the world to eliminate war. Once Germany, a 'nest of evil ideas', was defeated, good sense would reign. This was, he wrote, 'a war for peace':

> It aims straight at disarmament. It aims at a settlement that shall stop this sort of thing for ever. Every soldier who fights against Germany now is a crusader against war. This, the greatest of all wars, is not just another war – it is the last war![8]

Which of course it wasn't. Attempts were made to develop new institutions such as the League of Nations to manage conflicts and resolve them without war, and in 1928 there was even a new international treaty to abolish war, which had the effect not so much of stopping wars, but only of stopping them being declared. Any optimism about the resilience of this new international order did not survive the rise of Hitler. The Second World War broke out just over 20 years after the First concluded. After the Second World War the United Nations could do little because the Cold War meant that the veto-wielding permanent members of the Security Council were divided. There were many new wars bound up with the processes of decolonisation, which were in some cases followed by coups and civil wars. With industrialisation and easier trade there was no obvious profit in war, especially for the great powers, and potentially, because of nuclear weapons, they would be extremely destructive.[9]

Historian John Lewis Gaddis called this the 'Long Peace' in the mid-1980s,[10] and while there are increasing concerns that it will not last, for now it

---

8   H.G. Wells, 'The War That Will End War,' *The Daily News*, 14 August 1914, https://archive.org/stream/warthatwillendwa00welluoft#page/n5/mode/2up [Accessed 24/10/2024].

9   Carl Kaysen, 'Is War Obsolete?: A Review Essay,' *International Security* vol. 14, no. 4 (Spring 1990): pp. 42-64.

10   John Gaddis, *The Long Peace: Inquiries into the History of the Cold War* (Oxford University Press, 1987).

is still in place. Pinker, unlike Gaddis, was reluctant to acknowledge nuclear deterrence as a factor in the Long Peace. He sought to credit the decline of war to the civilising process, as reflecting a collective moral decision. As armed force described the problem, it could not be part of the solution. The idea of a balance of power was distasteful, consigning nations to permanent anarchy, assuming leaders would 'act like psychopaths and consider only the national self-interest, unsoftened by sentimental (and suicidal) thoughts of morality'.[11] Pinker denied that considerations of power might encourage states to avoid war. He saw no consistent effect at work and no correlation over history 'between the destructive power of weaponry and the human toll of deadly quarrels'.[12] His reluctance to accept that any good could come out of armed force might appear as a very liberal reaction, but it could end up avoiding the hard choices that are inherent in any defence policy and preparations to use violent means to achieve desirable ends.

Liberals expect wars to be fought in the line with the traditional Just War criteria, requiring not only a good cause but also proportionate means, respecting the distinction between combatants and non-combatants. This preference can be backed by arguments that inhumane methods are ineffectual and counterproductive. For example, failing to take care of civilian populations during an anti-terrorist campaign may just create more support for the terrorists, or that mass air raids boost rather than undermine civilian morale. But there are clearly limits to how far this argument can be taken.

Liberals thinking the unthinkable

Sometimes brute force works and the wrong side wins. Preventing their victory may require resort to illiberal methods. This issue comes into sharp focus with nuclear deterrence. It is hard to imagine a less liberal act than using a nuclear weapon against a populated area. It is therefore understandable that liberals have been uncomfortable with being in possession of a nuclear arsenal. Yet allowing an adversary a monopoly does not seem a good idea. One can imagine how the war with Ukraine might have developed if Russia had been under no restraints in the use of its arsenal. So long as great power relations are marked by distrust and antagonism, there is no obvious escape from a condition of mutually

11   Pinker, *The Better Angels of our Nature.*
12   Pinker, *The Better Angels of our Nature.*

assured destruction, in the hope that this will encourage caution and risk-aversion, which, up to now, has been the case. In these circumstances the liberal tendency is to argue at best for nuclear disarmament and at least for policies to ensure that nuclear weapons remain only the last resort, deterring nothing more than another's nuclear use. Even that leaves the quandary of preparedness, in which the horror of nuclear war can only be avoided by demonstrating readiness to fight one.

Away from the acute dilemmas of nuclear deterrence, there have been hopes that conventional warfare might become more 'humane'. This reflects the advances in weapon accuracy that allows for more precise targeting. Since the early 1970s it has been possible to use 'smart' precision-guided munitions to hit only what is supposed to be hit. These advanced systems not only added to Western advantages in warfare but also appeared to fit neatly with Just War criteria. This led to an assumption that, at least for the armies of developed countries, all casualties in war are avoidable. The old excuse that 'this is what happens in war' has become less acceptable. If only those targets that a commander desires to hit will be hit, if a building packed with civilians is struck that must reflect an indifferent cruelty rather than incompetence or just bad luck. And we know of instances in Syria and Ukraine where the same accuracy that makes it possible to avoid civilian targets makes it possible to score a direct hit. During the 1990s there was growing interest in forms of warfare that would allow the military to be kept separate from the civil, combatants from non-combatants, firepower from society, and organised violence from everyday life. Warfare could move away from high-intensity combat to something more contained and discriminate, geared to disabling an enemy's military establishment with the minimum necessary force. Opponents would be defeated by means of confusion and disorientation rather than slaughter. If this trend could be pushed far enough, then it was possible at some point to envisage a war without tears, conducted over long distances with great precision with as few people as possible – preferably none at all – at risk. No more resources should be expended, assets ruined, or blood shed than absolutely necessary to achieve specified political goals. This was the closest imaginable to a liberal military strategy.

Even with a regular war between major powers the idea that wars could be fought in this way was always optimistic. As soon as the fighting moved into urban areas then civilians would be at risk. Furthermore a lot of supposedly dual use facilities, including energy and communications systems, could be considered legitimate military targets, though their destruction could soon lead to the degradation of civilian life. The biggest problem was that the wars were not fought between regular armies but 'among the people',[13] with fighters moving in and out of civilian life, using schools and hospitals as sanctuaries, or at times being punished for their resistance by having their schools and hospitals attacked. And yet these were the wars to which Western countries found themselves drawn, with a growing readiness to use armed force to block the repressive policies of cruel regimes. This approach was even described as 'liberal interventionism' during the 1990s. From safeguarding the Kurds in Iraq in 1991 to providing relief to those caught up in the break-up of the former Yugoslavia, this approach quickly became a 'responsibility to protect'.[14] Instead of the necessity of confronting aggression as the singular case for the use of force (reflecting the priorities that stemmed from the principle of non-interference in the internal affairs of other states, as embedded in the UN Charter), intervention was now allowed, even with states who do not pose a direct threat, in the face of gross abuses of human rights and mass killing. According to this approach, when action is possible, passivity is tantamount to complicity, as for example with the Rwandan genocide in 1994.

Wars of choice and the liberal deficit

When it comes to these discretionary wars (sometimes called wars of choice), even for humanitarian objectives, the means will be judged against higher standards than would be the case in a defensive action against another's aggression. Activity must be shown to cause less harm than passivity. At the very least this requires effectiveness. Intervention in the affairs of another country should cause a notable improvement and certainly not make a bad situation worse. The liberal deficit in any intervention ought not to exceed the liberal credit. This sombre accounting tends to follow levels of casualties, especially as they are recorded by the media and social networks, tending to play down both the costs if illiberal forces triumph and also the relevance of

---

13   Rupert Smith, *The Utility of Force: The Art of War in the Modern World* (Allen Lane, 2005).
14   International Commission on Intervention and State Sovereignty, *The Responsibility to Protect*, Report of the Commission (International Development Research Centre, December 2001).

the classical 'strategic' factors of power, interest, honour and justice. Dwelling on larger strategic considerations can appear to be insensitive and heartless. Whatever the security case Israel had in Gaza after the Hamas attacks of 7 October 2023, it got lost in the desperate effect of their military operations to eliminate Hamas as a fighting force. And then they come up against questions of effectiveness. Liberal interventionism went out of fashion after long counter-insurgency and unsatisfactory campaigns in Iraq and Afghanistan, and the chaos that followed the toppling of President Gaddafi in Libya in 2011. They led to loss of life without evident benefit.

Regular forces seeking to eliminate guerrillas tend to give themselves considerable latitude in deciding who to imprison or kill. Western (if not Russian) counter-insurgency theory pays more attention to separating militants from possible sources of support, concentrating on hearts and minds to deny the enemy recruits, supplies and sanctuaries, which is less offensive to liberal sensibilities, although it can also exaggerate the benefits of sensitivity and kindness. At any rate the lesson from recent experience is that forces operating in areas where they were unwelcome leads to them getting bogged down and sometimes pushed out. A liberal intent of restraint at the start of conflict may not survive the experience of war. There may be practical difficulties, for example a lack of intelligence sufficient to support precision targeting, but most likely there will be a determined enemy fighting with its own methods to the point that without a change in strategy there will be no success, and this will lead to escalation. Even when every effort is made to show restraint and act with care the imperatives of war can result in harsh, physical actions which leave misery and grief in their wake.

Unless one accepts that the inherent illiberality of war invalidates any use of force, even in pursuit of liberal objectives, then it is best to acknowledge that force invariably carries these risks and that they cannot necessarily be avoided by means of tactical innovations. At the very least it requires paying much more attention to the interaction between the military and political strands of strategy when deciding upon the use of force and explaining its purpose to the public. After Iraq and Afghanistan, and because of Ukraine, there is less interest now in taking the military initiative in the name of liberal values and much more of a focus on the need to defend those values against aggressive states.

Bibliography

Angell, Norman. *The Great Illusion: A Study of the Relation of Military Power to National Advantage*. Cosimo Classics, 1909:2007.

Gaddis, John. *The Long Peace: Inquiries into the History of the Cold War*. Oxford University Press, 1987.

Howard, Michael. *War and the Liberal Conscience*. Maurice Temple Smith, 1978.

International Commission on Intervention and State Sovereignty. *The Responsibility to Protect*. Report of the Commission. International Development Research Centre, December 2001.

Kant, Immanuel. *To Perpetual Peace: A Philosophical Sketch*. Translated by Ted Humphreys. Hackett Publishing, 2003.

Kaysen, Carl. 'Is War Obsolete?: A Review Essay.' *International Security* vol. 14, no. 4 (Spring 1990): pp. 42-64.

Keegan, John. *A History of Warfare*. Knopf, 1993.

Levy, Jack S. 'Domestic Politics and War.' In *The Origin and Prevention of Major Wars*. Edited by Robert I. Rotberg and Theodore K. Rabb. Cambridge University Press, 1989.

Mueller, John. *Retreat from Doomsday: The Obsolescence of Major War*. Basic Books, 1989.

Pinker, Steven. *The Better Angels of our Nature: Why Violence has Declined*. Penguin Books, 2011.

Smith, Rubert. *The Utility of Force: The Art of War in the Modern World*. Allen Lane, 2005.

Wells, H.G. 'The War That Will End War.' *The Daily News*, 14 August 1914. https://archive.org/stream/warthatwillendwa00welluoft#page/n5/mode/2up [Accessed 24/10/2024].

20

Conclusion: Freedom Speaks

Paul Hindley and Benjamin Wood

This book has emerged at a time of acute crisis for liberal democracies. In June 2019, Vladimir Putin gave a comprehensive interview to *The Financial Times*, in which he argued that political liberalism was a spent force in global affairs. Sighting popular revolts against liberal norms in mature democracies, Putin decried mass immigration, multiculturalism and the contemporary plurality of gender identities and sexual lifestyles.[1] The heart of Putin's complaint was that notions of individual and international rights have become unmoored from the 'culture, traditions and traditional family values of millions of people making up the core population'.[2] Instead of freeing individuals to live in a global civilization, Putin suggested that the 'liberal idea has…come into conflict with the interests of the overwhelming majority of the population'.[3]

Here we see in operation Putin's doctrine of illiberal democracy.[4] In this account of politics, it is the role of the state to embody a highly bordered conception of national culture. What is stressed in such oversight is not freedom of speech or assembly, but the freedom of nations to put themselves and their cultural identity first. Within such a model, Russia, through its government, now claims for itself an expansive negative freedom, the freedom from cultural interference. Insofar as Putin's Russia possesses a coherent ideology, it is unapologetically neo-Eurasian. Instead of investing political value in universal rights, or a community of nations, the notion of national culture against globalisation is vehemently stressed. As Putin's

---

1   Lionel Barber et al., 'Vladimir Putin says liberalism has "become obsolete",' *Financial Times*, 28 June 2019, https://www.ft.com/content/670039ec-98f3-11e9-9573-ee5cbb98ed36 [Accessed 12/11/2024].
2   Barber, 'Vladimir Putin.'
3   Barber, 'Vladimir Putin.'
4   Fareed Zakaria, *The Future of Freedom: Illiberal Democracy at Home and Abroad* (W.W. Norton, 2007), p. 91.

court philosopher, the neo-Eurasist Aleksandr Dugin has summarised this trajectory:

> Eurasianism, recognising the pretence of the Western logos to universality, refuses to recognize this universality as an inevitability. This is the specific character of Eurasianism. It considers Western culture a temporary phenomenon and affirms a multiplicity of cultures and civilizations which coexist at different moments in a cycle. For Eurasists modernity is a phenomenon peculiar only to the West, while other cultures must divest these pretensions to universality of Western civilization and build their societies on internal values.[5]

For Dugin, cultures are not modes of universal humanity but are self-contained systems of meaning that possess coherence in and through their own internal workings. In this vein, liberalism has no philosophical basis for making universal claims, either about freedom or rights. Instead, says Dugin, there are a 'multiplicity of episteme built on the foundations of each civilization – the Eurasianist episteme for Russian civilization, the Chinese for the Chinese, the Islamic for Islam, the Indian for the Indian and so on.'[6] In practical terms, Dugin's commitments translate into a highly exclusionary and authoritarian ideal of national consciousness in which societies must be protected from dilution, hybridity and homogenisation. This is the very reverse of the cosmopolitanism and moral universalism that liberals have repeatedly championed since the 18th century. But the separatist world imagined by Dugin is not a distant spectre. The rise of ultra-nationalism in Russia mirrors similar developments across the world, in Italy, France, Britain, the United States, Hungary, India, Turkey, and Poland. Putin's relegation of liberalism speaks to a genuine ideological upheaval, one that seeks to refute the received wisdom of Western elites since 1945. Overshadowing and amplifying these developments is the existential threat of climate change. As weather patterns become more extreme, population displacement will intensify. Inevitably postwar inter-governmental agreements and organisations will begin to fracture under the pressure. We are already witnessing the diverse ways in which flows of desperate people are being weaponised by far right and nativist groups.

5   Aleksandr Dugin, *The Fourth Political Theory* (Arktos, 2012), p. 99.
6   Dugin, *The Fourth Political Theory*, p.99.

Climate change will be the best friend to the dictators and demagogues of tomorrow unless we act. At this perilous moment, the present writers are mindful of the ancient origins of the word 'crisis'. In Hippocratic medicine κρίσις (krisis) refers to the turning point in an illness which will either kill the patient or set them on the path to recovery.[7] Herein lies an important lesson. Our peril is an opportunity to choose a new direction midst our political infirmity. Liberalism needs to be refreshed, not simply defended. But if the fever of illiberal democracy is to break, we must be clear about the nature of the disease and our proposed remedies.

An appeal to humanity

At this time of upheaval, it is vital that we keep our first principles squarely in sight. Our response to one such as Dugin cannot consist of bland appeals to efficiency, reasonableness or generic beneficence. We must return to the central liberal affirmation of our common humanity. As the ancient playwright Terence expressed it: 'Homo sum, humani nihil a me alienum puto' ('I am human. Nothing human is alien to me').[8] As a consequence of this essential moral core, liberals should reject every mode of life which obscures basic human affinities and shared human needs. The chapters in this book have affirmed this humane vision again and again by their repeated rejection of both neoliberalism and populist nationalism. Against a world of ethnic fragments, liberals believe in human solidarity that crosses borders. Against greed and mindless accumulation, we stress the intelligent use of wealth for shared social ends. In an age so fixated on fences and borders, we reject the hollowness of so many of the divisions which animate nationalists, partisans and fundamentalists of all kinds. We oppose systems of political economy that are indifferent to poverty and the spiritual degradation of the individual. Nowhere are these impulses better expressed than in Voltaire's *Treatise on Toleration* (1763). Here Voltaire expressed the cosmopolitan hopes of the emerging Enlightenment. At the heart of this ambitious political, economic, and philosophical project was the unification of humanity under the banner of a universal culture, without distinction of nation, religion, or creed. Mocking the religious bigots of his own age, Voltaire observed:

7   Catalin-Stefan Popa, ed., *Soul and Body Diseases, Remedies and Healing in Middle Eastern Religious Cultures and Traditions* (Brill, 2023), p. 35.
8   This is a famous quotation from the Terence play *The Self-Tormentor*. A useful discussion of its social significance is found in Ashley Montagu's *Man's Most Dangerous Myth: The Fallacy of Race* (AltaMira Press, 1942;2001), p. 47.

> This little globe, which is merely a dot, revolves in space just like many other globes, in the vast extent of which we are all lost. A human being, who is about five feet high, is certainly a negligible entity in this creation. One of these imperviable beings says to one of their neighbours in Arabia or in South Africa, 'Listen to me, because the God of all the worlds has enlightened me; there are 900 million little ants like us on Earth, but there is only one little anthill that is cherished by God. He has hated all the others from the beginning of time. My anthill will therefore be the only one happy, and all the others will be eternally miserable.'[9]

In place of this xenophobic god of clan and territory, Voltaire seeks a deity which pursues neither fear nor favour. This is not the god of dogmatic sectarians, but the mirror and guarantor of a boundless conception of human reason. He possesses no single story, nor ethnic affiliation. His actions are not rooted within the conflicted domain of human history. His works are known, not by extra-sensory revelation, but through the coherence of nature. Under Voltaire's God, there is no Russian truth, Indian truth, Islamic truth, Western truth, or Chinese truth. There is simply truth. In His presence, the wars and skirmishes of nations and religions appear petty and senseless. In an attempt to instil a new and grander spiritual loyalty, Voltaire pleads for the rejection of hatred and bigotry 'in the interests of humanity'.[10] Akin to the earlier Stoic tradition of humanitarianism, Voltaire argued that the differences between social customs were inconsequential,[11] compared with the trans-cultural task of treating fellow human beings with compassion and justice. As Voltaire exhorts to the God of Reason at the end of the treatise:

> Grant that we may bear the burden of a short and painful life; that the slight differences in clothes that cover our fragile bodies, the differences between our inadequate languages, variations in all our ridiculous customs, imperfect laws and foolish opinions, differences between all the social conditions that are so important to us and so trivial to You; that all the little nuances that distinguish the atoms known as human beings may not become occasions for hatred and persecution![12]

9   Voltaire, *A Treatise on Toleration*, trans. Desmond M. Clarke (Penguin, 2016), p. 119.
10   Voltaire, *Treatise*, p. 13.
11   Voltaire, *Treatise*, p.124.
12   Voltaire, *Treatise*, p. 123.

We do not have to believe in Voltaire's high-minded Deism to appreciate the perspective being offered. Here we are taught to see the world as liberals. This god's-eye-view is the beginning of fraternity, tolerance and individual dignity. It is the essential inoculation against the numerous religions, sacred and secular, that attempt (often successfully) to wall us off from one another. For Voltaire, motives of 'justice, truth and peace'[13] become our indispensable tools for bringing the world's poisonous denominationalisms to an end. This is still, despite numerous defeats and false starts, the essential mission of liberal politics.

Liberalism's greatest gifts to the world remain the concepts of universal freedom and universal human rights. To be a liberal is to affirm that someone regardless of their particulars (their race, colour, creed, class, sex, sexuality, gender identity or (dis)ability), is in possession of equal moral and political worth. If ultra-nationalism affirms the irreducibility of nation and culture, liberals by contrast continue to insist upon the singularity of the human family, and the common right of all human beings to a large measure of dignity, justice, and liberty. We insist, contra Dugin, that such universalism is not a threat to particular communities, but rather an essential ingredient in the enhancement of human belonging. As liberals we believe that citizens with shared rights and mutual duties are in a far better position than a community defined principally by racial or clan consciousness. To possess an identity grounded in rights suggests a substantial conception of dignity. The rights-bearer is no mere appendage to some monolithic caste or class, but exists as a unique and unrepeatable person, to be valued on account of their unique personhood. This is the ethical centre of our liberal political creed; one we should not compromise for short-term political advantage or temporary popularity.

A recommitment to democracy

Perhaps the most pernicious charge against contemporary liberalism is that of elitism. There is sadly far too much truth in the accusation. Throughout the West, many liberal parties have become part of stale establishments, defenders of hideous hierarchies and unfeeling majorities. In this parlous state, liberal politics is unable or unwilling to conceive of liberty as liberation. Freedom becomes a byword for privilege and oligarchy. The cries of the poor and dispossessed are daily ignored under such regimes, in favour of glittering

13   Voltaire, *Treatise*, p. 131.

marketplaces, grand reforms and special interest groups. The gulf between communities and professional politics grows ever wider. In the end of course, such hubris is the death of liberalism. It is our view, and the view of many contributors to this volume, that in its current state liberal politics is failing to achieve even a meagre portion of its ideals. Inequality, economic injustice, and the spread of misinformation continue to erode fundamental democratic norms, and yet liberals are often bereft of an alternative story with which to challenge such public decay. This failure of articulation cannot continue. The prospect we face is that of an ailing and threadbare world, pocked and marked with nation-state fortresses, with the citizens behind those walls caught in noxious clouds of fear, hatred and egotism. If liberalism cannot solve the problems faced by ordinary people, then support for populist nationalism is only going to grow. The day that liberals think they have nothing to learn from voters (particularly the weakest and poorest), is the day they cease to be liberal and become conservative. At the beginning of the 20th century, the radical liberal Carlo Rosselli warned of this political stagnation in stark terms:

> Bourgois liberalism attempts to halt the historical process at its present stage, to perpetuate its own commanding position, to transform into a privilege what was once a right deriving from its undeniable pioneering work; it obstructs the entry of new militant social forces onto the stage of history. With its dogmatic attachments to the principles of economic libertarianism, private property, rights of inheritance, full freedom of initiative in every field, with the state as the organ responsible for internal policing and external defence), it has managed to shackle the dynamic spirit of liberalism to the transitory pattern of a particular social system.[14]

Here Rosselli brings us to an essential political truth. At its core, liberalism is a developmental doctrine; it is always work-in-progress. What freedom means in practice will be wrestled with afresh in each generation. As our knowledge and social awareness increases, so does our desire to extend rights and freedoms wider and deeper throughout society. There can be no final answer, no comprehensive solution which can crystalise the form of liberty for all time. There is nothing metaphysical about political freedom, nothing

---

14   Carlo Rosselli, *Liberal Socialism*, trans. William McCuaig (Princeton University Press, 1994), p. 87.

about liberal orders which puts the devoted political activist in touch with 'the one true way'. Indeed for liberals, there are many paths to social goodness, just as there are many roads to the formation of worthwhile lives. What is true of freedom is for liberals also true for democracy. Old social norms, political practices and institutions need to be continually renewed to make them more relevant and accountable to the people they are meant to serve.

As the world awaits the impact of a second Trump Presidency, we cannot help but reflect upon the fact that candidates who branded themselves 'moderate' and champions of pragmatism have again been defeated. They lost in part because they were unable to meet the real needs of the people. Their prescriptions were well-trodden, and their slogans recycled. They lacked the dynamic spirit of liberalism. They were unable to incorporate new and unruly social forces into their coalition. They did not see democracy as an unfinished project, but simply a prize to be won. This complacency represents a profound failure of political imagination and will doubtless be a gift to reactionary forces in the United States. But the insight here is a general one. If democracy is to survive in any meaningful form, then liberals need to take bold and decisive action in future proofing their economies and humanising their social institutions. A particular concern of this volume has been the democratisation of economic life. The proposals for universal basic income, works councils and greater power for local government are all attempts to renew and deepen the meaning of the word 'democracy'.

The recovery of community

If elitism and disconnection mar the conduct and reception of liberal politics so too do the twin gorgons of social and economic individualism. It is our belief (and the contention of this volume) that the revitalisation of liberal politics begins when we become acquainted with a social vision of freedom. Here liberty is neither caprice nor solipsism, but the ability of citizens to discover truth, beauty and justice together. There is no free life in a lonely competitive ego, but only in repeated patterns of care and well-wishing. In the peace and tranquillity of others, we find the key to our own serenity. As T.H. Green so vividly expressed this ethic:

> When we speak of freedom…we mean a positive power or capacity of doing or enjoying something worth doing or enjoying, and that, too, something that we do or enjoy in common with others. We mean by it

a power which each man exercises through the help or security given him by his fellowmen, and which he in turn helps to secure for them. When we measure the progress of a society by its growth in freedom, we measure it by the increasing development and exercise on the whole of those powers of contributing to social good with which we believe the members of the society to be endowed...[15]

In the end, there is no freedom which is not mutual, social and co-creative. There is no form of autonomy which is divorced from the lives of others, nor is there a life worth living which does not also include the gifts and burdens of life together. One of the implicit cries of this volume is that of William Morris' elegant moral formula: '[Fellowship] is heaven, and lack of fellowship is hell: fellowship is life, and lack of fellowship is death: and the deeds that ye do upon the earth, it is for fellowship's sake that ye do them'.[16] This is precisely what the young Mill found in the work of the romantic poet William Wordsworth. In his *Autobiography* Mill tells us of a mental crisis which almost drove him to suicide. What drew Mill away from this path of self-destruction was Wordsworth's heartfelt insistence that human beings were not mechanical devices whizzing along lonely tracks, but interconnected centres of love, compassion and creativity. If we wished to live rightly and fully, it was Wordsworth's contention that we needed to make these qualities daily real in ourselves. Particularly beloved of Mill was Wordsworth's ode *Intimations of Immortality*. In it, Wordsworth recalls the primordial consciousness of a child, its simple delight in the world, its overflowing love, and seemingly endless capacity for imaginative sympathy. As *Intimations* puts it:

> Though nothing can bring back the hour
> Of splendour in the grass, of glory in the flower;
> We will grieve not, rather find
> Strength in what remains behind;
> In the primal sympathy
> Which having been must ever be;

---

15 Thomas Hill Green, *Lectures on the Principles of Political Obligation and Other Writings* (Oxford University Press, 1986), p. 199.
16 William Morris, *A Dream of John Ball and A King's Lesson* (Reeves and Turner, 1888), p. 29.

In the soothing thoughts that spring
Out of human suffering;
In the faith that looks through death,
In years that bring the philosophic mind.[17]

Beyond the invisible cages of loneliness and solipsism, Wordsworth calls out in the name of liberality, that generous giving of ourselves to others. We are here invited to delight in the beauty and fragility of the world, while also sensing the suffering of others. For Mill these moods of expansive connection constituted the emotional backbone of his politics. As Mill recalled:

> What made Wordsworth's poems a medicine for my state of mind, was that they expressed, not mere outward beauty, but states of feeling, and of thought coloured by feeling, under the excitement of beauty. They seemed to be the very culture of the feelings, which I was in quest of. In them I seemed to draw from a source of inward joy, of sympathetic and imaginative pleasure, which could be shared in by all human beings, which had no connexion with struggle or imperfection, but would be made richer by every improvement in the physical or social condition of mankind...[18]

Thus, Mill's ideal became the unfolding progress of the human spirit and all that implied. All he found in Wordsworth, beauty, grace, joy, consolation, he wished for others. In the above quotation we observe almost the musical notes of Mill's liberalism: 'feeling', 'beauty', 'social', 'sympathetic', 'culture', 'improvement'. Drawing from these moral and aesthetic impulses, this book has argued that proper consideration should be given to the imperatives of community, the things we foster and seek together. Yet Mill, ever cautious, ever reflective, adds something vital to this high valuation of self-selfless conduct, which we must call distinctly liberal, namely the right to amend one's circle of belonging. Liberals are not against communities, only communities that one is not allowed to leave. As Mill puts the matter in *On Liberty*:

---

17   William Wordsworth, *The Complete Poetical Works of William Wordsworth, Together with a Description of the Country of the Lakes in the North of England* (Yay and Troutman, 1848), p. 388.
18   John Stuart Mill, *Autobiography* (Longmans, Green, Reader and Dyer, 1873), p. 148.

Society can and does execute its own mandates; and if it issues wrong mandates instead of right, or any mandates at all in things with which it ought not to meddle, it practises a social tyranny more formidable than many kinds of political oppression, since, though not usually upheld by such extreme penalties, it leaves fewer means of escape, penetrating much more deeply into the details of life, and enslaving the soul itself. Protection, therefore, against the tyranny of the magistrate is not enough; there needs protection also against the tyranny of the prevailing opinion and feeling, against the tendency of society to impose, by other means than civil penalties, its own ideas and practices as rules of conduct on those who dissent from them; to fetter the development and, if possible, prevent the formation of any individuality not in harmony with its ways, and compel all characters to fashion themselves upon the model of its own.[19]

These words possess a renewed potency today, when the world is getting ever smaller, but our tolerance for one another appears to be diminishing. It is the summative contention of this book that there can be no genuine fellow-feeling where sociability is demanded rather than invited. In this age of rising populism it is frequently supposed that the chief virtue of community is that we are fitted into narrow sameness, either by nation or ethnicity. But for one such as Mill this is nothing other than the tyranny of social custom. All forms of solidarity worth the name, must serve ends higher than community. Society must serve persons, cherish persons, and kindle the possibilities of persons, even if that makes the community at large a little less biddable, a little less profitable, and a little less efficient. In this spirit, our authors have attempted to imagine a social world in which everyone can realise the fullest degree of spontaneity, creativity, and initiative with and alongside others. There has been plentiful affirmation of a society in which every citizen has access to a generous measure of wealth, power, opportunity, and ownership. Freedom has been cast, not merely as the struggle for individual autonomy, but as a perennial and collective struggle against cruelty, prejudice, and political alienation. Reiterated throughout the volume are stern rejections of poverty, precarity and powerlessness in favour of a just and participatory economy, sustained by an active state and a flourishing civil society. Through these diverse interventions one can see a path beyond populism.

19   John Stuart Mill, *On Liberty* (Longmans Green and Co, 1859), p. 3.

The role of the individual

We end, appropriately enough for a volume of liberal politics, on a note of optimism. Despite the many dangers ahead, we believe that a great deal of social progress can be achieved through a widespread application of intelligence and sympathy. We believe that there is significant appetite among citizens to engage with and care for one another. We believe that much of the present suffering and inequality in Western societies remains avoidable. We continue to believe in the power of international co-operation as a means of curbing power and containing tyranny. But at the same time, we do not believe that such social improvements are possible nor secure unless and until enough of us are persuaded of the necessity of tackling injustice and preventable suffering. If we repeatedly pour into our institutions suspicion, greed, short-sightedness, and malice, no legal framework or policy can protect us from the outward consequences of our intentions. Look at the litany of scandals that have rocked the British state in recent years: The Windrush scandal, the post office scandal, the infected blood scandal, the Grenfell tower disaster. No-one can say that the UK government lacked the oversight or organisational capacity to avoid all these hideous events. What was evidently lacking related to the will.

This brings us to an essential theme of liberal politics, the moral primacy of the individual . Politics cannot make us good, kind or virtuous. All politics can do is clear the ground of impediments to human betterment. A generous and pluralistic politics provides us with many opportunities to seek truth, integrity and community. But we cannot find these things unless we are looking for them. We have to want a better future. Social peace will not arrive in our sleep. If the rise of populism has taught us anything, it is that democracy is not automatically a road to peace, prosperity and stability. It is an invitation only. As Mary Renault once wryly noted in one of her novels of ancient Greece: 'What is democracy…? It is what it says, the rule of the people. It is as good as the people are, or as bad'.[20] This is the plain truth. We cannot get more out of our politics than we are willing to put in to it. No system can generate curiosity, conscientiousness or the intention to address failure. Ideals matter, character matters, motives matter. A liberal society does not exist as a given. Neither is it achieved at a single moment in time, and then left to run as if on autopilot. Such a society runs (if indeed runs is quite the right word) on the beliefs, dreams, and aims of its members.

20 Mary Renault, *The Last of the Wine* (Arrow Books, 1954: 2004), p. 221.

On the surface this observation feels crushingly demanding. How can we, little selves that we are, embody the kind of political goods this book describes? But in liberal societies we are not called to be all-wise yogis, carrying the weight of the world on our shoulders. Rather we are invited to leave our door step and journey thoughtfully and considerately into the lives of others. In a liberal society we are encouraged, and not forced, to meet, learn, and work together. This book is a necessarily incomplete statement of what we might care about and what we might do. The policies detailed in these pages may date as time passes, but it is hoped however that the essential spirit sketched in these pages will continue to challenge and inspire in the years ahead.

Bibliography

Barber, Lionel, et al. 'Vladimir Putin says liberalism has "become obsolete". *Financial Times*, June 28 2019. https://www.ft.com/content/670039ec-98f3-11e9-9573-ee5cbb98ed36 [Accessed 12/11/2024].

Dugin, Aleksandr. *The Fourth Political Theory*. Arktos, 2012.

Green, Thomas Hill. *Lectures on the Principles of Political Obligation and Other Writings*. Oxford University Press, 1986.

Mill, John Stuart. *Autobiography*. Longmans, Green, Reader and Dyer, 1873.

— *On Liberty*. Longmans Green and Co, 1859.

Montagu, Ashley. *Man's Most Dangerous Myth: The Fallacy of Race*. AltaMira Press, 1942:2001.

Morris, William. *A Dream of John Ball and A King's Lesson*. Reeves and Turner, 1888.

Popa, Catalin-Stefan, ed. *Soul and Body Diseases, Remedies and Healing in Middle Eastern Religious Cultures and Traditions*. Brill, 2023.

Renault, Mary. *The Last of the Wine*. Arrow Books, 1954:2004.

Rosselli, Carlo. *Liberal Socialism*. Translated by William McCuaig. Princeton University Press, 1994.

Voltaire. *A Treatise on Toleration*. Translated by Desmond M. Clarke. Penguin, 2016.

Wordsworth, William. *The Complete Poetical Works of William Wordsworth, Together with a Description of the Country of the Lakes in the North of England*. Yay and Troutman, 1848.

Zakaria, Fareed. *The Future of Freedom: Illiberal Democracy at Home and Abroad*. W.W. Norton, 2007.

Appendix

Author Biographies

Sir Vince Cable was Member of Parliament for Twickenham from 1997 to 2015 and from 2017 to 2019. He served as the leader of the Liberal Democrats from 2017 to 2019. He also served in the Coalition cabinet as Secretary of State for Business, Innovation and Skills from 2010 to 2015. Vince is the author of *How to be a Politician: 2,000 Years of Good (and Bad) Advice* and *The Storm: The World Economic Crisis and What It Means*, amongst other books.

Andrea Coomber, KC (Hon.) is Chief Executive of the Howard League for Penal Reform. She has previously led JUSTICE and worked at INTERIGHTS, at the International Service for Human Rights in Geneva and at the South Asia Documentation Centre in New Delhi. Since 2019, she has served as a Lay Member of the House of Lords Conduct Committee. Andrea is a qualified barrister and solicitor in Australia.

Professor Emmy van Deurzen is a philosopher, psychologist and existential therapist who is the author of 20 books, which have been translated into two dozen languages. She has founded and co-founded numerous training and professional organisations and was the driving force behind the First World Congress of Existential Therapy. She is President of the worldwide Existential Movement, an international speaker and visiting professor with Middlesex University.

Dr Christopher England is the author of *Land and Liberty: Henry George and the Crafting of Modern Liberalism*, the history of a social movement that sought to alleviate inequality by redistributing urban rents. He has taught at the universities of Wisconsin-Madison, Stanford and Georgetown and currently teaches US History at Towson University, Maryland.

Ross Finnie was a Liberal Democrat Member of the Scottish Parliament from its re-establishment in 1999 to 2011. He was a cabinet minister throughout the coalition with Scottish Labour (1999-2007) principally as the Minister for the Environment and Rural Development. Prior to that he was a local councillor for 22 years.

Professor Sir Lawrence Freedman KCMG, CBE, PC, FBA is an academic, historian and author specialising in foreign policy, international relations and strategy. He is Emeritus Professor of War Studies at King's College London and the author of *Command: The Politics of Military Operations from Korea to Ukraine*. Lawrence was a leading member of the Young Liberal Movement in the late 1960s.

Paul Hindley is a doctoral research student in the department of Politics, Philosophy and Religion at Lancaster University. His research focuses on the theory and practice of neoliberalism. Paul is a Liberal Democrat activist based in Blackpool and a former member of the Social Liberal Forum Council.

Professor David Howarth is Professor of Law and Public Policy at the University of Cambridge, a Fellow of Clare College, Cambridge and a former UK Electoral Commissioner. He was Liberal Democrat MP for Cambridge from 2005-2010, serving as the Liberal Democrats' Shadow Justice Secretary, as a member of the Justice Select Committee and as a member of the Wright Committee on Reform of the House of Commons.

Noor Khan is a Press and Public Affairs Officer at the Howard League for Penal Reform. She has previously worked as a consultant for a firm specialising in policy and public affairs, helping small charities and NGOs achieve policy change. Noor holds an undergraduate degree in English Literature from King's College London and a Master's in Human Rights from University College London.

Gordon Lishman CBE is a British social and elder rights activist, Liberal Democrat politician, writer and former Director General of Age Concern England. He was awarded an Honorary Fellowship from the University of Central Lancashire in 2002. Gordon is the leader of the Liberal Democrat group on Burnley Borough Council and is also a senior member of the Social Liberal Forum.

Bob Marshall-Andrews KC is a KC and writer who was Labour MP for Medway from 1997 to 2010. As a result of his opposition to New Labour policies on civil liberties, a national magazine described him as 'the thorn in Tony Blair's red rose'. He holds an honorary doctorate from Bristol University. Bob has written several novels and his political memoir *Off Message* was published by Profile in 2011. He joined the Liberal Democrats in 2017.

Dr Helen McCabe is Associate Professor of Political Theory at the University of Nottingham. She works on questions around John Stuart Mill's socialism, feminism and egalitarianism, and his collaborative relationship with Harriet Taylor Mill, as well as contemporary questions around forced marriage, modern slavery, human trafficking, and honour-based abuse. Helen is the author of *John Stuart Mill, Socialist*.

Professor Matthew McManus is a Lecturer in Political Science at the University of Michigan and the author of *The Rise of Post-Modern Conservatism and The Political Theory of Liberal Socialism* amongst other books. His work explores themes of liberalism, democracy, liberal socialism and social equality. Matt is a member of the Democratic Socialists of America.

Michael Meadowcroft is a British author, politician, and political affairs consultant. He served as the Liberal MP for Leeds West from 1983 to 1987, following 15 years as a city and county councillor. Between 1988 and 2013 he served as a governance advisor in 35 new and emerging democracies. His MPhil was on Leeds political history and he regularly lectures and writes on Leeds local history, as well as contributing to the *Journal of Liberal History*.

Dr Andrew Phemister is an historian and the author of *Land and Liberalism: Henry George and the Irish Land War*. His research looks at 19th century agrarian and labour politics, popular activism, and political thought, and he is currently working on a history of boycotting.

Denis Robertson Sullivan has fostered a lifelong interest in the alleviation of homelessness and poverty. Denis has served as the Treasurer of the Scottish

Liberal Democrats, and an advisor to the Deputy Chair of a Development Corporation. He has been the Vice Chair of Shelter UK, Chair of Shelter Scotland, and a nonexecutive director of a Housing Association.

Edward Robinson is co-editor of the online journal *Land and Climate Review* and a former council member of the Social Liberal Forum.

Professor Helena Rosenblatt is Distinguished Professor of History and Political Science at the Graduate Center, CUNY. Her speciality is European intellectual history. Her latest work is *The Lost History of Liberalism: From Ancient Rome to the Twenty-First Century*, which has been translated into nine languages.

Dr Timothy Stacey is a researcher in sustainable futures at the University of Utrecht. His work considers the role of symbolism, ritual and myth in the formation of collective social and political identities. His work encompasses themes of ecological activism, political theory, and postulations of radical democracy. His latest book is *Saving Liberalism from Itself: The Spirit of Political Participation*.

Dr Stuart White is the Nicholas Drake Tutorial Fellow in Politics at Jesus College, Oxford, and Associate Professor in the Department of Politics and International Relations, Oxford University. Stuart's research focuses on egalitarian and non-authoritarian alternatives to capitalism. His publications include *The Civic Minimum* (2003) and *Equality* (2006). He is the author of the forthcoming book, *The Wealth of Freedom: Radical Republican Political Economy*.

Dr Benjamin Wood is a Leeds-based political theologian, writer, and Liberal Democrat activist. He is a Woodbrooke Associate Tutor, and a visiting researcher at the Centre of Religion and Public Life (University of Leeds). He has previously taught Theology and Religious Studies at Leeds Trinity University, the University of Chester, and the University of Manchester.